Metropolitan Latinidad

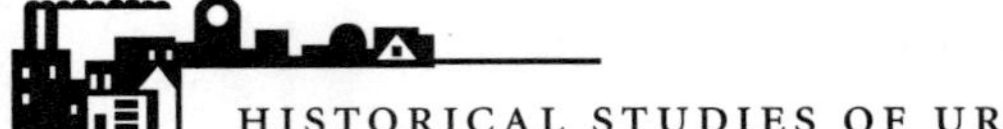

HISTORICAL STUDIES OF URBAN AMERICA

EDITED BY LILIA FERNÁNDEZ, TIMOTHY J. GILFOYLE, AND AMANDA I. SELIGMAN
JAMES R. GROSSMAN, EDITOR EMERITUS

Recent titles in the series

Alexander Wood, *Building the Metropolis: Architecture, Construction, and Labor in New York City, 1880–1935*

Leslie M. Harris, *In the Shadow of Slavery: African Americans in New York City, 1626–1863, With a New Afterword by the Author*

Tim Keogh, *In Levittown's Shadow: Poverty in America's Wealthiest Postwar Suburb*

Nicholas Dagen Bloom, *The Great American Transit Disaster: A Century of Austerity, Auto-Centric Planning, and White Flight*

Sean T. Dempsey, *City of Dignity: Christianity, Liberalism, and the Making of Global Los Angeles*

Claire Dunning, *Nonprofit Neighborhoods: An Urban History of Inequality and the American State*

Tracy E. K'Meyer, *To Live Peaceably Together: The American Friends Service Committee's Campaign for Open Housing*

Mike Amezcua, *Making Mexican Chicago: From Postwar Settlement to the Age of Gentrification*

Arnold R. Hirsch, *Making the Second Ghetto: Race and Housing in Chicago, 1940–1960, With a New Afterword by N. D. B. Connolly*

William Sites, *Sun Ra's Chicago: Afrofuturism and the City*

David Schley, *Steam City: Railroads, Urban Space, and Corporate Capitalism in Nineteenth-Century Baltimore*

Rebecca K. Marchiel, *After Redlining: The Urban Reinvestment Movement in the Era of Financial Deregulation*

Steven T. Moga, *Urban Lowlands: A History of Neighborhoods, Poverty, and Planning*

Andrew S. Baer, *Beyond the Usual Beating: The Jon Burge Police Torture Scandal and Social Movements for Police Accountability in Chicago*

Matthew Vaz, *Running the Numbers: Race, Police, and the History of Urban Gambling*

Ann Durkin Keating, *The World of Juliette Kinzie: Chicago before the Fire*

Jeffrey S. Adler, *Murder in New Orleans: The Creation of Jim Crow Policing*

David A. Gamson, *The Importance of Being Urban: Designing the Progressive School District, 1890–1940*

A complete list of series titles is available on the University of Chicago Press website.

Metropolitan Latinidad

Transforming American Urban History

A. K. SANDOVAL-STRAUSZ, EDITOR

The University of Chicago Press
Chicago and London

The University of Chicago Press, Chicago 60637
The University of Chicago Press, Ltd., London

Published 2025
Printed in the United States of America

34 33 32 31 30 29 28 27 26 25   1 2 3 4 5

ISBN-13: 978-0-226-83981-3 (cloth)
ISBN-13: 978-0-226-83983-7 (paper)
ISBN-13: 978-0-226-83982-0 (e-book)
DOI: https://doi.org/10.7208/chicago/9780226839820.001.0001

Library of Congress Cataloging-in-Publication Data

Names: Sandoval-Strausz, A. K., editor.
Title: Metropolitan Latinidad : transforming American urban history / A. K. Sandoval-Strausz, editor.
Other titles: Historical studies of urban America.
Description: Chicago : The University of Chicago Press, 2025. | Series: Historical studies of urban America | Includes bibliographical references and index.
Identifiers: LCCN 2024038376 | ISBN 9780226839813 (cloth) | ISBN 9780226839837 (paperback) | ISBN 9780226839820 (ebook)
Subjects: LCSH: Hispanic Americans—History—20th century. | Hispanic American neighborhoods—United States—History—20th century. | Urbanization—United States—History—20th century.
Classification: LCC E184.S75 M48 2025 | DDC 307.3/36208968073—dc23/eng/20241114
LC record available at https://lccn.loc.gov/2024038376

♾ This paper meets the requirements of ANSI/NISO Z39.48-1992 (Permanence of Paper).

Contents

Introduction

A. K. SANDOVAL-STRAUSZ

For at least half a century, urban history has fallen behind the pace of change in American cities. In the nation's largest metropolis, young people growing up in most neighborhoods in the 1970s would have heard Spanish spoken every day: perhaps in their own homes, possibly at school or work, almost certainly on the streets of the city. The most recent census had found that nearly one in six New Yorkers was Hispanic; in the Bronx, where I was born, the proportion was approaching one in three. And that was before the arrival of more than half a million new Latino migrants, who lifted their share of the city's population to 20 percent by 1980 and 25 percent by 1990.[1]

While most Latin American migrants to New York City arrived after mid-century, the community had been two hundred years in the making. Cuban sugar planters traveled to the city in the 1770s and established a substantial presence beginning in the 1830s. Puerto Rican sojourners began their own process of settlement two decades later, and over the subsequent hundred years, waves of merchants, political dissidents, and laborers established newspapers, mutual aid societies, and other civic institutions. They were followed by newcomers from across the hemisphere, making New York home to the greatest number of people of Latin American ancestry of any city in the United States.[2]

Yet if one of these *migrantes* or one of their descendants went to college to learn the history of the city, they might have been confused to find their community virtually absent from it. Urban historians had spent decades producing a wealth of information about everything from infrastructure, transportation, and finance to machine politics, vice districts, and Beaux-Arts to gender, immigration, and race. Especially race: by the 1980s, a generation of urbanists had definitively demonstrated that it was impossible to understand the history of cities and suburbs in the United States without recognizing the centrality of institutional and structural racism. Race, however, was almost always defined in terms of Black and white. So Latina and Latino collegians often found themselves asking, as I did with likely annoying regularity, "But professor, what about Latin people?"[3] It just seemed that because there were over a million and a half of us in New York City, we should be a much bigger part of its history. The question was not a new one—as we shall see, Chicanos and Puerto Ricans had already been asking it for more than twenty years. And by then there was a recent history of the city's largest Hispanic population: Virginia Sánchez Korrol was the first to systematically research the topic for her seminal 1983 book *From Colonia to Community*. But with that important exception, there was little else available to us that was relevant to the urban history literature.[4]

A decade later, a similar situation presented itself in Chicago. By the 1990s, the Windy City had been the foremost location for urban research in the United States for eight decades, ever since the emergence of the Chicago School in the 1910s. Mexicans and Mexican Americans had called the city home throughout those years, joined by a large Puerto Rican community beginning in the latter 1940s and a small Colombian one in the 1950s; and starting around 1970, the arrival of more than half a million new *migrantes* had dramatically increased the size, diversity, and vitality of Latino Chicago. Their influence was visible at every scale: the Hispanic undergraduate student group I advised was large and active, and it even included a recent community *reina*, Miss Little Village. My fellow graduate student Eduardo Contreras and I regularly traveled west to the Chicago Lawn neighborhood to teach English and to find sustenance at the local *taquerías* and *panaderías*. And within a few years, *Crain's Chicago Business* made national news when it reported that the Twenty-Sixth Street commercial corridor in Little Village was second only to the city's Magnificent Mile along Michigan Avenue in generating sales tax revenue.[5]

The historical literature on the city, however, still overwhelmingly hewed to the Black-white racial binary. Historians had long looked to Chicago to ask their biggest questions about race in the United States: they had inquired into the migrations that established its Black community, the origins of its severe racial segregation, the way that African Americans created churches, businesses, and associations, and their struggle for equality and political representation. This is not to say that no historical work on Latinos was available: there was, to be sure, the inspiration of Louise Año Nuevo Kerr's pathbreaking yet unpublished 1976 dissertation on ethnic Mexicans in Chicago; we could also look to Felix Padilla's 1985 book of historical sociology *Latino*

Ethnic Consciousness, which was based on his earlier fieldwork in the city. But much influential scholarship on Chicago Latinos was still in progress and appeared only at or after the new millennium. This was the case even with more present-oriented disciplines: Marta Tienda's series of sociological articles on Mexican migrants appeared only between 1999 and 2004, Eric Klinenberg's *Heat Wave* in 2002, and the anthropologist Nicholas De Genova's *Working the Boundaries* in 2005. Nearing the turn of the millennium, the historians who would write foundational histories of Latino Chicago were still graduate students, and to the extent that Latino urban history was being published, it was happening somewhere else than the Latino metropolis of the Midwest.[6]

That somewhere else was primarily Los Angeles. From its origins as an Indigenous population center for at least three thousand years and a Spanish settlement for more than two centuries, Los Angeles became the unchallenged center of historical research on Hispanics, especially ethnic Mexicans—a historiography that stretched from the first hagiography of Junípero Serra in 1787 to the works of the first Chicano historians in the 1960s. Moreover, since the mid-1980s, Los Angeles had come to challenge Chicago as the leading center of urban studies, with scholars drawing on more than one hundred years of English-language research and declaring the City of Angels the prime example of a polycentric or postmodern metropolis. In these same years, it became the leading site of research for a new generation of scholars who placed Latinos at the center of their analysis of how cities functioned.[7] In the field of Mexican American and Latino history, the 1993 publication of George J. Sánchez's *Becoming Mexican American* was a watershed event, demonstrating the intellectual promise of new community studies that fully interrogated both people and place within a broad theoretical framework. It served as a model for yet another generation of scholars, inspiring new histories of ethnic Mexicans in the region.[8]

Notwithstanding the quality and influence of the emerging Latino histories in all these cities, the ongoing efflorescence of new Latin American immigrant communities far outpaced the historical profession's capacity to chronicle them. Dramatic changes in national policy and international politics—especially the acceleration of U.S. interference in Latin American civil conflicts and economies, the debt crises in Mexico and other nations in Latin America, and the embrace of neoliberalism by Latin American governments—had set more migrants from a greater variety of countries into motion, and they had settled in a broader range of destinations. New places of origin gave rise to new communities, like the Salvadorans of metro Washington, DC. New destinations for older migrant flows led to growing Mexican communities in unaccustomed places like New York City and Atlanta.

And the combination of both factors resulted in communities of Guatemalan Mayans in Morganton, North Carolina; Ecuadorians in Ossining, New York; and Mexicans in Indiana's northern dunes, on town squares in Montana, and around the resort communities of Jackson Hole, Wyoming, and Steamboat Springs, Colorado. Whatever their origins and circumstances, by the 2010s, even the latest Latino communities that resulted from these changes were already two to three decades old—that is, old enough to merit histories of their own.

Metropolitan Latinidad was born of its contributors' wish for a more representative history of the urban and suburban United States. Both in terms of American cities' demography and transnational connections, we need a truly multicultural and multiracial urban history; a basic part of this must be studies of the fastest-growing group of metropolitan Americans.[9] The growing presence and importance of people of Latin American ancestry in the United States is by now well recognized, with various quantitative measures having been the subject of many years of journalistic coverage: Latinas and Latinos already constitute one in five Americans, we deliver more than half of all population growth, and if we were a country, it would have the fifth-largest economy in the world. But even more notable for our purposes is the fact that Latinos are already predominant in much of urban America. To take just one compelling indicator, in six of the ten most populous cities in the United States in the most recent census, Latinos are already the largest population of any demographic group, with a higher proportion of residents than either non-Hispanic whites or Black people; and that figure is expected to reach seven of the ten within a few years. Similarly, in the twenty-five most populous U.S. cities, Latinos are a majority in two, more than one-third of the population in eight, and over one-quarter of the population in thirteen.[10]

Given these figures, the time is long past when we can research, write, or teach urban history without giving a central place to Latinos. While it is true that history is a retrospective field as a matter of basic methodology, the urgency of rethinking our approach remains. Part of our responsibilities as urban historians is to describe the cities around us, so a central task before us is to explain how and why they look the way they do: to provide a historical analysis that helps us understand our present. Latino history must therefore be a fundamental concern of urban historians. But there are also important historiographical reasons we should want to see a new approach to urban history. The study of these indispensable Latino urban denizens also highlights important aspects of the development of cities that have not yet been fully accounted for in the historical literature: migrants as the human face of globalization, the many ways they shape metropolitan areas, new conceptions of race and identity, and the very different political alignments and economic conditions that result. What Vicki Ruiz, a giant in the field of Latina and Latino history, said almost two decades ago about the nation is even more true of its cities: "Nuestra América *es* historia americana. Our America *is* American history."[11]

By way of setting the stage for the main event, this introduction offers some essential historical and historiographical context. It begins with an account of the interwoven historiographies of urban and Latino history, then moves on to a four-part periodization of Latino urban history. It thereupon pivots to the subject matters and historiographical interventions of the contributors' twelve chapters, then concludes by outlining the major themes that emerge from this volume.

Latino history was born in the barrio. As a field, it has been intertwined with the study of cities throughout its historiography. Precisely because main threads of its intellectual genealogy have been interwoven with the urban, it has become essential to the ongoing development of this book's subject matter: Latino urban history, or, more broadly, Latino metropolitan history.

Latino history, as part of the broader field of Latino studies, was a response to the demands of people in urban communities who quite justifiably accused schools and universities of excluding them from their curricula. This played out simultaneously in barrios in the Southwest and on the East Coast. Chicano activists in the late 1960s and early 1970s insisted on lesson plans and college courses that would educate Mexican American students about their history and forthrightly explain the systematic subordination of their people in a region where they had lived for centuries. These demands emanated from barrios in the cities with the largest ethnic Mexican populations, starting with the East Los Angeles high school "blowouts" of March 1968, which inspired similar actions across the Southwest over the two years that followed. Consequently, the earliest Chicano studies programs were established at California State College in Los Angeles, and at the University of California, Los Angeles, the University of Arizona in Tucson, the University of Houston, and the University of Texas at Austin.[12]

In these same years, Puerto Rican activists in New York City also organized for educational reform. At the City University of New York (CUNY), Puerto Rican students began to enroll in significant numbers beginning in the mid-1960s but were taught curricula designed for overwhelmingly white student bodies. Understanding that they were a large part of the populations of the city neighborhoods served by these universities, they demanded classes that would both represent them and push back against public officials and popular culture that defined them as a problem; importantly, they mobilized together with Black students who had been making similar demands for their communities. In response, officials at CUNY established the Department of Puerto Rican Studies in 1970, with programs operating at schools including City College, Brooklyn College, Borough of Manhattan Community College, and Hunter College.[13]

As Chicano and Puerto Rican scholars searched for a usable past—one that would help them understand their place in a country whose historians had ignored them and whose mainstream culture belittled or villainized them—they found one in their neighborhoods and cities. In both Chicano studies and Puerto Rican studies, historians and other scholars identified densely populated Hispanic neighborhoods as a spiritual and intellectual taproot of community identity, thereby positioning urban places as fundamental to the entire field. Chicano scholars were initially strongly nationalistic but also settled on a geographically oriented narrative of identity. While they recognized that most of their coethnics were or until recently had been rural people, they identified the experience of being segregated into barrios as a necessary condition for Chicano consciousness. Among Puerto Rican Studies scholars, while the island was certainly the fundamental touchstone of collective identity and nationalism, it was also the experience of concentration in decaying urban neighborhoods, and the substandard and often dangerous housing, job discrimination, institutional deprivation, and police violence of their barrios that formed the immediate material basis of their organized protests—and the setting for so much creativity, from the Nuyorican poets to the first chroniclers of Puerto Rican New York.[14]

Looking specifically at Latino historians, we can see even more clearly how they studied cities in pursuit of their primary historiographical purpose: to disrupt long-standing narratives that had ignored them, erased them, or portrayed them as little more than victims of conquest. At a time when they were still giving conference papers and writing articles in the years before they published their first books, leading Chicano historians explicitly referred to their work as urban history. Albert Camarillo's first article in the second issue of *Aztlán* in 1971 was titled "Chicano Urban History," and an early historiographical essay declared that "Chicano urban history came into its own" in a session called "Chicanos and the City" at the 1973 American Historical Association meeting; it was followed at the 1974 Organization of American Historians meeting by the panel "Chicanos in the City." Indeed, from a fairly early date, Chicano historians saw urban history as central to the field: Juan Gómez-Quiñones and Luis Leobardo Arroyo observed in a 1976 *Western Historical Quarterly* review essay that "after labor history, Chicano urban history is receiving the most attention from doctoral candidates." This made a good deal of historiographical sense because their work shared a lineage with urban history. Both were part of the "new social history" and its emphasis on "history from the bottom up." Their focus was the historiography of the West: Chicano historians sought to explain the influence of the deeper past in ethnic Mexican community, identity, and socioeconomic status, and in particular the marginalization and subordination of Mexican-ancestry people in the region.[15]

This connection was even clearer as the first books in the field were published. Most of the early monographs were community studies of or in cities: Al Camarillo on Santa Barbara and Los Angeles, Richard Griswold del Castillo on Los Angeles, Mario T. García on El Paso, Ricardo Romo on East Los Angeles, Rodolfo Acuña on Los Angeles, and the introduction of mainland Puerto Rican history with Virginia Sánchez Korrol's book on New York City. Latino history was not necessarily asking the same questions as urban history, but the methodological similarities were unmistakable. Latino history was in one sense parallel to earlier moves in Black history that explained the centuries-long legacy of racism and its effect on African Americans' place in society; in another sense, it grew out of immigration history and the question of why Mexican Americans had followed a different path of historical development from earlier groups of immigrants from Europe.[16]

When this first generation of Chicano histories was published, scholars in both Western history and urban history saw them as representing an important new direction in their respective subfields. No less a figure than David Weber, for example, wrote in a 1983 article called "The New Chicano Urban History" that the first books by Camarillo, García, and Griswold del Castillo "exemplify a body of literature that represents the cutting edge of scholarship in southwestern history. The new social history, with urban history at the forefront, has helped bridge chronological boundaries in Southwestern history and has offered new information and fresh insight into Chicano communities and their relationships to the dominant society." And in that same article, the prominent urban historian Roger Lotchin described the books as a vital new approach to urban history, imbricating them into the field as much-needed explorations of new urban regions and new ethnic communities. This new direction, he wrote, "significantly broadens our understanding of urban history by carrying it into a relatively new geographic and ethnic subject matter. . . . Our knowledge of American cities was not informed by an understanding of either the urban West or our largest contemporary immigrant group. . . . These books will go a long way toward correcting this provincialism."[17]

There was indeed great promise here, because the field of urban history had been adding new approaches from an early point in its development. If we use the 1933 publication of *The Rise of the City* by the elder Arthur Schlesinger as the starting point for the field, we can get a sense of the growth of its subfields. In the decades that followed, urban history developed beyond its predominant focus on gradual social and economic change, with succeeding generations of historians authoring scholarly literatures on urban politics, immigration, labor, culture, race, gender, infrastructure, consumerism, sexuality, and environment—as well as specifically suburban variants of some of these as the field has recast itself under the more capacious rubric of metropolitan history.[18]

At this early point in what became Latino history, Chicano historians had perfectly positioned their work to fundamentally influence urban history in exactly the way that Weber and Lotchin identified—all that urban history needed to do was to overcome its East Coast, old-immigrant provincialism. It turned out, however, that that was too heavy a scholarly lift, at least at first. Weber also mentioned how "Chicano historians labored under a special handicap through much of the last decade" because widely read historians like Jacques Barzun and Henry F. Graff had dismissed the entire field of Chicano studies, deeming it hopelessly politicized as the product of community demands for inclusion (this despite the remarkably consistent complexion of Barzun's subjects especially).[19]

Urban historians largely ignored the city-centered Chicano and Puerto Rican scholarship for nearly twenty years. If we were to divide the reception of Latino history within urban history into periods, this would be the first of four, and it might easily be called "indifference." Until 1990, self-identified urban historians seldom included Latinos and Latinas in their writings, and they did not generally review such books as part of the field's developing historiography. One could search edited collection after edited collection and find virtually nothing on Mexican Americans, Puerto Ricans, or any other community constitutive of the Hispanic/Latino pan-ethnicity. Urban-historical research on immigration continued, but it was heavily canted toward "old" immigrant groups; and when urban historians wrote about race, they continued to think almost exclusively with a Black-white racial binary. So even though these subfields were interwoven with the same places and times and intellectual movements, only one of the two was actually thinking of them together.[20]

Why the indifference to this vital new approach to urban history? In search of an explanation, I queried the historians who first conceptualized their work in this way—the scholars whom Albert Camarillo called "that first generation naturally cutting their teeth in urban history." "One answer," offered Richard Griswold del Castillo, "was that many U.S. urban historians regarded Chicano history as regional and somewhat parochial with respect to the larger themes they were considering." Another sounded a similar note: "I think that urban history failed to incorporate studies in Chicano urban history for the same reasons that other subfields in U.S. history such as civil rights history, labor history, social history, et cetera, also failed: because they still did not see Chicano history as an integral part of U.S. history." He also suggested that "urban historians probably had the stereotype that Mexicans in the U.S. were primarily rural farm workers. The struggles of César Chávez and the [United Farm Workers] probably only added to this stereotype."[21]

Historians who studied Chicanos and other Latinos subsequently drifted away from urban history, partially because of the subfield's lack of engagement and partially in response to the exigencies of the profession and the community. Camarillo explained that Chicano historians felt a deep responsibility to pursue greater recognition for their subject within American history generally. "We had limited time and commitment . . . and I knew I needed to make an impact." This led Camarillo to work primarily with the Organization of American Historians because, he remembered, "I had to go to this big organization to do that." There was also a strong influence from students. Ricardo Romo observed that his undergraduates and graduate advisees retained the activist orientation of the first generation of Chicano scholars, and for that reason, they pursued the kinds of evidence and analysis that could help their communities: they researched civil rights activism, racial formation, social movements, immigration, and related subjects that were more directly applicable to political organizing and litigation in pursuit of substantive equality. Way led on to way, and it would be many years before the two fields began to converge once again.[22]

The four phases of Latino urban history—indifference, interest, recognition, and transformation—saw indifference giving way to interest in the early 1990s, with the second phase lasting through the late 2000s. In these years, a new generation of scholars published an expanding volume of articles and monographs on the subject, and a growing number of urban historians showed an interest in the place of Latinos in the field. The *Journal of Urban History* published its first article that meaningfully included Hispanics in its analysis in 1993. Over the five subsequent years, it followed up with an article and two extended review essays by Joseph Rodríguez after discussions between him and the journal's editor David Goldfield about the need for better coverage of this area. In all, the journal published six articles on Latino urban history across the 1990s and one in the 2000s. This period also saw the first awards given for research in the subfield: works of Latino history first garnered the Urban History Association's (UHA) article prize in 2004 and its dissertation prize in 2008. However, the clearest leading indicator of emerging work in the subfield—the number of papers on Hispanic themes at the UHA's biennial conferences—remained quite sparse, with only three in Pittsburgh in 2002, four in Milwaukee in 2004, and six in Houston in 2008.[23]

These years saw no shortage of monographs about Latinos in cities—the question was whether they asked the kinds of questions important to urban historians. Most of this scholarship, which appeared beginning in the early 1990s, was written by a new generation of historians studying ethnic Mexicans in the Southwest; they built upon the first wave of books from about twenty years earlier. Some of these works focused tightly on Hispanic communities, detailing their barrios, working lives, shared institutions, and patterns of protest and accommodation, but with less to say about their interactions with the city as a whole. Hence the *Journal of Urban History*'s *first* review of these books was titled "Mexicans in U.S. Cities"; Rodríguez noted that they did "not emphasize the urban dimension" and deemed most of them "not . . . urban history." That said, there were other works that directly addressed some of the basic subject matters of urban history, including municipal politics, labor and class relations, and immigration and ethnicity. Foremost among these was *Becoming Mexican American*, which deployed urban history methodologies like quantification and mapping and cited urban community studies at the top of the endnotes. Sánchez primarily addressed immigration and acculturation, interrogating the entire framework of assimilation theory by asking whether older models derived from European immigrants in the East and Midwest could accommodate Mexican newcomers to the Southwest. His research also inspired other historians, including Natalia Molina and William Deverell, to use the distinctive history of Los Angeles as a proving ground for urban-based inquiries into subjects like place identity, racial formation, health regulation, and policing.[24]

An equally important historiographical development in this "interest" phase was the emergence of scholarship on urban Latinos in new regions. A prime example was Zaragoza Vargas's *Proletarians of the North* (1993), which explored the history of Mexicans in Detroit and expanded upon this case study to offer trenchant observations about the entire Midwest. As the title suggested, this was very much a labor history, with Vargas emphasizing a number of interrelated points that defied older stereotypes: these Mexicans were industrial workers rather than agricultural ones, the skills they had honed in Mexico's railroad and other sectors drew U.S. companies to recruit them from a distance of two thousand miles, and the communities they built were as long-standing as substantial parts even of Mexican Los Angeles. Notably, as with Sánchez, Vargas's focus was on the first third of the twentieth century, before the mass repatriations of the Great Depression era. The migration of Mexicans to the United States in the final third of the century, which was roughly an order of magnitude larger, was implicit but not directly studied; and indeed, Vargas noted in *Major Problems in Mexican American History* (1999) that historians had done far too little work on the most recent decades. On a related note, while published during the decade that saw the largest number of immigrants to the United States in the nation's entire history, both works depicted communities that remained a very small percentage of their cities' overall populations—they were not yet a major force transforming entire cities.[25]

This was decidedly not the case in the other emergent regional historiography: the one that chronicled Cubans in metropolitan Miami. By the 1990s, that community's tremendous influence on the area was so economically, culturally, and politically apparent that the entire scholarly literature stood in the shadow of just how Hispanic that corner of the nation had become. As much was apparent when María Cristina García published *Havana USA* (1996), her enormously influential history of South Florida's Cuban community in which she explained the twisting and often unexpected path by which they became such a major force in the area and a huge demographic proportion of it. The same was true for similar work in other disciplines, as indicated by the subtitle of Alejandro Portes and Alex Stepick's sociological magnum opus *City on the Edge: The Transformation of Miami*. This literature also played another decisive role in Latino urban history because it moved the chronology firmly into the latter twentieth century, corresponding more clearly to the fast-rising number and proportion of people of Latin American ancestry in the United States.[26]

Finally, there was the study of Latino suburbia. This was key because it followed the field's broader attention to a metropolitan context as developed in books like *Streetcar Suburbs* and *Crabgrass Frontier*. But crucially, its origins were very different. Here, Matt García's *A World of Its Own* (2001) was highly influential in the way it carefully examined the particularities of ethnic Mexican migrant labor colonies and the way they became part of metropolitan geographies. Beginning his exploration in metropolitan Los Angeles, García pointed out how the nucleated camps that citrus workers had built were gradually absorbed into the area as suburbs rather than being one of the well-understood, largely transit-driven morphological types studied in other regions.[27]

Books like these that initiated or exemplified new directions within Latino urban and suburban history stood for some time as landmarks in their fields: they were not necessarily the only works in their areas, but they catalyzed a great deal of research among the next generation of scholars who, as we shall see, followed the trails blazed by their predecessors and thereby marked a new period in the scholarly literature.

The third phase of Latino urban history—a collective shout of *¡Manos a la obra!* that heralded numerous dissertations, articles, and books, followed in turn by leading figures and institutions recognizing Latinx history as a significant part of the field—began around 2010 and gained momentum for over a decade. This recognition was visible across a number of metrics. The *Journal of Urban History* published eighteen articles or review essays on Latina/o subjects during the 2010s, and from 2020 through 2023, there were seven such pieces in the journal. The UHA's conference programs have shown similar growth, with Latina/o-focused papers increasing rapidly: there were only six in Las Vegas in 2010, a number that rose to the mid-teens by the middle of the decade before crossing the twenty-paper mark in Chicago in 2016 and rising to more than thirty at the 2023 meeting in Pittsburgh. Other forms of institutional recognition also accelerated notably after 2010: the UHA gave awards to three dissertations, two articles, and three books on Latino urban history—this subfield, in other words, produced the winners between 20 percent and 30 percent of the time.[28]

The sheer volume of new books on Latino urban history in this period allowed for new analytical approaches to emerge alongside further elaborations of existing ones. The most distinctive and conceptually coherent of these was transnationalism, defined not simply as concerning people, goods, capital, and information that crossed borders but as ongoing interactions between places on either side of such borders and, in some cases, processes that operated beyond the control or logic of the nation-state. Jesse Hoffnung-Garskof's *A Tale of Two Cities* (2008) was an early exemplar that studied the way migrants and their ideas about development and popular culture bound the capitals of the Dominican Republic and the United States together in an extended exchange of intellectual and political influence. Historians also focused on ongoing crossings of the U.S-Mexico border, with Monica Perales's *Smeltertown* (2010) showing how El Paso's location shaped community, environment, and public health, and Geraldo Cadava's *Standing on Common Ground* (2013) emphasizing the border less as dividing and more as connecting Tucson and its Mexican hinterland, largely because of the huge volume of everyday crossings back and forth. Historians who took the transnational turn made many analytical points, but the most important ones have held that the scale and context of urban history should be extended geographically to show how large-scale, long-distance patterns of migration and return could shape entire categories of cities and other small urban places, and to show that globalization is instantiated in urban space right down to the level of individual blocks and households. Every history of a city, in this view, could be not just local but regional, hemispheric, or even global.[29]

Another of the major developments in this period was the ongoing elaboration of regional Latino urban histories. The historiography of the Latino Midwest centered on Chicago and flourished beginning around 2010. The scholars who wrote these histories took excellent advantage of key parts of the city's history and demographics, often citing the Chicago School to establish an intellectual pedigree and place their work at the center of the historical study of urbanism. The fact that the city's Latino community was both strongly Mexican and Puerto Rican was particularly important to Lilia Fernández's *Brown in the Windy City*, which broke away from the almost uniformly mono-ethnic character of most Latino urban histories to paint a more complex picture of Latinidad. Other scholars have contributed research on Latino communities in urban Michigan, Wisconsin, and Indiana, filling out the portrait of the entire region; this broad range of research culminated in a 2017 edited volume, *The Latino Midwest Reader*, that included material marking the full maturation of a Midwest Latino consciousness rooted in the region's old industrial cities and towns.[30] The Northeast has continued to be the leading center of research on Puerto Ricans, who continue as the most important subject of historical writing in this region, with the addition more recently of a promising emergent literature on Dominicans. For example, Llana Barber's *Latino City* (2017), which analyzes the kind of small postindustrial city in the region where many Puerto Ricans and Dominicans have been relocating from New York City, weaves their history into the broader question of the urban crisis. Jesse Hoffnung-Garskof's *Racial Migrations* (2019) takes up the much-understudied subject of Afro-Latinidad and moves the time frame of Latino urban history back into the nineteenth century, and Johanna Fernández's *The Young Lords* (2020) challenges our conventional understanding of postwar politics and its broader contexts.[31] The recent historiography's regional expansions also include the South, with research sites beyond the Miami area, including more conventionally Southern cities. There have been community studies in the region at least since Leon Fink's labor history *The Maya of Morganton* (2003), but it is only more recently that scholars have begun to ask more urbanistic questions, from Mary Odem's 2009 coedited volume to Sarah McNamara's recent book on Tampa; and Iliana Yamileth Rodriguez's research on Mexican Atlanta in this volume and her expected book will mark an important milestone in historical research in new parts of the Latino South.[32]

The theme of Latinx suburbia was also taken up by a new generation of scholars. While this might be taken as a Latino variant of the kind of work that Andrew Wiese did in his book on Black suburbia, the different origins of Latino suburbia that García pointed out involved a more complex metropolitan morphology. In *In Search of the Mexican Beverly Hills*, Jerry González used the municipalities of the Los Angeles area to explore the sharp disjuncture between spatial peripheralization and assimilation for Mexican Americans who moved to suburbia. Also working on suburban Los Angeles, Genevieve Carpio has shown in *Collisions at the Crossroads* (2019) how metropolitan space is itself implicated in the formation of racial identity and the privilege of moving from place to place in the modern metropolis. Most recently, this kind of work has been taken even further out to the metropolitan fringe, with Bobby Cervantes reengaging a newer category of *colonia* on the U.S.-Mexico border, showing how Latinos at the periphery were long involved in buying land, building homes, and struggling over power and resources as they were squeezed between expanding Texas municipalities.[33]

Historians also developed new approaches to the built environment, including Latino cultural landscapes, infrastructure, and institutions. Some built on the work of an earlier generation of geographers and planners who had identified distinctive place-identity features in places like Los Angeles and the Texas-Mexico borderlands: Daniel Arreola, in particular, authored a remarkable body of work including *Hispanic Spaces, Latino Places* (2004), which helpfully categorized places by characteristics like morphology, sequence of settlement, and relation to the border. This set the stage for a new generation of historians to research the theme of the complex and mutually constitutive interaction that created landscape, that is, the relationship between people and space. Lydia Otero, for example, showed in *La Calle* (2010) how mostly Anglo power brokers sought to use urban renewal to push Tucson's ethnic Mexicans out of their barrios and other areas of the city. Eric Avila's *The Folklore of the Freeway* (2014) interpreted the way Latino communities responded to elite efforts to make them sacrifice their homes and communities to the highway-building imperatives of civic leaders. And Kelly Lytle Hernández places Los Angeles at the center of what she repeatedly calls the nation's "carceral landscape," using the term to analyze a number of aspects of the phenomenon: the physical fact of prisons in the built environment, the way they have disproportionately removed Black men and Latinos from the city, and histories of urbanism, race, and punishment so intertwined that, as she points out, "men on the chain gang built the infrastructure and landscape of modern Los Angeles."[34]

Gender analysis, especially with regard to women, became a more consistent feature of Latino urban history in this period. From the beginnings of Latina history, key works took the form of urban community studies that were primarily concerned with labor, family, and sociability rather than urban morphology or municipal governance; these were exemplified by Virginia Sánchez Korrol's and Vicki Ruiz's landmark first books. The subsequent generation of scholars began to move the city from the site of gender analysis to its subject, revealing various points of articulation between urban life and gender. In most of their analyses, urban industrial labor was the main force driving change: this could be men's factory work transforming the household economy or women's introduction to wage labor transforming both family life and their relationship to the city, as described by historians like Monica Perales and Elizabeth Escobedo; or it could be the transition from a mostly male to a mostly female workforce, as in the case of Sarah McNamara's Ybor City. Partially overlapping with these dynamics were the more social concomitants of city life, with women's wage earning combining with the freedoms of the city to offer new options to Latinas—options that often engendered conflicts with parents and men in the community. Some scholars, including Lilia Fernández and Delia Fernández-Jones, emphasize how Latinas built upon these advances, rejecting attempts to limit their activities outside the home by engaging directly with city agencies in ways that flowed from their gender roles: making demands upon teachers and school boards, pursuing better municipal services in areas like recreation and sanitation, and seeking new uses for municipal antipoverty spending. In many cases these efforts led to direct involvement in urban politics and associational life, as Latina activists came to lead civic organizations and wield power as officeholders and policymakers. The fact that most of this research has been published within book chapters rather than as the central subject of monographs suggests that Latina urban history is an area with exceptional potential for further elaboration and innovation.[35]

This brings us to the recent past and present, the beginning of what we, the contributors to this volume, hope will become a period of transformation for Latinx metropolitan history. With Latino history rising within urban history, there is a real need for its practitioners to organize this growing scholarly current and to show why it must become, like African American urban history, an indispensable feature of the field, one without which it is impossible to understand present-day metropolitan America. (And as these essays show, we consistently look to the way that African American urban history transformed the field, seeking potential cues as to how we can follow our older-sibling subfield in driving critical inquiry and pathbreaking conceptual “turns” in the future.) Some of that work will involve the basic building blocks of a subfield: tasks like continuing to research and write community studies that document Latinx life in a variety of regional contexts, including established receiving communities but also expanding outward to newer settlements on the metropolitan periphery; showing how both panethnic and national identities formed in particular places and specific historical circumstances; and examining how these collectivities sought economic opportunity and political influence. In the process, we hope to find ways that Latinx metropolitan history can significantly revise long-standing narratives and assumptions about the trajectory of cities in the United States and the Americas.

Metropolitan history thus has a great deal to learn from Latino history's long engagement with the urban. At the most basic level, Latino historiography includes a great many community studies, which, while they proceed from different questions, are nonetheless methodologically parallel to past and present urban histories; it is easy to see the continuities that stretch from Camarillo, Griswold del Castillo, and Sánchez Korrol through to George Sánchez, Carmen Teresa Whalen, and other key historians of Latino urban America. Aside from the empirical information, Mexican American and Puerto Rican urban histories especially offer decades-long historiographies whose questions and turns can and should be studied as integral parts of the historiography of cities. It is certainly notable that some of the most influential scholars in Mexican American and Puerto Rican history have recently published books that explicitly address urban history or historiography.[36]

In this connection, it is also essential to recognize what Latino history has to gain from urban history. Perhaps the most important is an approach that emphasizes the future as much as the past, growth as well as expropriation—because as important as early Latino histories were, there was something they could not see because it was still over the time horizon of the future: the demographic transition that took “persons of Spanish language or heritage” from a few percent of the population to a projected one-third, including the aforementioned urban pluralities and majorities. The Chicano and Puerto Rican literatures were substantially articulated before it became clear how important ongoing migrations from Latin America were going to be in terms of demographics and urbanism. Latinx metropolitan history should therefore extend the analysis of those initial Chicano and Puerto Rican scholars in ways they could not have foreseen, including by positioning barrios not as artifacts of a fading past but as exemplars of a promising future. Here we see the potential fruits of a continued engagement with the idea of the barrio and *lo urbano* among Latinos.

If we think of this historiographical process as a rapprochement between two fields long alienated from each other—because my survey of two generations of leaders in the field of Latino history indicates that they have not generally thought of the field as still related to urban history—or as a reunification of divergent historiographies, there's a great deal of opportunity for fruitful reconsideration of the trajectories of both.

This volume is the first published collection of essays on Latino urban history. We offer both empirical research and broad rethinkings of the subfield as a way of surveying the existing literature and proposing an agenda going forward. Taken together, these chapters ask, What are we doing when we do Latino urban history? How have Latino communities been shaped by cities and in turn shaped them? And how does that change the field's master narratives? More broadly, we also hope to consider how Latino history might modify the approaches, methodologies, and contexts of urban history itself. In pursuit of this goal, *Metropolitan Latinidad* is divided into three parts—Metropolis, Neighborhood, and Hemisphere—each of which explores one of the geographies that is essential to writing a fully rendered Latinx metropolitan history.

Part 1, "Metropolis," focuses in part on individual cities or strictly urban settings and in part on suburbia because, for more than two decades, Latino populations have in absolute terms been growing faster in suburban areas than in either urban or rural ones. These chapters revisit some of the biggest long-standing questions or set pieces of urban and Latino history and ask what kinds of basic rethinking are made possible by the juxtaposition of these subfields. Pedro Regalado reinterprets the uprisings, riots, rebellions, and *disturbios urbanos* that shook the nation in the 1960s and 1970s, pointing out that some of these were Latino rather than (or in addition to) Black events and interrogating how this changes their meaning and allows us to see something new in them. Yami Rodriguez focuses our attention on two kinds of place-making in metropolitan Atlanta: how Mexican migrants, entering a landscape that offered no place to them, carved out social spaces at their places of work and how, as workers, these migrants literally built the metropolitan landscape itself. Thomas Sugrue inquires into the origins of inequality in newer Latino suburbs, looking for ways that older forms of mainly Black-white segregation managed to reinscribe themselves on the rapidly Latinizing crabgrass frontier of Long Island. Exploring greater Los Angeles, Becky Nicolaides sets up a comparison with America's other major immigrant-stock demographic, Asian Americans, asking what Wei Li's key term *ethnoburb* can reveal about the distinctive characteristics of Latino suburban development. In so doing, these scholars reveal new ways to historicize America's metropolitan fringe.

Part 2 is entitled "Neighborhood." Here, we turn our focus to the geographic scale at which the largest proportion of Americans have experienced the city for most of their lives; it has often served as a set piece for historians seeking a close-up look at urban life. While this might seem like an easier scale to analyze than others, it can be just as complex by showing how individual lives shape and are shaped by broader geographies and temporalities. It is at the neighborhood level that broad-gauge interpretive frameworks can best be tested and, in many cases, disputed. Sandra Enríquez takes a close look at El Paso's El Segundo Barrio, analyzing both a city on the U.S.-Mexico border and a neighborhood that exists right at the literal dividing line. She details how barrio residents implemented a housing plan that reclaimed adobe, revealing how Mexican American tenants challenged racial, political, and cultural erasure in the borderlands through direct participation in late twentieth-century urban redevelopment policy. Felipe Hinojosa looks into the spiritual life of New York City's Protestant Evangelicals in the 1970s, explaining how local congregations grouped together in a quest to create an active ministry that reflected their understanding of Christianity and was relevant to the lives of their parishioners and prospective converts. In the process, he contests some of the dominant narratives that undergird both religious histories and studies of the urban crisis. Llana Barber addresses the perennial question of pan-ethnic signifiers and collective identity, showing how the local setting fundamentally shapes the way that Latinos in actually existing circumstances have organized themselves for action using particular nomenclatures. She also explores what kinds of exclusions and misapprehensions may result when people ignore the specificity of urban context. Max Krochmal and Cecilia Sánchez Hill show how a single neighborhood in a single city—Polytechnic Heights in Fort Worth, Texas—is a microcosm of local ethnic and racial change in which immigrants from Mexico and Central America transform the demography and prospects of a once lily-white, then predominantly Black, now mostly Latino neighborhood; they also show how Poly is emblematic of larger social and political transformations. Michael Innis-Jiménez takes an even more closely focused approach, one centered on neighborhood Mexican restaurants in Chicago. He expands on a methodology recently taken up by Natalia Molina in *A Place at the Nayarit*, in the process displaying the full potential of microhistories to reveal the contours of everyday life in early twentieth-century Mexican settlements.

Part 3, “Hemisphere,” expands the scale of inquiry to show how Latinos in cities routinely extend the geographies of urban history. Cities have always functioned as central points of connection between distant places, but the presence of people from Latin America has reoriented the map and intensified the level of connectedness across national boundaries. While the idea of Atlantic crossings was very important to the development of the transnational turn in history, this section shows the ongoing intellectual payoff of considering urban history across the Americas. Looking back further in time than any other essay in this collection, Eduardo Contreras asks how the concept of Latinx might help us assess developments both in and beyond the United States; he inquires whether particular experiences or processes might have prefigured a Latino condition in the late twentieth and early twenty-first centuries. Mauricio Castro emphasizes the transnational geopolitics of the Cold War, showing how ideological struggles against communism shaped the development of U.S. cities. He begins with Miami and Havana but suggests that urbanism throughout the Americas was directly and clearly influenced by the Cold War. Monika Gosin analyzes how Afro-Latinos have experienced and responded to racialization in highly place-specific ways, demonstrating a new approach to racial formation that attends to the growth of minority-majority cities where non-Hispanic whites are not the largest demographic and race is shaped by locally predominant minoritized groups. She also pays close attention to the way racialization in the United States has been fundamentally shaped by hemispheric cultural currents in which Blackness was sometimes celebrated but more often denigrated or effaced.

There is a fair amount of distance between a conference, an edited collection, and a manifesto. But eight underlying areas of particular importance seem to emerge from our chapters: migration, politics, identity, landscape, transnationalism, empire, labor, and gender.

Migration: In almost every chapter in this volume, the Latinos and Latinas at the center of the story are migrants or migrants’ children. Indeed, one might easily venture that all Latino history is the history of migration.[37] Their arrival in metropolitan America is the fundamental material fact underlying their transformative history. The subsequent paths of influence vary tremendously: we foreground Latinos as protesters, builders, voters, entrepreneurs, employees, planners, evangelists, and students, all roles that have allowed them to shape their communities. While the sheer depth of historical time behind the Indigenous-Spanish presence remains an indispensable rationale for Latino history, a personal or immediate-family history of migration is the modal experience, and these chapters’ chronological focus certainly favors the more recent Latino past. Some of the chapters in *Metropolitan Latinidad* touch on the economic, political, imperial, or geostrategic reasons for these migrations. All of them analyze the changes wrought by the presence of Latinas and Latinos, whether demographic, urbanistic, social, electoral, entrepreneurial, or aesthetic. And a few deal with migrants' planned or actual return voyages to their place of origin. But in every case, these are histories of a people continuously on the move—at hemispheric, metropolitan, and neighborhood scales.

Politics: Latinos have been a significant factor in U.S. public life for decades, and in the past ten years, they have been forced into the white-hot center of national politics. The central theme has been their struggle to obtain a share of political power and public resources that is commensurate with the size of their population. Latinos' preponderance in many cities and suburban towns has meant that municipal politics offer the best chance at influence and officeholding, and several of these chapters look closely at local governance, apportionment, and grassroots mobilization. Our contributors also recognize how local issues can ramify in state, regional, national, and international struggles, and they attend to the challenges Latinos face as they attempt to define and position themselves among longer-established interest groups. These subjects have considerable historiographical potential: after all, the revitalization of urban history in the mid-1990s involved research that showed how national political trends originated or were shaped by municipal-level conflicts over race and resources. In an era when not just Latinos' choices and prerogatives but their very presence has been cynically politicized and consistently lied about, it is absolutely essential that we understand the place of Latinidad in politics—especially given the yawning gulf between America's dependence on Latinos and the way they have been repeatedly scapegoated in the nation's electoral and cultural conflicts.

Identity: One of the basic questions of Latino studies is, Who are Latinos, and why does this matter? The contributors to *Metropolitan Latinidad* engage with this issue in specific urban and suburban contexts, emphasizing actually existing processes of identity formation. We analyze collectivities in practice and in place, as close empirical work is a more revealing methodology than abstract debates over pan-ethnicity and terminology. These chapters show how the formation of Latinidad has been shaped by older and more pervasive cultural structures of whiteness and Blackness. They also explore other relevant comparisons, including the more recent and sometimes simultaneous formation of predominantly Latino and Asian American metropolitan enclaves. These contexts are essential because so many U.S. cities are now minority-majority municipalities in which white people are not necessarily the unmarked reference points in processes of racialization and minoritization. We also emphasize that even local and contingent identities form within larger cultural geographies that reach beyond the United States and into Latin America and other regions worldwide.

Landscape: The built environment is among the most fundamental parts of what makes a city a city or a suburb a suburb, and accordingly, we engage this aspect in all the forms in which it operates, from the physical to the social to the symbolic. At the most basic level, Hispanics have for decades been the group of Americans most disproportionately represented in doing the actual work of construction. Our contributors also emphasize the important role that Latino immigrants and expatriates have played in channeling essential resources like government spending, local capital, and mortgage and rent payments into cities and suburbs. Having done so much to create built environments, we explain, Latinas and Latinos were essential in occupying, ornamenting, and animating them as tenants, homeowners, entrepreneurs, consumers, activists, community organizers, placemakers, and institution builders. In many cases, their activities and aesthetics became the stuff of local controversy, especially when non-Latinos and even some Latinos began to object to and legislate against things like Spanish-language signage and street vending. In all cases, though, these chapters manifest the belief that landscapes are "good to think with"—that a close-in focus on everyday life in ordinary spaces is an indispensable part of urban and suburban history.

Transnationalism: Latinos are far and away the largest immigrant group and the largest transnational population in the United States. Their presence is an embodiment of globalization, and their migration to metropolitan areas concentrates its effects in specific localities. Latinas and Latinos thus present an excellent opportunity to study world-spanning processes at the human scale and in particular times and places—a useful alternative to theoretical abstraction and grand narrative. Migrants have created many kinds of connections between cities and across borders—connections whose persistence is essential to the very definition of transnationalism as a theoretical term (although, notably, these activities have been so common among Latinos as to be totally unremarkable). The essays in *Metropolitan Latinidad* remind us that Latin American migrants have maintained such connections for a very long time, affording us an opportunity to reconsider the temporal boundaries of Latinidad. They show how even small groups of migrants can shape the geopolitical strategies of a range of officialdom, from city councils to heads of state. And they demonstrate how transborder movements of people are not simply the side effects of capital flows but the origin and reason for subsequent flows of money, goods, and ideas.

Empire: The United States has been an empire for more than two centuries. This was true even before the 1823 articulation of the Monroe Doctrine, which positioned the nation as the rightful hegemon of all the Americas. Our contributors emphasize that Latinos in the United States, like their ancestors and coethnics in Latin America, have existed in a condition of coloniality. In terms of the specifically urban, work in this volume shows how the imperial reach of the United States created a hemispheric network of travelers to cities, one that allows us to think more broadly—not just in space but also in time—about a term like *Latinx*. These chapters also demonstrate that this condition of coloniality did not end at the point of migration: U.S. imperial imperatives often determined who would be forced to migrate, in which cities they would be incentivized to settle, and with which economic burdens or advantages. Moreover, our contributors remind us that the racial position of Latinos in metropolitan areas has been shaped by the unequal and largely predatory relationship between the United States and Latin America.

Labor: Urban and Latino historiographies share an important commonality in that both have long emphasized the importance of work, whether agricultural, industrial, domestic, or associational. Latinos have been a predominantly working-class and increasingly urbanized people for whom the pursuit of fairly compensated employment has meant ongoing struggles in astonishingly unequal metropolitan economies. Meanwhile, cities and suburbs have become totally dependent upon the labor of Latinas and Latinos, especially, but not exclusively, in the construction, childcare, agribusiness, food service, and maintenance sectors. The contributors to *Metropolitan Latinidad* thus return time and again to the basics of work opportunities, wage levels, and macroeconomic transformations (especially deindustrialization and neoliberalization) as foundational parts of our understanding of the Latino urban past. Because when we think about the right to the city (and suburbs), it makes sense to begin with the material fact of precisely whose labor has built and maintained these places.

Gender: Our contributors consistently read labor through gender. In one sense, this means elaborating on the way women's work has been essential to economic survival, cultural preservation, and community formation—a theme that has been fundamental to Latina history since the foundational work of Virginia Sánchez Korrol and Vicki Ruiz. They also emphasize the way that both men's and women's labor have undergirded the work of building homes and running businesses, as well as sustaining the sense of family that makes that work meaningful. In addition, their essays show how gendered labor is not just material but also cultural, because it has been essential to the performance of service and authenticity. They also raise the difficult issue of how Latinos have often excluded Latinas from institutional leadership and political power despite women's indispensable work in maintaining families and communities.

The trajectory of Latino history as part of urban history has been slow and sometimes frustrating, but things are quite unmistakably headed in the right direction. For two decades in the 1970s and 1980s, historians who understood Latino history as aligned with urban history were largely ignored. But a new generation of scholars kept at it in the 1990s—the decade of the greatest migration to the United States of any in history—by continuing to insist that Latino histories had something important to say about subjects of central importance to urban history. They inspired yet another generation of scholars in the new millennium to keep asking questions and making claims about the due and proper place of people of Latin American heritage in the cities in which they were becoming an ever greater proportion of the population. And as this collection hopes to demonstrate, we are now at the point of breaking out and not just challenging but revising long-standing ways of thinking in the field.

Urban history could serve as an example to the broader field of history, where progress has been somewhat slower. While there have been some real advances, Latinos and Latinas are still too often ignored or relegated to a sidebar. We still see too many big-think essays and plenary sessions that lack any reference to Latinos or our historical perspectives, even in areas where we could enrich the discussion. It remains the case that our experiences are often portrayed as merely appurtenant to other groups of minoritized people: what Aldo Lauria Santiago has called "the '. . . and Latinos' problem." And there are still too many grand narratives and analytic frameworks that get reiterated even though they do not adequately engage a multicultural America—and even when Latino histories have called them into question. We should therefore endeavor to keep writing metropolitan histories that show how Latino history can help renew and transform other fields and make them relevant and ready for the next generation of Americans.[38]

It is in this spirit that we offer *Metropolitan Latinidad* as what we hope is a measured and authoritative statement about the most important aspects of an agenda for Latino urban history. We approach this subject with humility, recognizing that there are a great many ways to pursue research in this area and that there is only so much that can be included in a single edited volume. For this reason, we wish to make clear that we regard this as an opening endeavor rather than a comprehensive one. We are acutely aware of the extraordinary diversity of origin and experience among Latinos living in very different circumstances throughout the United States, and we look earnestly forward to more scholarship on more people in more places. We have had the pleasure of learning about so much promising work from talented emerging scholars who could contribute to Latinx urban and suburban history. Ultimately, our most important purpose in *Metropolitan Latinidad* is to invite them to join us by offering them possible frameworks for conceptualizing their research. *¡Ojalá que nos acepten la invitación!*

Metropolis

1

Latinx Uprisings: Violence, Representation, and Social Movements in Urban America, 1960s–1970s

PEDRO A. REGALADO
Stanford University

In March 1968, the National Advisory Commission on Civil Disorders, better known as the Kerner Commission, issued its landmark report on the urban uprisings that erupted in the mid-1960s. In the analysis, the report's authors declared their oft-cited conclusion: "Our nation is moving towards two societies, one black, one white—separate and unequal." Later that year, hundreds of uprisings once again tore through U.S. cities following the assassination of Martin Luther King Jr. They persisted into the 1970s, reflecting a level of internal violence, writes Elizabeth Hinton, "on a scale not seen since the Civil War." Whether termed *riots*, *uprisings*, or *rebellions*, these events remain symbols of a turbulent era marked by the racial injustice the commission famously acknowledged.[1]

Yet the Kerner Commission's formulation of "two societies, one black, one white" belied what it offered about other parts of the nation. "Much of our report is directed to the condition of those Americans who are also Negroes and to the social and economic environment in which they live—many in the black ghettoes of our cities. But this Nation is confronted with the issue of justice for all its people," the commission declared, including "the people of Spanish surname."[2]

Though mentioned only briefly in the extensive report, Latinx Americans—at that time primarily Mexican, Puerto Rican, and Cuban migrants and their descendants—were slowly transforming America's social fabric.[3] The Census Bureau estimated that approximately nine million "persons of Spanish origin" lived in the United States by 1970—a sharp increase from approximately six million a decade earlier.[4] Activists criticized the bureau for its imprecision, which included overcounting in some areas of the country and undercounting in others. Despite these errors, it was clear that the population had experienced a dramatic increase.[5]

Most Latinxs resided in urban areas, a phenomenon reflected in the number of major cities where they made up a significant share of the populace. By one count, predominantly Mexican American Latinxs comprised about 17 percent of Los Angeles's 2.8 million residents in 1970. Similarly, in New York City, an overwhelmingly Puerto Rican population of Latinxs comprised more than 16 percent of 7.9 million New Yorkers. And in Miami, San Antonio, and El Paso, they represented nearly half or more of local inhabitants.[6]

As Latinxs labored to make their way in cities like these, urban life impressed its particularities on them. They confronted public and private discrimination in housing and employment, frequent police brutality, and scant electoral representation. Ongoing deindustrialization in Northern cities, where poet Pedro Pietri scribed a "Puerto Rican Obituary," and uneven industrial expansion in the American West and Southwest, where Lorna Dee Cervantes remembered life "beneath the shadow of the freeway," aggravated these hardships, framing how Latinx urbanites experienced the political economy of ethnic and racial change.[7]

In the same breath that the Kerner Commission recognized the injustices Latinxs faced, its report asserted that the community had "continued to keep faith with society in the preservation of public order." But this was not so. Puerto Ricans and Mexican Americans participated in dozens of their own uprisings from the mid-1960s and into the 1970s. As scholars have argued regarding the Black American uprisings of this period, these rebellions were not spontaneous acts of senseless mob violence. Nor were they political simply because participants were oppressed. Instead, as this chapter demonstrates, these pivotal moments in Latinx history repeatedly ignited in the context of long-standing grievances and demands involving young people, activists, parishioners, antipoverty workers, politicians, and a cross section of everyday residents.[8]

From this vantage point, a continental account of rebellion—from Chicago to New York, Hartford to Camden, Los Angeles to Albuquerque—offers a prism for examining the wide-ranging political commitments that emerged from Latinx urban America, as well as essential context for a deeper understanding of the era's racial politics more broadly. On the ground, mass violence directed at police or property symbolized an unabashed "right to the city" and empowered local leaders to exert greater pressure on elected representatives to address Latinx needs in housing, safety, services, and employment. In the process, they also opened opportunities for Latinxs and Black Americans to deepen their solidarities. Yet, if at the local level rioting formed one part of a complex communal revolt, it meant something altogether different at the federal level. For an emerging core of Latinx representatives in Washington, DC, rioting jeopardized their goal of crafting a cohesive "Spanish-speaking" constituency. The following pages chart these converging histories, highlighting how residents struggled against poverty, police violence, and political marginalization, and *for* power in the American city—a multifaceted episode in the broader Latinx urban experience that this volume explores.[9]

On the last day of the weeklong festivities of Chicago's first Puerto Rican Day parade in June 1966, a white patrolman shot and wounded a Puerto Rican man, Arcelis Cruz. Crowds gathered to condemn the officer, and widespread violence between onlookers and police soon erupted on Division Street near Chicago's Humboldt Park. Rioting spanned several days as residents scorched squad cars, smashed windows, and battled police with bricks, rocks, bottles, and scattered sniper fire.

Puerto Rican Chicagoans attributed their fury to long-standing anti–Puerto Rican discrimination, especially in the form of frequent police brutality that had been building up for several years. Writing just one year before the clash, one Puerto Rican editorialist warned that the time would "come when we will have war on Division Street because of a lack of understanding between police and our people." Thinking back years later, a different resident remembered that "lack of understanding" as the systemic criminalization of Puerto Ricans. "One very visible thing was police abuse," he recalled. "If you were Latino, you would get stopped and searched."[10]

Chicago's upheaval foreshadowed Latinx uprisings in cities across the industrial North, with police violence frequently serving as their catalyst. In 1967, a New York City police officer shot a Puerto Rican man, Reinaldo Rodriguez, alleging that the twenty-five-year-old had been wielding a knife. Later that evening, young protesters and hundreds of police officers confronted each other on the streets and avenues of East Harlem. Police shot and killed two residents, fueling greater chaos as rioting spread across the East River into the South Bronx. Mayor John Lindsay attempted to calm the revolt, engineering a truce between Puerto Rican youth leaders and Police Commissioner Howard Leary, but the respite was short-lived. Enraged young people cooled off after several days, but not before smashing windows and looting scores of businesses. Seeing an opportunity to condemn the mayor for his failure to attend to their three-month-old recommendations, the city's Puerto Rican Community Conference recognized "the riot as the expression of long years of frustration, anger and victimization of the Puerto Rican community."[11]

Rioting gripped New York just a year later when Puerto Ricans battled the city's Tactical Police Force on the Lower East Side, but it also took hold across the metropolitan region in smaller cities where Puerto Rican migrants put down roots after World War II. In July 1968 in Paterson, New Jersey, young Puerto Rican and Black protesters reportedly "firebombed buildings from roofs and bombarded automobiles with cinder blocks" after police arrested a Puerto Rican man for opening a fire hydrant. According to local leader José Rios, the community demanded a halt to police use of tear gas to quell disturbances, the removal of police patrol cars from Puerto Rican neighborhoods, and more recreational facilities for the city's Puerto Rican youth. Unrest spanned five days and ended in over 150 arrests.[12]

The following summer, seventy miles south in Trenton, several hundred people gathered to protest a police officer who shot a Puerto Rican teenager, Miguel Hernandez. According to local reporting, residents clashed with sixty helmeted police accompanied by K-9 dogs for three hours. The next day, some protesters carried placards that read "Puerto Rican Power" and demanded the release of Hernandez, who had been wanted on a warrant for breaking and entering and who lay in the hospital recovering from his wound. Similar to the events in East Harlem two years earlier, a local antipoverty official brokered a deal between police and crowds, promising that Hernandez would be released on bail after leaving the hospital. This time, the compromise seemed to have worked.[13]

For Puerto Ricans of the postwar diaspora, some who resettled in the industrial North in search of economic stability and others their progeny for whom the broken promises of the industrial city stoked a fiery Puerto Rican nationalism, police brutality was the match in the powder barrel of daily oppression. Poorly resourced schools, hospitals, and neighborhood services fomented community resentment. Substandard housing, in particular, typically emerged as the most pressing issue, one that residents and local elected officials frequently discussed during riot-driven negotiations. Beginning in the 1950s, many municipalities deployed federal resources to fund "urban renewal" projects intended to offer low- and middle-income residents better housing while revitalizing the urban core. Across the country, however, urban renewal "slum clearance" regularly displaced disproportionately poor and nonwhite tenants, including Puerto Ricans. In one of the most recognizable cases, the Lincoln Center for the Performing Arts on Manhattan's Upper West Side was constructed on the demolished site of a neighborhood that housed working-class Puerto Ricans living alongside Black and white-ethnic residents. But urban renewal also unfolded in smaller cities where redevelopment failed to address housing insecurity and signaled to many residents

FIGURE 1.1. Passaic, New Jersey, during the 1969 uprising. *Debris Is Strewn*, photograph by George D. McDowell, Philadelphia Evening Bulletin Photograph Collection, S413183B. Special Collections Research Center, Temple University Libraries, Philadelphia, PA.

that elected leaders—often liberal Democrats—were indifferent to the lack of adequate shelter as one of life's core necessities.[14]

This was the case in nearby Passaic, New Jersey, a municipality twelve miles west of New York City, which experienced three days of rioting in the summer of 1969 (fig. 1.1). Passaic received approximately $5.9 million (approximately $60 million today) in federal funds for three urban renewal projects by 1965. But before the decade was over, many of the city's six thousand Puerto Ricans rose up against housing insecurity by challenging the eviction of a mother, Petra Maldonado, and her eleven children from their small apartment. As in many other cities, municipal neglect facilitated private plunder. In the months leading up to the August 1969 eviction, landlords raised rents substantially, according to Odis Walker, the chairman of the Passaic Conference of Economic Opportunity, a local antipoverty agency. "The problem is much broader than one family," Walker maintained, observing that several thousand people in Passaic occupied 186 substandard dwellings that were "totally unfit for people to live in."[15]

The incident began after hundreds of Puerto Ricans marched peacefully on City Hall in support of Maldonado, against her landlord, and for better housing generally. It is unclear what exactly triggered confrontations between some residents and police, but skirmishes began in the evening and lasted three days. Witnesses saw Puerto Rican youth smashing shop windows, hurling rocks, and tossing firebombs, while other reports described hundreds of participants jeering at police as they moved through the streets. Amid the tumult, the Associated Press reported that "stores with Puerto Rican or Spanish names were carefully exempted, while shops adjacent were stripped."

Passaic's Housing Authority relocated Maldonado to a four-room apartment. Still, the driving force behind the initial protest—housing insecurity—did not seem to resonate with elected officials in the way demonstrators had hoped. That week, the New Jersey State Assembly passed a bill in an emergency session that allowed state funds for urban aid, including housing, to be diverted to pay higher salaries for police and firefighters.[16]

As the uprisings in these five cities suggest, the industrial North became a theater of Latinx rebellion rooted in police violence and the deeper systems of postindustrial oppression: by November 1971, more than three dozen Latinx uprisings had swept across cities in the region.[17]

Latinx popular violence was not confined to the nation's North, however—beginning in 1970, rebellions surged across the American West with increasing frequency. Among the most severe of these took place on August 29 of that year, when up to thirty thousand participants, mostly Mexican Americans from across the country, marched in a nonviolent rally in East Los Angeles (fig. 1.2). Known as the Chicano Moratorium demonstration, the gathering was intended to protest the high number of Mexican American deaths in the Vietnam War. Mayhem ensued when police provoked moratorium demonstrators, including families with children, with tear gas and nightsticks at Laguna Park after declaring the demonstration unlawful. One group of protesters stood up to the police, battling with them in the park and along Whittier Boulevard. The clash resulted in three deaths, including that of the Mexican American journalist Rubén Salazar, whom police killed when they fired a tear gas canister that struck him in the head as he sat at the Silver Dollar Cafe seeking a brief respite from the violence all around.[18]

Much like their Puerto Rican peers in the Northeast and Midwest, young Chicano activists perceived police murders and other brutalities as forming one aspect of a broader structure of domination targeting their communities. And like Puerto Rican radicals, including the Young Lords Party, underpinning this argument was the role of urban space in perpetuating a legacy of dispossession. For this reason, one element of the Chicano movement's goal of ending anti–Mexican American discrimination was, as outlined in *El plan espiritual de Aztlán*, struggling for the "control of our Barrios," which Chicano street battles with police vividly underscored.[19]

It was not long before young Mexican Americans and police clashed again. A month after the August melee, demonstrators and police collided

FIGURE 1.2. Chicano Moratorium demonstrators in East Los Angeles, 1970 (cropped). Los Angeles Times Photographic Archive, UCLA Libraries Special Collections.

after thousands of residents celebrated Mexican Independence Day in East LA. The confrontation ended in dozens of arrests and serious injuries. Then, on January 9, 1971, demonstrators struggled against police once more. The conflict originated when the National Chicano Moratorium Committee held a demonstration against police brutality targeting Chicanos that began in Boyle Heights and ended downtown, where a confrontation between police and protesters "erupted into a rock-throwing, club-swinging melee." "Over 50 Chicanos involved in the moratorium committee have been beaten or arrested by police in the past month," Rosalio Muñoz, committee cochair, told protesters before the riot. "We are marching to prove that we can protest peacefully, and that we will not be intimidated by police."[20]

Similar instances of Mexican American rebellion unfolded in Southwestern cities during the 1970s, beginning with Pharr, a small city on the Texas-Mexico border. There, Mexican Americans had vocalized their frustration with their local government in "months of protests against unfair politics, community inequality, and police brutality," writes the historian David Robles. In February 1971, a community demonstration calling for the ouster of the city's police chief and other officers escalated into a riot wherein police killed one bystander. Protests persisted, and the following year, Pharr elected its first Mexican American mayor.[21]

Uprisings continued that summer in Albuquerque's Roosevelt Park when police attempted to arrest a teenager among a crowd of several hundred young people. Heavily armed police battled protesters over two days as downtown Albuquerque lay in tatters.[22] Rebellion returned to Texas in 1973 after hundreds of Mexican American and Black residents in Dallas gathered to protest the killing of twelve-year-old boy Santos Rodriguez at the hands of a white police officer. The rally began peacefully but escalated when some protesters, agitated by the large police presence, hurled bottles at them and proceeded to smash windows and loot stores, resulting in the arrests of thirty people. In a city where they mutually endured police brutality, the reaction to Santos's death, Katherine Bynum notes, revealed "the frustration of Black and Brown activists who refused to silently bear the abuses of the Dallas Police Department."[23] And in 1977, Mexican Americans in Houston expressed their collective anger after police beat and killed Mexican American army veteran Joe Campos Torres. Dissatisfied with the officers' punishment, over one thousand community members protested Campos's death the following year, clashing with police in the city's Moody Park.[24]

By the late 1970s, the Latinx uprisings that had frequented American cities since police shot Arcelis Cruz in Chicago numbered more than seventy. Aggressive policing often lit the fuse, but the ensuing violence against property or police was typically paired with demands stemming from deep-seated grievances that reflected Latinx communities' growing sense of urban belonging. At the same time, situating these events within the broader social, political, and economic context of the era raises important considerations. Were these uprisings, as one scholar put it, the "unorganized face" of the radical social movements embodied by the Young Lords and Brown Berets? In what ways was unrest linked to the broader zeitgeist of more frequent uprisings in Black communities? And did Latinx mass violence precipitate the steep decline of industrial cities, as several of these instances were popularly remembered? Camden, New Jersey, offers a compelling case for examining such questions.[25]

Camden's Puerto Rican community emerged during World War II when local industries hired individuals from the island to fill wartime jobs. The city's largest manufacturer, Campbell's Soup Company, recruited about one thousand Puerto Rican men with the help of the War Manpower Commission. Before the decade was over, thousands more arrived seeking work in the Garden State's booming agriculture industry, picking and piling produce into baskets and trucks. While many workers returned to Puerto Rico at the end of their seasons, others put down roots in Camden. As a result, the city's Puerto Rican population grew from a few hundred in the 1940s to approximately twelve thousand by 1970 (this out of a total population of just over one hundred thousand).[26]

Puerto Ricans made Camden home just as its industrial fortunes turned for the worse. The city housed 224 business establishments that employed nearly thirty-nine thousand workers in 1947. Three decades later, those establishments dropped to 177, and the total number of production workers—the heart of the city's economy—dropped to 7,700. As in other Northern cities, postwar deindustrialization was paired with suburbanization and its racial politics. Before the war, whites accounted for roughly 90 percent of Camden residents. By the time the tumultuous 1960s concluded, they had made up little more than half of the city's population, with Black residents and, to a lesser extent, Puerto Ricans comprising the rest.[27]

The city's postindustrial transition brought high unemployment and declining public investment in housing and other public services, just as it did elsewhere in the state. And as happened in Newark, Paterson, and Trenton, police brutality sparked mass violence in Camden—a pattern repeated by police lieutenants Gary Miller and Warren Worrell on the night of July 30, 1971. That evening, the two patrolmen stopped Rafael Gonzales for erratic driving. They instructed Gonzales to exit his car. When he did, they beat him within an inch of his life. Carmen Villanueva witnessed the incident and later explained to a grand jury that Gonzales had fallen after the second lieutenant exited the patrol car and joined in, striking him on the head. "They started kicking him and hitting him with a nightstick. He was bleeding bad, and there was a pool of blood," she stated. The brutal assault left Gonzales in a coma. He died a few weeks later from the injuries that Miller and Worrell inflicted on him that evening.[28]

Following Gonzales's hospitalization, Camden's Puerto Rican community called for the suspension of the two officers, who had been assigned to the department's Strategic Relations Division—a group infamous for its rough tactics. When Mayor Joseph M. Nardi Jr. failed to act, 150 Puerto Rican community members and their supporters marched on City Hall carrying a large Puerto Rican flag and a banner of the Puerto Rican Liberation Front. Representatives among them met with the city's business administrator Joseph D. Dorris to provide the mayor's administration with a list of demands. Protesters called for the immediate suspension of Miller and Worrell, a complete investigation conducted by a grand jury, more Puerto Ricans on the police force, and censure by the mayor of the public safety director William Yeager and "his autocratic control of the police." They also insisted on Spanish-language interpreters to inform Puerto Ricans of their rights when arrested, along with competent public defenders.[29]

FIGURE 1.3. Latinx community leaders discussing their demands with Mayor Nardi and Public Safety Director Yeager at City Hall moments before the uprising began. Gil Medina pictured in the middle wearing sunglasses. *Conference Gets Under Way before Violence Cuts It Short . . .*, photograph by James Stewart, from *Courier-Post*, August 20, 1971. © James Stewart—USA Today Network.

Camden's police chief Harold Melleby charged officers Millar and Worrell with atrocious assault and battery, but the two were not suspended. A week later, on August 19, hundreds of Camden residents gathered at City Hall. This time, protesters' objectives included more than reforming law enforcement in the city. Among other needs, they pushed for community control of institutions, Puerto Rican employees in all departments and levels of City Hall, and more Puerto Rican personnel in the Camden Housing Authority, emphasizing, "We must have a voice in the running of city government."[30]

The demonstration began around noon, but Mayor Nardi refused to meet with community leaders until the evening, when the crowd had grown to approximately 1,200. While the two parties negotiated on the seventeenth floor of City Hall (fig. 1.3), the peaceful demonstration devolved into a brawl between police and many participants. One schoolteacher remembered witnessing police pushing people, including mothers with children, against a wall with their nightsticks. Only after that and the use of tear gas, she told reporters, did she see demonstrators or others throw bottles and stones.[31]

The rebellion plunged Camden into chaos for nearly a week. Hundreds were injured, several people were shot, the city's 328-member police force received backup from seventy-eight New Jersey state troopers, and its fire department struggled to keep track of fires. According to the local attorney Joseph Rodriguez, some fires were sparked by police tear gas: "It was hot.

Some of the tear gas that landed on their porches was dry, and fires were being started. So now, we even had people from the community forming fire brigades to put fires out because we didn't want to burn our own houses."[32]

The son of a Puerto Rican mother and a Cuban father, Rodriguez was among the handful of local Latinx leaders who met with city officials before and during the rioting, leveraging the community's rage to advocate for its needs. He was joined by a group of community-oriented professionals, including his brother, Mario, a former Camden city councilman and then commissioner for the State Division of Civil Rights; Hector Rodriguez, director of the state's Puerto Rican Convention; Angel Perez, director of the Community Organization for Puerto Rican Affairs; and Yolanda Aguilar de Neely, a Mexican American case worker at El Centro, Camden's social service center for Puerto Rican and other Latinx parents. Joining them too was Gualberto "Gil" Medina, a college student who helped spearhead the August 12 and 19 demonstrations (see fig 1.3).[33]

Medina represented a generation of Puerto Ricans who came of age in the city amid the era's radical social movements and proved more confrontational in their tactics than Rodriguez and his peers. Still, the senior at Rutgers and member of the Young Lords Party later underscored how the demonstration that preceded the riot drew from a wide spectrum of the community. "It wasn't just students," he remembered decades later. "It was a cross-section of Hispanics. It was a broad base, leaders of all sides of the spectrum, conservatives to the students. The whole mall was full of people." "This was not a protest movement of the young hotheads," he concluded. "It was far from that."[34]

Crucially, the outrage over Gonzales's beating also extended to Camden's Black leaders, several of whom had established strong relationships with the city's Puerto Ricans. Medina, for example, was a mentee of Charles "Poppy" Sharp, founder of the city's Black People's Unity Movement. Sharp had witnessed a riotous Camden before: in September 1969, violence erupted in South Camden after a large crowd confronted police attempting to arrest a man. The details of the incident were disputed, but gunshots rang out, claiming the lives of a police officer and a teenage Black girl. This time, recognizing Puerto Rican indignation, Sharp connected their communities' struggles against police. "I know I'm not speaking for many blacks in Camden," he stated, "but as a black man, and as a member of a suppressed minority, I know I speak for all blacks, including the silent ones because they know the next day it might be one of them whose rights are violated." His solidarity was clear: "We support the Puerto Rican community because we too have been victims of police brutality."[35]

The camaraderie these two groups forged during the early 1970s was not a predestined course. Puerto Rican migration to the city emerged in the cauldron of U.S. imperial policy that rendered Puerto Ricans' labor inexpensive to local companies like Campbell's Soup. Upon settling in Camden, these multiracial colonial subjects fostered ethnic-based community through churches, storefronts, and associations. But like their Black neighbors, Puerto Ricans also increasingly bore the brunt of police brutality, high unemployment, dilapidated housing, and little to no representation in city government. Ultimately, it was in the latter context that the Puerto Rican and Black communities looked to each other to develop a coalitional politics to guide the city's postindustrial future. Echoing his colleague Poppy Sharp at the Black People's Unity Movement, Omar Davis put it succinctly soon after the uprising began: "Only by unity can we lick this thing, together we are 75 per cent of this city. Neither of us can do it by ourselves."[36]

This spirit of solidarity was likewise present among some who looted downtown stores like Newman's Furniture and Sye Diamond's Shop. Responding to a journalist about his decision to participate in looting, one Black resident stated: "Frustration . . . It's even more than that . . . You know why we do it. Like, man, there's a limit . . . you get angry . . . you know you'll never get it any other way." He continued, "You know why this started. . . . It's what they did to [Gonzales]. We got angry just like the Puerto Ricans, and we figured it was time." In a moment seldom visible in the archive of urban unrest, this young person expressed kinship with his Puerto Rican neighbors, which he manifested by taking from the city what he wanted, concluding, "No one listens any other way."[37]

In the decades that followed the unrest, many perceived Camden's riot as the decisive moment in the city's postindustrial freefall. This has meant that Latinx rebellion has largely carried the weight of broader deindustrialization and housing decentralization. In reality, the uprising marked the culmination of those processes—and also of U.S. imperial ventures in Puerto Rico that compelled island residents to relocate to New Jersey. The rebellion became a pivotal moment when Puerto Ricans and their allies demanded greater governing power to ensure a more equitable distribution of metropolitan wealth. Realizing this vision would depend on several factors, including suburban management of resources, which, Howard Gillette writes, "determined the quality of life of residents in the region." As the 1970s progressed, it also hinged on how leaders in Washington interpreted Latinx mass violence as the era's urban liberalism teetered on collapse.[38]

While they opened opportunities for residents to improve local conditions, Latinx uprisings were often ignored by federal elected leaders who sought to build a pan-ethnic "Spanish-speaking" constituency beginning in the late

1960s. Until that decade, there had not been a cohesive sense at the national level of who so-called Spanish speakers, Hispanics, or Latinos were. Conceptions of Mexicans, Puerto Ricans, Cubans, and other Latin American and Caribbean migrants were mostly regional and subject to varying racializations. The Mexican American and Puerto Rican social movements of the 1960s helped reveal to a broader public the presence of these groups, as did the work of researchers studying their presence in cities.[39]

Black Americans became the principal targets for stereotyped portrayals that conflated race with a so-called culture of poverty beginning in the 1960s, but the theory had emerged in Oscar Lewis's depictions of Latinx urban life. The anthropologist's well-known books on Mexican and Puerto Rican "slum dwellers"—the revealingly titled *Five Families: Mexican Case Studies in the Culture of Poverty* (1959) and *La Vida: A Puerto Rican Family in the Culture of Poverty* (1966) offered audiences, including policymakers, a language for conceptualizing Latinx urban poverty as being rooted in identifiable cultural differences. These ideas were reflected in popular media, including the stage (1959) and screen (1961) productions of *West Side Story*, in which portrayals of Puerto Ricans as mercurial and violent were widely understood as documentary evidence of actual "slum" conditions and Puerto Rican temperament.[40]

As elected officials in Washington sought to position the growing number of Mexican Americans and Puerto Ricans in new ways, they were thus forced to confront the association between Latinxs and urban disorder that had been bubbling and that the prevalence of Latinx rioting threatened to exacerbate. Consider the December 1969 congressional proceedings to discuss support for a Cabinet Committee on Opportunities for Spanish Speaking People (CCOSSP)—a federal body intended to ensure that federal programs reached "all Mexican Americans, Puerto Rican Americans, Cuban Americans, and all other Spanish-speaking and Spanish-surnamed Americans." While some viewed the committee as little more than administrative excess, its proponents portrayed "Spanish speakers" as a deserving community, one that had "more Congressional Medal of Honor winners" than any other group in the country, and that, in the words of a different representative, "almost never ask for a handout." For his part, Los Angeles Democratic congressional representative Edward R. Roybal emphasized the group's poverty and underemployment while highlighting its military service and long history in the United States. Echoing the Kerner Commission, he also advanced the notion that they were "law-abiding Americans who had not resorted to riot and civil disobedience."[41]

This was a stunning claim. It would not have been surprising if Roybal had failed to recall the rioting in Trenton, a small city nearly three thousand miles away from Los Angeles, which had unfolded just months before he addressed his colleagues. But the congressman also ignored Puerto Rican uprisings in major cities like Chicago and New York that had erupted in 1966 and 1967. Meanwhile, Roybal's associate, New Mexico's Senator Joseph Montoya, worked a somewhat different angle in a Senate subcommittee hearing earlier that summer. In a statement to his peers, the covisionary of the CCOSSP ignored recent reality even as he seized upon the threat of Latinx uprisings as a political tool. "To date," he stated, "the Spanish-speaking American has not been duped or led astray by the apostles of hatred and violence whose only solution to problems is to tear down our social institutions instead of try to reform them." Studiously avoiding then-recent events in Chicago, New York, New Jersey, and Connecticut, Montoya warned that growing discontent among Spanish speakers would result in "serious civil disturbances throughout the Nation."[42]

Ironically, overlooking Latinx uprisings obscured the very conditions that Mexican American leaders like Roybal and Montoya aimed to expose, including police brutality, poverty, and lack of political representation. This omission also enabled federal officials to perpetuate the notion of docile and hardworking "Spanish speakers" in contrast to the perception of riotous Black Americans, undermining the solidarities these communities had fostered, especially in the industrial North. As Benjamin Francis-Fallon has observed of this crucial moment, "Hispanic Americans, so often disparaged in racist tales of the West or in damaging stereotypes of poverty-stricken ghetto dwellers—as obstacles to national progress—now found themselves embraced as part of an alternative history of noble cultural attributes deployed in the national service." But the "serious disturbances" that Montoya invoked did arrive. Less than a year after the CCOSSP hearings, Mexican Americans in East LA revolted against police violence, exposing the dissonance between federal leaders' public-facing rhetoric and the complex reality of Latinx street-level violence.[43]

The 1969 hearings unfolded against the backdrop of another major federal shift marked by waning support for War on Poverty programs that many Latinx communities had come to depend on. Antipoverty workers and organizations had become important brokers between residents and city officials during uprising negotiations and continued to serve in this capacity in their aftermath. In Chicago, this included the work of the Division Street Urban Progress Center established after the 1966 uprising. The center was intended to facilitate employment and help individuals apply for public assistance, which many were routinely denied, along with other community-oriented measures aimed at reducing poverty. However, federal funding for many such programs increasingly dried up as the Nixon administration aggressively redirected funds away from the Office of Economic Opportunity. At the same time, as I have written elsewhere, the network of Latinx business leaders in the president's administration blunted the more progressive claims of the era's Chicano and Puerto Rican radical movement leaders. With the hollowing out of the Great Society, they also stymied the more moderate demands on the part of antipoverty workers, including Yolanda Aguilar de Neely, the Camden Mexican American who helped to pick up the pieces after the 1971 uprising.[44]

Not long after the dust settled in Camden, Aguilar de Neely went on to operate the Camden County Office for Children in New Jersey. Testifying before a Senate subcommittee in 1978 about the lack of federal provision for childcare, she lamented: "In 1975, everything came to an abrupt halt. . . . [W]ith the introduction of title XX as the new funding source for not only daycare but all social services, the plans and dreams of the daycare community to eventually meet the needs of all children and families in Camden County came to a screeching halt." For the longtime Camden resident, childcare was a vital component of the solutions necessary to secure Camden's future, which (likely alluding to the uprising seven years earlier) she maintained was, in 1971, "beginning to show signs of trouble." Aguilar de Neely argued that day care allowed residents to find employment and fostered a sense of community. Frustrated with the changing political tide and the federal government's retrenchment from publicly funded day care for the poor, she concluded that under the Nixon and Ford administrations, the War on Poverty had morphed into a war "against poor people."[45]

The Latinx uprisings of the 1960s and 1970s marked an essential chapter in the history of urban activism in the United States. Without them, our account of the era's urban violence remains incomplete—a sign of Latinx history's significance to the field of urban history and beyond. As this chapter has demonstrated, these rebellions reflected the frustration and sense of dispossession that Puerto Rican and Mexican urbanites across the country endured. Sources suggest that young people were primarily responsible for looting, burning, shooting, and rock throwing. Yet a closer look at events surrounding these incidents reveals a complex relationship between violence and community demands: the former served as both a response to failed municipal leadership and a catalyst for fulfilling local communities' call for change, even when young people were not at the bargaining table. Despite sharing similar causes, the uprisings also resulted in outcomes deeply contingent on local contexts, although in most cases, they galvanized residents to become more deeply engaged in political action.[46]

It is essential to examine Puerto Rican and Mexican American uprisings together—not as a convenient grouping within the Latinx pan-ethnicity, but because they expose both fault lines and points of connection among Puerto Ricans, Mexican Americans, and Black people. At the national level, the 1969 congressional hearings that birthed the CCOSSP highlighted how some legislators ignored the prevalence of Latinx uprisings across the country or leveraged the specter of violence to advance the notion of one homogenized, patriotic, hardworking, and non-Black community. However, these approaches did not align with the reality at the grass roots, where Puerto Ricans and Mexican Americans often worked in coalition with Black neighbors who rose up alongside them in city after city. Nor did their project shield these communities from the national punitive turn that lay around the corner, evidenced by relentless instances of brutal police violence and, not least, the explosive rebellions they continued to ignite.[47]

2

"You Were the Ones That Called Us, Georgia": Mexican Construction Labor as Place- and Mythmaking

ILIANA YAMILETH RODRIGUEZ
Emory University

The Atlanta Committee for the Olympic Games (ACOG) was under a time crunch in April 1996. With less than three months until the beginning of the 1996 Centennial Olympic Games, construction projects, including sports venues and urban greenspaces, remained incomplete. "Blocks of rubble-strewn sidewalk on streets that were scheduled to be spruced up months ago," reported the *Washington Post*. "Giant mud craters that look like asteroid impacts. Traffic crawling through a maze of detours and closed viaducts." Billy Payne, a real estate lawyer and head of the ACOG, attempted to assuage anxieties by reminding the press of how much construction had already been accomplished: "We have literally transformed our city." In true Atlanta booster fashion, Payne, like others in the city, worked hard to convey an image of an excited community well prepared to take the international stage, observing that "the majority of our people have remained extremely supportive."[1] Atlanta politicians, business elites, and writers had been well practiced at selling "the city too busy to hate" since 1959, when Mayor William B. Hartsfield coined the phrase and boosters began to eagerly repeat it. The "mythology" of Atlanta was, by 1996, one that positioned the city as "not only a good place to do business, but hospitable, progressive, and racially harmonious."[2] With the Olympics, the ACOG and supporters hoped that successfully completing "perhaps the largest, most expensive and time-compacted urban face lift in years" would "display Atlanta as a symbol of racial tolerance and economic progress" to the world.[3]

While Payne centered the ACOG in narratives about changing Atlanta's built environment, the question of who would do the actual building remained. Mexican Consul General Teodoro Maus soon learned the answer. Maus had arrived in Atlanta in 1989, and his appointment as consul through the next decade coincided with key changes for the city, including an economic and development boom visible in the expanding construction industry and an increase in Mexican migrant arrivals. These shifting migration patterns, influenced by changes in federal immigration legislation and the growth of regional economies, coincided with preparations for the Olympics.[4] By 1996, Maus was established as a well-known figure and leader within Atlanta's Latinx communities due to his cultural, political, and advocacy work defending the rights of Mexican nationals, regardless of citizenship status, and other Spanish-speaking migrants living in the region. As the city approached its deadlines for the infrastructure that would showcase Atlanta to the world, an agent from the regional Immigration and Naturalization Service (INS) office telephoned Maus to discuss an unnamed city official's search for skilled, cheap laborers. Maus recalled: "The INS contacted me and said . . . 'for public relations purposes, from here until the end of the Olympics we're not going to be doing any enforcement.' And I said, you know I read the papers also, I know why. And they said, 'well, yeah that's, you know. If you can spread the word that they are welcome and they are not going to be persecuted, followed, taken, we'd appreciate it.' And the grapevine worked." *They* referred implicitly to Mexican laborers. Over the years, Maus remained vague about which city officials and agents had sought to recruit workers by encouraging a work environment (temporarily) free of immigration enforcement.[5]

Maus was clear, however, about the central role that Latinx—and even more explicitly Mexican—migrant labor had played in helping Atlanta build the infrastructure needed for the 1996 Olympic Games. In 2016, for example, Maus sat down with an interviewer to discuss the legacies of the Olympics. "When Atlanta won the Olympic bid," he remembered, "it was a great pleasure and then they [organizers] sat and said, 'and what do we do now?' . . . The only way was to bring a flock of Latinos, especially Mexicans, who are very fast in construction, who are very good."[6]

The telephone call reflected a continuation of the decades-long conflation of Mexicans with cheap labor and illegality in the United States, except this time from a Southeastern metropolis. For some community members, these migrant laborers also became part of a celebratory memorialization surrounding the 1996 games in a manner that furthered the racialized image of the "hardworking" Mexican who showed up to "transform" Atlanta. Thinking back to the Olympics twenty years later during a moment of rising national anti-immigrant agitation, Maus was asked by a reporter for the *Atlanta Journal-Constitution* about his opinion on local residents who wanted Latinx migrants to leave the region. Maus responded simply: "You were the ones that called us, Georgia."[7]

Mexican workers did not need the implied permission or encouragement of state actors—allies or not—to migrate to metropolitan Atlanta, however. The word-of-mouth "grapevine" of informal labor recruitment had been established more than two decades prior to the 1996 construction boom made possible by Mexican migrants. This chapter takes Maus's account of an unrecorded telephone call as the starting point for a local history that focuses on metropolitan development, racialized labor, community memory, gender, and placemaking. Here, placemaking is informed by critical geographers, urban planners, and ethnic studies scholars, and it describes the historical processes by which individuals and groups create places of economic, social, political, and cultural belonging for themselves and compatriots in often-hostile environments. The historian Natalia Molina's work on Mexican placemaking is especially instructive, as it raises "the question of *who* gets to define a place and *how* they do so" through the case of semipublic spaces such as restaurants. So rather than exclusively centering accounts from boosters, journalists, and civic leaders, the pages that follow narrate moments of metropolitan development from the bottom up, centering the laborers who constructed the changing national landscapes of the late twentieth century, particularly in the South and Sunbelt regions, which experienced construction booms in this era. Through oral history interviews and bilingual archival sources, I trace the experiences of Mexican men—at times directly, other times through the memories of their wives and children—who worked on roads, commercial buildings, residential subdivisions, and other construction projects that transformed the built environment of metropolitan Atlanta.[8]

At the close of the twentieth century, Mexican laborers were enmeshed in both literal and figurative placemaking processes across the region. These workers constructed buildings and roads that became early sites of community formation at a time when there were few public or private spaces to serve the social and cultural needs of a nascent, Spanish-speaking, working-class migrant community. By centering Mexican men's experiences within and in relation to the construction industry in metropolitan Atlanta, this chapter taps into the diverse "social memories" of labor and subsequent community formation that remade (sub)urban places. Writing on the systemic lack of historical markers to acknowledge minority histories in urban spaces, Dolores Hayden has proposed that an examination of the intersections of social histories and urban landscapes can help diversify the ways we understand place-based public histories. Although Hayden focuses on questions of spatial and historic preservation, her assertion that "social relationships are intertwined with spatial perception" offers an entry point for exploring the ways that Mexican workers made sense of their labor, its visible impact on the built environment, and the resulting memories that placed Mexicans at the center of a developing metropolitan history. In other words, examining how Mexican construction workers and their families created personal and communal connections to Metro Atlanta's built environment shows that they were not simply a transient, passive, exploitable labor pool made up of lone men with no personal or communal stake in the local landscape. While journalists and civic leaders' memories would come to associate Mexican laborers with illegality in a way that fit uneasily into narratives about Atlanta's ever-progressive march toward inclusive internationalism, Mexicans had their own experiences and ideas about the place they had been called upon to (re)make.[9]

Mexican Early Arrivals and Metropolitan Expansion, 1980s through the Mid-1990s

As a ten-county region (and the statistical region is even larger), Metro Atlanta underwent dramatic, primarily suburban expansion in the late twentieth century. This was emblematic of Sunbelt "boomtown" developments from Charlotte, North Carolina, to Los Angeles, California.[10] For Mexican migrants who arrived in Metro Atlanta before the late 1990s, the region differed from other growing Sunbelt cities in two important ways: first, there was little to no historical presence of established Mexican communities; second, the existent large, sprawling region necessitated a hypermobility of workers (who were visibly, racially distinct from longtime residents) in an often-hostile landscape. The Atlanta that Mexican newcomers encountered as they arrived in small numbers in the 1970s, and increasingly in the 1980s, was shaped by histories of racial violence and segregation that had long dispossessed indigenous peoples and disenfranchised African American communities. As the historian Tera Hunter reminds us, the residential developments in late nineteenth-century Atlanta were affected by existing railroads, uneven distribution of Reconstruction-era resources, and the rise of Jim Crow, which shaped the city's "physical and social geography." The legacies of such economically segregated and racialized geographies were reinforced at the metropolitan level by the ideological and residential reordering processes of white flight in the 1950s and 1960s, which shaped Metro Atlanta's northern counties into majority-white suburban places. Centering the experiences of Mexican construction workers in this era fills a gap in Kevin Kruse's account of white flight, which offers key attention to local matters of race, space, and politics, but less so to questions about the labor that built the infrastructure necessary to sustain an expanding white suburbia in the late twentieth century. As construction projects in majority-white northern counties like Cobb and Gwinnett continued to grow at a rapid pace from the 1970s through the 1990s, Mexican migrants were increasingly among the growing labor force that built the homes for a new generation of suburbanites.[11]

In the 1970s, Mexican early arrivals would have encountered a metropolitan region marked with historically racialized county lines and an emergent, spatially dispersed Spanish-speaking population. Beginning in the late 1950s, Cuban migrants began to settle in notable numbers around Metro Atlanta. By 1970, close to four thousand Cubans called the state of Georgia home, with the majority living in Fulton and DeKalb counties. While Cubans made up most of the Spanish-speaking population in the 1970s, there were sizable numbers of Puerto Rican, Mexican, and other Latinx migrants in the population. As Mexican migration continued steadily to the region over the course of the next decade, Mexicans came to be the majority, with a population estimated at 27,647 in the state by 1980.[12] Georgia's Mexican population increased steadily over the course of the 1980s. While some explained the increase in Mexican migration to "nontraditional" destinations with the passage of the Immigration Reform and Control Act, migration routes to Metro Atlanta were established prior to 1986, as demonstrated by the IRCA applications that migrants submitted in Georgia counties.[13]

From the 1950s through the early 1990s, which I characterize as the early years of Latinx community formation in Metro Atlanta, migrants' settlement and residential patterns reflected the reality of metropolitan sprawl. For construction workers in particular, the continued metropolitan growth during the 1980s and 1990s in the form of suburban housing and commercial buildings meant that many Mexican migrants settled into counties north of the city center that were experiencing high construction rates.[14]

One person who arrived in Metro Atlanta's northern counties in this era was Pepe, who left Houston in 1987 with a group of other young men who were among the first few thousand Mexicans in the local area. Born in San Luis Potosí, Pepe first migrated to Houston in 1987 in search of economic opportunities that were becoming rarer in rural Mexico at a moment of federal economic restructuring. From the 1970s through the 1990s, millions of Mexicans like Pepe encountered "joblessness, hardship, neglect, and growing economic marginalization" in their home country. In Houston, however, Pepe encountered another "moment of [economic] crisis" when he and others struggled to find work in the city. After a few months, Pepe was convinced by an uncle to take a chance on Georgia. His uncle, a carpenter and contractor, had various housing projects to complete in Metro Atlanta in the late 1980s, and he hired Pepe alongside six other men from Chiapas and Monterrey—all living in Houston at the time—to work on private residential builds in Georgia. The men worked primarily in the city of Duluth, located in rapidly growing Gwinnett County to the northeast of the city center.[15]

Because construction labor itself is a decentralized industry, commutes to work were unpredictable and often distant from the homes and apartments that Mexican migrants rented and shared around Metro Atlanta. Workers confronted spatial challenges of both getting to work and being hypervisible in an era when the Latinx community was still growing and remained geographically dispersed in counties including Cobb, DeKalb, Fulton, and Gwinnett. Thinking back to the 1980s, Pepe recalled how he and his coworkers were ridiculed by local residents for speaking Spanish when they stopped to buy coffee on the way to work and by white schoolchildren on buses who would yell at the seven men on their way to worksites. While the harassment the men faced was shaped by the fact that they were racialized people traveling long distances in a sprawling metropolitan region and therefore encountered hostility both in businesses and while in transit, Pepe's memories also pointed to a sense of social and cultural alienation that Mexican early arrivals felt in Metro Atlanta in this era. Prior to the mid-1990s, Mexican restaurants, stores, and sites of leisure were a rare sight in Metro Atlanta, which would change as the community dramatically grew from thousands to tens of thousands. Without the ability to see the near future, and after dealing with feelings of marginalization in local spaces for three years while working on residential construction projects, Pepe made the decision to move back to Houston in 1990.

While Pepe had alienating experiences during his first stint working in Metro Atlanta's construction industry, his ability to be part of and remain within an all-Mexican crew illustrated two interlocking realities. First, the region's context of white labor networks and white-owned construction companies, coupled with historical antiblackness in the building trades and diminishing union power, made this an industry very much defined by race and ethnicity. As Cameron Lippard explained in a 2006 study of the city's construction industry, this industry was "a microcosm . . . Atlanta and its economic system still use race and ethnicity to allow or restrict access to its economic prosperity, especially self-employment."[16]

In the context of a region steeped in continued legacies of antiblackness, the historian Julie Weise argues that some white Southerners in search of labor power adopted a "pro-immigrant conservatism" in relation to Mexican workers during the 1980s. While Weise's point refers to the agricultural fields of southern Georgia, a similar sentiment impacted a construction industry that would become increasingly Mexican and Central American by the close of the century. Available historical records do not show clearly stated intentions to hire Latinx over other local workers in this era within the construction industry. However, Natalia Molina's concept of racial scripts offers a mode for excavating the ways Latinx workers in this era were treated, and racialized, in relation to both Black and white workers in Metro Atlanta. In other words, the increasing "pro-immigrant" stance of those who stood to profit from a non-unionized and often undocumented labor force depended on the relational ways that Latinx workers were compared, often favorably, to local workers. One Emory professor of political science, for example, offered a "pro-immigrant" analysis steeped in stereotypes when asked about Atlanta's growing undocumented population, stating that "most immigrants are harder-working than native-born Americans."[17]

The "pro-immigrant" stance of builders and (sub)contractors also appears in newspaper accounts where celebrations of "Hispanic" workers painted them as a flexible labor source made up of primarily male day laborers, a status that allowed for temporary employment and was often accompanied by labor and wage exploitation. At one panel that included two builders and Consul Maus, an employer explained: "Let me say unequivocally that over the past eight to 10 years, the Hispanic labor market has been the salvation of residential construction in Atlanta. I don't have a clue where we would be were it not for that.... And while we do hear of exploitation, there have been tremendous opportunities also. Once, Hispanics were involved only in masonry. Now they are in all the trades." In the construction world of northern Georgia, at a time of outward growth from Atlanta's city center, a desire for cheap labor and the hiring informality of the industry facilitated an increased entry of Mexican and other Latinx workers, many of whom had limited English skills and had arrived in Metro Atlanta after being (in)formally recruited in other U.S. cities such as Houston by contractors, friends, and/or family members. The implied and overt racial dynamics of this "pro-immigrant" sentiment taking hold in the construction industry were critiqued by some local leaders, including those involved in advocating for Black labor and civil rights. Black leadership critiques of the growing migrant labor force were informed by local histories and contemporary realities structured by employment practices within certain industries. Lyndon Wade of the Atlanta Urban League, for example, argued that "these people [were] taking a lot of the jobs that historically had gone to blacks," while Earl Shinhoster of the NAACP elaborated on such critiques by focusing on the driving forces behind the growing undocumented labor force in Atlanta. "I don't blame the workers," Shinhoster told reporters, "I put the blame at the foot of the industries."[18]

Alongside the construction industry's increasingly "pro-immigrant" employment practices, which offered increased employment opportunities to individual (primarily male) migrant workers, the informal recruitment of Mexican construction laborers to Metro Atlanta in this era shaped a second reality for the workers and their families. Informal recruitment strategies resulted in both single male and familial migrations to Metro Atlanta. Regarding the gender dynamics of Mexican migrations to the region in the late twentieth century, oral histories, documentary evidence (photographs and film), and scholarly accounts point to early cohorts being made up primarily of single, often young men who did not view their migration to Atlanta as a permanent resettlement. Rather, unaccompanied men who were early arrivals tended to view their place in the city and surrounding suburbs as temporary, an economic venture that would allow them to support themselves and, often, their families in other U.S. and Mexican cities. This did not mean that there were no women and children who joined these early migrations to Metro Atlanta. Familial migrations and memories from this pre-1990s era point to the complex ways that construction workers and their kin networks made sense out of working and living in a new place with few public spaces that could reinforce cultural forms of belonging. To address the lack of such spaces, construction workers and their families played key roles in developing practices and spaces to support community formation.

Mina's experiences, for example, highlight the role that women played in supporting construction workers and sustaining culturally relevant communal practices in a region where Mexican migrants were still a "foreign" presence. Born in 1955 in the small town of Cedral, San Luis Potosí, Mina first arrived in Houston, Texas, in 1970 as a fifteen-year-old to work as a caregiver for a family member. In 1976 she married her husband, and soon thereafter had children. For five years, Mina worked in a Houston factory making wooden doors and windows until the factory closed. It was during this period, around 1981, that some family members asked Mina's husband—who owned his own vehicle—to give them a ride to their new construction jobs in Atlanta. After spending two weeks in Atlanta with his compatriots, Mina's husband returned to Houston only to announce that he had decided to relocate to Atlanta to work in the expanding construction industry to better sustain their binational family. Mina described the subsequent family decision-making process as having to choose whether her husband would migrate alone or whether she and the children would also move to Atlanta: "Well, what was I doing [in Houston] if I wasn't working? There was no sense in him being here and us there . . . [so] we began to sell everything, to pack, and that same weekend we left."[19]

In Metro Atlanta, the family of four shared a home with ten single men from Tamaulipas, Guerrero, and San Luis Potosí who were all working for the same construction company. Mina was the only woman within her small Mexican community, which resulted in her taking on the gendered labor of cleaning the shared home, grocery shopping, and cooking meals for the men to eat at home and at work. Some days she would take her children on special outings to visit her husband and the other young men at the construction site for lunch. The men, Mina explained, were always excited to share the progress they were making on a new house or in a new subdivision with her and the kids: "They were excited because they made so many houses, all beautiful. And there was a lot of work here, not like in Houston. Here there was a lot of forest where [they] could build homes . . . they would take us on the weekends to see the worksites—there was nowhere else to go, we didn't have places to hang out, so they would take us to see the houses." These memories tied to the built environment stay with Mina and her family in the contemporary moment. As we sat at her kitchen table going over the early years of living in Atlanta as a Mexicana and how that experience changed over the years, she shared, "There are some neighborhoods, these very pretty houses on Paces Ferry that my husband and my brother built. And they are pretty houses, mansions, and when I drive by with my granddaughters on that street, I tell them, 'Look, your grandfather built those houses.'" Mina's pride about the direct role her husband played in shaping Atlanta's built environment forms part of an archive—housed in the social memories of construction workers and their families, visible in the landscape for those in the know—that illustrates the development of personal connections to the built environment Mexicans navigated and, at times, quite literally built.[20]

Participation in the construction industry offered migrant laborers and their families not just economic opportunities but also possibilities to develop personal, direct connections to the built environment of a new city that had few to no markers of Latinx presence in the public sphere.[21] Just as Mina held fond memories of the homes her husband and others built in Metro Atlanta, other Mexican migrants had similar experiences. Brenda Lopez Romero, Georgia's first Latina official elected to the state's House of Representatives, shared similar sentiments of pride regarding the Mexican role in building up Metro Atlanta's signature infrastructure. Born in Cuernavaca, Morelos, Lopez Romero left Mexico at age five to reunite with her father, who was working in Atlanta's construction industry during the 1980s. As Lopez Romero shared in an oral history interview about her first memories of arriving in Atlanta: "We would drive around downtown with some of the buildings and especially with what we call spaghetti junction, which is the intersection of 85 and 285, you know my dad would always tell me that he built those. He built the bridges because that's one of the places where he worked. And to know that we have this infrastructure that is directly on the hard work and sweat of individuals like my father is very important to me and why eventually I grew this very personal stake in our state, and ownership in our state because it was my father who quite literally helped build it." Through pointing to the literal, and visible, transformation that her father brought to Metro Atlanta's built environment, Lopez Romero illustrated how buildings and highways served as some of the first local sites that informed individual and communal identity formations by offering tangible proof of a Mexican presence bringing important changes to the region. As both Mina and Lopez Romero demonstrate through their recollections, relatives of construction workers noted how traveling to construction sites served as a form of leisure at a time when there were virtually no options for accessible leisure spaces in Metro Atlanta—and also as a form of laying claim to a new place through built environments that would otherwise not read as "Mexican" or "Latinx" to other residents.[22]

The gendered dimensions of placemaking were evident in the ways individuals recounted their memories about the 1980s. By attending to the laboring lives of both men and women in this history about experiences within the construction industry, the gendered dimensions of "homemaking" take on a new meaning. While often associated with women's reproductive labor within private homes, homemaking takes on a second sense when discussing men who built literal homes in the public sphere. Focusing on the histories of construction workers and their loved ones, then, allows us to elaborate not just a labor network but also a social world shaped by gender and kinship as ethnic Mexicans established themselves in Metro Atlanta. While men's labor and its relationship to the built environment is the focus of this chapter, it is important to pause and reflect on the significance of the reproductive labor carried out by women like Mina that made establishing familial roots in Georgia possible. For example, while the men worked and the children attended school, Mina spent her time visiting various grocery stores where she analyzed spices and searched for proper ingredients to feed her loved ones culturally appropriate food. It was, in other words, the food, care, love, and sacrifices of their wives and children who relocated to Georgia, or the promises of reunification with kin in Texas or Mexico, that made living and working in a place like Metro Atlanta "worth it" (and possible) for many ethnic Mexican men in this era.

Working in the construction industry offered some of the earliest placemaking opportunities to Mexican migrants in ways not immediately visible to those outside of the community. Like Pepe, who worked building residential homes between 1987 and 1990, other workers who belonged to all-Mexican work crews often found, or rather created, opportunities on the job site for community and placemaking. While some work crews were diverse in terms of home states in Mexico, others were highly regionalized and became increasingly so as early arrivals established direct migratory routes between Atlanta and two types of sites: hometowns in Mexico and "traditional destination" cities in the United States where they had established kinship connections through stepped migration practices prior to moving to Atlanta. This was illustrated in another migrant's account of working in Atlanta in the 1980s.[23]

In 1978, at age fifteen, Ricardo left his small town in San Luis Potosí to work in Houston's service industry: "I came with the hope of [finding] work, to help my family, my parents." The young man worked as a dishwasher for a while, then as a busboy. Ricardo joked that busboy was the highest position he could hold at the restaurant with his limited English and lack of formal education, so he soon decided to leave his service job to work in construction. For the next few years, he worked with a company building bridges in Houston. While living and working in Houston, Ricardo kept up a cyclical migration pattern, traveling regularly to San Luis Potosí to visit his wife, Epifanía, and his parents. During one of his Mexico trips to visit Epifanía and their newborn son, Ricardo received notice from a brother-in-law that there were new work opportunities in Georgia. While planning the move, Ricardo found himself depending on other male early arrivals to find work opportunities, including Epifanía's eldest brothers, who had migrated from Texas to Georgia in 1980. Once Epifanía's brothers settled into Lawrenceville (Gwinnett County), the two men began to work in the construction sector, specifically in framing for new homes, and they welcomed Ricardo into the family business.[24]

Although the Mexican community in Metro Atlanta was still quite small in the 1980s, Ricardo met other Mexican men outside of his crew while doing construction work, and he began to build local knowledge about the migrants' home states from the specific work the men did while building houses. In that era, he recalled that many of the men in Lawrenceville had hometowns in San Luis Potosí and Guerrero. Hometowns, and the intricate networks of family and friends that formed the labor network "grapevine," played a key role in the specific type of construction work Mexican men would enter while living in Metro Atlanta. Ricardo described the construction crews who did the initial framing for houses, "los frameadores," as being made up of mostly men from San Luis Potosí. The same went for those who laid the cement, "los cementeros," while the men who placed the roofing tiles, "los ruferos," tended to come from Guerrero.[25] Painters, "los pintores," for a time hailed heavily from

Veracruz, and later from the state of Coahuila. This was a process of identity formation on the construction site, where migrants used Spanglish to take on the name of the construction materials they worked with as both a job title and a mode of differentiating skills and regional or local identities between construction workers. Within the informal practices of hiring and working in construction, Mexican men drew on this identity formation to claim their specific skills. At a time when migrants were few in number and may have felt at odds with a new destination in the South, the Mexican regionalisms that existed within Metro Atlanta's construction crews offered a sense of community to Mexican men. Their worksites were at once spaces of community making and identification—however, these sites were also increasingly targeted for immigration enforcement in the 1990s.[26]

Constructing and Marketing an International City, 1995–1996

Atlanta's Mayor Maynard Jackson was explicit in his vision for the 1996 games. The Olympics had to capture "the twin peaks of Atlanta's Mount Olympus," which included a first step to prepare the city for the event and a second step to cement a positive legacy. To this end, Mayor Jackson implemented the Corporation for Olympic Development in Atlanta nonprofit, which was tasked with both assisting in preparing the city's built environment for the international stage and securing a legacy for Atlanta that was not centered on population decline, disinvestment, and inequality. Such stated goals no doubt played a role in the continuation of the celebratory tone around the city's Olympic moment and tacitly encouraged making positive connections between the games and the region's demographic shifts. While Mayor Jackson and the ACOG were building upon politicians' and boosters' efforts to internationalize the city that had begun in earnest during the 1970s, what differed by the 1990s was the growing number of Latinx and Asian migrants who offered a more "international" community profile for the organizers and politicians to consider.[27]

The years and months leading up to the April 1996 construction crunch included both celebrations of an internationalizing city and an increase in regional immigration enforcement. The 1993 Cultural Olympiad, for example, resulted in *Mexico: A Cultural Tapestry*, a joint effort by the ACOG and the Mexican Consulate that brought Mexican artists and performers to showcase music, art, and dance to Atlantan audiences. While Consul Maus joined the venture to uplift Mexican culture, he remained critical of the regional realities his compatriots and other Latinx migrants faced in the South. In a 1993 interview, Maus declared: "The image of the U.S. as a giant melting pot is more of a cultural myth than a reality here . . . [The United States is] open [to immigration] because you are still in a growth phase. You still need immigrants just as you did 100 years ago. And the jobs that the immigrants take are generally those that Americans would refuse to accept, just as newly arrived immigrants took similar jobs 100 years ago." While Maus spoke in the context of a stalled North American Free Trade Agreement (NAFTA) in 1993, his critiques of NAFTA were informed by Mexican labor experiences in Georgia: local police committing violations such as entering private homes to demand legal documentation from residents, labor exploitation in the construction industry, and regional INS raids.[28]

In January 1995, for example, Thomas P. Fischer, the director of the Atlanta Immigration and Naturalization Service office, led a raid of the Olympic Village construction worksite where undocumented men were laying concrete. Men running to hide in unfinished buildings and sewers was one of many images of the fear and violence sowed by enforcement agents during preparations for the games. The raid resulted in thirty-seven undocumented workers being detained and deported to Mexico. It remains unclear where and how the concrete subcontractor, United Forming Inc., first recruited its Mexican employees. Regardless, the presence of undocumented Mexican workers at Olympic construction sites showed that, despite the ACOG's stated commitment to job training programs for local residents, contractors were willing to hire non-union labor at cheaper rates.[29]

By the summer of 1995, Latinx immigrants were at the center of regional workplace raids by INS agents in northern Georgia. As illustrated in previous pages, Mexican migrants were not solely working on Olympics-related construction projects but also on many sites of (sub)urban expansion and revitalization spurred by the games and a booming economy. The increased visibility of racialized migrants on construction worksites made them targets for policing. Fischer unleashed a new wave of terror upon Metro Atlanta through Operation SouthPAW, or Operation Protect American Workers. Again, rather than focus on fining the contractors recruiting undocumented laborers, as stipulated by the 1986 Immigration Reform and Control Act but rarely enforced, INS chose to go after individuals. Between June and July 1995, workers were detained at construction sites including a public library, elementary schools, apartment complexes, residential subdivisions, and a supermarket. On at least one morning when fifty-five workers were detained, reports stated they were "all Mexicans."[30]

SouthPAW in 1995 preceded the construction time crunch of early 1996, when the infamous telephone call was made to Consul Maus. The Olympics were neither the sole nor the primary catalyst for metropolitan expansion or increased Mexican migration to Metro Atlanta, although experts have recognized the games as a "milestone" for narrating the region's changing demographics in the late twentieth century. The everyday lived experiences of Mexican migrants in 1990s Atlanta show that the city and region were far from the welcoming, internationally minded place boasted of for the Olympics. Both English- and Spanish-language local media extensively covered how Mexican laborers were policed, detained, and deported in the lead-up to the 1996 games. The hypocritical local climate that migrants, particularly the undocumented, navigated in this era was on full display as the 1990s saw a further dramatic increase in immigration enforcement activity, leading into the 2000s, which brought the implementation of laws targeting undocumented migrants.[31]

Immigration Enforcement and Ma(r)king Disposable Laborers, Late 1990s–2000s

There's no proof of whether the INS kept its verbal promise to Consul Maus and, by extension, to undocumented Mexican workers. What newspaper records do show, however, is that the 1990s—including 1996—saw efforts by the INS to detain and deport undocumented, primarily Mexican workers from Metro Atlanta. Following the games and into the late 1990s, Metro Atlanta witnessed the continuation of two booms that appeared to be interrelated—the continued and dramatic expansion of suburban residential construction and the increased and sustained arrival of Mexican migrants. During this decade, the regional and national construction industry was increasingly filled with Latinx laborers. The high representation within construction was evident in industry data, with Latinx workers making up an estimated 9 percent of the industry's labor force across the United States in 1990. This number increased to 10 percent by 1995, and to 15 percent by the close of the decade in 2000. In the Metro Atlanta case, Latinx workers most often had specialty businesses (e.g., drywall, masonry), while white people remained in more lucrative general contractor roles. This mirrored national trends, with data on specialty occupations within the industry further illustrating the overrepresentation of Latinx workers as drywallers (58 percent), concrete layers (55 percent), roofers (47 percent), and general laborers (45 percent) by the early 2000s, in comparison to a mere 9 percent of Latinx workers who held construction managerial positions.[32]

As the laboring migrant population grew in Georgia from the late 1990s through the early 2000s, so did anti-immigrant sentiment. This era saw rhetoric used by media, local leaders, and workers alike that painted Latinx workers—Mexicans, more specifically—as an "illegal" presence. One 1996 *Atlanta Journal-Constitution* article detailed the discovery of thirty-four undocumented Mexican migrants being held in a small horse trailer outside of a local motel. An INS agent gave his take on the matter: "Atlanta has been a boom town recently . . . Where ever [*sic*] you have a lot of job opportunities, you have people coming in to take those jobs, including illegals."[33]

Although Mexican construction workers shared memories of discrimination and alienation in everyday life prior to the late 1990s, their specialized skills as construction workers sometimes offered a way of distinguishing themselves as desirable labor. Pepe, for example, returned to Atlanta in 1992 after his workplace in Houston flooded, leaving him without other employment options. During his two years in Houston, Pepe took it upon himself to join different work crews to learn the skills necessary to become a *maestro*—a worker with extensive on-the-job experience and skills who can teach others, sometimes taking the role of crew leader. Two years in Houston had also given him access to English-language classes held in the community. Upon returning to Atlanta, Pepe had the confidence to lead his own crew and find work. The men drove around Metro Atlanta to find worksites in areas they knew were under development. They would go into subdivisions, "and one would just start asking . . . 'do you need framers?' and they'd tell you yes, and they would give you the plans." Pepe further explained why he had success finding work as a Mexican man in this era: "In that time there were still white crews, and they would take two weeks on a house. And we would do it in five, six days . . . and regardless, they would come in [to work] at eight, nine, and they would leave at five. And us, we stayed until it was done."[34] In this quick summary, Pepe highlighted once again the way race and ethnicity structured not just the construction industry's crews but also the implicit expectations that Mexican workers felt were placed upon them by employers. Pepe's memories show how a lack of labor regulations, historical racial scripts that associated Mexican labor with affordability, and genuine pride in one's own "hard work" were all part of telling a nuanced labor migration history.[35] Despite some economic gains for Mexican migrants living and working in Metro Atlanta, the remainder of the 1990s was marked by attempts to make English the official state language, the criminalization of day laborers, and the continued refusal by state authorities to allow undocumented people access to driver's licenses.

By the early 2000s, it was common knowledge in Metro Atlanta that Latinx workers made up a large proportion of construction laborers, as well as laboring in manufacturing and poultry processing in northern Georgia, agriculture in southern Georgia, and service sectors across the state. The pushback to this reality came from multiple sources, including legislative actions that further cemented Georgia—and by inclusion, Metro Atlanta—as a place hostile to undocumented migrants, who were often racialized as Mexican or Latinx. In a rapid expansion of anti-immigrant legislation, authorities in Georgia aimed to make life uncertain and difficult for undocumented migrants at the county and state levels. The 287(g) program, for example, was established in Metro Atlanta's northern counties in 2007. The program facilitated cooperation between local police departments and Immigration and Customs Enforcement in an effort to facilitate the arrest, detention, and deportation of undocumented migrants. Meant to seek out "aliens" who were possibly involved in "violent crimes, human smuggling, gang/organized crime activity, sexual-related offenses, narcotics smuggling and money laundering," 287(g) proved one of many policies that further criminalized people of color perceived as undocumented migrants.[36]

By the 2010s, there was no way for Metro Atlanta to pretend it was a welcoming place for all. In 2010, for example, the state university system's board of regents voted to ban undocumented students from Georgia's top five public universities. The following year witnessed the most direct attack on the broader undocumented community, as Georgia officials passed the Illegal Immigration Reform and Enforcement Act of 2011, or HB 87, which further criminalized undocumented migrants by implementing electronic verification systems at worksites and increased fines for migrants caught using false documents for employment purposes.[37]

The impacts of anti-immigration rhetoric and policy had real, damaging, and lasting impacts on undocumented communities, including construction workers. The Salvadoran journalist Mario Guevara, for example, took it upon himself to travel around the Metro Atlanta region to find and report on the nightmarish and increasingly common sight of abandoned construction vehicles along roads and highways. In 2016, Guevara documented vacant white work vans for his reporting and articles on Immigration and Customs Enforcement activity in the region and soon started to share videos of the vans on Facebook in an effort to find kin of those disappeared by a violent system of state enforcement. The videos, shared as a livestream, focused in on details that loved ones might recognize—a sweater, a bag of food items, a cup of coffee that was still steaming. Where once construction sites themselves were racialized sites targeted by INS agents, today mobile tools of the trade have been equally racialized and policed to the detriment of undocumented workers. While for some of us white work vans with ladders strapped on top are a marker of home and pride in labor, for immigration enforcement they represent easily targeted, undesirable, disposable laborers.[38]

Conclusion

The contributors to this volume were asked to answer a shared question—What should Latinx urban history be doing programmatically? The preceding pages answer this by focusing on methods for excavating histories not found within traditional archives. Especially in places dubbed "new destinations" for Latinx migrants, it is important to center community memories and stories that circulate orally. Furthermore, Latinx urban history should follow the tradition of Latinx and ethnic studies to center the lived experiences of marginalized communities. By doing so in relation to urban history, it becomes possible to narrate histories of placemaking and building from a bottom-up and, as shown here, worker perspective. The memories of these construction workers, their nuanced, real experiences, show how individual and communal relationships are developed in relation to the built environment over time. Such relationships then factor into questions, realities, and challenges of ethnic community formation in a new city. If we ignore the lived experiences of such workers, then myths about a "city too busy to hate," of an Atlanta that is a welcoming place for migrants, of Latinxs being a new presence in the South, about economic pull factors and lack of agency for migrant laborers, will persist.

Regarding the case of Mexican labor migration to Metro Atlanta, it is important to note that Mexican labor is by no means the sole presence in the industry, although it is highly represented. Especially in conversations about so-called new destinations for migrant laborers where construction was a major industry for hiring such workers, it is important to consider buildings and other construction projects as migrant and ethnic placemaking projects—or as the editors of *Sunbelt Rising* put it, as "texts for identifying the material contours of a region." By extending our understanding of historical texts to include buildings and infrastructure built by Latinx workers in the late twentieth and early twenty-first centuries, those of us invested in capturing underrepresented histories of placemaking can expand the archival sources we use in examining and writing Latinx urban histories.[39]

In this moment, the residential subdivisions, apartment complexes, stadiums, and roads built by Mexican construction workers and their colleagues have been joined by new "texts" that are highly visible within Atlanta's built environment. This includes, for example, Atlanta's renowned Mexicana artist Yehimi Cambrón, whose work seeks to create "monuments to immigrants in the South." In a political climate where public memorialization remains highly politicized, Cambrón's murals unapologetically center undocumented, DACAmented, working-class, queer, young, and elder migrants that form an essential part of Metro Atlanta's social fabric. In one mural titled *Monuments: Atlanta's Immigrants*, located near the Mercedes-Benz Stadium, Cambrón's father sits at center stage surrounded by young migrants and monarch butterflies. As Cambrón explains, her choice to surround Atlanta's diverse migrants with foliage and monarch butterflies was an effort to create a "sanctuary landscape" with symbolism used by immigration activists globally. Whether or not urban historians take up the task of recording and preserving such histories, community members, activists, and organizers are already leading the way to ensure future generations know who has been part of—and who has built so much of—Atlanta, Georgia.[40]

3

Latinos on the Crabgrass Frontier: Migrants, Immigrants, Race, and the Transformation of Postwar Suburbia

THOMAS J. SUGRUE

New York University

In early June 2019, a huge crowd, nearly fifty thousand strong, gathered on the streets of Brentwood, a section of the town of Islip, Long Island, to celebrate the annual Puerto Rican and Hispanic Parade. Enthusiastic participants cheered as traditional Ecuadorian dancers, a Mexican ballet troupe, Salvadoran military veterans, a Puerto Rican cultural group, and thousands of other marchers passed by, carrying flags and banners representing their places of origin. Parade goers danced to the beats of salsa, cumbia, and ranchera music.[1]

The postwar housing developers who transformed the potato farms, pine barrens, and marshes of Islip into one of metropolitan New York's largest suburbs could not have imagined Suffolk Avenue thronged with Spanish-speaking people. They had envisioned Islip as a place where whites could flee the nation's largest city, its economic woes, and, especially, its rapidly growing Black and Latinx populations. Islip was a typical postwar suburban landscape, with low-slung commercial buildings, strip malls, gas stations, and countless ranches, tri-levels, Cape Cods, and colonials, mostly built between 1950 and 1980.

Fifty miles east of New York City, with a population today of 335,000 sprawling over 106 square miles, Islip expanded exponentially during the postwar boom, funded by a massive infusion of federal highway and military spending and underwritten by federal home mortgage programs. Today, Islip is still majority white. But it is now home to one of the largest Latin American populations in the suburban Northeast; that population accounts

Some material from this chapter appeared in my unpublished expert report for *Flores v. Town of Islip*, 448 F.Supp.3d 267 (E.D.N.Y. 2020).

for about a third of the town's residents. Latinx Islip is very diverse, hailing from twenty-one Spanish-speaking countries. A majority comes from three places: El Salvador (32,400), Puerto Rico (22,000), and the Dominican Republic (11,000), with growing numbers of newcomers from Ecuador (5,800), Honduras (5,500), Mexico (5,400), Colombia (4,800), Peru (4,300), and Guatemala (4,000). Islip's Latinx population is concentrated in the town's northwestern section, largely in three areas: Brentwood, where the annual parade takes place; North Bay Shore; and Central Islip, the latter also home to most of the town's nine-thousand-strong Black population. Islip's northeastern and southern sections, including the waterfront, along the Great South Bay and most of Fire Island, are largely white.[2]

We have few compelling scholarly frameworks for understanding suburbs like Islip, especially in the Northeast, which have attracted diverse Latinx newcomers from throughout the Caribbean, Central America, and South America into a region shaped by long-standing Black-white binaries, different from the better-studied suburban communities of metropolitan Los Angeles, where Mexican Americans have long been the predominant Latinx group.[3] Islip, like countless other suburbs in the Northeast and Midwest, rose as a sprawling, middle-class, overwhelmingly white postwar suburb like those described in canonical histories of suburbanization by Kenneth T. Jackson, Robert Fishman, Delores Hayden, and Lizabeth Cohen.[4] But it also became a "new immigrant gateway," shaped by a massive shift of immigrant settlement away from central cities. By the early twenty-first century, a majority of Latinx immigrants to the United States and a majority in the Northeast lived in suburbs, many of which are like Islip.[5]

Despite this momentous demographic shift, many historians and social scientists continue to analyze suburbanization using a framework that emerged in the mid-twentieth century. Suburbs then and now are characterized as aspirational places, the embodiment of "the American dream." Living in suburbia is a symbol of upward mobility; owning a suburban house is evidence of "making it." Much recent scholarship on immigrant suburbanization dusts off the old tropes of Americanization and assimilation. "Growing numbers of suburban areas," writes the Brookings Institution demographer William H. Frey, "are achieving what might be termed 'melting pot' status."[6]

The experience of Islip suggests another framework for thinking about Latinx suburbanization, especially in the multiethnic Latino suburbs of the Northeast, where newcomers have created new landscapes that reflect both their national heritages and an emerging pan-Latinx identity. The process of Latinx suburbanization in Islip is neither assimilation nor integration. Islip's Latinx residents live in a place deeply shaped and constrained by New York's long history of racial exclusion, exploitation, and predation. They did not build their new community from scratch. Rather, they settled in a suburban space shaped by long-standing racial categories, stubborn workplace discrimination, and persistent residential and educational segregation. Understanding Latinx suburbanization requires a close examination of local and regional real estate markets, suburban governments and schools, labor markets, and other local institutions both in creating new opportunities and new identities and in reshaping rather than unraveling century-old racial disparities.

The Changing Face of Suburbia

Postwar suburbs like Islip embodied what Lizabeth Cohen calls the consumer's republic, competing with urban downtowns by offering residents retail, dining, and services in roadside shopping centers and regional malls. Islip's commercial landscape has evolved since the 1950s, as new retailers, many now Latino, have revamped midcentury storefronts buildings to attract Latinx customers. Major thoroughfares, especially in Brentwood and Central Islip, are lined with Latin American eateries and shops tucked into aging strip malls, including Dominican bars and dance clubs, Colombian bakeries, and several Salvadoran restaurants, ranging from fine dining to takeout *pupuserías*. The town still has some older delicatessens and pizzerias with vintage postwar signs, but nearly as many *bodegas* and *taquerías*. Along Suffolk Avenue are dozens of Latin American establishments, including a Peruvian deli across the street from a restaurant selling Venezuelan and Colombian food. The aisles of local supermarkets sell food and beverages from nearly every part of the Americas. Many of Islip's Latinx-run businesses are brightly painted in blue, yellow, and red, their facades emblazoned with bright yellow and red signs, a colorful updating of the staid white and gray wood-framed and red-brick colonial revival buildings that dominated the postwar landscape. Many commercial buildings that catered to postwar whites have been adapted for reuse, especially churches like the Iglesia Evangelista Cristo Te Llama, the Iglesia Pentecostal Unida de Dios, and the Iglesia de Dios, which occupy three storefronts along Pine Aire Avenue in two adjoining, largely vacant strip malls. Even decades-old Catholic parishes have made changes to appeal to their Latinx parishioners, erecting multilingual signs advertising Spanish-language masses and hanging icons of the Virgin of Guadalupe near their altars.[7]

Islip's many postwar subdivisions, with modest, detached aluminum-sided houses surrounded by trees, manicured shrubs, and picket fences, sometimes look unchanged from a half century ago. But that continuity is often superficial. The town's new migrants, unburdened by postwar white suburban notions of nuclear family and domesticity, have repurposed single-family houses to accommodate extended families and boarders. At some houses, garages have been converted into accessory apartments, their large aluminum hanging doors removed and walled over, their facades punctuated with residential doors, double-sash windows, and air conditioning units. At night, lights and the flicker of televisions shine from the curtained windows of basements converted into living quarters. At the end of the workday, pickup trucks and cars pack into expanded driveways that have often replaced front lawns altogether, evidence that houses originally built for nuclear families are now home to several working adults. Even those parts of suburban Long Island that most resemble the postwar "crabgrass frontier," with predominantly white and better-off residents, live in a Latinized landscape, dependent on Latinx workers to preserve the suburban idyll of prosperity and domesticity by mowing lawns, trimming shrubs, cleaning bathrooms and kitchens, caring for preschoolers, and cooking meals.[8]

Latinx newcomers have also altered one of the most characteristic features of postwar suburbia, what the historian Kenneth T. Jackson calls its culture of automobility. Islip is crisscrossed by expressways and wide roads, scarred by acres of surface parking lots. But many of those parking lots, especially near train stations and home improvement stores, now serve as informal, outdoor hiring markets where, in the mornings, men gather, drink coffee, and wait to be picked up for work as day laborers in landscaping or construction. Even though Islip's roads are clogged with traffic, especially during rush hour, and most workers of Latin American descent rely on cars to get to work, it is not unusual to see people walking along the edges of major streets, most of which do not have sidewalks. Islip is by no means a walking city. Its infrastructure is not particularly pedestrian-friendly. But the worn-out grooves in the greenswards along many of the town's roads are evidence of a new pedestrian life that could scarcely be imagined in the car-oriented postwar years.[9]

Latinx newcomers also remade Islip's recreational spaces, sometimes with little conflict but more often with controversy. Soccer fields, large and small, have proliferated. By the 1990s, three large, intensely competitive *fútbol* leagues—the Interamerican Soccer League, the Nassau and Suffolk Soccer League, and the Long Island Hispanic Soccer Association, all with teams often organized by national heritage—attracted cheering crowds, waving national flags, to their matches. Islip also has a large soccer training center run by the family of its most prominent Colombian bakery, La Espiguita.[10] But the town's parks have also become sites of contestation, especially because of evening gatherings of Latino men who drink beer, play cards, listen to music, and sometimes brawl. Town officials have long fought to stem the Latinization of town parks. Brentwood's José Vasquez Park, named for a local man killed in the Vietnam War, was closed in 1979, after neighbors complained of "loitering" and vandalism. For more than a decade afterward, the park was largely ignored by Islip's Parks Department, fenced off and strewn with litter. Rey Rodriguez, a local activist, complained that closing the park was "a slap in the face to the Hispanic community." In 1986, Latinx residents led a six-hundred-person march to demand the park reopening, but town officials stalled. Finally, in 1992, Islip agreed to sell most of Vasquez Park to a housing nonprofit, setting aside a portion for a pocket park designed mostly for small children.[11]

A few miles away, Brentwood's Timberline Park served as a recreation area by day, with shabby soccer and baseball fields and picnic areas, and as a gathering space for Latinx men by night. After a 2009 murder in the park, Islip officials renamed it Roberto Clemente Park, stepped up aggressive nighttime policing there, and pledged to relandscape it, with disastrous consequences. In 2013, the park was closed for reconstruction, and because of municipal corruption and neglect, it became a toxic waste site. Between mid-2013 and spring 2014, the town's contractor dumped about forty thousand tons of construction waste containing wire, glass, rebar, and asbestos in the park. Later tests at the site also discovered banned pesticides, petroleum products, and toxic metals, including antimony, cadmium, chromium, arsenic, and lead. For months, town officials dodged complaints from Brentwood residents and then, when confronted with photographic evidence of the dumping, scrambled to remove some debris and cover the dump with topsoil. Members of Brentwood's Latino community and civic leaders accused town officials of environmental racism for permitting the dumping and ignoring residents' complaints. The park remained closed until late July 2017 for a full cleanup, and the contractors and town officials faced both criminal and civil charges. It is hard to imagine one of Islip's mid-twentieth-century parks, constructed as picturesque idylls in predominantly white neighborhoods, so ravaged.[12]

Geography and Inequality

For all the changes that have remade Islip, it is still a racialized landscape, the legacy of a century of pervasive racial inequality in the metropolitan Northeast and Midwest. Islip has long been one of the most segregated places in the United States, a process that has shaped and constrained opportunities for its growing Latinx population.[13] The magnitude of residential segregation in the town can be measured by the index of dissimilarity, which calculates the percentage of a minority group that would have to relocate for the distribution of the group in every area to be the same as the group's representation in the overall population. In simpler terms, the index of dissimilarity measures the evenness of a minority group's distribution across a geographic area. The index ranges from 0 (not segregated) to 100 (totally segregated). A community with a value of 30 or less is considered to have a low level of racial segregation, a range of 30–60 indicates moderate segregation, and any value greater than 60 is considered highly segregated.[14] In 1990, Islip's Latino-white index of dissimilarity was 61.0. In 2000, Islip was more segregated, with an index of 68.5. In 2010, that figure had risen to 70.7.[15]

What explains the high degree of segregation in Islip? One might hypothesize that Latinos, especially those from poor or working-class backgrounds, are clustered in areas with cheap housing, like Brentwood and Central Islip. Indeed, there is much evidence that high housing costs in parts of Islip have limited the options available to working-class Latinos.[16] But this seemingly commonsensical explanation is belied by the fact that many parts of the town, including those that remain overwhelmingly white or have just recently attracted Latino residents, also have stocks of relatively affordable housing.[17] If Islip's Latinos had full access to the town's housing market, one would expect to find them represented in larger numbers in affordable but predominantly white parts of town, not overwhelmingly concentrated in the town's northwestern section.[18] Current patterns of segregation are rooted in the town's long history of racial politics, economics, and especially housing.

Islip's Long Latinx History

Islip's distinctively Latinx landscapes and its deep and persistent racial segregation must be understood with a long-term perspective. Islip was a suburban space embedded in layers of inequality that accumulated over time. Each of those layers can be understood separately, but each must also be understood in relationship to the others. First, Islip's Latinos bore the burden of the town's long history of racialized inequality that predated their arrival beginning in the 1930s. They arrived in metropolitan New York in multiple diasporas at moments when policymakers were devising new systems of racial classification and using racial categories to value property and labor. Second, the Latino experience was indelibly shaped by Latinos' relationship to the still-deep Black-white binaries that shaped the geography and labor markets of postwar suburbia. Latinx Long Islanders found unprecedented opportunities but also a racially and ethnically segmented labor market. Third, Latinos confronted a racialized system of policing created and maintained by white public officials who saw nonwhites as prone to criminality, viewed immigrants as a threat to order, and wielded the tools of harassment and brutality with few checks. Fourth, Latinx migration into a region with a long history of Black-white residential division, I argue, shaped and constrained housing opportunities available to Islip's Latinos. Their fate was linked to the transformation of a real estate market in which racialization and financialization operated hand in hand. Fifth, the town's racialized geography of public education shaped housing markets and exacerbated inequality.

Between the late 1930s and the early 1960s, a small community of Latinx newcomers settled in Islip. The first were Puerto Ricans, who arrived at the end of the Great Depression and the beginning of World War II, most recruited to work in service, maintenance, and groundskeeping jobs for Pilgrim State Hospital, one of the largest psychiatric facilities in the country, then located in the northwestern corner of the town.[19] More came to Long Island during World War II, when local employers faced a serious labor shortage and began to recruit workers of color to fill jobs.[20] In the mid- and late 1940s, still more Puerto Ricans came to the area to work as agricultural laborers, harvesting potatoes, fruit, and other crops, some as part of a 1948 recruitment effort by the Suffolk County Farm Bureau.[21]

From their first settlement in Islip, Puerto Ricans, many with mixed European, indigenous, and African ancestry, faced stigmatization, reinforced by government policies and popular ideologies that racialized them. In New York during the 1930s, as Lorrin Thomas discovered, the federal government issued identification documents to Puerto Rican–born U.S. citizens residing, using racial descriptions such as "dark," "olive," "ruddy," "regular brown," "light brown," "dark brown," or "colored." Not a single Puerto Rican applicant for a federal ID in New York during that period was classified as "white," not even those who appeared very pale in the photographs that accompanied their application forms. Puerto Ricans confronted a binary or one-drop rule about race, leading them to be racialized as nonwhite.[22]

Notions about the racial inferiority of nonwhites were widespread in mid-twentieth-century America, but they found particularly fertile soil in Islip. Just a decade before the first Puerto Ricans arrived, Islip was the center of Suffolk County's large and active Ku Klux Klan, whose membership peaked at ten thousand (about one in seven county residents) in the mid-1920s. The Second Klan, fueled by anti-immigrant sentiment, anti-Catholicism, and racism, appealed to white fears that immigrants were taking their jobs, corrupting American government with foreign ideologies, promulgating dangerous religious ideas, and diluting white racial purity through intermarriage.[23] Two Klan units, the Junior Order for Boys and the American Krusaders, had their

Long Island headquarters in the Islip hamlet of Bay Shore. Klansmen in full cloaks and hoods, some riding hooded horses, gathered for midnight rallies and paraded through Islip. At a massive KKK rally in a field in East Islip in June 1923, 25,000 people witnessed the induction of 1,400 new Klan members. Klan membership translated into political power: Islip KKK members won elections in Suffolk County in the mid-1920s. The flagpole in front of the Islip Town Hall long bore a plaque stating that it had been donated by the Islip branch of the Ladies of the Klan.[24]

Even as the Klan waned institutionally in Islip and nationwide by the end of the 1920s, its anti-immigrant and racist ideologies persisted, playing a key role in shaping the experience of the town's first Latinos, as it did in places as diverse as suburban Los Angeles and southern Texas.[25]

The fact that many Latinos spoke Spanish as a first language further limited their opportunities and generated nativist hostility. Beginning in the mid-twentieth century, many white people began using the derogatory term *spic* or *spik* to refer to Latinos, derived from the phrase "no speak English." Even second- or third-generation Latinos who spoke English inflected with a "Spanish" accent were still often branded as outsiders and inferior by the English-speaking majority. The stigmatization of Spanish speakers has been a persistent problem in Islip, including regular complaints of discrimination against those who spoke accented English, the inadequacy of Spanish-language instruction in the town's schools in the 1970s and 1980s, the failure of Suffolk County to provide Spanish language assistance to voters, and a high-profile but unsuccessful effort to an enact English-only law in Suffolk County in the late 1980s and first half of the 1990s.[26]

The designation of Islip's first Latinx residents as nonwhite and linguistically un-American meant that in many realms of everyday life, notably employment, they found themselves relegated to an inferior status. On Long Island, many found themselves confined to what had long been defined as "Black jobs." In 1947, for example, the *Long Islander* newspaper wrote that "dark-skinned, Spanish-speaking workers, who are United States citizens, are being recruited from the farms and in the small villages of Puerto Rico . . . They are young men, for the most part, somewhat small of stature, but strong and enured to hard work in hot weather." The notion that dark-skinned people were particularly suited to hard work in hot climates was one of the hoariest clichés in American culture, used to justify chattel slavery and, later, the concentration of people of color in grueling and poor-paying agricultural jobs.[27] Employers also channeled migrant women into conventionally Black jobs, especially household service, notoriously unregulated and exploitative. In 1955, the New York State attorney general Jacob Javits issued a report to the state legislature documenting how Long Island employment agencies recruited domestic workers from Puerto Rico and the Virgin Islands and held them "as nothing more than indentured servants," paying them poor wages and threatening them with arrest if they left their employers.[28]

In the decades following World War II, the pace of Latinx suburbanization increased as Long Island's manufacturing sector expanded rapidly. The northern and western sections of Islip, with cheap land and good highway and rail connections to New York City, attracted a growing number of firms relocating from deindustrializing Brooklyn and Queens. Nearby were Long Island's aircraft and electronics manufacturers, which expanded massively during the Cold War. Whites monopolized the region's best-paying blue-collar jobs, especially in the military-industrial complex, but smaller, nonunionized firms, many of them defense subcontractors with slim profit margins, found Puerto Ricans and later other Latinos as a ready source of cheap labor.[29]

The construction of new houses, factories, offices, malls, and highways also created thousands of well-paying jobs on Long Island, but the building trades were clannish and discriminatory, confining nonwhite men to entry-level, heavy-lifting jobs. Raul Martinez, a Puerto Rican construction worker, offered a grim description of his experience on the job. "We're the last to be hired and the first to be fired," he told a reporter in 1971. On the job, he faced harassment by resentful white coworkers, who vandalized his car, "put chalk in the fingers of his gloves or in his pockets," and stole his tools. "When you try to improve yourself," he lamented, "They do everything in their power to break you."[30]

The shared experience of workplace discrimination brought together Puerto Ricans and African Americans in Long Island into an intense period of protest in the mid-1960s.[31] In 1963, Lincoln Lynch, the head of Long Island's chapter of the Congress of Racial Equality (CORE), announced a campaign to challenge the "bastions of segregation and debasement of Negroes and Puerto Ricans" in Suffolk and Nassau Counties. For the next four years, nonviolent protesters targeted businesses for refusing to hire African American and Puerto Rican workers, including the Franklin Savings Bank, which had a branch in Central Islip, the Gardiner Manor Shopping Center, near the growing Latino settlement in Islip's Bay Shore area, and the Long Island Railroad, the Long Island Lighting Company, and the New York Telephone Company, all of which served Islip. At best, these local protests led to token gains, not fundamentally altering Islip's labor market.[32]

Local activists also pushed for the expansion of opportunities in public sector jobs, which had been an important avenue for upward mobility for

Blacks and Latinos in nearby New York City. In 1963, CORE targeted discrimination against workers of color in Long Island's public parks. And in 1967, Black and Puerto Rican activists demanded the hiring of nonwhites by Islip's Street Department, which remained all-white. Both efforts, however, led to few gains. Five decades later, when Islip was nearly one-third Latino and more than 10 percent of the town's Latinos worked in natural resources, construction, or ground maintenance jobs, the municipal government employed only two Latinos out of 105 full-time parks and recreation workers and just 11 Latinos out of 136 full-time street and highway workers.[33]

From middle of the twentieth century onward, Islip's Latinos remained primarily employed in insecure, poor-paying service work and manual labor, like landscaping, housekeeping, childcare, eldercare, non-unionized construction, and food preparation. "The Long Island economy," wrote the anthropologist Sarah Mahler, who conducted fieldwork in Islip in the 1980s and early 1990s, "produced many thousands of low-wage, dead-end jobs that few natives would take." As a consequence, Latinx workers in Islip often held more than one job to make ends meet. Latinx households frequently relied on the labor of several family members to cover housing, transportation, food, and other expenses.[34] Moreover, many of the jobs available to Latinos on Long Island were informal or unregulated, offered few benefits, and subjected them to degrading work conditions, health risks, long hours, and wage theft. Islip's informal labor market took material form in the landscape of parking lots turned into outdoor hiring halls.[35]

Despite its history of discrimination, Islip was a magnet for new waves of Latino migrants from the midcentury on forward, in part because of the presence of a small but increasingly visible Latino community. Islip's Latino population began a long, steady expansion beginning in the 1960s. Joining the town's established Puerto Rican community were refugees from Cuba who fled the island in the wake of the Cuban Revolution. In 1980, another wave of Cubans, many of African descent, arrived in Islip after the Mariel boatlift.[36] Salvadorans arrived in large numbers in Islip after 1979, most of them fleeing rural parts of El Salvador that were ravaged during its brutal civil war, eventually becoming the town's largest immigrant community.[37] Colombian immigrants to Islip similarly fled their country's long and bloody civil conflict, which was particularly intense between the early 1980s and a 2016 ceasefire agreement.[38] Islip also attracted many Latinos fleeing New York City's economic troubles and expensive housing for the suburban region's increasing demand for care workers, landscapers, and house cleaners, especially as the postwar suburban white population aged in place. During the late twentieth century and early twenty-first century, Latinos from the Dominican Republic

(New York City's largest immigrant group) and Mexico (who began moving to the city and suburbs in the early 2000s) began moving to Islip.[39]

Like their Puerto Rican predecessors, many new Latino residents of Islip were branded as nonwhite, particularly Dominicans, post-Mariel Cubans, and Colombians, who often had some African ancestry. In addition, Latinos of indigenous descent—especially Salvadorans—were also stigmatized as racial others because of their skin color and physiognomy. Latino immigrants also experienced the negative impact of what Leo Chávez calls "the Latino threat" narrative, in which Latinos are depicted as dangerous, threatening, criminal, or unlawful.[40] By the late 1960s, as the nationwide "war on crime" intensified, the Suffolk County Police Department (SCPD) began profiling and harassing Latinos in Islip. In 1969, Puerto Rican and Black students at Central Islip High School held a school boycott to protest police harassment. Student leaders were outraged by an SCPD patrolman who "displayed his shotgun and used unnecessary force" at a school dance at which eight students were arrested. In 1971 and 1972 alone, the SCPD received 130 sworn complaints about police brutality, largely from residents of Brentwood and Central Islip. Local activists, led by the Council of Puerto Rican Organizations, protested police violence and launched a wave of lawsuits.[41] In a high-profile effort to curb police brutality, the Puerto Rican Legal Defense Fund and the NAACP Legal Defense Fund brought a class action lawsuit against the police, leading federal judge Robert Weinstein to find that the SCPD deployed excessive force and used racial epithets "in a substantial number of cases," leading many minorities to "feel abused."[42]

The outcry against police violence and discrimination spurred a series of high-profile investigations of the SCPD by the Suffolk County Bar Association (1980), the Suffolk County Human Rights Commission (1989), the New York State Department of Investigation (1989), and the U.S. Equal Employment Opportunity Commission (1995). Twice, once in 1983 and again in 2009, the U.S. Department of Justice (DOJ) filed civil rights lawsuits against the SCPD.[43] In 1986, the DOJ entered into a consent decree with the SCPD concerning discriminatory hiring practices. In 2014, in response to a series of hate crimes targeting Latin American immigrants and persistent complaints of police harassment and discrimination against Latinos, the DOJ entered into a second agreement to oversee nearly every aspect of the SCPD's relations with the community. As of 2024, both consent decrees remained in force. The SCPD had been under continuous DOJ supervision for more than forty years.[44]

Growing anti-immigration sentiment on Long Island at the turn of the century intensified conflicts over policing and public policy. In the late 1990s and early 2000s, Long Island saw the rapid spread of white supremacist groups who painted anti-immigrant graffiti and attacked immigrant day laborers. White teens clashed with Latino students in Islip's schools.[45] At the same time, a panic over Latinx street gangs, especially La Mara Salvatrucha, or MS-13, which had grown rapidly in central Long Island, fueled anti-immigrant animus and calls for more aggressive policing, including targeted stops of Latinx drivers and arrests of teens suspected, often wrongly, of gang affiliation. In 2016, the Suffolk County Sheriff's office announced that it would cooperate with the Department of Homeland Security in detaining undocumented immigrants, but the policy was quickly struck down as impermissible under New York state law.[46] Still, anti-immigrant sentiment and fears of crime were not so easily disentangled. In a July 2017 speech about MS-13 in Brentwood, surrounded by cheering SCPD officers, President Donald Trump told the police, "Please don't be too nice," infamously instructing them not to protect the heads of suspects as they were loaded into police cars. *El Diario La Prensa* denounced Trump's "false narrative" of crime and his defense of police abuse at a moment of growing community agitation against the SCPD's practices. Between 2013 and 2017, Latinos had filed at least 134 complaints against the SCPD, while Latino Justice, a civil rights organization, sued the department on behalf of twenty-one plaintiffs.[47]

The Segregated Suburb

The racialization of Islip's Latinos through racial classification and prejudice, labor market discrimination, and policing reinforced a deep and enduring pattern of residential inequality. When Latinos moved into Islip, they arrived in a place with an already-segregated housing market. Islip's housing market was typical of twentieth-century suburban communities, segregated first through the widespread use of racially restrictive covenants, which sometimes targeted Puerto Ricans.[48] Even after the U.S. Supreme Court ruled in 1948 that racially restrictive covenants were unenforceable, racial restrictions shaped real estate practices in central Long Island for decades to come. Postwar Islip's racial geography was also shaped by federal housing programs, including the Home Owners' Loan Corporation, the Federal Housing Administration, and the Veterans Administration, all of which underwrote racially segregated housing developments.[49]

Viewed as nonwhite, Islip's Puerto Ricans had few options. Many moved into neighborhoods with established Black populations, largely in the northwestern section of the town. In this respect, Islip's history of racial suburbanization diverged from that of Mexican American suburbanization in the

VENTA DE LOTES
$695 MEDIO ACRE
20,000 pies cuadrados (10 lotes de ciudad) Cerca de Bayshore Long Island. A una hora de Nueva York por tren y carretera.
R. PEREZ
221 W. 21 St., N.Y.C. - OR 5-3710

FIGURE 3.1. Advertisement for lots in Bayshore in *Ecos de Nueva York*, October 25, 1953.

Pomona Valley outside Los Angeles, where, as Genevieve Carpio argues, "Latinas/os maintained relative racial privilege" in housing markets over African Americans, even as both were marginalized by whites.[50] In Central Islip, the most urbanized section of the town, Blacks and Puerto Ricans were confined to blocks near the Long Island Railroad tracks that were lined with small, wood-framed houses dating from the late nineteenth century. Beginning in the 1970s, Central Islip's Carleton Park neighborhood, which was built in the early 1950s as temporary housing for defense workers, became increasingly Black and Latino, with landlords preying on nonwhite renters who had few choices in Islip's housing market.[51] Housing conditions there were so abysmal that the town eventually had the area cleared for redevelopment.[52]

Latinx newcomers also found housing in Brentwood and North Bay Shore, especially in areas that were largely undeveloped and unzoned in the 1940s and 1950s but convenient to the Pilgrim State Hospital and the industrial zone along the town's western edge. In the 1940s, some Islip landowners began advertising in New York's Spanish-language press, offering inexpensive lots in the area (fig. 3.1). Some Latinx newcomers learned about cheap property there through personal or familial connections. Elizabeth Guanill, a *puertorriqueña* whose family moved to Islip in 1943, recalled that her father heard from a friend about property available for "$150 an acre, ten dollars down, ten dollars a month."[53] The first Latinx settlements in these sections of the town resembled *colonias*, informal settlements of Mexican migrants in periurban areas along the Texas-Mexico border or exurban Los Angeles, as well as informal settlements on the periphery of many Latin American cities, where newcomers settled on small plots of land, usually lacking infrastructure and built their own homes.[54] Guanill recalled that "Brentwood is more like Puerto Rico than Manhattan is," because its residents lived in houses rather than tenements and used their lots to raise chickens and grow vegetables and fruits.[55]

While many Latino newcomers found the prospect of living on Islip's suburban fringe attractive, they also faced real hurdles. Getting funds for home construction was difficult in the conventional, racially discriminatory housing finance market. In Brentwood and North Bay Shore during the 1940s and 1950s, many lived in tents or temporary tar-paper cabins until they saved up enough to begin construction.[56] Josephine Festa's family, who moved from Brooklyn to North Bay Shore in the 1950s, followed a cousin who lived there in "a little shack." Festa recalled that her father bought a nearby plot of land and, "with thoughts of the future," dug a basement and eventually self-built the family house.[57]

Other Latinos settled in a small segregated development, nicknamed "Tan Town" for its racially mixed population, in North Bay Shore, close to the busy Sunrise Highway, cordoned off from surrounding neighborhoods by a fence and accessible only by a single entrance along a back street. The owner of Tan Town, Louis Mazza, who also ran a notorious local bar, profited by offering rundown houses for rent and small parcels of land for sale. Tan Town was invisible to most of Islip's residents, although on various occasions, the town targeted Mazza for code violations. Some of the small shacks still stand today, mostly as outbuildings in what has today become a mobile home park.[58]

The settlement of nonwhites in marginal, undeveloped areas was, as Andrew Wiese has found, a common pattern in Long Island. As long as Latinx neighborhoods were cordoned off from white areas and invisible, they attracted little white opposition.[59] But the growth of Islip's Latino population in the postwar years both alarmed white residents and created new opportunities for predatory real estate practices, especially in mostly white Brentwood neighborhoods. In 1959, *Newsday*, Long Island's largest newspaper, investigated civil rights and housing and reported that members of the Suffolk Real Estate Board "openly admitted . . . that unscrupulous realty dealers in the county were 'blockbusting'—using racial prejudice as a lever to panic homeowners into selling at a loss."[60] The practice attracted the attention of New York's attorney general, who warned in 1960 that "unethical real estate operators were telling homeowners in long-established white neighborhoods that Negroes or Puerto Ricans were buying homes in the same blocks."[61] Blockbusting stirred up animus toward Latinos and signaled to whites that northwestern Islip neighborhoods were risky.

While some brokers stoked the fears of white homeowners, blockbusting was an isolated phenomenon in Islip. Brokers had a greater interest in catering to the demands of the hundreds of thousands of whites who settled in the town in the postwar years. By 1960, Islip was the largest town in Suffolk County; in 1980, the town's population reached its peak of 330,000 people. Like most midcentury American suburbs, Islip became a refuge for mostly middle-class whites who looked back in their rearview mirrors with a mix of romanticism and disdain toward the rapidly changing neighborhoods they left behind in Brooklyn and Queens. They expected that Islip would be segregated. Real estate brokers, bound by a code of ethics that forbade the introduction of "incompatible" groups into white neighborhoods, were eager to comply.[62]

The housing patterns set during the postwar years proved very resilient. Islip remained racially segregated, and discriminatory housing practices persisted, even after the incremental passage of fair housing legislation in New York State in 1950, 1955, 1961, and 1964. The federal government followed suit, enacting Title VIII of the Civil Rights Act in April 1968, which forbade housing discrimination on the basis of race, color, religion, or national origin nationwide. A month later, Islip enacted its own ordinance forbidding housing discrimination, joining forty other New York municipalities that had already passed similar laws.[63] Enforcing civil rights laws, however, proved challenging. New York's local, county, and state levels tasked with addressing housing discrimination complaints have had limited resources and have struggled to fulfill their mandates. The enforcement of federal fair housing law was largely delegated to the U.S. Department of Housing and Urban Development, which primarily depended on local, nonprofit fair housing agencies to investigate discrimination and bring litigation, or the DOJ, which litigated only major cases of "pattern and practice" or "general public importance."[64]

In Islip, real estate professionals developed tactics to preserve the racial homogeneity of neighborhoods and dodge the laws without attracting the notice of homebuyers, renters, or public officials. Those tactics included refusing to provide information to Latinx renters or homebuyers about available properties in white neighborhoods, lying about the availability of particular listed properties in predominantly white rental complexes, or simply refusing to show rental units or homes to minority renters or homebuyers. One of the most common tactics was racial steering—refusing to show nonwhites homes for sale or rent in white neighborhoods and vice versa, best summed up in comments a Long Island broker told a potential white homebuyer in 1969: "I could take you to places where Spanish people live, where colored people live. You don't want that."[65] From the late 1960s well into the twenty-first century, a staggering number of investigations into housing discrimination by local fair housing organizations, the federal Department of Housing and Urban Development, the Islip and Suffolk County planning departments, and various journalists and scholars found pervasive discrimination against both Blacks and Latinos.[66]

For decades, conventional mortgage lenders had discriminated against Latino homebuyers, regularly denying them loans. But beginning in the late 1990s, encouraged by the deregulation of home finance, banks and mortgage brokers suddenly flooded into Latino neighborhoods in Islip, profiting from the rise of subprime and predatory lending. In 2005–2006, just before the global financial crisis, Brentwood and Central Islip had the highest rates of high-cost mortgage lending on Long Island. Predatory lenders, like NationsBank, named in a 2007 lawsuit filed by Brentwood residents Luis Turcios, Aurora Velasquez, and Elise Velasquez, offered high-interest mortgages for rundown houses that had been appraised for far more than they were worth. In its ruling in the Turcios case, a state court noted that NationsBank targeted buyers who "were typically Hispanic, working as marginally employed blue collar workers residing in the Bay Shore, Brentwood or Central Islip communities." Victims of predation paid a high price. In 2014, 35 percent of homeowners in Brentwood and Central Islip had "underwater" properties, meaning that they owed more on their houses than the houses were worth. These two heavily Latino sections of Islip ranked in the bottom 5 percent of all communities in the entire United States by percentage of underwater properties.[67]

Islip's long history of discriminatory housing and predatory lending explains the distinctive features of its Latino landscape. It explains why Latinos remain overwhelmingly concentrated in northwestern Islip. And it explains how the town's Latino landscapes diverge from those of the postwar crabgrass frontier. Suburbanization and homeownership have long been synonymous, but because of discriminatory lending practices, Islip's Latinos have long been more likely to rent than the town's whites and are more vulnerable to exploitative landlords. Immigrants moving to Islip were an easy target for landlords who converted little postwar ranches and Cape Cods into boardinghouses while letting their properties deteriorate. Latino tenants were often afraid to file complaints against their landlords for fear of being evicted and tossed into a discriminatory housing market where they had few options. Whether renters or homeowners, Islip's Latinos continue to live on the financial brink in the town's segregated housing market, a fact that explains the disappearance of the single-family homes of the crabgrass frontier. By the early 1990s, Islip had an estimated twelve thousand accessory apartments—units carved out of existing single-family homes, including in basements, garages, and attics.

The division of homes was sometimes the result of desires to keep extended families united. But it was also a survival strategy.[68]

Whether they are renters or owners, Islip's Latino residents are substantially more likely than white residents to pay a greater portion of their income on housing and to experience inferior housing conditions. In 2015, just 42 percent of Islip's white residents paid more than 30 percent of their income for housing expenses, compared to 60 percent of Latinos. Not surprisingly, the areas where residents bore the highest burden of housing costs were Central Islip and Brentwood. And Latinos usually paid more for less. In 2015, the town of Islip reported the number of households by race that experienced at least one of four "severe housing problems," which included lacking a kitchen, lacking complete plumbing, severe overcrowding (more than 1.5 people per room), or severe cost burden (over half of household income spent on housing). Even Latinos approaching middle-class status are more likely to live in inferior housing than their white counterparts.[69]

The inequities in Islip's housing market and the town's long history of stigmatizing Latinos poisonously combined to create and reinforce educational disparities in Islip. In a 2019 report on housing discrimination on Long Island, *Newsday* quoted a real estate agent engaged in racial steering: "What I say is always to women, follow the school bus. You know, that's what I always say. Follow the school bus, see the moms that are hanging out on the corners."[70] Her comments point to one of the most important legacies of housing segregation in Islip: separate and unequal housing creates and maintains separate and unequal education. White homebuyers are keenly attentive to school district boundaries out of a mixture of racist assumptions about nonwhite children and their parents, but even more because of huge gaps in school funding by district by race. Where you live in Islip has high stakes for your children's education, especially because the town is fragmented into twelve local school districts, each with its own tax base. School district boundaries, as Amy Wells writes in a recent study of public education on Long Island, shape disparities in educational outcomes. Boundaries, she writes, "demarcate different property values, tax rates, public revenues, private resources, working conditions, family income and wealth, parental education levels and political clout." In wealthier districts, schools can pay teachers higher salaries; purchase up-to-date curricular materials, computers, and laboratory equipment; and support costly extracurricular programs, including athletics. Wealthy districts can also rely more on donations by well-to-do parents to bring all sorts of "extras" to schools, from classroom supplies to expensive sports equipment.[71]

The schools that serve the majority of Islip's Latinos are underfunded compared to those serving the town's whites. Of the four districts with the lowest per-pupil spending, three (Bay Shore, Brentwood, and Central Islip) are majority or plurality Latino. The four districts with the highest per-pupil spending (Connetquot, Bayport/Blue Point, Hauppauge, and Sayville), by contrast, are all more than three-quarters white.[72] One of Islip's wealthiest and whitest districts, Connetquot, spends over $13,000 more per student than its poorest and most Latino district, Brentwood.[73]

History, Inequality, Identity

Islip's early twenty-first-century landscape, as we have seen, has been at once built and rebuilt by Latinx suburbanites, those who, like Elizabeth Guanill or Luis Turcios, moved to the suburb to pursue the (often elusive) dream of homeownership. Whether they picked crops, assembled aircraft parts, hauled construction materials, cleaned houses, trimmed hedges, or cared for children and the elderly, they were drawn to Long Island by its seemingly endless supply of jobs. But they found themselves in a suburban place whose long history of discrimination, segregation, exploitation, and predation profoundly limited their opportunities.

That history has had unintended consequences. Migrants from widely disparate parts of Latin America, speaking different dialects, with different familial histories and different understandings of race, have increasingly found themselves living in the same neighborhoods, bound together by a common linguistic heritage, but more importantly by the effects of racialization and the shared experiences of discrimination and segregation. That shift has resulted in the pan-Latinization of institutions that had originally served residents of a single nationality. Brentwood is home to two of Islip's many Latino-serving nonprofits: Adelante, founded in 1966 by Puerto Rican residents but transformed into a cultural organization serving Latinos of different backgrounds, and CARECEN-NY, an organization founded in 1983 to support Salvadoran refugees but now dedicated to providing legal support to Spanish speakers of all backgrounds.[74] Islip residents also celebrate Hispanic Heritage Month (a banner celebrating it hung at the Brentwood Public Library when I conducted research there in October 2019) with a slew of cultural events and readings. They dine in restaurants that are at once rooted in national culinary traditions but also create new syncretic and fusion cuisines.[75]

Of all the events that foster a sense of community among Islip's Latinos, none is more prominent than Brentwood's annual Puerto Rican and Hispanic Parade, which attracts tens of thousands of people to the streets of Brentwood every spring. The parade's history encapsulates the evolution of Islip's Latino community over time. Founded in 1967 to celebrate Puerto Rican culture, it was renamed the Puerto Rican and Hispanic Parade in the early 1980s as the town's Latino population grew more diverse. As musicians and dancers, marching bands and filiopietistic floats, pass the huge crowds along Suffolk Avenue, Latinx residents of Islip still celebrate their national heritages but also understand themselves as sharing a common identity, whether they hail from the Dominican Republic or Pueblo, Mexico or rural El Salvador. A 1999 account of the parade described the competition between ranchera and salsa performers. One parade watcher, Magda Rodriguez, who had lived in Brentwood for two decades, described her experience. "At first we didn't get along well, but here we are all together and I love it because now I can learn about many cultures, while maintaining my Puerto Ricanness."[76]

Above all, Islip's history of discrimination, segregation, and inequity has also forged a common sense of grievance and created new opportunities for mobilization against racial inequality and injustice. Islip's Latinos, who have recently bonded together to fight for voting rights, against anti-immigrant policies and unjust policing, and for better municipal services, schools, and parks, is a reaction to the process of racialization in the United States but also, critically, the result of a growing sense of common interests, more than just a common linguistic heritage, one that grows out experiences of marginalization.[77]

As we look out onto the suburbanization of Latinx Americans, especially those in places like Islip with a long and troubled history of segregation and exclusion, the tired assimilationist frameworks make little sense. Suburbia today is less a model of upward mobility than a place where historical spatial inequalities lay the groundwork for new forms of inequality. The legacies of the crabgrass frontier and of suburban whiteness have not been washed away by a new diversity, but rather, they have taken on new form, in old skins, during the era of mass migration from the Caribbean, Central, and South America. In bearing the burden of past policies and practices that created segregated suburbia but adapting to new realities of work and housing, the Latinx history of Islip suggests a new direction for understanding the unresolved issues of race and place in suburban America.

4

Are Latino Suburbs Ethnoburbs? And Why It Matters

BECKY M. NICOLAIDES
Huntington-USC Institute on California and the West

The history of Latino peoples in metropolitan America is increasingly a suburban story. The suburbs have seen rising levels of ethno-racial diversity, upending many assumptions about the balance of power and race across metro areas. The numbers are fairly astounding. While in 1970, Black Americans, Asian Americans, and Latinos comprised just 10 percent of the American suburban population, that proportion had risen to 45 percent in 2020. From another angle, by 2010, a majority of all three populations lived in suburban areas—54 percent of Black Americans, 63 percent of Asian Americans, and 61 percent of Latinos (up from 50 percent in 1990). As of 2020, Latinos were the largest nonwhite suburban group in seventeen major metro areas, including five in California, four in Texas, and three in Florida, as well as in New York City, Las Vegas, and Phoenix.[1] Immigrants were also part of this shift. By 2000, fully 52 percent of the foreign-born population lived in the suburbs, many of them settling there directly upon arrival.[2]

Suburbia, then, deserves much more attention when it comes to understanding the Latino metropolitan experience. Suburbs were places where people settled, built communities and lives, and at times engaged in politics. And many were built upon foundations of white racial exclusion, with well-developed toolkits for maintaining that exclusivity. But what would happen

This work received the financial support of the European Commission Erasmus + Initiative, "Urbanism and Suburbanization in the EU Countries and Abroad: Reflection in the Humanities, Social Sciences, and the Arts" (2021-1-CZ01-KA220-HED-000023281). The European Commission's support for the production of this publication does not constitute an endorsement of the contents, which reflect the views only of the authors, and the commission cannot be held responsible for any use which may be made of the information contained therein.

to these places once they transitioned away from whiteness? And how did these dynamics play out across different ethno-racial landscapes?

In my research on Los Angeles, at the leading edge of suburban diversification—a metro area where people of color came to outnumber whites in suburbia by 1990 and as suburban homeowners by 2010—I found that crossing ethnic borders in the scholarship on suburbia can yield some fruitful questions and insights.[3] Los Angeles is rife with Latino and Asian suburbs. As I started delving into the weeds of their suburban histories, it became clear that the scholarship on Asian suburbanization was quite well theorized and could offer useful frameworks for analyzing suburban spaces of all ethnic groups. The nascent scholarship on Latino suburbs has rarely cited this work on Asian suburbs. It has existed in an entirely separate lane, offering its own powerful insights but not engaging useful concepts from scholars of Asian suburbanization.

This article contends that there is much to be gained by merging these lanes using suburbia as its main spatial focus. Rather than compare Latino suburbs to Latino *urban* spaces, it compares them to other suburban areas, particularly Asian suburbs, where the spatial constraints and presence of ethnic residents present a more equivalent context.

In the Asian American suburban literature, one of the key organizing concepts is the ethnoburb, where Asian ethnic identity was on full display in the built landscape and where ethnic businesses, professions, and residences were encouraged, robust, and interdependent. In the ethnoburbs, Asian Americans could claim full cultural citizenship, a sense of belonging and inclusion. These were spaces of ethnic empowerment, where ethnic wealth and community resilience were amassed and celebrated.[4] While offering a useful typology of Asian suburban community, the ethnoburb concept also raised questions about whether it could be applied to other kinds of ethnic suburbs.

My research led to some unexpected turns. I began with the assumption that when ethnic groups settled in suburban communities, as the ethnoburb model posits, they would have relative freedom to shape those places according to their own cultural proclivities. What I found instead was a process of much greater nuance, variation, and contestation. Ethnic identity could not always be freely expressed in suburban places: it could be suppressed by both coercion and consent. My search for "ethnoburbs" of Los Angeles revealed more of a spectrum of suburban communities inhabited by Asian and Latino residents alike—some robustly ethnic, others clinging to well-established "white" traditions even after whites had left. Moreover, Latino suburbs diverged from the typology in certain important ways. This mattered because whether a community accepted ethnicity in its midst ultimately shaped dynamics around ethnic power, wealth, belonging, and cultural freedom. These were the stakes.

The story of Latino and Asian suburbs in Los Angeles was shaped by global inequalities between Latin America and East Asia, reflecting disparities inherent in the globalization of the world economy. Mexico and Central America sent immigrants who were predominantly "transnational migrants from below," people escaping poverty, war, and political upheaval. Difficult conditions in home countries, moreover, reinforced loyalties to family and communities of origin, fueling a robust remittance culture.[5] By contrast, human and capital flows from Asian nations like China, Taiwan, and Hong Kong brought greater wealth. Asian immigration included a fair share of working-class people—but they were outnumbered by highly skilled white-collar workers, professionals, and entrepreneurs. Chinese business owners and investors brought capital to America, enabling them to create an ethnic economy "from the top."[6] The Los Angeles suburbs reflected this uneven playing field, with these deep divisions shaping the history of ethnic suburbia.

Learning from Asian American Suburban Studies

In metropolitan Los Angeles, suburban ethnic diversification was accelerating from 1970 to the early 2000s.[7] But even in the midst of these trends, white suburbs continued to matter. The historical narrative that has been so well established to this point—emphasizing the primacy of white suburban homeowner politics and culture, with their values of individualism, privatism, putatively color-blind meritocracy, and entitlement—remains vitally important to our understanding of metropolitan places and the perpetuation of inequality.[8] In perhaps less noticed ways, white suburbs established norms and praxis that deeply influenced the historical trajectory of some suburbs undergoing diversification. Yes, white suburbs could resist ethno-racial newcomers altogether. But in other cases, they shaped how new ethnic suburbanites might carry forward local political cultures and lifeways. Since the 1980s, in fact, the suburban narrative had become a variegated one, with a host of new players, politics, and everyday practices: some building upon long-standing white suburban cultures and others introducing wholly new suburban values.

Asian American suburbanization emerged as a main thread of this unfolding story. Perhaps because Asian Americans gained an early foothold in the suburbs in the post–World War II era and emerged as the "most suburban" of all ethnic groups, scholars began studying them earlier.[9] One key concept was spatial assimilation, the idea that when people moved to certain types of communities—especially suburbs—that process helped assimilate them to mainstream America. This theory applied particularly to European American ethnic groups, who were able to move into racially segregated suburbs and gain the advantages of whiteness through that move.[10] But scholars like Min Zhou, Yen-Fen Tseng, and Rebecca Kim questioned whether this process held for non-European ethnics.[11] This related to the racialization of Asian Americans, which placed them (along with Latino people) in the "middle" of the American racial hierarchy, somewhere below whites but above African Americans. While they didn't occupy the "bottom," they didn't necessarily possess the advantages of whiteness, either.[12] This racial othering obstructed full social acceptance by the white mainstream, rendering wholescale assimilation essentially unachievable purely on racial grounds.

The geographer Wei Li took this idea further. She devised the concept of ethnoburbs—"suburban ethnic clusters of residential and business districts" that acted as crucial hubs of ethnic business, immigrant community, and political solidarity. These were suburbs where ethnicity not only survived but thrived, countering the assimilation framework altogether. As the spatial successor to urban Chinatowns, the ethnoburbs attracted both upwardly mobile Chinese people moving out of Chinatowns as well as Chinese immigrants who bypassed the inner city to settle directly in suburbia. Li found evidence of ethnoburbs in the Asian American suburbs of LA's San Gabriel Valley, particularly among Chinese immigrants. She argued that ethnoburbs had certain key traits. Ethnic businesses and institutions reinforced a strong sense of ethnic identity in the place itself. Ethnoburbs were nourished by transnational flows of people, capital, and commodities, especially in the context of post-1980 globalization and immigration from Asia. The vibrancy of ethnicity in "ethnoburbia," moreover, was bolstered by two additional, interrelated patterns: the persistence of ethnic clustering (as opposed to gradual spatial dispersal) and the continued influx of new immigrants into these suburban enclaves.[13]

In the ethnoburbs, the ethnic population and economy were tightly linked. This synergy provided familiar consumer goods, opportunities for entrepreneurs and professionals, and immigrant jobs—all in one suburban place. This ethnic economic base was crucial to the formation and continued growth of ethnoburbs. While acknowledging the economic diversity of ethnoburban populations that included both ethnic millionaires and poorer immigrants, reflecting the polarized nature of Asian immigration in general, Li highlighted the overall wealth of these communities. They were continually infused by Chinese investment capital. In the larger scheme of LA's economy, these entrepreneurs and investors precipitated an important shift—from the decline of LA's Anglo growth machine toward the rise of "immigrant growth machines," often centered in the suburbs.[14] In Los Angeles, the anchor ethnoburb in the San Gabriel Valley was Monterey Park, soon joined by San Gabriel, Rosemead, Alhambra, Hacienda Heights, and Rowland Heights, among others.

The economic development of the ethnoburbs revealed their growing power and clout over time.[15] Broadly speaking, they evolved from ethnic service centers to global economic outposts. In the 1970s, the first Chinese shopping center with a grocery store and restaurants opened in Monterey Park. It was followed gradually by Chinese American banks, realty companies, medical and dental practices, travel agencies, and beauty salons. By the 1980s, Chinese investors and businesspeople joined forces to open large shopping areas and supermarkets—including the popular chain 99 Ranch Market, which spread across California, Seattle, Honolulu, Las Vegas, and Phoenix. Asian malls became key social and commercial hubs, reviving a suburban form—the mall—that many had written off as "dead." By the 1980s and 1990s, ethnoburbs were fully linked to the global economy. Suburban global ties showed up especially in the FIRE (finance, insurance, and real estate) sector. Real estate companies, for example, began marketing directly in Asia, especially as more and more Chinese nouveaux riches saw investment in American suburban real estate as a safe bet. Other global enterprises included import-export and logistics, making the ethnoburbs a focal point of international business, investment, and capital circulation. The ethnoburbs built up remarkable economic strength, enabling them to weather economic downturns and recessions, evident in their comparatively lower unemployment and commercial vacancy rates than county averages.[16]

The timing of ethnoburbia's initial emergence, moreover, was propitious, to say the least. Ethnoburbs developed right on the heels of Proposition 13 (1978), the state's tax-cutting measure that decimated local municipal revenues. With fresh, steady infusions of transnational wealth, ethnoburbs were replenished and strengthened financially at a time when most municipalities were struggling to make ends meet. From another angle, Prop 13 had the unintended effect of shifting the property tax burden away from more settled white suburbanites and onto newcomers of color, who bought into suburbia in rising numbers after 1980, when housing costs were spiking. They missed the advantages enjoyed by those long-term white residents who benefited from their racially privileged access to affordable homes in the postwar suburbs and the tax advantages of staying put.[17]

Even with their wealth and capital investments, the ethnoburbs came to embody the inequalities inherent in globalization itself, reflected in disparate streams of immigrants who arrived from Asia, from the wealthy to the working class. Some ethnoburbs, for example, had significant numbers of local kids who qualified for free school lunches, and there were shocking reports of sweatshop conditions in Asian-owned worksites.[18] Clearly, the amassing of ethnic wealth did not guarantee that its benefits would be shared.

In ethnoburbia, ethnicity was visible and expressive. It was there to see in Chinese language signage, businesses, Asian malls, and in architectural flourishes on private suburban homes. This ethnic assertiveness was never a given but was the product of a protracted series of hard-fought battles with white suburbanites resistant to change—a story well documented in foundational works on Asian suburbs, especially Monterey Park, which stands as a well-studied archetype in this literature. These victories resulted from several factors, including a strong network of Asian American legal, research, and social service groups in greater Los Angeles, which helped mobilize crucial support from local Asian American lawyers, professors, and professionals who lived in Monterey Park and had the expertise to wage effective political battles. They also formed alliances with Latinos who recognized their shared plight. In these suburbs, a sophisticated base of human relations work underlaid the formation of ethnoburbia.[19]

Ethnicity, then, was vividly experienced—and sometimes readapted—*within* many American suburbs, exploding a plethora of suburban stereotypes of conformity, whiteness, and blandness. Moreover, the class diversity of these suburbs complicates the older spatial assimilation model, which posits that movement into suburbia meant automatic upward mobility and assimilation. The fact that suburban living has come to mean a variety of *class* experiences challenges the idea that a suburban address automatically confers white middle-class advantage.[20]

If ethnoburbs were centers of robust ethnic life—economic, cultural, social—other suburban settlements of Asians were much less so. Many Asians settled in more dispersed patterns, in contrast to the ethnic clustering model.[21] Their ethnicity was rendered invisible in spatial terms, as suggested by the evocative descriptor *invisiburb*, coined by Emily Skop.[22]

Even in some suburbs with an ethnic Chinese majority, that identity could also be suppressed. In these communities, ethnicity in the built landscape was consciously concealed through local policies such as limiting foreign-language signage, zoning against retail and housing density (to discourage ethnic business districts), and enacting design review guidelines that implicitly targeted Asians to protect Anglo-American landscapes. White suburban city councils usually led the way, but they soon gained the support of local Asian American leaders and residents. Yet the proximity of ethnoburbs like Monterey Park and San Gabriel was a critical advantage to these same Asian

American residents. They had easy access to the best Chinese grocery stores, restaurants, and services nearby without having to alter the look of their own town. Many expressed NIMBY attitudes toward ethnoburbia itself, crucial to protecting the class advantage of their Anglo-looking suburbs.[23]

In Asian suburbs, then, ethnicity existed along a spectrum. On one end were ethnoburbs, sites where ethnic investment, culture, and community were allowed to fully flourish. The ethnoburbs helped Asian American communities amass ethnic wealth and even political power, building economic resilience during hard times and the capacity to buoy their communities. On the other end of the spectrum were Asian suburbs where ethnicity was suppressed. That suppression could occur in the realms of the built landscape, retail, public culture, housing, politics, or ethnic entrepreneurship.[24] In these suburbs, ethnically Asian residents butted against static suburban spaces, less amenable to infusions of ethnic lifeways and culture, adhering more to existing Anglo suburban norms—even when those spaces were no longer Anglo.

Are Latino Suburbs Ethnoburbs?

The next step, then, is to consider how we might relate these concepts to Latino suburbs. What kinds of communities did Latino suburbanites develop? Did they lend themselves to ethnic assertiveness, expressiveness, and belonging? And were they instrumental in building ethnic wealth, resilience, and even political power?

Scholarship on Latino urbanism and Latino suburbs offers a useful starting point for thinking through these questions. Particularly helpful are works by Genevieve Carpio, Clara Irazábal, Laura Pulido, Laura Barraclough, Jerry Gonzáles, and Wendy Cheng—who all focus on metropolitan LA. Their work emphasizes the concept of the right to the suburb—the right of Latinos to claim a place in suburbia. The battle to break through white barriers and establish themselves in suburban communities was, without question, a crucial first step. Often confronting hostile white resistance and racist real estate practices, they managed to purchase homes and establish themselves in these communities. They displayed pride of ownership in their homes, some joined clubs and parent-teacher associations, and many sought to make "positive contributions to their new communities," as Jerry González has noted.[25]

The next step was to assert their values in the community, an effort that was sometimes at odds with existing white suburban norms. Perhaps the most vivid example of this was simply the act of embracing multiracialism itself. Wendy Cheng's profile of the west San Gabriel Valley (the same suburbs as Li's study) found that Latino and Asian American residents championed inclusionary, multiracial values that contrasted starkly with the outlook of many white suburbanites and that reflected a conscious desire to distance themselves from whiteness itself. Residents in these suburbs revealed a deep-seated comfort with difference and a desire to raise their children in a multiracial community. They were, in essence, expressing an emergent multiethnic suburban ideal.[26] Other studies have explored how Latino suburbanites fought for the right to live in suburbia free of harassment (especially against the undocumented), to express their cultural practices (like *charrería* or car cruising culture), and to assert themselves politically.[27] In a few cases, middle- and working-class, native-born and immigrant Latinos united in solidarity against the old-guard structure of white power in struggles for decent affordable housing and education.[28] An important contrasting work by G. Aron Ramirez revealed a more nuanced story of the Mexican American suburban experience, in which Mexican American homeowners opposed the local presence of Latino businesses as a means of protecting the middle-class identity of the community.[29]

As with Asian suburbs, Latino suburbs existed across a continuum. At one end were the areas just described, including suburbs such as Pico Rivera and Santa Fe Springs, where ethnic assertiveness was strong. At the other end were suburbs where Latino cultural and political expression was more muted, often suppressed through measures spearheaded by old-guard whites alarmed by ethnic changes transforming their communities. While some Mexican American leaders, newly risen to power, joined these efforts, they were likely acting from a defensive and tenuous position during an era of rabid anti-Latino sentiment—they hoped that assimilation to local ways could help deflect that hostility. Conflict, consensus, and internal divisions course through many Latino community studies and aptly describe the social dynamics in many Latino suburbs, spaces of contestation over the look, feel, and identity of these places. In the following pages, I explore these themes from two angles: built environments and economic functions.

BUILT ENVIRONMENTS

One hallmark of the ethnoburb is ethnic expression in the built environment. The work of James Rojas is especially useful here. More than thirty years ago, he described the "enacted Latino landscape" of East LA, an area with both urban and suburban qualities. This area exemplified what has become known as Latino urbanism, with streetscapes turned into vibrant public spaces.[30] Rojas described how residents of East LA used their front yards, driveways, sidewalks, and streets as places to mingle and exchange goods. Streetscapes became "spontaneous, dynamic and animated" landscapes, culturally expressive spaces that served multiple functions. Residents used residential spaces to sell goods, with fences along front lawns holding up items and delineating the "selling space." Homes incorporated ethnic touches like Mexican-style courtyards. And front-yard fences were ubiquitous, creating places where people converged and socialized.[31] Small, modest homes were thus transformed into evocatively Latino social spaces, serving social, economic, and cultural purposes, often in very public ways. This challenged, above all, the suburban value of privatism. Rojas concludes that a growing Latino population created a "new cultural landscape out of the existing suburban form of East Los Angeles." These spatial practices could have political implications, fostering the sort of interaction that might propel civic incorporation and activism.[32]

How ubiquitous was this sort of "enacted Latino landscape" across the suburbs? Notably, Rojas's description of the "enacted Latino landscape" closely resembles an ethnoburban landscape, and he was describing an unincorporated, basically suburban area that was not subject to strict regulations on land use. We don't yet have a well-defined framework of Latino suburbanism as a kind of corollary to Latino urbanism, a much better-developed concept. It arises, I believe, from the variations present across Latino suburban landscapes, with ethnicity suppressed in some areas and expressed in others.[33]

My evidence suggests that in many suburban areas, Latino residents encountered a more static, unbending built landscape—one controlled by local land use regulation—that didn't always lend itself to practices of "enacted Latino landscapes." In incorporated places especially, strong traditions of local rule empowered suburbs to use zoning and other regulatory powers to support local needs, protect property, and promote certain landscape aesthetics. Generations of white suburbanites had honed these local powers, developing highly effective municipal toolkits to control land use and social behaviors. They used these powers to exclude the poor and people of color, hoard wealth, and protect idealized landscapes of single-family homes set in yards. This grassroots authority was a hallmark of suburban governance, bestowing on individual suburbs a particularly robust responsiveness to their relatively small populations—especially homeowners—who were invariably concerned about protecting property values and "quality of life." In contrast to large cities where elected leaders were often far removed from their constituents, in smaller suburban municipalities, local self-determination was more of a lived reality. Suburbanites refined these tools in different ways: some to circumvent civil rights laws, others to enhance local authority over immigration, and still others to support traditional Anglo suburban aesthetics.[34]

Suppressive land use measures in the suburbs of Southeast LA, the center of Latino growth in LA after 1980, illustrated how this worked. Suburbs there essentially used their powers to outlaw enacted Latino landscapes. In some cases, these efforts pitted middle-class Mexican American homeowners against recently arrived immigrants who engaged in practices like street vending and yard sales to make ends meet. Suburbia's distinctive power to control land use offered tools to suppress such practices, which had the effect of marginalizing recent immigrants and the poorest members of these communities.

As immigration from Latin America increased after 1980, predominantly Anglo suburban leaders began backing measures that banned the markers of enacted Latino landscapes—street vending, vivid paint colors on homes and businesses, certain forms of outdoor socializing, and yard sales. Attempts were even made to regulate Spanish-language signage. While their stated goal was to restore a more traditional, residential suburban aura, these measures also expanded policing authority over immigrants in the name of public health, order, safety, and aesthetics. They were part of a broader anti-Latino and anti-immigrant movement in California and the nation at this time.[35] Laws against pushcart vending—which targeted Latino immigrants selling popsicles, fresh fruit, and the like—were passed initially in the southeast suburbs at the leading edge of ethnic diversification: Norwalk, Cerritos, Lakewood, Hawaiian Gardens, Downey, Pico Rivera, Signal Hill, and Long Beach. Typical penalties were a $500 fine or six months in jail. Whittier required a $50 annual license, as well as a $30 fee for fingerprinting and photo, a deterrent to new cash-strapped immigrants. Similar measures spread into southeastern suburbs like South Gate, Huntington Park, Montebello, Bellflower, and Hawthorne. In Huntington Park, vendors who couldn't show a driver's license or California ID card were subject to a citation and confiscation, which could mean the loss of a vendor's livelihood.[36] In June 1990, authorities there confiscated 32 coconuts, 85 watermelons, 120 mangoes, 743 bags of pork rinds, 53 churros, and 72 bags of spiced fruit. In Black and Latino Compton, a special enforcement team forced vendors out of the city and into unincorporated territory. Communities like Lakewood and South Gate also passed measures banning piñatas in the park. And as part of a cluster of measures South Gate passed in 1993, when the immigrant Latino population was rising rapidly, local leaders outlawed spontaneous games of soccer in the park and began requiring permits.[37]

Yard sales also came under increasingly heavy regulation starting in the 1980s, which tended to penalize poor Latino residents. As part of Rojas's enacted Latino landscapes, yard sales were a source of essential income for economically marginalized residents. The historian Margaret Crawford notes that such measures reflected the view by suburban leaders that a garage sale once or twice a year could be a "wholesome event" for eliminating residential waste, but more frequent sales bordered on outright commerce, which contradicted suburban residential norms.[38] In the 1980s, new suburban ordinances limited the number of days a resident could hold a yard sale (usually either once or twice a year), required a paid permit, and prohibited announcement signs on public rights of way. Suburbs passing such measures included Azusa, Arcadia, El Monte, Pasadena, Pomona, and Sierra Madre, and by the 1990s, Glendale, Santa Monica, Inglewood, Artesia, Beverly Hills, Downey, South Gate, Maywood, Gardena, and Monterey Park. Azusa was an early adopter as it tipped toward a Latino majority. Suburban leaders there passed a measure in the early 1980s restricting yard sales to two per year. They quickly got pushback, prompting them to exempt impoverished seniors who depended on yard sales for income and were allowed to hold monthly yard sales. The LA County Board of Supervisors took cues from these suburbs, passing its own measure in 1993 limiting yard sales to two per year and allowing only one posted sign, which applied to all unincorporated areas of the county. Repeat offenders could be charged with a misdemeanor and fined one thousand dollars. By contrast, more lenient rules applied in the City of Los Angeles, which allowed five sales per year but also required a permit and the paying of taxes on all sales. Enforcement was an ongoing challenge, and in some areas—including East LA—yard sales persisted despite the measures.[39]

The suburb of South Gate also pushed to outlaw Spanish-language signage and the use of bright paint colors on homes. In 1985, South Gate's predominantly white planning commission proposed an English signage ordinance, making it the first suburb in Southeast LA to do so. While local officials claimed that English signage was needed to ensure public safety ("so police and paramedic units know where they're going") and clarity to customers, they also took cues from fights brewing in Monterey Park. Local Latino residents immediately objected, noting the folly of such a measure in a region long defined by Spanish-language place-names. While most of the Anglo city council and the police chief saw no need for the ordinance, Henry Gonzalez was the lone councilman to back it. The city council ultimately dropped the measure, but that same year, it formed a Design Review Committee for the first time, reflecting a shift toward greater regulation of the built landscape.[40]

Twelve years later, a controversy over regulating paint colors revealed an intraethnic rift among local Latinos. In 1997, Latino leaders in South Gate proposed a measure outlawing bright colors on houses, allowing only more muted palettes like gray and beige. They believed this rule would help define a coherent identity for South Gate, instead of the current "hodgepodge" look. They also claimed that citizen complaints prompted the measure and that they were mainly from second- and third-generation Latinos—not Anglos. Even some immigrants objected to the bright colors. Yolanda Arias, a native of Colombia and decade-long resident of South Gate, described the "neon" paint as "ugly." She noted: "I sound racist. I'm not racist. But people coming from Mexico, people coming from other countries, they should know that this is America, that here it is different. . . . They put down this country with those colors." Henry Gonzalez, South Gate mayor at the time, also relayed a concern among Latino homeowners that bright hues would depress local property values. Defending the bright colors, the local artist Leo Limon asserted: "It's part of our cultural identity. It's the colors of feathers and birds and trees, and the Latino population sees that and uses that." These disagreements revealed a multiplicity of opinions among immigrants as well as American-born Latinos, suggesting that consensus was elusive when it came to Latino landscapes. Immigrants also brought with them certain ideals of urban space, class, and race that could shape their own aesthetic preferences, similar to Chinese immigrant residents in San Marino who shunned the trappings of ethnoburbs. While the paint control measure was ultimately dropped by city officials after it drew negative media attention, it can be seen as part of a broader push to preserve an Anglo-American landscape.[41]

In the face of such regulations, some suburban Latinos sought subtle work-arounds. One of these was the use of cantera stone. In her study of home designs in Los Angeles, Austin, and Phoenix, Sarah Lopez has shown how cantera stone added subtle Mexican touches to local architecture that were fairly invisible to "white" eyes. It was a way of folding ethnic elements into suburban home designs, similar to feng shui in Asian suburbs, that would not overtly announce itself as ethnic. In so doing, it conformed to the precepts of "design assimilation," a practice evident in some Asian American suburbs where residents conformed to existing Anglo design aesthetics.[42]

Together, these suppressive spatial measures signified the desire for a particular feel, the recognizable touchstones of white Anglo suburban Americana—English-language signs, homes in soft colors, tidy green yards used in the "right" way.[43] It was perhaps no coincidence that the proliferation of corporate-built suburbs in the 1970s and later—with the strictest spatial controls thanks to the powerful tool of covenants, conditions, and restrictions (CC&Rs)—happened right in the midst of suburbia's rapid ethno-racial diversification. CC&Rs became a sweeping instrument for policing suburbia's appearance into a bland, Anglo-normative environment, devoid of any recognizable identity, ethnic or otherwise. In the Latino suburbs of Southeast

LA, the burst of regulatory efforts in the 1980s and 1990s illustrated an aggressive response to the infusion of Latino practices and alterations of the built environment.

Asian ethnoburbs initially met similar resistance, but Asian and Latino residents fought protracted battles there to secure the right to introduce ethnic elements into their community landscapes, electing local Chinese leaders like Lily Chen and Judy Chu who advocated for these rights.[44] With the advantages of transnational wealth, professional expertise, and support from Asian American legal, research, and social service agencies, the ethnoburbs had deep resources to support these campaigns. In Latino suburbs that were contending with economic disinvestment, a poorer populace, and substantial numbers of undocumented immigrants, such battles were harder to fight. In campaigns against yard sales, pushcart vending, and bright house colors, both white and Latino suburbanites pushed for an aspirational suburban ideal that was being eroded by economic decline and demographic change. Moreover, internal schisms between Latinos who were native born versus immigrant, middle class versus working class, could impede ethnic unity and the kind of collective uplift that occurred in both Asian ethnoburbs or even Latinized urban spaces. Together, these factors set Latino suburbs apart from Asian ethnoburbs.

ECONOMIC FUNCTIONS

In most basic demographic and social respects, Latino and Asian suburbs shared certain traits. They both received ethnic newcomers, driving the process of suburban diversification. Yet in other respects, they diverged profoundly, particularly in the very different positions they occupied in the global and regional political economies. As noted earlier, Asian suburbs benefited from heavy infusions of transnational wealth during a period of rapid economic growth in Asia, prompting investors to seek safe havens for their assets. They also received a stratum of immigrants who were highly educated and well financed, some arriving with prior business experience. The Latino suburbs of Southeast LA, by contrast, received immigrants from countries facing very different challenges, including economic crises, political instability, and war. The southeastern suburbs then had to contend with two heavy economic burdens—first, they lay right in the heart of LA's deindustrialization zone, and second, they received immigrants who generally arrived with fewer resources and received low wages.[45] These two categories of immigrants exemplified globalization's bifurcated flows of humans and capital, and their contrasting contexts would shape the political and social dynamics of these suburbs.

As a result, the economic landscapes of Latino suburbs diverged from the ethnoburb model in several key respects. To begin with, most Latino suburbs had small-scale, ethnic service economies focused on small mom-and-pop businesses like *bodegas*, *panaderías*, *taquerías*, bridal shops, insurance agencies, and international money-transfer agencies, catering to the everyday needs of residents. Like many barrios in urban areas, businesses found it difficult to secure the kinds of financing needed to expand their operations. This contrasted with the more heavily capitalized businesses of Asian ethnoburbs, infused by trans-Pacific investments. Moreover, in Latino suburbs, immigrant entrepreneurialism did not receive the same kind of civic support. In fact, in some cases, local suburban leaders opted to court non-Latino business over Latino entrepreneurs for reasons relating especially to the precarious position of their communities in the region's changing political economy.

The southeastern suburbs, once the center of industrial strength in Los Angeles, suffered the devasting effects of plant shutdowns in the 1980s, which decimated local economies and sent town leaders scrambling for recovery strategies. They often sought out the most heavily capitalized businesses to help fill the gaping void left by factory closures. The stories of South Gate, Huntington Park, and neighboring towns illustrate how this played out in suburban contexts.[46]

South Gate's economic recovery strategy focused on improving the suburb's image and attracting outside capital and investors. It targeted federal and state redevelopment dollars, as well as capital from American and Asian investors. Unlike the ethnoburbs of the San Gabriel Valley, which were heavily infused by transnational Asian investment capital, in southeastern Los Angeles, Latino capital played a much smaller role. Instead, town leaders pursued Anglo and Asian capital in the form of retailers, industries, and warehouses. Ultimately, they placed retail at the center of their recovery strategy, retail owned mostly by non-Latinos. This approach was part of the drift in the suburbs of Southeast LA toward what William Fulton characterized as "urban extraction"—enterprises that would "suck from a community whatever economic vitality might remain."[47]

In the 1970s and 1980s, South Gate and neighboring suburbs began their economic recovery efforts using the traditional tool of urban redevelopment. From 1972 to 1980, eight of the towns created eleven redevelopment districts, giving local governments direct control over about seven square miles of territory, including the power of eminent domain. In South Gate, leaders overcame an initial distaste for redevelopment—fearing it would mandate the construction of low-income housing—but they had come around by the early 1980s. Henry Gonzalez, a UAW union leader with vivid memories of what was lost in the local GM shutdown, was a vocal champion, assuring residents that federal block-grant dollars were desperately needed to spruce up infrastructure and bring back jobs.[48] In the mid-1980s, South Gate's Community Redevelopment Agency launched a two-pronged effort to this end. First, it instigated a campaign to improve South Gate's landscape and image in order to reassure prospective business and industry that the suburb was ripe for investment. This broad cleanup effort included crackdowns on informal housing, which had spread widely, an $8 million street improvement project around two commercial areas, graffiti abatement, and a public information program "to foster local pride." The suburb also funneled HUD money into business facade improvements while skirting the local housing crisis.

Its second effort was to begin rebuilding South Gate's economy. It attracted a "food park," essentially a small cluster of fast-food chains, extended $2.2 million to HON Industries, an Iowa-based office furniture manufacturer, to occupy the shuttered Firestone plant, and built a twenty-two-unit senior citizen apartment complex. These efforts created 175 minimum-wage fast-food jobs and 350 jobs at HON. The Community Redevelopment Agency continued to offer low-interest loans, bonds, and other incentives to business and commercial prospects. By 1990, the Community Redevelopment Agency had brought in over $10 million in federal grants. It purchased the shuttered GM lot for $12 million, and despite ambitious plans to develop it into a $60 million industrial park—creating over three thousand jobs—it ended up using a good portion of the land for much-needed schools and a handful of small factories. The shuttered Firestone factory later came to house warehouse space, apparel makers, an adult school, and other light industry.[49] By the 1990s, South Gate had about 185 factories, the vast majority of which had fewer than twenty workers each. But industry was outpaced by wholesale in terms of overall sales, signaling the growing importance of the logistics economy. Yet even as industry persisted in South Gate, what remained was a shadow of its former self: the number of factories had earlier topped six hundred, employing between twenty-five thousand and thirty-seven thousand workers. By the 1990s, that old economy had been essentially gutted.[50]

It soon became clear these older economic development strategies were falling short. South Gate then pivoted toward retail. That move was catalyzed in part by Proposition 13, the 1978 property tax reduction measure that drastically cut municipal budgets across the board, leaving all communities scrambling to make up the difference. Many turned to retail as the answer, since every city received "one penny of sales tax for every dollar of retail sales," as William Fulton noted. The result was "a complete reversal of local planning policies," away from building new housing and industry and toward retail.[51]

In this context, a new retail landscape emerged in these Latino suburbs: shopping areas geared to Latino customers but financed by Anglo and Asian investors. Some were the product of "ethnic gentrification," a process that transformed declining shopping strips into thriving ethnic commercial areas. Others were redevelopment projects that planted new American-style shopping centers atop old industrial sites. A key pioneer was Pacific Boulevard in Huntington Park. In 1976, the city council launched a multimillion-dollar redevelopment project to revitalize the Boulevard, a once-thriving Anglo suburban shopping area in steep decline because of white flight. The Anglo city council enlisted Seal Beach–based Watson Associates to revamp the strip by transforming it into a Latino shopping area. They saw the writing on the wall and committed to the suburb's newest demographic and thus gained an early retail foothold in the Southeast. La Pacifica, as it came to be known, was designed by Anglo architects and developers who used Mexican stylistic flourishes to convey a new ethnic identity. The styles were something of a mishmash—mixing Mexican, mission revival, Aztec, and rural Andalusian. Old storefronts were subdivided into small, long, narrow stores that were rented to mom-and-pop establishments selling clothes "para toda [la] familia," shoes, music, and food. Street vendors completed the scene, hawking everything from razors to *chicharrón* (fried pork rind). The overall effect, wrote one observer, was festive, exciting, and chaotic. While many tenant shopkeepers were Mexican, others were from Korea, Iran, Vietnam, Nicaragua, Cuba, and the Netherlands, all gearing their wares to Latinos. However, the owners of these commercial properties were non-Latino, suggesting that this was an unseen example of Fulton's "urban extraction."[52]

Similar shopping plazas were developed in later years. In nearby Lynwood, Plaza Mexico was built by two Korean developers and anchored by a La Curacao department store that was owned by two Israeli immigrants. (La Curacao, an appliance and electronics chain, was well known for offering credit to undocumented immigrants.) And Plaza Alameda in Walnut Park was the work of Primestor Development, an Anglo-owned developer geared to minority markets. In most cases, the developers devoted careful attention to creating an authentic Mexican ambience, even if reifying nostalgia.[53] An awakening by developers to the potentials of the Latino marketplace drove some of this effort, led by people like Bob Rodino, founder of Latinvest. He worked to create an awareness of Latino market potential in Los Angeles, driven by the twin motives of social justice and profitability.[54] While all these shopping areas were designed for Latino customers, and indeed came to serve as vibrant community hubs, their ownership lay in non-Latino hands, compromising the accumulation of ethnic power and wealth in these suburbs.

That disconnect was strong in South Gate. Certainly, there were some Latino entrepreneurs there, such as the Guatemalan immigrant Alvaro Cristales, who rose from working as a janitor to running his own janitorial service; Brian Gonzalez, who co-owned Casa de Gonzalez Car Dealership; and Debby Gonzalez, who owned South Gate Jewelers. Yet there were also Latino-oriented stores run by non-Latinos, such as the Tres Hermanos clothing stores, a chain owned by Lebanese immigrants.[55] For the most part, South Gate leaders and policy did not warmly support Latino entrepreneurs, perhaps because they brought less capital, ran smaller operations, and tended not to join the South Gate Chamber of Commerce, which might have helped them build supportive networks. For example, Dan Kang, a second-generation Korean American, was manager of Care-Tex, his family's garment-dyeing firm. With about $5 million in annual sales and thirty-eight employees, Care-Tex was touted as a local success story in South Gate. On the flip side was David Rodríguez, who opened Nana's Restaurant with a $75,000 nest egg. He complained that South Gate authorities gave him a hard time "almost every time I try to advertise with flyers or banners. . . . You still need permission for this and permission for that." If he had to do it again, he mused, he would never have chosen South Gate. A 1994 RAND report confirmed Rodriguez's sense of the local climate for Latino entrepreneurs, noting that instead of bolstering small immigrant businesses, South Gate tended to target them for regulatory violations. In the southeastern suburbs, moreover, Spanish-speaking merchants were generally not active in local chambers of commerce because meetings were conducted in English. While some formed their own chambers of commerce in response, they were separated from a traditional stepping stone to local leadership.[56]

Over time, South Gate's retail-driven development strategy more emphatically embraced corporate American over Latino businesses, especially in a number of industrial site conversions. South Gate's El Paseo shopping center offers a good example. It opened in 2001 on the site of a former oil-tank farm and was cited by one developer as a "turning point" for Latino-oriented retail: it was filled with American chain stores and restaurants like Ross, Marshalls, Applebee's, Chili's, and, of course, Starbucks—with South Gate one of the gigantic chain's leading sellers of Frappuccinos. The developers forecasted four hundred new jobs at the complex. South Gate chose Starbucks over what some locals dubbed "amigo stores," even as Latinos accounted for over 90 percent of the population. (One notable exception was the Latino-owned coffee chain Tierra Mia, which originated in South Gate and whose success ironically attracted Starbucks to the community.[57]) A similar American-style shopping center—the Azalea Center—opened ten years later on the former site of American Concrete & Steel Pipe Co, once a major factory in South Gate.

In South Gate, these shopping centers reflected consumer demand in the area, particularly among the more Americanized children of immigrants, based on door-to-door surveys done by the developer Primestor.[58] Residents wanted the "architecture, restaurants, and stores that they saw elsewhere," said Steve Lefever, South Gate's director of community development, saving them the drive to places like Long Beach or Cerritos. The councilman Gil Hurtado added: "Outside of that, we had nothing but small mom-and-pop shops. When the shopping center opened, it gave us something." That included the $2.6 million the Azalea Center generated in sales tax during its first year.[59]

In other areas of LA, such as Baldwin Park and Santa Ana, similar decisions sparked more pushback from residents who resented the lack of support for immigrant entrepreneurs and their customers. The suburb of Baldwin Park, in the San Gabriel Valley, was populated mostly by Latinos, with smaller groups of whites and Asians.[60] Immigrant-centric retail started out strong there, with numerous check-cashing businesses, Latino groceries, bridal shops, and Mexican western-wear stores. But by 2008, Baldwin Park's Mexican American city council began discouraging these outlets. They passed a moratorium on new payday-loan and check-cashing businesses, seeing these as predatory entities that gave the community a bad image as "poor." They also pushed forward a redevelopment plan to demolish one hundred small businesses and eighty homes to replace them with American chains like Claim Jumper, Applebee's, and Chili's. In part, this push reflected the change of local leadership—mostly second-, third-, and fourth-generation Mexican Americans who controlled local politics—although the suburb itself was divided between immigrants and American born. As the councilperson Marlen Garcia put it, "We're striving to insure Baldwin Park doesn't look like Tijuana," while Mayor Manuel Lozano said, "We don't want the fly-by-night business, the 'amigo store.'" American chains, they believed, fulfilled the consumer desire of American-born Latino residents and conveyed something upscale. Immigrant residents like Rosalva Alvarez felt differently: "I'm proud of my roots. I was born in Mexico and raised in this country. I agree we need some change. But what they want to bring here is totally unrealistic. Applebee is good, but a Kabuki? And a Trader Joe's? Come on, I don't even go to Trader Joe's." Local immigrant entrepreneurs resented the initiatives, which threatened to put them out of business. A similar dispute erupted in Santa Ana, in Orange County, sparking tensions between Mexican Americans and their immigrant coethnics. As Sam Romero, owner of St. Teresa's Gift Shop in Santa Ana, quipped of one Mexican American leader pushing for Anglo retail, he "broke every glass and mirror in the house so he wouldn't have to see a Mexican."[61] The chilly reception toward Latino entrepreneurs not only shaped the ethnic flavor of these suburbs but also exacerbated cleavages between American-born and immigrant Latino residents.

While American businesses in Latino suburbs may have reflected consumer desire and success in attracting mainstream retail—thus avoiding the fate of retail neglect common in many poor, minority neighborhoods—it also represented non-Latino investment capital. This stood in sharp contrast to the San Gabriel Valley ethnoburbs, where ethnic wealth was amassed in Asian-oriented retail strips and malls, helping turn these communities into global economic outposts. That process gave localities, as Wei Li put it, "a chance to better integrate the ethnic economy into mainstream economic affairs, take advantage of immigrants' skills and resources, adopt alternative strategies during periods of recession, and strengthen their position in the globalized economy."[62] In short, the ethnoburb leveraged ethnic investment and resources into a source of ethnic power and resilience. In the Latino suburbs of Southeast Los Angeles, those assets were absent.

In South Gate, one consequence of its retail choices was a community disconnect: many of the area's business owners and workers did not live there—they commuted in from surrounding cities. At the Sealy mattress plant, for example, only 10 percent of employees lived in South Gate because, as a manager put it, not enough locals had adequate English skills to fill factory positions. Census figures confirmed that about 13 percent of residents actually worked in South Gate in 1990 and 2000. This trend contributed to a leadership void, since fewer local business leaders would follow the traditional pathway to political leadership.[63] In turn, South Gate, Maywood, Bell, and other southeastern suburbs suffered a series of catastrophic political corruption scandals in the 1990s and early 2000s, a sign of the dampened civic capacity in these suburbs.

Conclusion

The Latino suburbs of Southeast Los Angeles followed a different path of development from ethnoburbs, given the myriad efforts to suppress Latino features in these communities. In the suburbs of Southeast LA, the center of Latino suburban growth after 1980, this resistance came in two waves. The first, from 1980 to the 1990s, coincided with the related trends of harsh anti-immigrant sentiment more broadly, deindustrialization which devastated local suburban economies, and very rapid demographic turnover from white to

Latino in these suburbs. Local leaders—mostly white and a small but growing number of Latinos—responded with measures to diminish the full expression of Latino built environments, everyday spatial practices, and entrepreneurship, and in so doing to shore up familiar suburban traditions to stave off perceived threats of decline. By contrast, Asian ethnoburbs dodged the challenges of deindustrialization—the San Gabriel Valley did not suffer the plant closures that ravaged south Los Angeles—and existed in a relatively stable economic landscape.[64] And in the Asian ethnoburbs, the white flight that ushered in demographic change also happened at a slightly slower pace than in the Latino suburbs.[65]

During the second wave of resistance, after 2000, an additional driver of ethnic suppression may have also played a role—the influence of second- and third-generation Mexican Americans in these suburbs who leaned more toward "mainstream" Anglo-American tastes. In the ethnoburbs, the immigrant population remained on a constant upswing from 1960 to 2010 and came to outnumber native-born residents by 2000. This confirms Wei Li's characterization of ethnoburbs as constantly refreshed by inflows of immigrants. In the Latino suburbs, by contrast, the proportion of immigrants peaked around 1990 and then began to decline as the native-born Latino population rose steadily, suggesting that the American-born children of immigrants were acculturating to Anglo-normative styles of living. Immigrants occupied a more marginal position, with a weaker public presence to push for more Latino-style suburban space. A couple of caveats are worth mentioning. First, the U.S. Census may have undercounted undocumented immigrants in the heavily Latino suburbs—although even that act suggested their marginalization in civic life, if they were reluctant to move out of the shadows. Second, anti-immigrant crackdowns and legislation tended to hit Latino communities harder than Asian ones.[66] The waning voice of Latino immigrants in these suburbs—especially the undocumented who lived on the margins—worked against a confident claiming of ethnic space in suburbia.

This foray into ethnic suburbia in Los Angeles suggests important contrasts across different groups and spaces. While both kinds of suburbs benefited from immigrant arrivals who stabilized local economies, the subsequent economic divergence raises questions for further research. First, the issue of the direction of transnational flows of capital: in the ethnoburbs, capital apparently flowed from Asian home countries into the United States to be invested in businesses, real estate, and the community itself. This was facilitated partly by the greater wealth in the rising economies of these feeder countries, which also sent large contingents of wealthy and well-connected migrants. By contrast, those coming from Mexico and Central America were often poor, arriving with few resources and pressing concerns about impoverished families back home.[67] This generated the robust remittance culture that characterized life among Spanish-speaking migrants in LA and beyond who were determined to help relatives and communities back home. This meant that capital flowed in the opposite direction, back to home countries through remittances and investment via hometown associations. More research is needed to substantiate this premise, comparing remittance patterns of Mexican and Chinese Americans, for example, and the impact of these patterns on investment in American communities.

Second, given that Asian ethnoburbs had significant numbers of Latino residents in their midst, it raises the question, To what extent were Latino people in heavily Asian ethnoburbs encouraged to express their own ethnicity in built landscapes, ethnic businesses and professions, and local politics? Did the warmth of welcome there extend to Latinos? Studies by Leland Saito and Wendy Cheng begin to get at interethnic relations in these communities, yet more research on these larger questions of ethnic assertiveness in multiethnic suburbia will help paint a clearer picture of the social and power dynamics among these different groups.[68]

While the theme of ethnic suppression in Latino suburbia looms large in this story, there is evidence to suggest that Latino suburbanites have found ways to assert their cultures through housing and businesses in recent years. Signs of "gentefication" have appeared in Bell, Huntington Park, and South Gate, with the opening of millennial Latino-owned businesses like coffee houses, breweries, and bakeries geared to "hipster" customers.[69] Another example is the handful of brightly colored McMansions in South Gate. These suburban structures are potent symbols of ethnic expressiveness and financial investment in American suburbia. They are rebuilds of the original modest housing in this working-class suburb, suggesting an evolution over time toward greater ethnic assertiveness and acceptance in suburbia, even despite earlier political efforts against this. These homes contribute to a changing suburban landscape, they may be a harbinger of future change, and they remind us that suburbia remains a dynamic, diverse setting for ethnic identity itself.

Neighborhood

5

Adobe Homes for the Sun City's Mexican Barrio: Community Housing Alternatives and Creative Self-Determination in El Paso, Texas

SANDRA I. ENRÍQUEZ
University of Missouri–Kansas City

In December 1979, the Southside Low-Income Housing Development Corporation (SLIHDC) proposed an innovative project before the El Paso City Council. Since its inception in 1977, the SLIHDC, a group of tenants from El Segundo Barrio—the city's historical Mexican American border neighborhood—had worked arduously to develop a multiyear strategy to improve living conditions and stop its destruction.[1] The organization requested $500,000 from the city's Community Development Block Grant (CDBG) to address substandard barrio housing. Federal funds would enable the SLIHDC to construct a new apartment complex and rehabilitate a dilapidated tenement. The plan also incorporated several creative approaches, including housing cooperatives, self-help and sweat equity models, and, most importantly, adobe and passive solar construction techniques. The proposal became a critical step in putting forward a new vision for South El Paso's future at a time of uncertainty, displacement, and revitalization.[2]

Despite the unanimous recommendation of El Paso's Community Development Steering Committee, the city council questioned the project's feasibility. Council members criticized the proposal for replicating ongoing redevelopment activities and high construction costs for a "novelty" project, and they doubted that adobe met federal regulations. Alderman Jim Scherr questioned low-income tenants' ability to make informed decisions for an operation of such magnitude and suggested they add businessmen and other experts. Carmen Felix, an organization representative, responded that, although tenants made up the SLIHDC's board, the plan had ongoing guidance from architects, university professors, lawyers, paid consultants, and even a National Council of La Raza (NCLR) housing specialist. Finally, after an hour of intense debate, Alderman David Escobar declared: "These people want to help themselves. I think we ought to support them 100 percent." Amid cheers and applause, the council authorized the pilot project in a 4–2 vote. Through the environmentally sustainable and low-cost adobe homes, the SLIHDC visibly resisted the long-standing political and geographic erasure of the Sun City's ethnic Mexican past, present, and future.[3]

The city council's support came as a surprise. For over a century, white political and business leaders had declared the Southside and its Mexican population to be obstacles to El Paso's urban and economic development. As a working-class migrant community, El Segundo Barrio confronted decades of intentional segregation and some of the worst living conditions in the country due to disinvestment by absentee property owners and city officials alike. By the 1960s and 1970s, these power brokers sought to revitalize the city by transforming El Segundo Barrio into the "Gateway to Mexico." Southside tenants organized in opposition to the forced displacement, urban neglect, and political disenfranchisement they had experienced for generations. The threat of El Segundo Barrio's destruction galvanized the community to challenge top-down redevelopment plans and put forth their own visions for the future of the border neighborhood.[4]

The story of the SLIHDC's adobe homes reveals a bold and radical community-controlled revitalization plan that provided practical solutions to the urban crisis. Designed by Mexican American and Chicanx working-class tenants, this ambitious neighborhood strategy centered on what they called "creative self-determination"—innovative and viable alternatives centered on their culture, socioeconomic needs, and lived experiences in a transnational neighborhood. The SLIHDC's adobe housing efforts demonstrate how barrio residents challenged racial politics and erasure in a border city through direct grassroots participation in urban redevelopment while operating with the limited tools afforded to minoritized and disinvested communities in the late twentieth century.

Although many early works on Chicanx history concentrated on the Southwest, recent scholarship has often departed from the region.[5] While this growing body of literature is rightfully expanding the breadth of the Mexican American experience, Southwestern barrios are far from being overstudied. Not only was the field born in the barrio, but these older communities are critical to understanding Latinx urban and metropolitan history. For example, despite scholarship on long-standing barrios that often chronicles stories of demolition and displacement, neighborhood destruction also energized the Latinx civil rights struggles of the 1960s and 1970s.[6] South El Paso and the SLIHDC formed part of a vast grassroots movement in which barrio residents challenged structural racism by demanding access to affordable housing, social services, better education, and economic uplift.[7] Furthermore, their efforts showcase how Latinxs in long-existing barrios actively fought to save their communities from the bulldozer.[8]

Older barrios can also illuminate the intersections of Latinx activism and twentieth-century urban policy. The Great Society's antipoverty programs provided millions of dollars to disinvested cities and mobilized working-class Black and Brown communities through welfare and economic justice activism.[9] However, the country's political realignment in the 1970s resulted in significant budget cuts to antipoverty programs under the umbrella of the U.S. Department of Housing and Urban Development (HUD). New federalism policies during the Nixon administration exacerbated urban and housing policy deregulation while incentivizing private market redevelopment. Dwindling access to federal funds posed many difficulties for Black and Latinx working-class communities. Many neighborhood-based redevelopment efforts faltered without sustainable funding, while others turned to the private sector for survival. But as the SLIHDC's efforts illustrate, community organizations challenged privatized revitalization and found creative ways to address substandard housing and disinvestment before the era of gentrification.[10]

South El Paso's housing activism did not happen in a vacuum. The barrio's location on the U.S.-Mexico border emphasizes the importance of locality in Latinx urban and metropolitan development. In his 1980 study *The Chicanos of El Paso*, the historian Oscar J. Martínez argued that "El Paso affords the student of ethnic relations an excellent setting for analyzing social change in a Chicano urban community."[11] *La frontera*, the border, is a fluid but contested space where life "goes on" in a highly racialized, policed, and impoverished environment on the margins of two nations. Despite living in a "Latinized" space and accounting for a majority of the population, ethnic Mexicans endured the ubiquitous limitations of life in the borderlands. In this place, ethnicity, citizenship status, class, and even tenancy complicated notions of exclusion and belonging.[12] Latinx border communities faced a duality of being hypervisible and invisible, expendable and indispensable, in the city's growth and development. The SLIHDC's housing struggles reveal these very contradictory dynamics. As a working-class tenant community, Southsiders lacked a political voice and experienced profound poverty. But these exact circumstances led barrio residents to conceive transformative and imaginative solutions to the Sun City's most visible form of disinvestment: its decaying housing.

The history of El Paso's early settlement and development explains why the SLIHDC's adobe homes were a powerful intervention in the city's political landscape. Ethnic Mexicans have never charted the course of El Paso's politics or urban identity despite making up most of its population. Unlike other Southwestern cities founded under Spanish colonial rule, El Paso consolidated as a community only with the arrival of the railroad in 1881. For much of the region's history, Mexican settlements were located to the east, in towns like Ysleta, Socorro, and San Elizario, or south of the Rio Grande in what is now Ciudad Juárez. There was no significant settlement in present-day downtown El Paso until 1827, when Juan María Ponce de León obtained a land grant from the Mexican government and built an adobe hacienda. In the aftermath of the Mexican-American War, white merchants and traders purchased the land from Ponce de León and formed a few scattered settlements. Although El Paso was "a sleepy, dusty village of about 800 souls," the Anglo minority firmly established political and economic control over the development of the borderlands. By the end of the nineteenth century, railroad lines connected the desert city to national and international markets. Subsequently, El Paso experienced a population boom and rapidly transformed into the region's most prominent industrial, commercial, and transportation center.[13]

Over the following decades, power brokers transformed the area into an American cultural landscape. Boosters promoted the town as one of "progress and modernity" destined to become the powerhouse of the Southwest and sought to differentiate it from its sister city across the border. The built environment became the symbol of a new racialized social order. For centuries, inhabitants of the borderlands had relied on the desert's natural resources—*tierra y sol* (earth and sunshine)—to construct earthen structures. With little access to mass-produced construction materials, white "pioneers" created buildings in the Territorial style, which blended adobe with "American" decorative brick elements.[14] Like the Sun City's racial relations, this harmonious architectural style was short-lived.

For white newcomers, progress meant the erasure of the city's Indigenous and Mexican built environment. As early as 1883, local newspapers reported on a campaign to eradicate adobe structures. One proclaimed that "the removal of the ancient adobes, with all their bad associations, mean[t] a new life for El Paso. Let the buildings be erected there-on be worthy of the finest business site in the place." As white El Pasoans waged war against "uncivilized" and "primitive" adobe structures, they tapped into the area's natural resources to build an Anglo-American city. The region's desert valleys and mountains provided ample access to clay, limestone, shale, gravel, and sand, raw materials needed to manufacture cement and brick. Leaders capitalized on the ready access to these supplies to construct "handsome brick and stone" structures for modern El Paso. By the early 1900s, booster materials advertised El Paso as the "Reinforced Concrete City"—the antithesis of the "Mexican town of adobe and straw" of the past.[15]

Power brokers cemented the Sun City's racialized urban landscape in the early twentieth century. Known as the "Ellis Island of the Southwest," El Segundo Barrio served as the entry point for refugees fleeing the political violence and economic turmoil of the Mexican Revolution. While many journeyed to other parts of the United States, some settled in South El Paso for the city's booming industries.[16] City leaders quickly blamed the influx of ethnic Mexicans for the Southside's poor housing and impoverished conditions. Medical professionals, local officials, and businesspeople racialized refugees, characterizing their presence in the congested Mexican quarter as a recipe for epidemics. Following the Public Health Department's recommendations, the city council launched a cleanup in South El Paso to keep disease away from American homes. This multiyear campaign condemned and demolished "filthy adobe huts" and subjected barrio residents to "baths" in a government disinfecting center. Although framed as a public health necessity, these efforts seldom addressed the area's dire poverty, poor infrastructure, and outright neglect. Ultimately, the cleanups only worsened living conditions and depicted ethnic Mexicans as foreign, unassimilable, and expendable.[17]

The cleanup campaign set the stage for South El Paso's inadequate housing in the twentieth century. The destruction of adobe homes and *jacales* (mud-plastered huts) necessitated the fast construction of replacement housing to keep working-class Mexicans confined to the Southside. With the support of city officials, real estate developers rallied the community to build "healthy" brick tenements as viable, modern, and sanitary alternatives for the "large foreign population of workers." Historically, South El Pasoans have referred to these "modern tenements" as *presidios*, or prisons. These large two-story brick buildings in the later Territorial Revival style were substandard from the start, as they lacked proper ventilation, heating, plumbing, and running water. For decades, *presidios* physically illustrated working-class ethnic Mexicans' place in El Paso's political, social, and economic landscape.[18]

Like many barrios across the Southwest, El Segundo became a segregated refuge for generations of ethnic Mexicans in the Sun City. In addition to El Paso's racialized politics, the borderland's exploitative economy confined twenty-five thousand ethnic Mexicans to the barrio for much of the twentieth century. Local leaders often touted the Sun City's abundance of cheap labor to attract new industries. Access to an extensive labor pool on both sides of the border enabled enterprises to keep wages down.[19] These economic dynamics limited barrio residents' ability to rent or purchase homes in other parts of the city. Despite these restrictions, ethnic Mexican families cultivated meaningful kinship networks among neighbors, created community institutions to meet their needs, and fashioned the Southside into a transnational walking neighborhood with the "sights and sounds of two cultures."[20]

In the postwar era, the barrio became vital to restoring the city's status as the powerhouse of the Southwest. City leaders saw Mexico's emerging Programa Nacional Fronterizo (a federal program investing in infrastructure and tourism for border cities) as an opportunity to attract binational tourist dollars through a revitalized downtown. The barrio's geography could also play a critical role in fomenting the Border Industrialization Program (an effort to attract foreign industries to northern Mexico through a cross-border twin plant concept). Ultimately, a blank slate in El Segundo Barrio signaled new possibilities to reimagine the front yard of the United States.[21]

Although El Segundo Barrio had been under siege for nearly a century, the 1960s ushered in aggressive redevelopment tactics for the neighborhood. In 1963, the signing of the Chamizal Treaty ended a hundred-year international boundary dispute in which the United States ceded six hundred acres from South El Paso to Mexico and displaced five thousand people. Ten years later, leaders enforced the city's housing code against the Southside following a deadly tenement explosion. In eighteen months, the Tenement Eradication Program razed ninety structures and uprooted over eight hundred families. By the mid-1970s, South El Paso's population fell from twenty-five thousand to about ten thousand people. Southsiders believed this "systematic destruction of the barrio" meant an overall scheme to remove ethnic Mexicans from the area and profit from it.[22]

The mass displacement resulting from urban redevelopment efforts fueled community action. Established in 1975, the SLIHDC's parent organization, La Campaña Pro la Preservación del Barrio (Campaign to Preserve the Neighborhood), battled against the Southside's destruction to deliberately preserve its residential and cultural character. An outgrowth of a local Chicanx movement, this multifaceted struggle led by Mexican American working-class tenants demanded low-income housing construction and community control over South El Paso's future development. As the housing movement intensified, city officials applied for federal funds from HUD's Urban Development Action Grant (UDAG) to address substandard tenements and redevelop "The Gateway to Mexico," a commercial strip leading to the international bridge. Conflicting plans complicated the already-strained relationship between barrio residents and city hall. La Campaña and other Chicanx organizations opposed the UDAG application because it lacked community input. After much conflict, harassment, and numerous protest letters to HUD officials, the Sun City received $2.3 million to construct affordable housing in South El Paso.[23]

Implementing top-down renewal policies in the border barrio faced numerous obstacles. First, UDAG required commitment from private investors, who deemed low-income Southside housing unprofitable. Second, federal programs depended on urban renewal and eminent domain to acquire land affordably. The constant speculation over barrio development made land costs skyrocket as property owners held out for the highest bidder. In addition, Texas state law required local governments to hold urban renewal referendums, a measure El Pasoans defeated three times. Finally, HUD regulations prohibited the concentration of low-income housing in poor communities. These stipulations caused many delays, and in 1981, HUD pulled $1.7 million in unused UDAG funds.[24]

To bring their voices and visions to the forefront of barrio development, residents formalized La Campaña's efforts by establishing the SLIHDC in 1977. Through this nonprofit organization, Southsiders could funnel CDBG funds to build housing and bypass obstacles set up by local leaders and state laws. The SLIHDC's board intentionally reflected the barrio's primarily low-income tenant population and acted on residents' input and recommendations from allied experts. One of La Campaña's protest letters to HUD argued that "the barrio has the necessary will, skills, and manpower to accomplish its own regeneration. What is needed is the professional expertise and knowledge of implementing such a delicate task." SLIHDC members believed that Southsiders' firsthand experiences with urban disinvestment could translate into expertise, so they held informal meetings to develop a community-generated neighborhood strategy.[25] The SLIHDC also created an advocacy planning team that included lawyers, university professors, nonprofit organizations, an NCLR housing specialist, and Mack Caldwell, whose local architecture firm had ample experience building low-cost housing and Chicanx and Yaqui community planning projects in Arizona. These experts listened to barrio residents, provided relevant information, and helped formulate grant proposals.[26]

The SLIHDC created a two-pronged strategy to protect the neighborhood's residential character: building cost-effective multifamily housing and prioritizing construction in vacant lots. La Campaña activist Oscar Lozano explained that Southsiders lamented that El Segundo "was already scarred by many empty lots" due to the city's tenement demolition policy. Infill housing would expedite new unit construction while helping Southside residents fight the expansion of industrial and commercial uses in the barrio. The organization concentrated on El Segundo's western section because the twin plant program had targeted the area as an ideal warehouse location with easy access to the international bridge. To combat this threat directly, the SLIHDC purchased an industrial lot across from Sacred Heart Church to build its pilot adobe project. In 1981, when the owner of 714 S. Mesa advertised the lot as "ideal for Twin Plant Operation," the nonprofit mobilized to purchase the property. The SLIHDC thus effectively converted industrial lots into residential zoning and halted what they deemed incompatible land use in the barrio.[27]

The SLIHDC ensured that its revitalization strategies did not impose an economic burden upon barrio residents. After decades of community demands for housing, federal funds enabled the city to build new affordable—not low-income—housing in the barrio. For example, the city's UDAG plan promised the construction of sixty-four single-family dwellings through Section 235 subsidies. Meanwhile, El Paso's Community Development Program earmarked CDBG money for a tenement rehabilitation loan program to entice owners to bring their properties up to code. While these things are commendable, Southsiders knew that very low-income families would not benefit from these efforts. According to a socioeconomic survey from the Department of Planning, Research, and Development, 67 percent of barrio families earned less than $4,000 annually. Although Section 235 provided low-interest mortgage subsidies, the UDAG program also required potential homeowners to qualify for a bank mortgage and pay a portion of the down payment and closing costs. As barrio families faced banking discrimination and had scant opportunities to save money, very few would become homeowners. Furthermore, tenement owners who used CDBG rehabilitation loans increased rents, pushing out tenants from the remodeled units.[28]

In contrast to city programs, the SLIHDC's plan strategically centered residents' socioeconomic status to prevent gentrification. Activists knew these city-led efforts would continue aggravating El Paso's critical housing shortage. Leaders noted that "it [would not] be enough simply to provide new and rehabilitated units. These units must be provided [while] recogniz[ing] the desire of present barrio residents to remain there and to own or control their housing." Moreover, SLIHDC members argued that new construction needed to be available at costs that "very low-income people can pay." Most believed the project should provide "quality, but not luxurious" options, as Southsiders thought they didn't "need big luxury apartments." After several community meetings, the SLIHDC drafted a viable alternative that proposed the construction of affordable vernacular housing and mobilized the skills and power of barrio residents.[29]

The SLIHDC combatted erasure by celebrating the barrio's cultural past through the built environment. The Chicano activist Oscar Lozano recalled that residents chose adobe "because [it] is a traditional building form [and] building material. We saw it as something viable, inexpensive, and something traditional that the people had been getting away from." Many barrio residents had experienced living in adobe dwellings, either in Mexico or in older tenements and single-family homes scattered across South El Paso. Adobe also met low-cost construction goals. The architect Mack Caldwell advised residents that adobe could be "the most practical way to go" because it was cheaper than brick or cement. Furthermore, adobe was easy to manufacture in El Paso's desert environment, lasted longer, and required little maintenance.[30] The adobe structures thus became visible representations of Mexican and Indigenous cultures that had been suppressed in El Paso for over a century.

The SLIHDC also rooted its housing plans in concepts of environmental sustainability. Much of South El Paso's activism developed in the context of the energy crisis. Throughout the 1970s, barrio residents built parks and created home and community gardens that capitalized on El Paso's primary renewable energy source: sunshine. *El Mestizo*, a local Chicanx newspaper, urged its readers to explore solar energy applications: "In many cities, including El Paso, *gabacho* groups have organized efforts to exploit and monopolize solar energy. Meanwhile, *La Raza* has used solar energy for thousands of years. In the past, we used simple and effective sunlight methods." Community members also argued that the Sun City offered ample solar power that could be easily incorporated into the designs. Oscar Lozano recalled, "sheetrock buildings are not useful for the environment [or] for the people. Adobe was an alternative that could be brought back." As an already-energy-efficient building material, adobe provided insulation by storing heat and coolness, meeting barrio residents' goals for environmental conservation.[31]

The SLIHDC created an innovative adobe housing prototype for working-class communities (fig. 5.1). Although passive solar designs sounded expensive, the architect Mack Caldwell argued that they could be integrated "by simply designing and placing windows to the south, utilizing a solar overh[ang] to shield the windows from the hot summer sun, and keeping north walls well insulated and windowless or nearly so." Caldwell recalled proposing the idea to the SLIHDC: "I thought it was appropriately low-tech, cost-effective, and perfectly suited for adobe construction. I explained how it worked, that it could save the tenants money on their winter utility bills, and that there would be more natural light and ventilation for the units." With Caldwell's technical support and expertise, Southsiders approved using this energy-efficient method in their housing units.[32]

FIGURE 5.1. The activist Carmen Felix standing by a model of the SLIHDC's pilot adobe building, 1979. Box 30, folder 73, *El Paso Herald-Post* Records, Library People Files, MS348, Special Collections Department, University of Texas at El Paso Library.

The organization's choice to build only adobe homes was also a political articulation of Mexican American identity. The plan coincided with a period when adobe was making a comeback in El Paso and the Southwest. Months before the SLIHDC's approved proposal, the *El Paso Times* reported that "the mud from which El Paso was built may be oozing back into the city's future" and that the Sun City sat "squarely in the path of a brown wave of the sun-dried brick." Demand for this type of construction grew as white newcomers settling in El Paso often looked to purchase adobe homes because of their aesthetics, Southwestern and Spanish artistry, and energy-efficient characteristics. Local architects generated interest by designing exclusive custom-made residences in the city's "best" neighborhoods, with costs ranging between $135,000 and $160,000 (about $550,000 to $665,000 in current dollars).[33] Deemed "El Paso's first passive solar adobe home[s]," these innovative structures purported to bring the "tradition of adobe to today's homeowner through modern design and building techniques." This "rediscovery" persuaded the West Texas Council of Governments to commission a report on the region's capacity for adobe production. Beyond pointing out the obvious answer, the study also concluded that local demand for adobe bricks could support a $12.2 million industry, an opportunity local leaders capitalized on by requesting HUD funds to establish an adobe-brick-making factory. The SLIHDC identified this sudden curiosity for adobe as yet another campaign to erase ethnic Mexicans from the city's landscape. Thus, barrio residents' efforts to reclaim adobe became a vehicle to challenge cultural appropriation and the political forces whitewashing the city's role in eradicating adobe over the previous century.[34]

Despite the enthusiasm for adobe, local leaders and federal entities placed numerous obstacles in the path of the SLIHDC's housing projects. Much of the contempt for earthen structures remained embedded in El Paso's housing code, which had for decades hindered the use of adobe. In addition, the success of the city's brick manufacturing industry undermined other construction materials, with members of the Bricklayer's Union advocating the abandonment of adobe to save "American labor" from Indigenous and Mexican workers. These long-standing conflicts led local officials to question the material's integrity and cost-effectiveness. As a CDBG-funded project, barrio residents also needed HUD approval for their plans—but HUD banned adobe in public housing projects in 1979, claiming it provided poor insulation. While local authorities and the West Texas Council of Governments lauded affluent homes' innovative application of this cultural tradition, these entities frowned upon low-income Mexican communities using adobe.[35]

Barrio residents attributed this bureaucratic red tape and lack of support from HUD and the city council to their ethnicity and class status. SLIHDC members demanded that local and federal authorities acknowledge the adobe construction boom in the Westside and Upper Valley—the city's whitest and wealthiest neighborhoods. Southsiders also cited the accolades and awards that Mack Caldwell and John Edmonson, one of the exclusive custom-made home builders, had recently won from HUD for their energy-efficient adobe designs. These racial and class biases only hardened barrio residents' determination to fight for adobe. As La Campaña member Oscar Lozano recalled: "We got a lot of flak from the city, opposition [and] hesitancy from building inspectors and others that tried to denigrate the value of adobe. And the more they attempted to dissuade us from using adobe, the more we fought for it until eventually it was allowed." Southside residents joined a group of builders, architects, and engineers to challenge adobe restrictions. In 1980, the City of El Paso's new housing code permitted the use of adobe in building construction. HUD also approved South El Paso's projects and began feasibility studies for implementing adobe in low-income housing construction.[36]

The interior design choices of the SLIHDC's adobe homes also reflected the Mexican American community's cultural and social needs. Activists and residents lamented how redevelopment dismantled key features of Chicanx culture, noting decisions that "sacrifice[d] the middle-class standards to accommodate the person who would live in the homes." Caldwell recognized that while white families deemed closets a necessity, Mexican families found that these "amenities" wasted valuable living space. Through discussions with residents, Caldwell realized that nixing closets helped maximize each unit's living area since families stored their belongings in chests or other furniture. Floor plans also illustrated how barrio culture shaped architectural plans (fig. 5.2). Large families faced difficulties finding housing as both the Housing Authority of the City of El Paso (HACEP) and landlords turned them away. Each SLIHDC adobe building featured a variety of floor plans to meet the demands of the Southside's diverse household sizes, with two- and three-bedroom units to keep families under one roof. Because barrio elders objected to being relocated to senior living facilities in high-rise public housing, SLIHDC housing included efficiency units so they could stay in "the same buildings where relatives are living to maintain the Mexican Chicano culture of a tightly-knit family." In contrast to city renewal plans, the SLIHDC embraced multigenerational family life and kinship networks as core principles in their housing philosophies.[37]

The SLIHDC's plan blended elements of the past into their visions for the community's future. One grant proposal explained that "architectural design w[ould] meet the health, safety, and comfort needs of the future residents, w[ould] be durable and energy efficient, and w[ould] harmonize with the environmental and historic character of the Southside Neighborhood." Even though the earth-tone stucco adobe structures would contrast with the red brick *presidios*, the new homes reflected barrio cultural sensibilities. To achieve this, SLIHDC members incorporated the appealing qualities of tenements into multifamily exterior designs.[38] Although substandard, *presidios* represented much of the Sun City's Mexican and Mexican American experience. Relegated to life in the tenements, barrio residents actively transformed areas in and around these sites through their daily practices. Tenants adapted the *presidios'* courtyards into informal outdoor gathering areas and the surrounding streets into the barrio's public social spaces, reflecting concepts later identified as Latinx urbanism.[39] Residents worked closely with Mack Caldwell to incorporate these community-defining characteristics into their plans. The buildings featured enclosed common courtyards and slightly modified second-story open-air walks to provide tenants with "more amenable outdoor space." Residents demanded their housing plans conform to El Segundo's historic urban character by adhering to street grids, preserving existing alleys, and maintaining the no-setback requirement for front lawns.

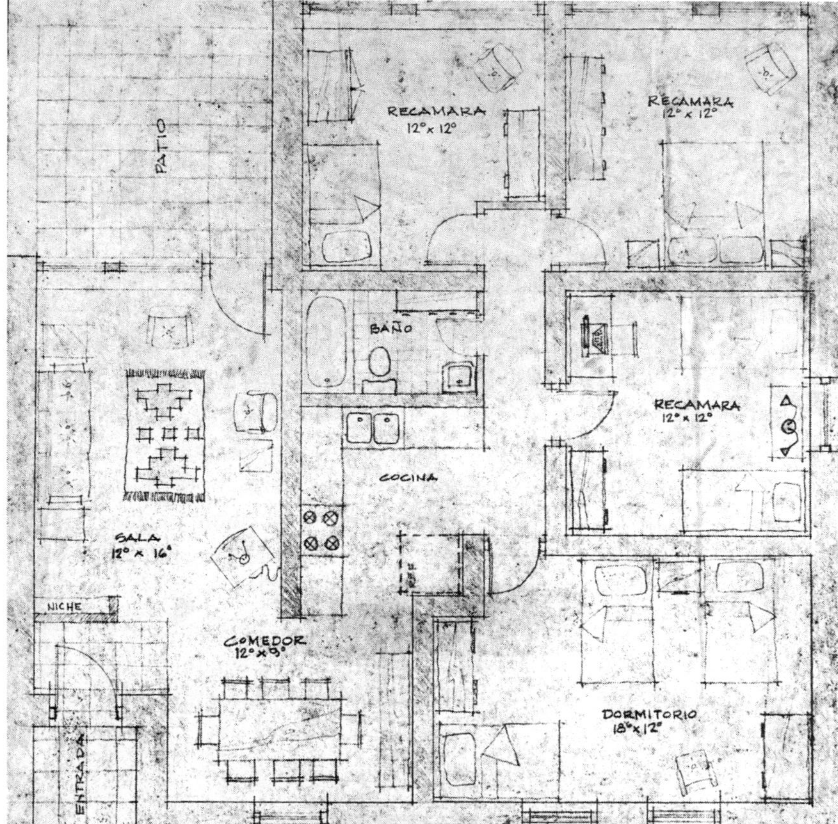

FIGURE 5.2. Plans for a four-bedroom apartment designed by the architect Mack Caldwell. The SLIHDC addressed the needs of barrio residents and families through their interior designs and different floor plans. Box 3, folder 7, Renate Caldwell Papers, MS257, Special Collections Department, University of Texas at El Paso Library.

In effect, the SLIHDC's plan proposed pragmatic ways to rebuild the neighborhood without compromising the fundamental aspects vital to life in the barrio.[40]

Building a healthy community meant creating pathways for meaningful employment to raise living standards for barrio families. Southsiders earned among the lowest wages, and the area suffered the highest unemployment rates in the city, often fluctuating between 15 percent and 25 percent. To combat economic distress, La Campaña employed barrio youth to paint murals and perform minor housing repairs over the summer. Following this model, the SLIHDC implemented self-help concepts to cut building costs and provide employment opportunities. Before the Reagan administration repealed the Comprehensive Employment and Training Act, the SLIHDC obtained funds to hire barrio school dropouts to build the adobe homes. Under the guidance of Mack Caldwell, Victor Vega (the organization's housing coordinator), and contractors, youth employees learned construction skills while working thirty hours a week. The hired crews also participated in a one-month adobe-making training led by barrio elders knowledgeable in the craft.[41]

The SLIHDC extended the self-help model to the adobe building's future residents by requiring them to provide sweat equity. The organization's board carefully reviewed applications and prioritized longtime tenants invested in preserving El Segundo Barrio. Once selected, families assisted with basic construction tasks such as laying tile floors and taping, floating, and painting walls (fig. 5.3).[42] In 1988, Arcadio and Maria de la Luz Gonzalez were selected for a two-bedroom unit at 714 S. Mesa. The Gonzalezes, both in their sixties, enthusiastically worked for three weeks to put the finishing touches on their new home. Although Mrs. Gonzalez had never handled a paintbrush before, she did not mind helping to stay within budget. Another future resident, Maria Estrada, had long awaited a new apartment with her family. When interviewed by the *Times*, she exclaimed: "We'll lay tile. We'll paint the walls. We'll even post guards out at night if we have to. But this apartment seems as if it belongs to us."[43]

The construction process fostered collective community power for future residents. Based on *mutualista* (mutual aid) concepts, the SLIHDC organized residents into *colectivas* (collectives) to cultivate a sense of common purpose and belonging. Families residing in the adobe multifamily buildings were expected to pool their resources into an escrow account to pay utilities, taxes, insurance, and maintenance costs. This framework enabled the SLIHDC to create a contingency fund ensuring that no family paid over 25 percent of its adjusted income in rent. *Colectivas* continued self-help programs as families cared for their buildings and learned budgeting and financial management to become economically independent. In a 1992 interview, Carmen Felix reflected: "Our co-op program has really been successful in that the tenants feel the[y] own the property and they are more inclined to care for it the best way possible. The families make decisions about their housing that a homeowner would normally make."[44]

Life in the adobe buildings created a deep sense of pride and ownership over El Segundo's redevelopment. Virginia Castruita, a resident at 623 S. Florence, told the *Times*, "I know this property is not mine, but I feel proud of living here. I think I have the best two-bedroom apartment in the whole of South El Paso, and I mean to keep it that way." The adobe buildings represented

FIGURE 5.3. A work crew during the construction of an adobe building, ca. 1980s. The SLIHDC involved barrio residents in self-help efforts, including the physical construction of the structures. Box 9, folder 10, Chicano Services Section of the UTEP Library Collection, MS191, Special Collections Department, University of Texas at El Paso Library.

the barrio's long struggle for better housing and control over its destiny. The structures' architectural designs and materials symbolized the reclamation of the neighborhood's Mexican American past and present and the values of the community. Despite not having the financial resources to redevelop the community holistically, Southsiders leveraged their cultural assets, the strengths of their families and kinship networks, and their sense of place. As Maria Estrada expressed to the *El Paso Times*, "ten years from now, we hope people will be able to see our progress."[45]

After years of protests led by groups like La Campaña and the SLIHDC, Mexican American tenants achieved significant victories. The 1980s and 1990s marked a substantial wave of low-income housing construction in the barrio. According to the activist Oscar Lozano, there was "a building spree," especially in South El Paso's eastern sector, which "stopped gentrification and brought more people to the area." The SLIHDC's efforts alone resulted in forty-four affordable rental units spread across four adobe buildings and two renovated tenements. In the mid-1990s, the nonprofit initiated a small homebuyer program for barrio residents. Through CDBG funds, grants, and bank home loans, the SLIHDC built ten low-cost single-family adobe homes. The CD program sponsored other nonprofit housing projects and provided loans to property owners to rehabilitate their tenements and bring them to code. In addition, the City of El Paso invested millions of federal dollars into rehabilitation and facilitated the construction of HACEP's new public housing in the barrio.[46]

Another notable accomplishment—at least on paper—was the City of El Paso's commitment to preserving El Segundo's residential and cultural character. In 1986, SLIHDC members worked closely with local officials to implement a zoning rollback for the barrio's western sector. To rectify incompatible land uses, the city council designated twelve blocks, including the commercial corridors that connected the El Paso and Ciudad Juárez downtowns, as a Special Residential Revitalization District. This effort would prevent the expansion of new businesses in the area, invest federal funds to rehabilitate substandard housing, and protect barrio residents from displacement. A testament to the SLIHDC's work in the community, planning officials recognized this as a "positive action by the City Council [that] reconciled a classic disparity which has existed for over fifty years—property owner rights versus human rights of families to decent habitation." Although commercial and industrial encroachment continued to threaten the area, barrio residents leveraged this promise to halt unregulated development.[47]

Despite the hard work and commitment from residents and activists, the SLIHDC confronted a changing political and economic environment that constantly undermined their neighborhood preservation strategies. The SLIHDC did prevail in the face of policies that favored market-oriented solutions to urban disinvestment.[48] The organization's innovative methods and philosophies were lauded by experts and recognized as a model of delivering responsive and sustainable low-income housing. In 1980, the NCLR identified their adobe housing projects as having potential for national replication.[49] Unfortunately, the SLIHDC's initial reliance on federal funds limited any opportunity to scale up its housing strategy. As a working-class Mexican tenant community, Southsiders historically faced lending discrimination, and low household incomes made partnerships with local bankers and the private sector virtually inconceivable. Private investors never found new housing, let alone low-income housing, as an attractive or profitable investment for South El Paso. With no immediate alternatives, the SLIHDC depended on the $8.5 million in CDBG funds that HUD allocated to El Paso annually. In an attempt to return decision-making power to local communities, HUD awarded city governments these competitive grants to address blight in low-to-moderate income areas.[50] While barrio tenants contended with the realities of federal deregulation and the privatization of housing in the late twentieth century, they also confronted the unique effects of these policies along the U.S.-Mexico border.

Without federal oversight, community development programs across the nation were riddled with problems that restricted neighborhood organizations' access to the resources needed to revitalize their communities. A 1978 audit revealed El Paso's less-than-stellar record, as officials diverted CDBG funds from low-income areas and spent them on citywide public works projects. Amid these revelations, HUD threatened the city's future funding.[51] Although the community development program strongly supported the SLIHDC's pilot projects, obtaining CDBG monies to sustain the organization's initiatives became a logistical nightmare. In 1980, despite unanimous approval from the Community Development Steering Committee, the city council cut $588,000 allocated for an eighteen-unit adobe building from the final CDBG budget. Claiming that the nonprofit had unspent grant money (due to a two-week delay in project implementation), council members shifted the SLIHDC's funds to build a clinic in Ysleta and a pool in the Southside. In 1984, the community development program awarded the SLIHDC a $400,000 loan to continue its housing projects, but the city council withheld the funds for three years, forcing the nonprofit to "run into and overcome one bureaucratic obstacle after another." Council members stalled SLIHDC building activities for many reasons, including an alleged City Charter provision prohibiting a "lame duck" council from voting on contracts, requesting the nonprofit obtain a $35,000 grant match, and ignorance about passive solar designs. According to an *El Paso Times* article, Mayor Jonathan Rodgers simply wanted the project scrapped because he thought "it provide[d] too few apartments for the price." Despite the SLIHDC's potential to raise living standards in El Segundo Barrio, local officials prioritized other projects. Between 1975 and 1989, HUD awarded the City of El Paso nearly $115 million in CDBG funds to address poverty in the community. Without HUD's bureaucratic oversight, city authorities used money from these grants for capital improvements, street repairs, drainage, and community facilities outside the barrio.[52]

The SLIHDC's battles with city hall over CDBG funding demonstrate how local governments thwarted the bold visions of working-class neighborhoods. Although barrio residents were skeptical of city leaders and their intentions toward South El Paso's revitalization, they knew collaboration was integral to the success of their housing program. Victor Vega, then executive director of the SLIHDC, reflected these sentiments in a letter to the city council. "The tremendous amount of time, energy, and sacrifice which were involved in the development of SLIHDC's Housing Plan will be more than justified if City Council and SLIHDC together can mobilize the commitment and resources which are essential for its implementation," he wrote. "SLIHDC was created by Southside residents and its plans are designed to see that the residents of South El Paso receive the respect, the preparation, and the living conditions which are essential for creative lives."[53] Unfortunately, scarce funding and city council disinterest hindered the nonprofit's momentum and its ability to improve housing for barrio residents on a larger scale.

By the late 1980s, the SLIHDC faced fundamental challenges as the country's financial instability made the continuance of their projects uncertain. In an era of dwindling federal funds and privatized urban redevelopment, grassroots organizations born of Black and Latinx freedom struggles turned to community development corporation (CDC) models to institutionalize their efforts. CDCs enabled organizations to increase capacity and expand services offered in their neighborhoods through private funds, philanthropic grants, and federal money. However, this often contradicted their organizations' founding principles and philosophies. To create financial sustainability, neighborhood-based groups adapted to private market pressures and the stipulations of funding entities, often leaving behind the very communities they served.[54]

Although the SLIHDC received NCLR support—which provided technical assistance and seed money to Chicanx CDCs—the organization did not transition into a more extensive and full-fledged economic development engine.[55] Instead, the nonprofit maintained its grassroots operations to ensure Southsiders continued to control their multifamily housing projects and future barrio development. By the mid-1990s, the SLIHDC moved beyond solely relying on CDBG monies and worked with philanthropic and private grants as well as bank loans to carry out its single-family homeownership program.[56]

Some El Pasoans criticized the organization's small-scale approach to revitalizing El Segundo. Alfredo Diaz, a former barrio resident, condemned Carmen Felix and the SLIHDC for "holding back Downtown development," claiming they helped only a few families who were "not El Pasoans, but are either illegal or resident aliens, are uneducated, don't pay taxes and drain the social programs." Felix and the nonprofit understood their limitations and the border barrio's delicate dynamics. She noted: "Every year we have done something significant with the intent to keep the [Southside's] residential character. Our organization can say clearly and with much pride that we have been a catalyst at keeping this area alive." Under her leadership, the SLIHDC employed a sensible approach to housing very low-income Mexican American families (figs. 5.4 and 5.5). The nonprofit's adobe homes provided a framework for other local organizations as the Sun City entered the new millennium.[57]

FIGURE 5.4. The SLIHDC's first adobe building completed in 1982. Photograph courtesy of the author.

FIGURE 5.5. An adobe housing project completed in 1987. Despite the El Paso City Council's bureaucratic obstacles to access Community Development Block Grant funds, the SLIHDC continued to build passive-solar adobe apartments across the Southside. Photograph courtesy of the author.

Despite decades of activism, challenges particular to the U.S.-Mexico border aggravated El Paso's ongoing low-income housing crisis. With an already-precarious economy based on low-wage and labor-intensive industries, neoliberal policies such as the 1994 North American Free Trade Agreement exacerbated economic challenges across the borderlands. NAFTA accelerated a decades-long relocation of American manufacturing industries to Ciudad Juárez to cut operating costs. By 2000, 22 percent of El Paso's population fell below the poverty level. High unemployment rates aggravated housing shortages in the region. Local planning officials determined the city needed at least twenty-five thousand low-income housing units, with other estimates citing thirty thousand to forty thousand. El Paso's history of underinvesting in affordable housing resulted in pockets of need beyond South El Paso. Unable to find housing, ethnic Mexicans settled in *colonias*, the undeveloped city outskirts. Still dependent on federal housing subsidies and CDBG funds, local leaders now looked to nonprofits and charitable organizations to house El Paso's predominantly Latinx residents.[58]

As a veteran organization, the SLIHDC's strategies provided useful regional models. What began as a response to the destruction of the city's historic Chicanx barrio paved the way for building low-cost, environmentally sustainable housing. When *colonia* residents organized around housing issues in the mid-1990s, the emerging nonprofits adopted concepts employed by Southsiders, such as self-help, mutual aid, and even adobe construction, to provide affordable and safe housing for all El Pasoans. For example, the nonprofit Organización Progresiva de San Elizario (Progressive Organization of San Elizario), whose members lived in one of the oldest settlements in East El Paso County, implemented a passive solar adobe and sweat equity housing program to improve living standards in their rural community. With support from HUD's Office of Rural Housing and Economic Development, the U.S. Department of Agriculture, and the University of Texas at El Paso's Energy Center, the nonprofit's adobe homes sparked low-income homeownership among San Elizario's residents. Just like generations of El Segundo Barrio tenants helped build El Paso throughout the twentieth century, their bold visions for regenerating the Southside shaped the future development of low-income housing in the region.[59]

In 1983, Jay Ambrose, the managing editor of the *El Paso Herald-Post*, wrote a commentary piece prompting readers to recognize what the nation could learn from its largest border community. His report described a joke an out-of-town chaplain made during President Ronald Reagan's visit to the Sun

TABLE 5.1. El Segundo Barrio's Economic Demographics in 2022

	Total Population	*Percentage Hispanic/Latino*	*Median Household Income*	*Below Poverty Level*
United States	333,287,557	19.1%	$74,755	12.6%
Texas	30,029,572	40.2%	$72,284	14%
El Paso County	868,763	82.9%	$53,424	21.3%
El Paso City	677,456	81.6%	$52,645	21.7%
Segundo Barrio Census Tract 19	1,982	89.7%	$13,952	60.3%
Segundo Barrio Census Tract 20	2,189	98.1%	$14,531	57.3%

Note: U.S. Census Bureau, American Community Survey (ACS) 1-Year Estimates Subject Tables: Table S1701, Poverty Status in the Past 12 Months (2022); Table S0601, Selected Characteristics of the Total and Native Populations in the United States (2022); *Census Reporter*, ACS data, Census Tracts 19 and 20; U.S. Census Bureau, ACS 1-Year Estimates. Retrieved from *Census Reporter Profile Page for El Paso, TX* (2022), https://censusreporter.org/profiles/16000US4824000-el-paso-tx/, accessed November 1, 2023.

City. The chaplain said, "God follows people everywhere they go, even to 'strange and distant places'" like El Paso. Although Ambrose admitted the city's "strangeness," he reminded his readers that, "at a time when Hispanics are becoming the biggest minority group in the country, El Paso could serve as a kind of model project on how the two groups could get along better. . . . As is already happening, the two groups enrich each other." Four decades later, outsiders' perceptions of border cities remain unchanged. Many imagine the heavily urbanized southern border as a desolate and open place where "invading migrants" threaten the very fabric of American society. But as Ambrose suggested, the Sun City can be invaluable to our understanding of U.S. history.[60]

Today, El Paso is the twenty-second-largest city in the United States and the epicenter of the Borderplex region, which includes Ciudad Juárez, Mexico, and Las Cruces, New Mexico. The Borderplex is home to 2.5 million people who form the "largest bilingual and binational workforce in the Western Hemisphere." According to U.S. Census data, El Paso's population totals 677,456, with 82 percent identifying as Hispanic or Latinx. Notwithstanding the major political, educational, and socioeconomic strides Latinxs have made over the past decades, the group still trails the city's white minority. As noted in table 5.1, El Paso's median household income in 2022 was $52,645, and 21.7 percent of its population fell below the poverty line, significantly lagging Texas and the United States. Although the Sun City has experienced demographic and economic growth in the twenty-first century, its residents continue to earn low wages and face housing insecurity. These struggles are evident in the fact that HACEP is Texas's largest public housing agency and the fourteenth largest in the country.[61]

While El Paso's history shows that Latinx demographic growth and mainstream visibility do not equate to automatic political power, Southside struggles serve as a reminder that grassroots activism is foundational for social change. Social and economic problems linger in El Segundo, but the realities of life in this border neighborhood continue to galvanize its residents and generations of barrio descendants. In recent years, Southside leaders and institutions like Sacred Heart Catholic Church mobilized to welcome a new wave of refugees and asylum seekers into the community by providing them shelter, food, and humanitarian support. Over the past decade, residents challenged urban redevelopment plans threatening the neighborhood's survival. And in 2020, when the El Paso County Commissioners voted on a map that omitted half of the neighborhood from the boundaries of a potential historic district, current and former barrio residents and their allies rallied to force a revote. Their efforts paid off in November 2021 when the National Register of Historic Places named El Segundo Barrio a National Historic District. These legacies of barrio activism illustrate that small actions can lead to transformational collective action.[62]

In these contexts, the history of the SLIHDC provides an example of how Latinxs challenged political disenfranchisement and late twentieth-century urban redevelopment policies. The SLIHDC's adobe homes were more than just a novelty. They visually represent a community's transformative, pragmatic, and bold solutions to long-standing urban neglect and exploitation on the U.S.-Mexico border. Although their efforts to regenerate and uplift South El Paso faced constant obstacles and setbacks due partly to the limits of devolution and private-market-led urban revitalization policy, Southsiders' actions reclaimed the borderlands' cultural landscapes to address neighborhood conditions. The SLIHDC members' determination, intellect, and love for their community resulted in the construction of new low-income housing and saved El Segundo Barrio from the bulldozer.

South El Paso's adobe homes demonstrate that Latinx metropolitan history can still benefit from community-based studies analyzing Southwestern barrios. The intersections of Chicanx activism and urban history remain understudied and offer many avenues for future inquiry. The story of this border barrio raises important questions. How would American cities look if urban policies truly supported the bold visions of the most historically disinvested communities? And how would urban policy differ if it considered the localized complexities of border cities like El Paso? Examining Mexican American and Chicanx border barrios sheds light on how Latinxs have transformed urban landscapes and actively claimed their right to the city amidst tremendous transnational, political, and economic pressures. As communities on the margins of city, state, and federal government policies and priorities, long-standing Chicanx and Latinx barrios like El Segundo have been at the vanguard of creating low-cost and environmentally sustainable housing and have developed human-centered alternatives to urban revitalization. These are essential lessons in an era of rapid climate change and a nationwide low-income housing crisis. Mexican American tenants' tenacious visions for South El Paso and their collective labor to build adobe homes in the Sun City provide a blueprint for a viable solution.

6

Gods in the City: Acción Cívica Evangélica and Latino Religious Politics in New York City, 1969–1978

FELIPE HINOJOSA
Baylor University

> Also, seek the peace and prosperity of the city to which I have carried you into exile. Pray to the Lord for it, because if it prospers, you too will prosper.
>
> JEREMIAH 29:7 (NEW INTERNATIONAL VERSION)

> *Time* magazine would do well to recognize that the Pentecostal phenomenon does not belong only in its religious pages, but rather, at the forefront of new analysis of the dynamics of political activity among Third World peoples.
>
> REV. RAYMOND RIVERA, pastor of Melrose Reformed Church and cofounder of Acción Cívica Evangélica (1974), Bronx, NY

During the late summer of 1976, a series of arsons threatened Protestant Latino churches on New York City's Lower East Side. The Damascus Christian Church went first, followed by the Emmanuel Spanish Baptist Church, and a few weeks after that, the pastor at Iglesia El Divino Maestro received a phone call from an anonymous caller shouting, "Your church will be next!" The slow response by police to investigate these crimes prompted over thirty Latino pastors from across the city, brought together by the newly formed Acción Cívica Evangélica, to march seven blocks from Damascus Christian Church to the East Fifth Street police station. They marched to pressure police to investigate. The Rev. José Caraballo, who served as president of Acción Cívica and was one of the leaders of the march, threatened that if nothing was done, Latino pastors "might have to resort to vigilante groups because of inadequate police protection." Noting that other houses of worship were also being targeted in apparent hate crimes, Caraballo added, "synagogues in the area that are vandalized seem to get much more police response than we do." That caught the attention of Mayor Abraham Beame, who quickly assured the pastors that "the police department would intensify efforts to prevent vandalism of churches, particularly on the lower east side."[1]

That a group of Latino pastors marched in such an organized fashion and grabbed the attention of the mayor's office so quickly was a result of their work with Acción Cívica Evangélica, which emerged in the mid-1970s as the largest and most influential Latino religious organization in New York City. Started in late 1974, the group practiced a distinct blend of Evangelicalism and social justice that reflected the values of tens of thousands of congregants from over forty denominations and more than five hundred Pentecostal and mainline Protestant churches across the city. Acción Cívica partnered with government officials, community organizers, pastors, and church leaders to address the issues that most affected Puerto Ricans and other Latinos in the city: hunger, affordable housing, and jobs. At its height, the organization raised more than $3 million in federal, state, and local grant funds for its job training programs, elderly care, and classes for pastoral leaders, as well as its school lunch programs in the Bronx, Manhattan, Brooklyn, and Queens that fed more than forty thousand young people.[2]

Fueled by both their deep faith and a sense of social responsibility, Acción Cívica's leaders believed that the church could not be complete "unless the Good News of the congregation leads to the well-being of the community." What some religious leaders called "holistic ministry," or in Latin America, "misión integral," Acción Cívica's politics and activism represented a shift among a new generation of Latino pastors asking new questions about the social implications of the Gospel and about the place of Latino Pentecostals in urban politics. In addition to providing a moral base for antipoverty work in the city, Acción Cívica gave Latino religious leaders unprecedented access to the mayor's office and moved them out of the shadows and into the center of New York City's politics in the 1970s.[3]

This is a story as much about changing trends in theological thinking in the late 1960s and 1970s as it is about New York's financial crisis, the civil rights movement, and the remaking of urban liberalism itself after the initial dismantling of the social safety net. The 1970s was the decade when, as the historian Kim Phillips-Fein bluntly put it, "the old American dream fell apart."[4] In 1975 unemployment reached 8.9 percent, the highest it had been in the postwar era. In New York City, Mayor Beame laid off more than 3,700 city workers, including 400 police officers and 150 firefighters, after dire warnings about the city's "metastasizing debt" in the 1970s. As unemployment rose, the number of people on public assistance skyrocketed to 1,255,721 in 1972 (up from 322,921 in 1960) as one out of every eight New Yorkers struggled to make ends meet.[5]

In the midst of financial turmoil, demographic change was also transforming New York City yet again. In the years after World War II, the Puerto Rican population grew from 61,463 in 1940 to 612,574 in 1960. Migration to the mainland, and to New York City in particular, was fueled by federal industrialization efforts on the island that gave massive economic incentives to businesses and corporations but left the rural and unemployed population with few options for work.[6] For thousands of Puerto Ricans, migration to the mainland, and New York City in particular, was a matter of survival.

When Puerto Rican migrants arrived in New York, they re-created pieces of the Caribbean, with Spanish-language churches, bodegas, and Caribbean music across the city. And for many, Pentecostalism offered a sense of hope in this new and frigid land. This included families like the one Felipe Luciano grew up in. Luciano, a civil rights icon and Puerto Rican Young Lord, had an activism, style, and public-speaking skills shaped and influenced by those fiery Pentecostal sermons he grew up hearing in East Harlem.[7] And those sermons and churches were everywhere across East Harlem. In referencing a popular radio ad, the Puerto Rican poet Piri Thomas once wrote of East Harlem, "We got more storefront churches than Carter has liver pills."[8] In the late 1960s, Latino Pentecostals were hiding in plain sight across New York. This new religious marketplace cropped up in tandem with increased urbanization that, as the historian Jon Butler has argued, "created the conditions and opportunities that inspired religious activity and expression" across New York City.[9] So, it made sense that this era saw Pentecostal movements led by the children of those Puerto Rican migrants to save the city from urban decline and to introduce it to Jesus Christ, or as the popular phrase proclaimed, "New York *para Cristo*" (for Christ)—a phrase that was also applied to cities across the country: Newark *para Cristo*, Los Angeles *para Cristo*, and so forth. These grassroots movements for spiritual and social reform, fueled by a wide range of players, including Acción Cívica, "transformed the political economy from the ground up."[10]

Acción Cívica Evangélica came on the scene at a moment of intense change and joined preaching and prayer with organizing and political action in a way that few Latino faith-based groups had done prior. Latino Pentecostals had a reputation for keeping to themselves, for staying away from the evils of the city, and for seeing themselves as living in the city but not belonging to the city. Heaven was their real home. The writer Piri Thomas captured this sentiment when he chastised Pentecostals for ignoring the indignities of poverty, the cockroaches, and the "horrors of decaying rotten tenement houses and garbage littered streets."[11] For a large majority of Latino Pentecostals, these maladies were temporary. The real gifts were in heaven, reserved for those who lived a faithful and obedient life on earth. No matter of social service or community engagement could transform one's body and spirit or bless the neighborhood. If Pentecostals practiced social services, and many did, they served church members or other believers in need of employment, health care, or a place to live.

That's what made Acción Cívica's work so significant. They were a Pentecostal organization that emerged out of the city, shaped by the politics of the civil rights movement, and with a young generation of church leaders eager to merge their spirituality with an ethic of social service. What changed? In 1970s New York City, high rates of poverty and limited educational opportunities inspired a new generation of Latino pastors, many of whom were immigrants or migrants themselves, to preach a Gospel message that spoke to both personal and systemic issues. And they preached this message in churches on Sunday mornings and in their communities every other day of the week. Their sermons, and the activism that followed, counter the assertion by some religious studies scholars that the late 1960s, with the assassination of Dr. King and the rise of Black and Brown militancy, was to blame for the death of the religious left. A focus on Latino Pentecostals in the 1970s tells a different story.

This was not only a phenomenon in New York City. Across the country, Latino clergy and leadership gained influence in the 1970s even as organizations like the National Council of Churches, known for its lack of engagement with Latino churches, struggled to raise money and lost membership.[12] As the liberal Protestants shrank in influence and power, Latino Pentecostals (and Catholics and mainline Protestants) filled the gap as a powerful moral voice in the midst of the austerity politics of the 1970s. This chapter tells their story by taking a grassroots and hyperlocal approach to help explain the "phenomenon," as Rev. Raymond Rivera called it, that was Acción Cívica.

The Roots of Acción Cívica Evangélica

The American city has long been the fixation of Christian missionaries. Throughout much of the twentieth century, the city was characterized as the place where God did not live, where poverty and crime evinced godlessness, and where white missionaries arrived to introduce God to the city and its "jungles of terror."[13] In the late 1960s and early 1970s, nothing captured this dynamic better than the 1968 book *Run, Baby, Run* and 1970 movie *The Cross and the Switchblade*. The film was an adaptation of Nicky Cruz's book, which sold millions of copies and was translated into more than thirty languages.[14] But it was its big-screen adaptation that most inspired Latino Christians. The motion picture told the story of David Wilkerson, a small-town preacher who moved to Brooklyn to minister to Puerto Rican gang members. Touched by a *Life* magazine article, Wilkerson made his way to New York City to quite literally "save" Puerto Ricans.

Against the backdrop of New York City streets, the film's Wilkerson (played by Pat Boone) is always calm, collected, and certain that God is on his side. While initially rejected by Nicky Cruz (portrayed by Erik Estrada) and the very gang members he has come to save, Wilkerson finds acceptance among a small, quiet, and passive Puerto Rican Pentecostal church. Church leaders seem to be at a loss for how to deal with the problems of the neighborhood: drugs, prostitution, violence. And of course, Wilkerson steps in to provide the magic antidote to crime: the blood of Jesus. This was one of the first films to document the Latino religious experience in the city, to explain the evangelical concern for a decaying urban America—but more importantly, it spoke to an entire generation of Latino Christians who felt left out of the promises of the American dream.

Latino pastors saw the city in much the same way as their white counterparts. While they held a deep sense of responsibility to do something about social and economic injustice, they also saw themselves as saviors, carrying a message of hope that offered both personal and social transformation. "God raised up John Three Sixteen [one of the largest Latino Pentecostal churches in the country at that time] as a lighthouse in the midst of the ghetto city," preached one Latino pastor in New York City.[15] One exception to this was the work of the Rev. Leoncia Rosado Rousseau, affectionately known as "Mama Leo," who organized grassroots ministries focused on drug rehabilitation, gang members, and sex workers during the middle part of the twentieth century. While this chapter does not focus on Mama Leo's efforts, it is her work and vision that laid the groundwork for faith-based social services in New York City.[16] Mama Leo's ministry to the "outcasts of society–the drug addicts, gang members, prostitutes, and alcoholics" shaped the lives of many New Yorkers, including Nicky Cruz.[17] She was also legendary for having rejected a $12 million grant from the Rockefeller Foundation after it demanded she remove references to "Christ" in her programming. The story goes that she sternly responded, "You can keep your $12 million, I will keep my Christ."[18]

Pentecostalism is tailor-made for a faith politics that includes Nicky Cruz and Mama Leo. As a grassroots movement within evangelical Christianity, its emphasis on divine healing, speaking in tongues, lively worship, and organic intellectualism has long made it an appealing counter to the stale and hierarchical features of Catholic and mainline traditions. And while it gets a bad rap for being heaven focused and apolitical, the truth is that Pentecostalism has a long social services tradition of providing housing, food, health care, and sanctuary to immigrants and refugees, although they have preferred to focus on fellow Pentecostals in need.[19] This tradition is rooted in their reading of the Bible but also in the urban conditions that helped their particular brand of faith thrive: inequality, eclectic politics, diverse populations, and confined urban spaces. Robert Orsi observed a similar phenomenon when he argued that "much of what constitutes the distinctive character of modern American Protestantism arose in response to cities."[20] Nicky Cruz and Mama Leo's work offers a complicated portrait of the faith politics that Latino Pentecostals practiced in the city. They also highlight how Pentecostalism opens spaces for organic intellectuals to rise up and speak to the needs of migrants in the city.

While New York City attracted some of the best religious minds of the twentieth century—theologians like Paul Tillich and Reinhold Niebuhr and humanitarians like Dorothy Day—Latino religious leadership rose up from the margins, fueled by movement: migration and itinerant preachers. No preacher had a greater influence in the years before World War II than the Mexican Pentecostal Francisco Olazábal, also known as "El Azteca." When Olazábal hosted a series of evangelistic revivals in East Harlem in 1931, people showed up in the thousands. In the midst of an economic depression, and with a community that lived in the shadows of New York City, Olazábal's preaching brought people together. Olazábal would go on to start one of the largest churches in New York City and another ten mainline and Pentecostal denominations across the city of New York. How and why Pentecostalism connected with Puerto Ricans on the island and in New York City in such significant ways has much to do with how the faith "resymbolized the supernatural worldview of Catholicism" and offered people direct access to the supernatural and the possibility for both physical and spiritual healing.[21]

Liberation, Holistic Ministry, and Puerto Rican Poverty

In the 1960s and 1970s, Puerto Ricans made up the largest Latino group in the city and the second-largest minority group behind African Americans.[22] Searching for economic opportunity in New York City meant working in mostly low-wage jobs in hospitals, restaurants, and hotels, and above all in New York's declining manufacturing industry. Puerto Rican families were thus trapped squarely at the bottom of the economic ladder. In 1960, for example, 34 percent of Puerto Rican families made less than $3,000 a year, compared with 27 percent of Black families and 12 percent of white ones. Another 54 percent made just slightly above the $4,000-a-year poverty line, making it almost impossible to find decent, safe, and affordable housing. In those years, over 40 percent of Puerto Ricans lived in crumbling homes, and over 85 percent of them lived in the poorest four neighborhoods of the city.[23]

In the late 1960s, amid national and global revolutionary movements, the Puerto Rican Young Lords rose up in East Harlem, a neighborhood overrun by Robert Moses and destroyed by urban renewal in the 1950s and 1960s.[24] In the late 1960s and early 1970s, the Young Lords cleaned up the streets of East Harlem, occupied the First Spanish Methodist Church (twice), and occupied Lincoln Hospital in the South Bronx to bring attention to the poverty and racism that plagued Puerto Ricans and other communities of color. In 1969, they captured the imagination of an entire city—and they did so from the pulpit of a sacred space, the First Spanish United Methodist Church on the corner of East 111th Street and Lexington Ave.

On a cold Sunday morning in December 1969, the Young Lords occupied the church and, as the historian Johanna Fernández beautifully articulated, "transformed the occupied building into a staging ground for their vision of a just society."[25] The occupation of the First Spanish Methodist Church took place against the backdrop of slum clearance and an urban crisis that, as Luis Aponte-Parés argued, was "unweaving the work of a generation: the deterritorialization of a whole community."[26] The Young Lords carried their own style; they were fashionable, articulate, and bold. And while none of the Young Lords proclaimed to be a practicing Christian, they knew the Bible, they recited its versus, and they spoke of the politics of Jesus in ways that worried Pentecostal leaders across the city. Could their church be the next one to be occupied?

On the flip side of that fear and concern was a growing sense of social responsibility among some Latino religious leaders. One of the strongest voices in this regard was Rev. Raymond Rivera. When the Young Lords occupied the church in 1969, Rev. Rivera was a young minister serving at El Camino Pentecostal Church in Brooklyn's Sunset Park neighborhood. For him, the Young Lords "represented Puerto Rican manhood in the urban context . . . they connected urban Puerto Ricans to the larger struggle for Puerto Rican independence on the island."[27] His fascination with the Young Lords prompted him to visit the First Spanish Methodist Church during the occupation. There he reconnected with Felipe Luciano. "There we were," wrote Rivera, "two childhood friends, who had grown up in the same church. I had become a minister and he a political revolutionary."[28] Rivera would go on to support the work of the Young Lords, serving as a "bridge builder and reconciler" between multiple organizations and churches that began to follow the lead of the Young Lords in the 1970s.[29]

But it was faith in Jesus Christ, not revolutionary politics, that drove Rev. Rivera to become one of the strongest religious voices for social justice in the 1970s. Raised in East Harlem and Brooklyn, Rivera was a gifted preacher and a budding community organizer. By day, he worked with welfare recipients as part of the city's Council on Poverty. But by night, he ministered to the people of Sunset Park. In *Liberty to the Captives*, his book describing his more than forty years of ministry in New York City, Rivera outlined the differing ideologies that tugged at his heart. "I would tell my congregation: 'Suffer now and your reward will be in heaven. Only God can change things.' Then, during the day, I would tell people with whom I worked, 'You do not have to suffer. We can change the system now!' "[30] That duality led him to ask deep and probing questions about his ministerial and political work: "Did the message of Christ speak to our personal situations as well as to our collective situations?"[31] The antipoverty work of Rev. Rivera and other Latino pastors in the 1970s carried forward much of the boldness and audacity of the Young Lords, even as they dared not engage revolutionary politics. Instead, they represented a piece of the larger tradition of the dialectic of revolution and reform, accommodation and resistance, so central to Latino religious politics. If the Young Lords created a vision for community control, health-care justice, and art as politics, and freedom for Puerto Rico in the late 1960s, it was New York City preachers that carried their message, albeit reformed and spiritually grounded, into the financially troubled 1970s.

Rev. Rivera's political and ministerial work merged at a moment when Christian theology itself was changing. Shaped by uprisings in Latin America and the civil rights movement in the United States, liberation became a central theme that at once contextualized theology away from its Eurocentric focus and spoke of God being on the side of the oppressed. Liberation theology, as it came to be called, radically transformed the theological landscape in the late 1960s. The historian John McGreevey contends that the "crucial conjunction of immigration, Vatican II, and civil rights protest" in the 1950s and 1960s together pressured church leaders to address racial injustice and urban poverty and situated the church as a site of struggle.[32] That shift came on the heels of a global realignment whereby Christians in the Third World began questioning the authority of the institutional church and its role in the world. This made an important impact on Latino Christians in the United States and moved the church to deal with its exclusions in ways it had not done before.[33] But theological realignments of the era did not emerge without a fight. Widespread resistance to desegregation efforts remained a staple of churches in the urban North, especially in white Catholic churches, where the opposition to integration remained overwhelming into the 1970s.[34] In fact, it was the church's engagement with civil rights politics and marches that shook white religious leaders and sparked much of the backlash to integration from Southern Citizens' Councils to Northern white Catholic neighborhood associations.[35]

Among the Pentecostal leadership in New York City, the political and economic focus of liberation theology did not always resonate. They believed that there remained a personal dimension that required salvation and a commitment to follow Jesus Christ. This was a holistic view of ministry that organized for social justice—but without sacrificing the Evangelical call to share the Gospel and live a life committed to the church and to follow Jesus. Holistic ministry emphasized the personal and the corporate, making the work for social justice a necessary component of following Jesus Christ.[36] For Pentecostals like Rivera, antipoverty and the struggle for social justice provided only partial salvation and partial reform. The real change, they argued, would happen only after the second coming of Christ. "The aim of the gospel," argued Orlando Costas, "is to liberate man from his total situation. . . . No dichotomies here . . . [but instead] a holistic vision of God's mission to the world and the church's role in it."[37]

Acción Cívica and the Religious Fight to End Poverty

Rivera's blending of faith and politics blossomed at El Camino Pentecostal church in the late 1960s. His connections with antipoverty work in the city helped the church secure a grant to operate a summer day camp housed at the church. The program brought in counselors from other churches, named a director from another Pentecostal church, and served over one hundred children that summer. According to Rivera, this was the first time that a local Pentecostal church had received an antipoverty grant from the city.

As significant as this was, Rivera's community work also opened his eyes to what he saw as the invisibility and official neglect of the Puerto Rican community. Nowhere was this clearer than in how New York City distributed its War on Poverty funds. In 1967, the city identified twenty-six poverty districts, areas that it defined as having high concentrations of poverty, and established grassroots community groups to help each poverty district receive its share of War on Poverty dollars. At the time, Puerto Ricans constituted more than 15 percent of the total New York City population. They were younger, had less formal education (only one in five had completed high school, and only one in one hundred had a college degree), were often the lowest-paid in the city, and at least 85 percent lived in neighborhoods that had been designated as high poverty. The problem was that they were neither represented nor supported in proportion to their population numbers. Of the fifty-five members that represented the twenty-six poverty districts, only eight were Latino.[38] Representation on the Council of Poverty mattered precisely because Puerto Ricans in the city were at or near the bottom in every major poverty index.[39]

But not everyone agreed that Puerto Ricans were being cut out of antipoverty dollars. Commissioner Major Owens of the Community Development Agency pushed back against accusations that the city had ignored Puerto Ricans. Instead, Owens accused Puerto Rican leaders of using "gangster methods" to get the attention of city officials. Puerto Ricans fired back, saying the city's antipoverty programs were run by a "black clique."[40] Charles Gadsen, cochairman of the Council of Black organizations in South Bronx, then got involved, charging Puerto Ricans with racism and using mob tactics to get their way.[41] The back-and-forth recriminations continued until February 24, 1970, when, taking a cue from the Young Lords, Puerto Rican leaders, many of whom were preachers, stormed city hall and occupied the building, demanding an equal voice in matters having to do with how antipoverty funds were distributed. Rev. Rivera led over a hundred Puerto Rican protesters to city hall and took over the capital budget hearing for more than ninety minutes. One *New York Times* reporter noted that the protesters "arrived shouting, cheering, and waving the Puerto Rican flag."[42]

The protesters accused the mayor's office of ignoring the needs of the Puerto Rican community, and in one of the most explosive moments of the chaos, Rev. Rivera shouted: "We want you to listen. The mayor has totally ignored us. The money allocated for programs does not get down to the Puerto Rican community. This system perpetuates human misery in our community."[43] When called out for being out of order, Rivera shouted back: "We're tired of being out of order, brother!" Crucially, in a move to set the record straight and ease tensions between Blacks and Puerto Ricans, Rivera affirmed that his group was "not against the blacks getting a fair share of poverty aid," but he insisted that they were there to highlight the inequity in the distribution model that left out a majority of Puerto Rican communities.[44]

The rest of the meeting was a blur. Police armed with nightsticks attacked the protesters and forced them out. Raul Reyes, another protester who served as executive director of the Puerto Rican Community Development Project, was slammed against the wall and struck by police. In the days that followed, Reyes would orchestrate the withdrawal of the Puerto Rican Community Development Project from its association with the city's antipoverty work and community action programs. Instead, the project would begin to operate independently. The frustrations did not stop there and continued into the mid-1970s. As a result, new organizations emerged as powerful advocates for the Puerto Rican community. Into that void stepped Acción Cívica Evangélica.

At the time of its founding in 1974, Acción Cívica was the first ecumenical movement in a city that was home to six hundred Latino churches.[45] Religious networks of Pentecostals and mainline Protestants, which in the postwar era had grown dramatically across the city, made Acción Cívica unique in terms of connections to their organizing base. No one had the reach, or access, to grassroots Latino leadership in quite the same way that Acción Cívica did. And in the context of a looming financial crisis in the city, that access proved hugely important for Latinos. But even more importantly, it was Acción Cívica's connection to Joseph Erazo, who served from 1974 to 1978 as special assistant to the mayor and director of special programs. All that meant was that Erazo was city hall's chief troubleshooter. No Puerto Rican held a higher position in the Beame administration, and Erazo was good at what he did. He already had a strong track record in city politics prior to serving under Mayor Beame. From 1963 to 1967, he was Democratic district leader and member of the party's New York County executive committee, where he served as counsel to a number of Puerto Rican community organizations and was active in the city's urban coalition.[46]

What he lacked in political power he made up for in political influence. His little office two doors down from the mayor meant that he had access to Mayor Beame at any given moment. Erazo's connections and his ability to find money made Acción Cívica a viable and powerful organization almost from the start. "They have done what it can take an organization 20 or 25 years to do," Erazo told the *New York Times* in 1976, "and that is a miracle. I don't know how you could look at it any other way."[47] Erazo was not wrong, but he also made it easy for Acción Cívica by essentially opening up city hall to this group of religious leaders, giving them powerful access to city resources.

The work of planning and organizing Acción Cívica came out of long meetings late into the night at which Latino pastors gathered to push for what they believed was their "fair share of resources for our community," said Rev. José Caraballo, the group's first president and cofounder.[48] Acción Cívica's leaders wanted to take "an active role in solving problems," but they struggled with problems of their own. The board was almost entirely male. While it was a cause for some concern, there's no evidence that Latino pastors moved in any serious way to bring more women on board. There were also denominational differences that played themselves out in theological debates.

But these issues rarely kept the money from flowing. In its first year, Acción raised more than $900,000, and by 1976, it had received $3 million in federal, state, city, and private funding for everything from sponsored lunch programs distributed daily to children across the city to youth programs and eldercare. And where it had started in the basement of the parish house of the First Baptist Church off 115th Street in East Harlem, in 1976, it received an additional $53,000 to move their office to a more central location on 125 East Twenty-Third Street. This brought the work of Acción Cívica closer to the

New York City Mission Society and a host of other faith-based organizations doing similar work.[49]

Acción Cívica began under the leadership of Rev. Raymond Rivera (Reformed Church), Rev. José Caraballo (Pentecostal and Acción's director), Rev. Jose B. Valencia (Baptist), and Rev. Edmundo Morgado (Methodist).[50] Each leader worked with Latino pastors in every borough. One of the largest, Trinity Christian Church at 880 East 180th Street in the Bronx, also became one of the most active congregations. In 1975, it operated a bilingual day-care center that served 250 children and helped renovate over fifty housing units in the neighborhood. In addition to that, the pastor, Bernardo Lopez, organized over twenty job training seminars with hopes of opening more in churches across the city. Many of the pastors had little to no training, and some had barely graduated high school.

The limited training they did have often came from neighborhood Bible schools with no formal accreditation. That also changed in the 1970s when New York Theological Seminary (NYTS), led by the school's president Bill Webber, began offering theological training for Black and Latino pastors with the opportunity to also earn a bachelor's degree. The program originated as a collaboration with Adelphi University in 1973, when it welcomed its first twenty-five students. By 1975, enrollment had grown to over one hundred ministers.[51] Rev. Rivera was one of those students. NYTS, which had a reputation for traditional theological studies and for training pastors and missionaries for global service, all of a sudden found itself in the midst of a changing theological landscape. In the 1960s, NYTS had struggled with low enrollments and a sense that the education it provided was irrelevant to the urban crisis that faced the city. But its troubles were not unique: theological schools across the country faced strong challenges in the midst of the changing political and theological atmosphere of the 1960s.

Even as some seminaries and churches celebrated record financial surpluses that spurred on new construction, soaring enrollment, and new programming in the postwar era, most of the same schools stood frozen in the face of the moral questions raised by the Black freedom movement. Frustrated with their own theological education, young, mostly white seminarians insisted on putting their theology to work by marching against segregation, working with churches on antipoverty campaigns, and attuning themselves to the urban political movements of the day. For some students and seminary professors, like NYTS's President Bill Webber, the rage of the Old Testament prophets and the teachings of Jesus in the New Testament had something profound to say about power, injustice, and social change. By establishing a program for Black and Latino pastors, along with other financial moves that revitalized the institution, NYTS counted its enrollment in 1976 at 453 students, up greatly from only a few years previous.

The new and fresh interpretations of the Bible appealed to a rising generation of Latino pastors intent on making the Bible relevant to their social context. "How," they wanted to know, "do I go out and translate [the Bible] in my community?"[52] That translation work—taking the scriptures to the streets and asking questions about social change and the implications of the Gospel—proved fundamental to students studying the Bible in the 1960s and 1970s. "I went to NYTS," Rev. Rivera told me during an interview at the Latino Pastoral Action Center in New York City, "to answer the question of, How is the Gospel holistic? Does the Bible respond to personal and systemic issues?"[53] The answer for Rivera, and Latino Pentecostals of his generation, was a resounding yes. Fueled with this new vision of ministry, Latino Pentecostals became a force in New York City—not through the paternalism of the David Wilkersons of the world or the National Council of Churches, which for the most part ignored the experiences of Latinos, but with a faith that moved them to action, a faith that inspired them to work for a just city.[54]

Even as Acción Cívica continued to grow and thrive, New York City's financial situation worsened. In fact, as early as 1974, when Abraham Beame began as mayor of New York, it had been clear that the city was in deep financial trouble. The manufacturing economy had all but vanished, family income had dropped by 18 percent, and a new generation of Puerto Ricans had come of age in an economy that could not offer them the same opportunities for economic stability that previous waves of European immigrants enjoyed. The problems started in earnest in 1969, and over the following five years, "the city lost 219,000 jobs in manufacturing, 83,000 in sales, and 10,500 in finance, insurance, and real estate."[55] By 1975, it had become abundantly clear that city leaders had no clear plan, nor did they have much federal help, to address the crisis. President Ford rejected the idea of federal intervention and instead blamed the crisis on the city's financial mismanagement, inflated pensions, government salaries, and social services, or the "welfare burden."[56]

Rather than crediting the War on Poverty with lifting people out of destitution and giving the young a sense of social responsibility, the New York crisis was put forward as proof that Lyndon Johnson's Great Society had failed. The disinvestment in neighborhoods, suburbanization, highways, and the decline of manufacturing, all of which played a bigger role in the crisis, were conveniently ignored as central factors in the city's decline. When threats of municipal bankruptcy forced Mayor Beame to take on more debt, antipoverty programs like Acción Cívica suffered. Regardless of the vision and hope that Rev. Rivera and Rev. Caraballo had for the city, it was not enough to sustain an organization that had done its best to give people a helping hand. While Acción Cívica survived with the insider help of Joe Erazo in Mayor Beame's office, the election of Mayor Ed Koch in 1978 signaled the end for Acción Cívica. Koch came in with a new attitude that questioned the role of city government, he criticized welfare programs, and he rarely brought up the city's powerful civil rights legacy. He blamed Mayor Beame for lacking vision and for making the city's financial outlook only worse by borrowing more money at a time when, according to Koch, he should have been slashing budgets.

New York City's fiscal crisis was the main reason for Acción Cívica's decline, but it was not the only one. Aside from the problems brought on by the fiscal crisis, some of the churches involved in programming with Acción Cívica were accused of having their youth "teaching Bible classes" or of religious proselytizing and offering "kickbacks" to pastors (in reality, pastors required youth workers to tithe 10 percent of their income back to the church).[57] Acción Cívica responded to Rep. Elizabeth Holtzman's accusations in a report where its members denied every accusation. None of it mattered. The damage had been done.[58] When exactly Acción Cívica's work ended is not clear, but the organization did not last long after Holtzman's accusations. Rev. Rivera, in an interview conducted years later, attributed the end to a "lack of funding sparked by an investigation from the mayor's office."[59] Years later, Rev. Rivera would continue Acción Cívica's work with a new organization called the Latino Pastoral Action Center, founded in 1992 in New York City.

Conclusion

Pentecostalism in New York City was familiar and known; it looked and sounded like Puerto Rico, spoke its language and moved at its pace, and became a fixture in the boroughs where Puerto Ricans first settled. But this was not happening only in New York. Across the country, Latino religious communities (mainline, Pentecostal, and Catholic) were the boots on the ground in neighborhoods doing the kind of antipoverty work that most thought had fizzled out. In Houston, Los Angeles, Chicago, and San Antonio, groups like Communities Organized for Public Service and the United Neighborhood Organization, rooted in the grassroots community organizing of Saul Alinsky, took on city infrastructure, education, and poverty, and helped Latinos get involved in local politics.[60]

These days, Latino religious politics seem to be inextricably linked to conservative politics. That comes as no surprise to those who study Latino religious communities and to those of us who grew up in the church. Those politics are, at least in part, rooted in the 1970s when Latino religious groups entered the political fray and struggled to blend their liberative social politics with their Evangelical and conservative religious commitments. In this case, the two went hand in hand. As committed as Acción Cívica remained to restoring neighborhoods, its work was part of a larger shift toward neoliberal policies that reimagined the city through increased privatization and a heavy dose of private-public partnerships. In other words, the work of New York City politicians matched well with the desires of Pentecostals to save the city both economically and spiritually. Acción Cívica's network of churches across the city, their informal economies, and their strong political connections to the mayor's office by way of Joe Erazo all set the conditions whereby Latino Pentecostals established connections with New York City politicians at the highest levels as they sought to reorganize the economic order block by block.

Writing about Latino religious politics means being attentive to the multiple political expressions taking root across place and time. But that analysis cannot be divorced from the reality that religious groups are guided by larger theological commitments that many times stand at odds with grassroots activist movements, whether antiwar or Black and Brown Power movements. As I have shown, urban politics in the 1970s demonstrate how religious groups created mutual aid societies and antipoverty work even as they remained true to their belief that they were in the city but not of the city, that justice would come only as a heavenly reward. This is what makes Acción Cívica's story so compelling. It shows us the careful and meticulous work of Latino Pentecostals as they merged faith and politics in an urban context. And this is a story that continues today. From Catholic churches in North Carolina and Atlanta helping to orient new immigrants to the People's Church in East Harlem turning its sanctuary into a food pantry during the COVID-19 pandemic, Latino religious politics remain as vital today as they were in the 1970s. The tradition of faith-based activism continues, even if it is mostly ignored by mainstream media outlets. The reason, at least in part, is rooted in the organizing base that religious leaders have access to in churches. The theological revolutions in the 1970s that fueled Acción Cívica made a grassroots impact in boroughs across the city largely due to the sheer number of people in churches that made up the organization. And that's the case across the country.

Acción Cívica was short-lived, its strongest years were from 1974 to 1978, but in its brief time, it revealed how a powerful network of churches, in the midst of theological shifts, financial uncertainty, and a rising tide of conservative religion, became an important player in New York City politics. The truth is that no other Pentecostal group of the era came close to doing what Acción Cívica did, and its legacy can be seen in the faith-based movements that have emerged since: Alianza de Ministerios Evangélicos Nacionales in the 1990s in California and the Latino Pastoral Action Center in New York City. Moreover, Acción Cívica's place in New York City is yet another example of why Latino religious communities and politics should be brought into the historiographical mainstream. It's not so much about the lack of studies on religion in urban contexts as much as the profession's failure to study and cite the work that already exists.

In this chapter, I focused on New York City, not because it is characteristic of Latino religious politics in the 1970s (no one place is) but because it offers a starting point to examine the relationship between religion and politics in urban America in the 1970s. In the postwar era, increased Latino immigration and migration to urban centers from Los Angeles to Houston to New York City radically changed the religious landscapes of these areas, creating new coalitions among religious and nonreligious community leaders. Acción Cívica arose in New York City at a time when both urban and theological contexts were changing and at a moment when the city found itself on the verge of bankruptcy. Pentecostals flourished in New York City because they recognized the importance of holistic ministry, of blending the secular and the sacred, and because they believed that their faith had something significant to say about poverty, housing, and the rights of people to live lives of dignity.[61]

7

The "Puerto Rican Exception" and the Limits of Latinidad in Urban History

LLANA BARBER
University of Minnesota

One of my favorite paintings by the artist Carlos Jesus Martinez Dominguez (a.k.a. FEEGZ) is a graffiti-style piece in bright, primary colors with a yellow silhouette of the Caribbean islands in the top right corner. Directly below Cuba and Jamaica in the same vibrant yellow paint is the text, "Not Spanish Not Hispanic Nor Latino . . ." followed by "ANTILLANO SOY!!" in huge, capital block letters. The piece is one of several in which Martinez Dominguez dismisses pan-ethnic terms like *Latine* or *Hispanic* and instead proffers the Caribbean as an alternative regional identifier. Martinez Dominguez, a Dominican and Puerto Rican interdisciplinary artist based in New York City, has long been outspoken in his criticism of the term *Latino*. While *Hispanic* is often dismissed as too aligned with Spain—the colonizing power—Martinez Dominguez notes that the *Latin* in *Latin America* or *Latine* is equally European focused; it just substitutes multiple European countries for Spain. He argues that Dominicans, Puerto Ricans, and Cubans should acknowledge the shared regional history of the Caribbean, particularly its significance in the African diaspora, and the array of cultural similarities that pervade the region. "Caribbean means that I am not drawing this strict line between me and a Jamaican just because of language. And we can see the *plátanos* we eat instead of the language we speak."[1]

Martinez Dominguez argues that the term *Latino* involves an embrace of European connections at the expense of acknowledging African and/or Indigenous roots. In addition, he contends, the diversity of different national-origin groups gets erased under the rubric of Latinidad. In particular, smaller, poorer, or darker Latine groups are not given equal representation nor access. In recent years, social media conversations under the hashtag #LatinidadIsCancelled have made similar arguments. As Tatiana Flores explains:

"Latin America as a construct is Eurocentric to the degree that its conceptual boundaries perniciously exclude African diaspora spaces. . . . Black erasure, sadly, is built into the concept of latinidad." Alan Pelaez Lopez, who coined the hashtag in 2018, points out that Latinidad is often enmeshed in a form of respectability politics that promotes the most privileged Latines as the norm, "#LatinidadIsCancelled was supposed to critique not only the concept of 'race,' but the ways in which U.S. latinidad has created an ideal latinx citizen: white & white mestize, cis-het, thin, normatively attractive, able-bodied, and 'respectable.'" The term *Latine*, these critics argue, whitewashes and domesticates the community it purports to describe, leaving many outside its borders.[2]

After the publication of my first book, *Latino City: Immigration and Urban History in Lawrence, Massachusetts, 1945–2000*, Martinez Dominguez reached out to congratulate me and also to challenge me on the title. I defended the choice, explaining that the book is explicit throughout in its focus on Puerto Ricans and Dominicans, but that part of the history I was recounting was their efforts to forge and mobilize a pan-ethnic identity with others of Latin American descent, and that they did that as Latines (or more precisely, as *Spanish*, *Latins*, *hispanos*, and so on). I also weakly mentioned that titles are marketing terms, which surely only strengthened his point. This chapter marks an effort to take seriously and engage with his criticism.[3]

Martinez Dominguez was not alone in his aversion to the pan-ethnic emphasis in my title. In his *Journal of American History* review of *Latino City*, the renowned Chicano studies scholar Rodolfo Acuña (author of the landmark 1972 book *Occupied America: A History of Chicanos*) wrote, "Barber is a socially conscious scholar, but the flaw of her book is that its title falsely assumes that the term Latino is factual." Acuña strongly argued against the use of *Latino* in the title, dismissing the term as politically aspirational, not grounded in people's lived identities. "Today, the majority of Mexican and Latino scholars craving the unity of all Latinos has arbitrarily constructed this identity hoping that the wish will become a reality." Acuña instead urged a focus on national origins: "A Latino nation does not exist. Latinos in Lawrence have identities—Puerto Rican and Dominican. . . . There is a necessity for Latino unity, but labeling someone Latino does not make it so." Ultimately, he dismissed pan-ethnic terms, not as a local organizing strategy, as I had tried to depict them, but as a national political ploy: "Barber emulated the obsession of Latino leaders nationally to make Latinos or Hispanics the majority population; numbers give the illusion of power."[4]

There is a wide-ranging and important debate over pan-ethnic terms within Latine studies, and my aim is not to recapitulate it here.[5] Rather, my goal is to explore the significance of the debate for urban history specifically, to reckon with what we might gain or lose with a pan-ethnic framework. I would like to think through the ways Latinidad might be useful, or even perhaps necessary, in understanding U.S. urban history and the ways it might be limiting or misleading. Pan-ethnic terms already define fields of scholarly inquiry (the title of this volume is a case in point). For better or worse, the field of Latine studies exists; indeed, it has been hard won through generations of activism. If this ship has sailed, how do we steer it? I would like to explore potential ways to mitigate the risk of erasure and whitewashing seemingly inherent in the pan-ethnic lens. To do so, I take the urban history of stateside Puerto Ricans as a case study, examining how it fits within, challenges, or encourages us to reconceptualize Latine urban history as a field. My focus here is on the postwar and urban crisis eras (mid-1940s to mid-1990s), but some of what follows is relevant to other periods as well.[6]

Acuña's criticism assumes that only national-origin identities are salient for individuals of Latin American descent, but that is not always true. In my research on Lawrence, Massachusetts, the first Latine-majority city in New England, pan-ethnic identities were essential to grassroots organizing efforts. Tens of thousands of Puerto Ricans, Dominicans, and other Latin American nationalities settled in that small, postindustrial city in the late twentieth century, where they encountered a highly segregated landscape that had been economically devastated by suburbanization and deindustrialization. Scapegoated for the city's crisis, they experienced economic and political marginalization as well as fierce and sometimes violent bigotry from their white neighbors. In this context—people from multiple Latin American nationalities struggling in a highly racialized environment that lumped them together and stigmatized them—pan-ethnic organizing was absolutely critical, and a pan-ethnic identity, while not replacing nationality, became meaningful and resonant. Pan-ethnic organizations like the Alliance of Latins for Political Action and Progress played essential roles in advocating for Puerto Ricans, Dominicans, and other Latines in the city, and the Puerto Rican "Spanish coordinator" at the local community action council, Isabel Melendez, worked tirelessly on behalf of Dominican and other Latin American immigrants while promoting pan-ethnic Hispanic empowerment in the city. Beginning in 1979, a pan-ethnic cultural celebration, Semana Hispana, brought together an array of Latin American nationalities each summer, promoting an ideal of "Hispanic" unity while highlighting diverse national cultures. The Hispanic Week festival was also part of a broad, pan-ethnic effort to mobilize Latine people in Lawrence politically, registering voters at the celebration and later participating in a successful pan-ethnic voting rights lawsuit against the city aimed at remediating Latine disenfranchisement and dilution of their political power.[7]

Dominicans, Puerto Ricans, and other people of Latin American descent ultimately transformed Lawrence: reversing its population decline; revitalizing its streets, downtown, and other public spaces; and building a bilingual, bicultural, and transnational economy to replace the industry that had fled. This transformation required a struggle, and Latinidad—creating and mobilizing unity across national-origin groups—was a key part of that fight. This does not mean that national identities were erased or minimized, or that tensions did not exist between different groups—just that the exclusion and bigotry Latines faced in Lawrence transcended ethnic divisions, and so their activism transcended those divisions as well. The pan-ethnic category thus became resonant and meaningful. This Latinidad was forged at the grassroots level, not by national leaders or elites, and it was not only organizers and activists who embraced it. In the context of highly racialized struggles over public space and the right of Latine people to even be in Lawrence (including a 1984 riot in which Latine and white Lawrencians faced off in the streets with rocks and Molotov cocktails while white rioters shouted "Who's American? We're American" and "Go back where you came from" at their predominantly Puerto Rican neighbors), pan-ethnic claims were broader and more popular than just elite political discourse. A 1979 photograph of the Essex Street housing projects in Lawrence showed graffiti proudly declaring "Latin Place, No Honkeys."[8]

Lawrence's history makes clear that it is essential to acknowledge Latinidad as both a process and an identity category relevant to many of our historical subjects. Further, mobilization around the identity category enabled substantial Latine activism that ultimately transformed U.S. cities in countless ways, long before the U.S. Census created the Hispanic category in 1980. Other urban historians have documented this as well: Eduardo Contreras artfully details how and why pan-ethnic categories became resonant and politically useful in midcentury San Francisco. Johanna Fernández explores how the Young Lords used the term *Latino* in the late 1960s to capture and create solidarity with the Chicano movement and the non–Puerto Rican Latines who had joined the Young Lords. Felix Padilla famously documented these pan-ethnic dynamics in Chicago in the early 1970s. Pan-ethnic identification was not universal or automatic, however; it occurred in certain cities in certain eras, depending on complex circumstances. It was often tenuous and fraught, in need of constant reinforcement and negotiation. Acuña is correct that historians cannot assume unity or shared experiences among people of Latin American descent. Instead, we must carefully excavate the instances when our historical subjects endeavored to create such unity—fragile and contested as it often was.[9]

Cristina Beltrán cautions us not to abandon pan-ethnicity, but instead to approach "Latinidad as action—as something we do rather than something we are." Pan-ethnic solidarity, she argues, is "less *found* than *forged*." This is particularly relevant for urban historians because cities have long been the sites of such forging, particularly among poor and working-class Latines. Milagros Ricourt and Ruby Danta's classic study of "hispanas" in Queens, New York, for example, showcased the pan-ethnic connections created by women from many Latin American backgrounds through their shared struggle to build their lives in the 1980s and 1990s. In an expensive city and with few resources, these women created pan-ethnic networks of support and connection through "convivencia diaria," a shared daily life. If "Latino is a verb," this type of grassroots latinando, so to speak, is precisely the purview of urban historians. Dismissing Latinidad out of hand would blind us to the ways everyday people crafted and used it to build lives for themselves in U.S. cities.[10]

Even so, when historians write about "Latines," we are often being anachronistic at best, describing people in ways they would not have described themselves at that time. Some of this is inevitable as language evolves. The problem arises if the use of anachronistic terms distorts people's lived realities, elides aspects of their pasts, or erases certain groups' experiences. Acuña argues that the very use of the term *Latino* implies a solidarity and unity that did not exist. The argument of Martinez Dominguez (and #LatinidadIsCancelled) goes further, claiming that it implies a unity premised on racial exclusions and thus inhibits a far more radical potential solidarity based on shared historical experiences, social positioning, and the "roots" and "routes" of the African diaspora.

To flesh out the argument in "Antillano Soy," how would the urban history of Puerto Ricans, Dominicans, or Cubans in the mainland U.S. look different if we considered these groups as part of a Caribbean diaspora rather than as Latines? What if we dropped Spanish language or Latin American heritage as the main thematic connection and saw instead the complex multicultural, post- and decolonial Black diasporic history of the Caribbean as the common connection? Such a focus would undoubtedly draw our attention to Afro-Caribbean experiences or to the ways many white Caribbean migrants came equipped with their own versions of anti-Blackness, prepared to take a place at the top of a racial hierarchy. A diasporic Caribbean focus would encourage us to consider the history of Dominicans, Cubans, and Puerto Ricans alongside that of Jamaicans, Haitians, and other Afro-Caribbean communities. It would encourage us to focus on the Caribbean diaspora's complex relationship with African Americans in U.S. cities, including—for many, but certainly not all—shared neighborhoods and experiences, related processes of racialization, and transculturation.

A Caribbean diasporic lens in post–World War II urban history might foreground the Northeast and Florida. This regional emphasis would illuminate the impact of deindustrialization and suburbanization on the Caribbean diaspora, highlight the significance of segregation and disinvestment during the urban crisis era, emphasize the role of Blackness and anti-Blackness in shaping diasporic experiences in U.S. cities, and flesh out the mechanisms of privilege that enabled Cuban Miami to become the "capital of Latin America." The impact of U.S. imperialism would become particularly glaring, not only in the colonized space of Puerto Rico but also in Panama, the Dominican Republic, Cuba, El Salvador, Nicaragua, Guatemala, Haiti, and elsewhere. Migration from the circum-Caribbean region, our "American lake," is absolutely incomprehensible without reckoning with the long history of U.S. intervention in the area. While the United States has interfered in other parts of Latin America as well—the Central Intelligence Agency–backed overthrow of Salvador Allende in Chile springs instantly to mind—the circum-Caribbean region is by far the most U.S.-invaded space in the world. A diasporic Caribbean focus would force us to reckon with that, bringing an analysis of U.S. imperialism solidly into U.S. urban history.[11]

Ultimately, however, both Latine and Caribbean diasporic frameworks risk losing the specificity of different groups' experiences, the dramatic diversity of Latine and Caribbean peoples, and the impact of regional and local conditions. National origin, skin color, class background, economic status, gender, sexuality, and so on, all shaped Latine urban experiences in ways that cannot be overstated, and cities in different parts of the country offered radically different receptions. The racism facing many Latines before the 1990s was not united by any national policy, stereotype, or discourse vis-à-vis all Latines; racism varied from place to place, depending on regional history, local political economy, and the race and class makeup of the predominant Latine group. In truth, the racism faced by Latine peoples has never been uniform or monolithic, and thus privileged or oppressed circumstances for one group in one place cannot be read as privilege or oppression for all. Different Latine communities had distinct struggles and require distinct histories. If we recount these specific histories under too broad of a Latine banner, we risk erasing and distorting Latine experiences.

As urban historians, we are highly attuned to the local; we recognize the particularities of each distinct urban environment, and we strive to draw conclusions that emerge from, synthesize, and respect each city's specificity. We must be no less careful in the conclusions we draw about urban Latine communities. How do we collectively craft a narrative that does equal justice to experiences as divergent as, for example, that of Cubans in Miami, Mexican Americans in Los Angeles, and Puerto Ricans in the Bronx? If we accept the salience of the pan-ethnic label and define "Latine urban history" as a field, then the conclusions we draw and the stories we tell must emerge from, synthesize, and respect the experiences of all the different groups that fall under the Latine banner. Is that even possible? As historians, can we find a way to use *Latine* that mitigates the dangers enumerated here—that respects diversity, resists minimizing Blackness and Indigeneity, and fully incorporates the experiences of smaller, poorer, or darker Latine groups?

As scholars in the incipient field of Latine urban history, we must actively struggle against the homogenizing function of the pan-ethnic lens. One possible way to do this may be to center the experiences of marginalized Latines, not only recounting their histories but also recasting and reimagining the broader narrative through the lens of their specificity. How do we see Latine history differently when we foreground Indigenous or Afro-Latine experiences, working-class or poor Latine experiences, queer Latine experiences, and so on? I argue that Latine history cannot be told solely from the perspective of the majority or the most privileged without losing its rich texture and complexity, and without obscuring the stunning history of Latine oppositionality and resistance. If there is to be a broad, pan-ethnic narrative, it must emerge from an aggressive attention to the margins.

There was an explosion of scholarly and media attention to Latinidad in the 1980s, the "decade of the Hispanic," after the census introduced the Hispanic category, and as the number of Latines in the nation grew dramatically. As the renowned cultural theorist Juan Flores declared, "By the 1990s, 'Hispanic' and 'Latino' [were] everywhere." Celebratory accounts of Latine progress and incorporation, however, were often interrupted to discuss "the Puerto Rican exception." Puerto Rican poverty, unemployment, welfare use, and other negative socioeconomic indicators diverged significantly from those of other Latines, and Puerto Ricans were frequently blamed for these disparities, accused of clinging to a "culture of poverty" that impeded their upward mobility. This attention to the so-called Puerto Rican exception, Flores noted, actually preceded the "decade of the Hispanic," as accounts of New York immigrant and ethnic communities had also long bracketed Puerto Ricans as disappointing outliers: "New York Puerto Ricans have long been viewed or construed as the 'exception,' the extraneous ingredient in the melting pot or ethnic pluralist stew, salad bowl, or mosaic. The assimilationist thrust involved in ethnic and immigrant analogies has gone accompanied by the social pathologies of the 'Puerto Rican problem.'" Long-standing, head-shaking accounts of the Puerto Rican exception were then recycled in the 1980s and 1990s, as pan-ethnic accounts of Hispanic growth, progress, and potential were emerging. "In the 1990s, as the Hispanic giant rouses from its slumber, the Puerto Ricans are still the 'exception' to the pan-ethnic rule, the 'problem' even among their own kind."[12]

Why look closely at the "Puerto Rican exception" in the postwar and urban crisis eras? If Puerto Ricans were distinct from most Latines at the time—not only in their socioeconomic indicators but also in their U.S. citizenship, the timeline of their mass migration, their relation to African Americans, their urban concentration and segregation levels—what do their experiences offer to a broader pan-ethnic narrative? The answer is twofold: first, as recounted earlier, any vision of Latinidad that is not grounded in the specific experiences of diverse, marginalized Latine groups is simply not viable. As Flores explains, "The adequacy of the embattled 'Latino' or 'Hispanic' concept hinges on its inclusiveness toward the full range of social experiences and identities." Second, Flores argues that "the 'exception' may also be the paradigm." Displaced by the forces of U.S. imperialism, having to reckon with urban disinvestment, forging a social position vis-à-vis African Americans: Puerto Ricans were not unique in any of these experiences. In other words, the structural factors that accounted for Puerto Ricans' social positioning in this era shaped other Latines' experiences as well, and the extreme disparities these factors created for Puerto Ricans help make them visible to a degree they may not otherwise be. Examining the "Puerto Rican exception" provides a methodology and set of questions that may help us understand the history of other Latine groups as well.[13]

Attention to the diversity of Latine experiences is particularly essential for urban historians, as the spatialized inequality of the urban crisis era generated and magnified these differences. The so-called Puerto Rican exception was partially the result of coloniality, as I discuss more subsequently, but it was also the result of Puerto Ricans' concentration in cities from which capital, resources, and opportunities had been removed. As Nicholas De Genova and Ana Y. Ramos-Zayas remind us, disparities between Latine groups do not reflect inherent cultural characteristics; rather, they reflect how different groups are perceived and treated by the state and by those with economic or discursive power. What we see by centering Puerto Rican experiences is that the disparities also reflect different positioning in an unequal racial geography as white flight and urban disinvestment spatialized racial inequality in the half century after World War II.[14]

The Latine presence in U.S. cities accelerated beginning in the 1980s, but mass Puerto Rican migration began much earlier, in the late 1940s and 1950s. Between 1940 and 1970, nearly a million Puerto Ricans moved to the mainland, initially concentrating in New York City, with 88 percent of stateside Puerto Ricans living there in 1940. They gradually dispersed but remained overwhelmingly concentrated in Northeastern cities.[15] Puerto Ricans, like African Americans, were arriving in these cities at the same historical moment that white flight, deindustrialization, and disinvestment were eviscerating them. As Puerto Ricans and African Americans from the South were moving into New York, for example, white residents were moving out in a massive flight to the suburbs. Between 1940 and 1970, the city lost nearly two million white residents as the suburbs surrounding the city boomed, largely restricted to white families through an array of discriminatory developer, realty, and bank practices. New York City lost another 1.3 million white residents between 1970 and 1980.[16] Puerto Ricans and African American migrants from the South arrived in U.S. cities just in time to see the jobs disappear; the employment, educational, and health-care opportunities that drove many to migrate evaporate; the modern, comfortable life they had hoped for vanish in the crisis city. In New York, young Puerto Ricans faced racial attacks from white youth on the streets, bitter anti-desegregation fights in New York City public schools, criminalization and brutality from the police, the decimation of the City University of New York during the city's fiscal crisis, a public health nightmare of lead paint, tuberculosis, and underfunded public hospitals, and a public safety debacle of shuttered fire stations, arson for profit, and a political economy in which criminalized work was some of the only work around. Indeed, not only did Puerto Ricans and African Americans arrive at the very beginning of urban crisis; their presence and their rebellious outrage at their treatment were part of what spurred white people and businesses to continue to seek out the homogeneous, segregated spaces of the suburbs.[17]

Centering Puerto Rican urban history foregrounds Latine experiences with segregation and disinvestment and the power of structural anti-Black racism in shaping Latine experiences. The metropolitan political economy of the urban crisis era maintained white supremacy by containing Black presence and protest in urban areas from which investment and resources fled, then heavily and violently policing those areas. Puerto Ricans were forced to find or carve out for themselves places within that urban crisis landscape, and many found themselves trapped, similar to or alongside African Americans, in urban neighborhoods from which capital, resources, jobs, and opportunities had been stripped. As a result, Puerto Ricans encountered segregation, discrimination, stigma, and poverty to an extreme degree.[18]

Among Latine groups during this era, Puerto Ricans were also most likely to share neighborhoods and circumstances with African Americans and to develop shared resistance strategies. Recent work, especially that of A. K. Sandoval-Strausz, has argued that Latines played a major role in revitalizing U.S. cities in the late twentieth century and contributed to ending the era of urban crisis by the mid-1990s. Focusing on Puerto Ricans, however, as the "exception" to some of the relative privilege, success, or mobility of many other Latine groups, foregrounds the fact that many Latines also suffered profoundly from urban crisis and that it constrained their choices, created downward socioeconomic mobility, and sometimes ruined or even took lives. Puerto Ricans, similar to African Americans, experienced racialized unemployment and poverty, substandard housing and displacement, residential segregation, neighborhood disinvestment, inadequate public services, police abuse, political marginalization, rampant and unchecked discrimination, and quotidian bigotry during the urban crisis era. These aspects of the urban crisis are the root of the Puerto Rican "exception."[19]

Puerto Ricans were concentrated in central cities during the crisis era to a degree absolutely unparalleled by other Latine groups. In 1979, for example, the majority of Latines (51 percent) lived in central cities. Yet this pan-ethnic lens hides a massive divergence: a stunning 79.2 percent of Puerto Ricans lived in central cities, versus only 45.6 percent of Mexican Americans and just 33.7 percent of Cubans. Further, nearly all of the central cities where Puerto Ricans lived were in the Northeast and Midwest, in the Rust Belt, where deindustrialization and suburbanization were devastating urban economies and creating a new geography of racial segregation: predominantly white suburbs surrounding Black (and Puerto Rican) "inner cities." Puerto Ricans' position in this racial geography was reflected in a level of segregation from non-Hispanic whites that diverged sharply from that of other Latines. An analysis of both 1970 and 1980 census data by Douglas Massey and Nancy Denton found that "the high level of Puerto Rican segregation from Anglos is exceptional." This segregation was "exceptionally high" even after controlling for socioeconomic differences; in other words, this segregation was not just about Puerto Rican poverty. While some theorized that the greater presence of Afro-Latines among Puerto Ricans (relative to Mexicans and pre-Mariel Cubans) was responsible for this extreme segregation, Massey and Denton found that, even when they controlled for Black identification, Puerto Ricans still "stand out for their high segregation from Anglos." In other words, Puerto Ricans in the 1960s and 1970s were highly segregated *as* Puerto Ricans, not only as Black people or as poor people (although being also Black or poor definitely increased segregation levels). Massey and Denton concluded that "Puerto Ricans, alone among Hispanic groups, face a serious risk of becoming part of an isolated urban underclass cut off spatially from the rest of American society." A key part of the Puerto Rican exception was this extreme level of segregation in an era when opportunities were largely spatially determined.[20]

While noting that Puerto Ricans were not quite as segregated as African Americans, Anna Santiago and George Galster confirmed that Puerto Ricans' "pattern of high segregation from Anglos most closely resembles the experience of Blacks and is quite distinct from the experience of other Latine sub-populations." The two other major Latine groups at the time, Mexicans and Cubans, were only moderately segregated from non-Hispanic whites, and their segregation levels declined as their socioeconomic status improved. Both Cubans and Mexicans, however, were highly segregated from non-Hispanic Black people (or it would probably be more accurate to say that Black people were highly segregated from Mexicans and Cubans, but Massey and Denton did not discuss segregation as a process, just as an effect). Puerto Ricans were far more residentially integrated with Black people than Mexicans or Cubans were. Though still moderately segregated from Black people, Puerto Ricans were far more residentially integrated with Black people than with white. Massey and Denton noted, "No other ethnic group that has been studied in the United States—Hispanic or European—displays such a pattern of systematically greater integration with blacks than with Anglos." In cities of the Northeast and in Chicago, levels of Puerto Rican segregation from white people were comparable to those of African Americans.[21] An analysis of 1980 census data concluded that, among Latines, "Puerto Ricans are clearly at greatest risk of being denied equal access to spatially determined resources like education, health, security, and employment." Extreme Puerto Rican residential segregation mirrored that of African Americans during the urban crisis era. Far more than other Latine groups, Puerto Ricans were spatially isolated from white America, sharing the circumstances of segregation and urban disinvestment with Black people, and often even sharing the same neighborhoods.[22]

Segregation in Rust Belt cities made Puerto Ricans particularly vulnerable to deindustrialization. Puerto Ricans had been recruited into industrial labor in the postwar era, and they were disproportionately concentrated in manufacturing, particularly in the apparel industry. Deindustrialization resulted in mass Puerto Rican unemployment. A 1976 U.S. Commission on Civil Rights report noted that manufacturing was "the greatest single source of employment" for Puerto Ricans. From 1950 to 1970, however, New York City lost

274,000 manufacturing jobs, more than a quarter of its previous total. Then from 1970 to 1975, the city lost nearly the same number of jobs *again*, in just five years! By 1990, New York retained only one-third of the manufacturing jobs it had in 1950. The entire sector had been decimated, and Puerto Ricans had been hit the hardest, leading to shocking levels of unemployment. This was exacerbated by the fact that many professional degrees and licenses in the U.S. territory of Puerto Rico were not recognized on the mainland, and the 1976 report noted as well that racial, ethnic, and sex discrimination were barriers to job opportunities for Puerto Ricans.[23] In a chapter despairingly titled "Decline within Decline," Andrés Torres and Frank Bonilla noted that as New York City underwent a fiscal crisis and economic restructuring from 1970 to 1980, Puerto Ricans were the only group to "suffer an absolute decline in employment in the region."[24] In summary, Puerto Ricans arrived in stateside cities in the postwar era at the same historical moment that the jobs they came to fill were disappearing. The historian Carmen Teresa Whalen thus calls Puerto Ricans "displaced labor migrants," who came to find work but instead found themselves displaced from urban economies as industry fled Northeastern and Midwestern cities.[25]

Being displaced from urban economies yet segregated within urban neighborhoods suffering from disinvestment led to extreme levels of Puerto Rican poverty and joblessness (which, of course, exacerbated Puerto Rican segregation). A 1964 study found that Puerto Ricans suffered the highest poverty rate of any group in New York City, as well as the lowest education levels, the lowest income, and the most inadequate housing. "The Puerto Rican New Yorker is caught today in a poverty trap," the study concluded. "His low occupational status dictates low family income; his low income condemns his children to limited educational opportunities and achievement, which in turn sentence him to a low occupational status with low pay, and so on and on." The authors projected with foreboding that "in the New York City of today he will not escape the trap, nor will his children, nor his children's children." In 1960, 40 percent of housing units occupied by Puerto Ricans were "deteriorating" or "dilapidated," and only slightly more than half of Puerto Rican households lived in sound units with all plumbing facilities. Puerto Ricans paid dearly for this miserable housing; in the mid-1950s, they were charged more in monthly rent ($49) than either white ($37) or African American families ($43).[26]

In 1960, Puerto Ricans' median earnings were less than those of both white and Black workers in every occupational category in New York City. Impoverished mothers turned to welfare: in 1969, 328,000 New Yorkers relied on welfare; by 1972, 1.25 million did, and 40 percent of the city's welfare recipients were Puerto Rican. Puerto Ricans' socioeconomic position was exacerbated during the city's fiscal crisis in the mid-1970s. By 1977, the median income for Puerto Rican families was just $10,499, below that of African American families ($13,999) and half that of white families ($20,998). The 1976 U.S. Commission on Civil Rights report noted that 85 percent of New York City's Puerto Ricans lived "in low-income neighborhoods of the Bronx, Brooklyn, and Manhattan. Some of these areas include the worst slums in the nation." That same year, the *New York Times* proclaimed, "The greatest concentration of human misery in this trouble-beset metropolis is among the million-member Puerto Rican community." The exceptional poverty of Puerto Ricans was not limited to New York City. Nationally, in 1959, Puerto Rican families earned only 71 percent of the national average. By 1979, they earned only an abysmal 49 percent of the national average. The March 1975 Census survey noted that Puerto Ricans were the poorest of all Hispanic groups. The annual median income for all U.S. families was $12,836, but for stateside Puerto Rican families, it was just $7,629, substantially below Mexican American ($9,498) and Cuban and "other Spanish" families ($11,410).[27]

While the Puerto Rican exception was generally marshaled to contrast Puerto Ricans with earlier European immigrants or other Hispanic groups, many observers noted that Puerto Rican poverty was "exceptional" compared with that of African Americans as well. The Puerto Rican Forum noted in 1970, "In the present climate of concern for the plight of the American Negro, there remains widespread unawareness of the fact that in occupational status, family income, and educational achievement the Puerto Rican New Yorker is below the deplorable level of the Negro New Yorker." A 1991 *Atlantic* article noted, "Practically everybody in America feels some kind of emotion about blacks, but Puerto Rican leaders are the only people I've ever run across for whom the emotion is pure envy. In New York City, black median family income is substantially higher than Puerto Rican, and is rising more rapidly. The black home-ownership rate is more than double the Puerto Rican rate. Puerto Rican families are more than twice as likely as black families to be on welfare, and are about 50 percent more likely to be poor."[28]

The tone of such commentary often implied that this reality was surprising, as if somehow African Americans were supposed to be at the bottom of the ladder, and their prosperity relative to Puerto Ricans somehow upset the natural order. *Time* magazine, for example, noted in 1978 that "Puerto Ricans are *even* more hard pressed than New York's ghetto blacks." Some observers, like Andrés Torres, explicitly noted that African Americans faced the long legacy of anti-Black racism and wondered why Puerto Ricans were not faring better: "How do we explain the greater inequality and powerlessness of Puerto Ricans, a people who bear a lesser burden of racism?" While I am not interested in making an argument about whether Puerto Ricans had it "better" or "worse" than African Americans, I am deeply interested in what specific factors contributed to the dismal socioeconomic indicators for Puerto Ricans in this era. The lack of a Spanish-language infrastructure certainly played a role, but in fact that is just one small part of the puzzle.[29]

The Puerto Rican exception was not simply about Puerto Ricans' position in the racial geography of the urban Northeast—a position they often shared with African Americans—it was also about the colonial status of Puerto Rico. Attention to Puerto Rican experiences draws coloniality and empire firmly into the U.S. urban historiography. Puerto Ricans were not immigrants in U.S. cities; they were imperial migrants, driven from the periphery to the heart of empire. Many arrived in New York City with the critical perspective of colonial subjects, aware that U.S. rule had distorted their home country. In the early 1950s, as Puerto Ricans were moving to New York City, an independence movement on the archipelago was being violently repressed, including mass arrests and extremely punitive sentences, a "gag law" criminalizing advocacy of independence and the possession of a Puerto Rican flag, and even the aerial bombing of U.S. citizens in the Puerto Rican towns of Jayuya and Utuado. Whatever their views on independence, Puerto Rican migrants were certainly aware of U.S. rule in their home country. In 1957, the famed Afro–Puerto Rican author and activist Jesús Colón wrote a story in which the narrator exhorted his grandmother not to leave the colonized space of Puerto Rico to join her family in New York City: "I know there is need and poverty all around you. And discrimination and economic and cultural oppression there. Something called imperialism sees to it that these things are not wiped out. . . . Still I think I ought to tell you that the most important men and forces interested in keeping people poor and ignorant and fighting wars one against the other, have their offices in one short street in this New York to which your relatives are trying to bring you." For Puerto Rican migrants, there was no refuge from American empire. Instead, they came only closer to its center, right into the belly of the beast. While migration brought them nearer the wealth and power of the metropole, borders of segregation and discrimination kept most of them from accessing that wealth and power (as the Nuyorican poet Pedro Pietri lamented of Puerto Rican workers in New York "who came to this country to make a fortune / and were buried without underwears").[30]

Promoting Puerto Rican migration to mainland U.S. cities in the postwar era was part of a strategy to ensure the stability of the colonial state and to revamp Puerto Rico into a Cold War model of capitalist development for newly decolonizing nations. U.S. colonial rule in the early twentieth century had transformed Puerto Rico into a one-crop export economy, reliant on producing sugar *for* the United States and consuming overpriced imports *from* the United States. This colonial sugar economy created an impoverished agricultural proletariat in Puerto Rico, including a massive reserve of "surplus" labor. Widespread un- and underemployment, as well as miserable wages and working conditions, were exacerbated by the Great Depression, and Puerto Rican labor and nationalist protests grew increasingly militant in the 1930s. Concerns about "overpopulation" had long permeated colonial discourse; rather than blame exploitative economic structures for impoverishing Puerto Ricans, colonial officials blamed Puerto Ricans for reproducing. They worried that a growing mass of impoverished and increasingly radicalized Puerto Ricans posed a threat to both the colonial economy and U.S. rule on the island. In the 1940s, as U.S. and Puerto Rican politicians negotiated a transition to commonwealth status—a type of semicolonialism in which Puerto Rico has a limited form of self-government while remaining subject to the sovereignty of the United States—emigration from Puerto Rico was widely touted as a solution to the island's putative overpopulation problems.[31]

In 1947, Puerto Rico commenced Operation Bootstrap, a massive economic development program designed to attract U.S. investment through a series of (what would today be called neoliberal) incentives, particularly tax exemptions, low wages, and open access to the U.S. market. The goal was to rapidly develop Puerto Rico and thereby demonstrate the miraculous growth potential of capitalism. Widespread Puerto Rican poverty, however, was incompatible with the island's role as a "showcase of democracy." The industrial and tourist-sector growth that resulted from Operation Bootstrap did not generate nearly enough new employment to solve the island's economic problems. The (qualified and temporary) successes of Operation Bootstrap thus came to rely on the exportation of Puerto Rico's "surplus" population. The removal of hundreds of thousands of Puerto Ricans to the mainland United States and the remittances they sent home to families in Puerto Rico were essential to improving economic indicators on the island.[32]

While the migration of Puerto Ricans reflected their agency and aspirations, the Puerto Rican government actively promoted and facilitated emigration as an economic development strategy for the island, although its official, highly disingenuous policy was that it neither encouraged nor discouraged emigration. The colonial state worked to place Puerto Ricans in stateside jobs and played a major role in providing social services and advocacy for stateside Puerto Ricans. Importantly, Puerto Rican and U.S. officials cooperated to dramatically reduce airfare between the island and the mainland, making emigration feasible even for low-income Puerto Ricans. The metropole was invested in the emigration of Puerto Rico's poor, as continued economic crisis on the island could lead to increased advocacy for independence or potentially communist agitation. As Edgardo Meléndez carefully documents, U.S. and Puerto Rican decision-makers considered migration "a means of providing social, political, and economic stability to the colonial regime in Puerto Rico at a crucial juncture in time for the American government." Key to the Puerto Rican exception was the reality that Puerto Rican migrants in the postwar decades were overwhelmingly working-class, structurally "surplus" labor in the "overpopulated" colonial economy. Once exported to stateside cities, many quickly became "surplus" in the disinvested postindustrial urban economy as well.[33]

Puerto Rican urban poverty in the postwar era contributed to vicious stereotypes of Puerto Ricans as diseased, dirty, and poor: a population of welfare abusers and delinquents. But media disparagement of Puerto Ricans had begun in the 1940s, even before deindustrialization displaced Puerto Ricans from urban economies. It should not be surprising that Puerto Rican migrants were stigmatized virtually on arrival in stateside cities, given that the entire colonial project at the turn of the twentieth century hinged on portraying colonized subjects as racially inferior, uncivilized, immoral, sickly, and ignorant. Efforts to maintain and justify U.S. power in Puerto Rico (and other occupied spaces of the Caribbean) relied on and perpetuated a derogatory and stigmatizing discourse. Portraying Puerto Ricans as inferior served to justify U.S. rule on the island, but it led to a frenzy when those defamed colonial subjects moved to the metropole. The media wrote hysterically about the "Puerto Rican problem," blaming the new arrivals for overcrowded housing, unemployment, illnesses, and crime. As Meléndez describes, "News articles emphasized the 'tropical' character of these people, their inclination to go into welfare, and their ignorance of the English language." U.S. Americans might have been persuaded that Puerto Ricans were an acceptable population to rule over, but not to live beside. By the 1960s, Puerto Ricans were derided for their putative "culture of poverty" and later accused of being an "underclass" without the cultural resources for upward mobility. This stigma both emerged from and reinforced Puerto Ricans' "exceptional" poverty and segregation.[34]

The racialization of Puerto Ricans was also related, but not reducible, to Puerto Rico's place in the African diaspora. Postwar estimates of the proportion of Black Puerto Ricans in stateside communities ranged from 9 percent to 33 percent. Puerto Ricans had varying levels of African descent and varying phenotypical presentations that might result in their being ascribed a Black identity in the United States. Similar to the one-drop rule that rendered any individual with partial African ancestry definitively Black, the presence of

Puerto Ricans who were read as Black interspersed throughout the New York migrant community contributed to rendering the entire group definitively nonwhite. As Puerto Ricans and African Americans remained overwhelmingly segregated into urban areas, white privilege became spatialized in the movement of capital, resources, and opportunities to suburbia—a structural form of anti-Black racism. Thus, Puerto Ricans, as a group, experienced some of the effects of this structural anti-Blackness, even if, as individuals, they would not have identified or have been identified as Black.[35] Yet the racialization of Puerto Ricans was not reducible solely to anti-Blackness. As discussed earlier, the racialization of Puerto Ricans began as part of the colonial project and became more elaborate during the postwar migration boom. To be Puerto Rican was to occupy a particular racial position, not between Black and white, but distinct from them both. Of course, one could be a Black Puerto Rican or a white Puerto Rican, but to be a Puerto Rican at all in the urban crisis era was to belong to an already racialized group, by which I mean a group that was pervasively stereotyped, that faced extreme prejudice and bigotry, and that was systematically denied equal opportunities in housing, employment, and education. This racialization of Puerto Ricans occurred at the intersection of anti-Blackness, xenophobia, and coloniality. No other Latine group has been racialized in quite the same way.[36]

Puerto Ricans had a complex relationship with African Americans. Afro–Puerto Ricans felt the bitter sting of both anti–Puerto Rican and anti-Black bigotry. As Pablo "Yoruba" Guzmán, one of the founders of the New York Young Lords, articulated it, "Before people called me a spic, they called me a n——."[37] The historian Johanna Fernández has done excellent work highlighting the shared circumstances of Puerto Ricans and African Americans in the crisis era, particularly in New York City: "Common lived experiences pushed black Americans and Puerto Ricans together. Both lived in an urban environment where poverty was qualitatively different than before, marked by economic restructuring and structural unemployment, combined with the shared experience of police brutality in the streets and the various forms that racism took in northern cities." In addition, Fernández demonstrates how "common traumatic schooling experiences laid the groundwork for cross-ethnic collaboration, particularly in the face of white backlash against integration in the late 1960s." As Andrés Torres explained, "since the 1950s, blacks and Hispanics—particularly Puerto Ricans—have been drawn together in an alliance of survival" in New York City. Many Puerto Ricans, however, even those partially of African descent, were reluctant to identify with the struggle of Black Americans, given the pervasiveness of anti-Blackness both in the United States and in Latin America. Puerto Rican organizations often competed with African American organizations for scarce resources and opportunities, and they frequently had different priorities or visions of progress.[38] But other Puerto Ricans came to recognize that urban Black and Puerto Rican communities were facing similar obstacles in the crisis era and began to embrace Black struggles and solidarity. Although such solidarity was not without tension, scholars have documented the myriad ways it flourished at the grassroots level, particularly in New York City: shifting attitudes and identities, generating transcultural networks of support, alliance, and friendship, and giving birth to innovative cultural hybrids like the music of boogaloo. Puerto Ricans and Black Americans organized together in the realms of labor, housing, welfare, and education rights, against police abuse, and in pursuit of electoral power. Of equal importance, they developed shared urban cultures of survival, resistance, and celebration during the crisis era.[39]

Among the many resistance strategies Puerto Ricans shared with African Americans was rebellion. As Elizabeth Hinton has powerfully documented, hundreds of Black neighborhoods erupted in rage and protest during the urban crisis era. These insurgencies were a form of political rebellion against the structural violence of segregation and disinvestment, as well as the concrete violence of police abuse. What is less well known is that Latine communities also "rioted" in the crisis era (as Pedro Regalado's chapter in this volume details), rebelling against police violence, poverty, unemployment, displacement, inadequate housing and public services, marginalization in city governance, widespread discrimination, stigmatization, and bigotry. Puerto Ricans, "exceptional" among Latines in the level to which they suffered from urban crisis, were particularly likely to rebel: more than two-thirds of these Latine rebellions involved Puerto Ricans, even though they were only a small proportion of the country's Latine population, and Puerto Ricans also participated in many of this era's African American uprisings. Beyond these insurgent moments, Puerto Ricans created revolutionary social movements as well (often including, alongside, or inspired by Black activists). The radical vision of groups like the Young Lords and El Comité were shaped by the distinct structures of racism dominant during the urban crisis, particularly racialized disinvestment, displacement due to urban renewal projects targeting neighborhoods of color, and the collapse of public services. Puerto Rican revolutionaries occupied the city's spaces and repurposed them to serve the people: squatting in buildings set for demolition during Operation Move-In or occupying Lincoln Hospital or the "People's Church" to provide better care for their communities.[40]

Trapped in the decaying metropole, many stateside Puerto Rican activists dreamed transnationally of a decolonized Puerto Rico, challenging the U.S. repression that shaped their circumstances and denied their self-determination, including famously hanging a Puerto Rican flag from the crown of the Statue of Liberty in 1977. Of course, Puerto Ricans also engaged in less spectacular but profoundly essential community and political organizing around education, labor, housing, and language and voting rights. One of the saddest ironies of the narrative of Puerto Rican exception is that even though Puerto Rican activism laid so much of the groundwork that allowed later Latine communities to endure and advance, Puerto Ricans were subsequently derided for their apparent lack of progress compared to these other groups. In the depths of the urban crisis, Puerto Rican neighborhoods did not suffer silently; rather, they gave birth to activism and social movements that helped make U.S. cities viable for poor and working-class people of color. And Puerto Rican activism that was revolutionary or insurgent exposed the lie of American meritocracy; it articulated powerful critiques of racial capitalism and U.S. empire and communicated inspiring visions of what true freedom or equality might look like.[41]

By the early 1990s, the persistence of concentrated Puerto Rican poverty generated fears that Puerto Ricans, alongside African Americans, were forming a permanent "underclass" in the nation's "inner cities." A controversial article in 1991 deemed Puerto Ricans "the other underclass," noting that while "most people think of inner-city poverty as a black phenomenon. . . . Puerto Ricans are the worst off ethnic group in the United States." Fearful rhetoric about the "underclass" obscured a far more complicated reality. As scholars looked closely at the 1990 census data, it became evident that Puerto Ricans had actually experienced tremendous economic growth throughout the 1980s. In addition, a new mass migration had begun that included many professional-class Puerto Ricans, individuals better situated to prosper stateside than earlier "displaced labor migrants." Adjusted for inflation, the median household income per capita for Puerto Ricans increased 29 percent over the 1980s, the highest increase for any major racial or ethnic group. In 1979, Puerto Ricans' income trailed that of other Latines significantly, but by 1989, the average household income per capita of Puerto Ricans was essentially equal to that of Latines overall: in other words, as a group, Puerto Ricans had closed the income gap with other Latines and eliminated the Puerto Rican "exception," at least in terms of income. In addition, while Puerto Rican median household income per capita had been only 85 percent of non-Hispanic Black income in 1979, Puerto Rican income slightly exceeded Black income in 1989. By the early 1990s, as the discourse on the Puerto Rican exception was increasing in volume and stridency, Puerto Ricans were actually no longer that exceptional socioeconomically, neither compared with Latines as a whole nor compared with African Americans.[42]

It is important to keep in mind, however, that if Puerto Ricans, taken as an aggregate in 1990, were doing only as well as other Black and Latine people, that is a quite limited index of progress. In 1979, Puerto Ricans made 45 percent of non-Hispanic whites' income; by 1989, that had increased to 53 percent. As Puerto Rican income just barely squeaked above half of what white people earned, it was clear that Puerto Ricans' exceptionality vis-à-vis other Latines was only a small part of the problem. Equally troubling, the aggregate data obscured a significant divergence in economic conditions for Puerto Ricans. Puerto Ricans in Northeast and Midwest cities continued to struggle, while the growing number of Puerto Ricans in the Sunbelt were experiencing most of the gains. As a 1994 report from the National Puerto Rican Coalition explained, "The community has polarized into two groups: one shows significant movement into white-collar occupations, significant gains in education, and movement to the Sunbelt; the other, mostly non–high school graduates, live in the decaying neighborhoods of the older cities where crime, drugs, and the AIDS epidemic seem out of control." The improved economic position of Puerto Ricans in the aggregate actually hid massive disparities. Puerto Ricans in metropolitan Los Angeles, for example, had the highest per capita income ($12,032) among the areas sampled. This was nearly 80 percent of the overall average per capita income in metro LA. On the other end of the scale was Lawrence, Massachusetts: Puerto Ricans in the Lawrence metro area had a per capita income of only $4,228, a paltry 35 percent of what other residents in the metro area earned. In the 1980s, Puerto Ricans who remained concentrated in disinvested urban neighborhoods in the Northeast suffered, but many of those who managed to escape or evade the urban crisis and settle in the suburbs or the Sunbelt were thriving. The racialized metropolitan political economy at the root of the urban crisis had not disappeared; some Puerto Ricans were just managing to carve out a new place within it.[43]

Discussions of the Puerto Rican exception did not long outlive the urban crisis era. There are many potential reasons for this, and I can only speculate here. As segregation, concentrated poverty, and disinvestment in the "inner city" yielded to reinvestment, gentrification, and displacement in the 1990s, the very idea of a distinctly urban "underclass" seems to have lost its salience. Generations of Puerto Rican activism substantially increased Puerto Ricans' access to education, language rights, employment, housing, and political representation, and this has undoubtedly played a role in improving Puerto Ricans' economic circumstances. With the growth of a substantial undocumented immigrant population in the late twentieth and early twenty-first centuries, it is also possible that Puerto Rican citizenship—albeit second-class citizenship—gained increased significance and provided a degree of economic privilege within certain labor markets. The substantial dispersion of Puerto Ricans out of New York City and other Northeastern cities often improved their economic circumstances and may also have improved the ways they were depicted and perceived, defusing the distinctly anti–Puerto Rican stigma that had crystallized in an earlier era. The movement of Puerto Ricans to places like South Florida, where being Latine became associated with relative privilege, not deprivation, may have played a role in mitigating bias and discrimination. It is also possible that the national discourse around Latinidad that gained prominence in the 1990s and 2000s—particularly the perception of Latines as hard workers and family oriented—may have come to outweigh the specific stereotypes that had plagued Puerto Ricans. This is fertile ground for future research.[44]

We must be careful, however, not to prematurely celebrate the end of anti–Puerto Rican stereotypes. Instead, we should interrogate how stigmatizing discourses about Puerto Ricans have persisted and evolved and how they may have been incorporated into narratives about Latines more generally. While the broad brush of pan-ethnicity can often efface the experiences of smaller or marginalized groups, the reverse can also occur: the experiences of a highly visible (or sensationalized) few can shape how the broader group is viewed. Did the stigmatizing discourse of the Puerto Rican exception shape broader perceptions of Latines? Does the criminalization of Latines and their persistent depiction as lawbreakers originate not only in fear-mongering about illegal Mexican border crossings and Central American gangs but also in colonialist and distinctly urban stereotypes about Puerto Rican delinquency and rebelliousness? As I documented in *Latino City*, both immigration and welfare reform legislation in 1996 were shaped by the fear that the United States might become a "welfare magnet" for the world's poor. This "welfare magnet" discourse relied on and recycled long-standing depictions of Puerto Ricans as welfare abusers, extending a colonialist stigma to others in Latin America and throughout the Global South. Documenting the specificity of Puerto Rican historical experiences is therefore essential to understanding the creation of contemporary narratives and the treatment of Latines more broadly.[45]

Examining the Puerto Rican exception compels us to consider the history of racial capitalism in U.S. cities and of U.S. empire in the Caribbean. It demands we confront the exploitation and displacement of colonialism. It obliges us to reckon with anti-Black racism, segregation, and disinvestment and to take note of instances of solidarity and shared radical vision with African Americans. Puerto Ricans were not the only Latine group whose historical experiences are illuminated by such critical attention, however. If, as Juan Flores suggested, the "exception" might also be the "paradigm," then centering the history of Puerto Ricans offers a powerful methodological model for Latine urban history more broadly.[46]

Although the discursive hullabaloo over the Puerto Rican exception may have quieted, many Puerto Ricans still struggle with poverty, both in Puerto Rico and in diaspora, and the structural causes for that poverty have not disappeared. And, of course, coloniality continues to distort the island's economy and drive migration. This is particularly evident in Puerto Rico's twenty-first-century debt crisis and the colonialist financial domination of PROMESA (Puerto Rico Oversight, Management, and Economic Stability Act), and most tragically in the deaths, devastation, and renewed waves of migration after Hurricane Maria in 2017.[47] Puerto Ricans' unrestricted right to migrate gains a lot of attention, especially in comparison with the brutal barriers to migration for other Latin American and Caribbean peoples. But little is said about Puerto Ricans' right to stay home. As gentrification—spurred by colonialist economic policies—transforms Puerto Rico, activists are loudly trumpeting Puerto Ricans' right to the island: their right to remain there and thrive, to access housing and public spaces, and to determine its future. May this history of Puerto Rican struggles in diaspora strengthen their call.[48]

8

Latinx Palimpsest: Remaking a *Colonia* on the Edge of Aztlán

MAX KROCHMAL AND CECILIA SÁNCHEZ HILL

University of New Orleans and Texas Christian University

On August 1, 2017, at least five hundred protesters marched on the city hall of Fort Worth, Texas. Led by a group of Latinx college students and allies of all colors wearing red, the demonstrators traversed the city's frontier-era brick Main Street past downtown skyscrapers, chanting in both English and Spanish and carrying signs reading "No to SB 4." "*¡El pueblo, unido, jamás será vencido!*" they yelled, announcing their presence under the leadership of a new organization, United Fort Worth. News helicopters circled overhead, their deafening rotors competing with the crowd's noise. A series of speakers called on City Council members to voice their opposition to the recently passed state Senate Bill 4, a "show me your papers" statute requiring all law enforcement agencies to ask detainees about their citizenship status. Even the city's chief of police opposed the law, warning that it would have a chilling effect on immigrant communities, making it harder for officers to find and question witnesses, receive timely reports of crimes, and otherwise "protect and serve." Other cities across the state had filed suit to prevent the bill's implementation, but Fort Worth city leaders held back. United Fort Worth spokespeople demanded that the city council join the fray by endorsing the lawsuit. After the march, protesters went inside and testified before the council, offering heartfelt accounts of migration, discrimination, and the desire for inclusion. Two weeks later, they did so again—more than 150 speakers in total, outnumbering their restrictionist opponents 10–1. Yet the council majority sat unmoved, feigning bare interest in the testimonies before giving rote speeches justifying their inaction. After midnight, they voted 5–4

Briana Salas, Lucius Seger, and Evaliza Fuentes also contributed to this paper as part of a graduate seminar at Texas Christian University in the fall of 2021.

against joining the litigation. Those voting with the majority, which included the mayor, were all white Anglos, while the minority included one white, one Hispanic, and two Black members.[1]

Fort Worth remains unknown to much of the nation, the self-described "Cowtown" located "where the West begins." But it is the thirteenth-largest city in the United States (and the fifth largest in Texas), a "majority-minority" municipality of over 900,000 residents, the seat of the 2.1 million-inhabitant Tarrant County—yet still the forgotten stepsister of Dallas next door. The city traces deep roots to both the Jim Crow South and the Juan Crow Southwest, reflecting the nation's histories of genocide, enslavement, and conquest. The 2020 U.S. Census found that non-Hispanic whites remain the largest single ethno-racial group, although they account for just 36.63 percent of the city's population. Latinx peoples represent the second-largest group (34.81 percent), followed by Black residents (19.21 percent) and people of Asian descent (5.11 percent)—all of whom were likely undercounted. Few indigenous people inhabit the former frontier settlement stabilized by (and named for) a military post created to eliminate Indians.[2]

Despite its diverse demographics, Fort Worth operates as the fiefdom of a few powerful families—oligarchs whose names adorn the city's museums, hospitals, and universities.[3] An electoral outlier nationally, it is the largest U.S. city with a Republican mayor, at the heart of the nation's largest "red" county. Voter turnout in local elections rarely exceeds 10 percent and sometimes dips as low as 6 percent, while countless more voters remain disfranchised as a result of a broken immigration system that depends on undocumented workers but impedes naturalization, criminal records in a "justice" system that targets Black and Latinx people, recent voter ID laws, and other forms of suppression. The city fathers can easily buy candidates for local office, and through 2022, only one of the council's single-member districts had ever elected a Latino (and never a Latina). By most measures, the old Jim Crow and Juan Crow caste systems persist.

The 2017 uprising against SB 4 shook the city's power structure and began to transform the landscape of local politics.[4] Occurring in tandem with a parallel campaign against police brutality led by African Americans, it announced the entry of an organized, independent bloc into local politics, threatening the downtown growth machine and its ostensibly color-blind conservative political consensus for the first time in decades.

Underneath the surface, however, for more than a century ordinary Latinx people had engaged in the making and remaking of Fort Worth. In a story with parallels across much of the Southwest, small numbers of Latinx immigrants had built much of the city's basic infrastructure and industry beginning in the 1880s. They formed a *colonia* that fostered a cohesive ethnic community despite being split geographically across town. Over generations, activists in the barrios developed new hybrid Mexican American and Chicano/a cultural formations. Still, as late as 1970, people of "Spanish origin or descent" represented only 8.5 percent of the city's population. They remained "in the waiting room" of Fort Worth history and politics. Most non-Hispanic observers still perceived the city's Latinx residents as relative newcomers, colorful, foreign and, in any case, contained and inert.[5]

Then, over the fifty years that followed, new waves of migrants, mostly from Mexico, radically altered huge swaths of the city. Spanish is now the lingua franca in many areas, Latinx-oriented businesses predominate inside the Interstate 820 loop, and real Mexican food has become the city's most visible cuisine. Immigrant enclaves sit on top of reinvigorated older barrios and push outward into historically White and Black sections. The city can be understood only as a Latinx palimpsest, a landscape experiencing rapid change from newcomers who are building new communities amidst the older but still visible *colonia* as well as on top of the heritage of Jim Crow and Juan Crow segregation.

A closer look at the many layers of Fort Worth's history demonstrates that much of the city's growth has depended upon generations of migrants who built the city's basic infrastructure and, more recently, have created vibrant communities amidst the ashes of urban disinvestment. Even as local politicians demonize or marginalize immigrants, including via the selective incorporation of long-term Hispanic residents, Latinx newcomers are remaking the city in their own image, buying property, opening businesses, and organizing their neighbors to create a rising tide that is lifting all of the city's boats.

Fort Worth's Latinx *Colonia*

In 1880, four years after the railroad arrived in Fort Worth, fourteen Mexicans appeared on the census records, a first for the city.[6] Although most passed through Fort Worth seeking work, thousands chose to stay. By the 1910s, Mexicans lived in a few different barrios and began forming a strong, if dispersed, community. They held large gatherings (of two thousand people in 1917 and six thousand in 1924) to celebrate Mexican Independence Day, raised money for the Red Cross, encouraged "their countrymen" to support the United States during World War I, and went on strike to demand higher wages and shorter workdays.[7] City leaders did not always welcome the new residents. Referring to them as "idle Mexicans" and "surplus Mexicans," as the *Fort Worth Star-Telegram* did, local officials worked alongside the Mexican consulate, local welfare agencies, and community centers to remove four thousand Mexicans from the city in 1921.[8] Throughout that spring and summer, the *Star-Telegram* reported on multiple trainloads, each with hundreds of Mexicans, leaving the city for Laredo and then to Mexico.[9]

A neighborhood known as La Corte had formed downtown near the Trinity River by the 1930s. It was home to more than a hundred Mexican families and housed the district's separate institution for Mexican children.[10] In a 1930 report, this "Mexican school" received one of the lowest scores; it required "extensive rehabilitation, additions, and repairs" but was not included in plans for repairs.[11] The report also noted the increasing population of Mexican children near A. J. Chambers Elementary School, which at the time was "completely surrounded by negroes" amid a decreasing white population. District staff contended that the campus would need no further attention because they could instead convert it into a Mexican school. The Fort Worth Housing Authority later demolished the neighborhood to make room for the white-only Ripley Arnold Public Housing project. Many of the demolished barrio's displaced Mexican families then faced hostility as they attempted to move into historically white communities whose residents tried to restrict Mexicans to the east of Main Street in the city's still diverse Northside neighborhood. According to G. A. Walls, the superintendent of the Mexican Presbyterian Center, they "settle[d] in one place . . . not because they are Mexican but because it would be better for them."[12]

At the end of World War II, most Mexicans and Mexican Americans in Fort Worth lived in two communities, the Northside and Southside. Both areas produced leaders, many of them veterans, who spoke loudly to city officials about their communities' needs. Gilbert C. Garcia organized a branch of the newly founded American G.I. Forum in 1949 after meeting Dr. Hector P. Garcia in Corpus Christi, Texas. According to Linda Garcia, Gilbert's wife, he could not stop talking about Dr. Garcia's ambitious plans for the organization. Linda organized the Ladies Auxiliary, and they both worked with the Forum throughout the 1950s. By decade's end, the *Fort Worth Star-Telegram* reported that Gilbert had helped increase the paid poll taxes of Mexicans from just fifty to two thousand, assisted students in preparing for and staying in school, mediated between businesses and Mexicans who alleged discrimination against them, campaigned successfully to get the police department to hire a Mexican American, and established a Boy Scout troop that Garcia described as "American as ham and eggs."[13] Gilbert and Linda continued their activism into the early 1960s through the Viva Kennedy clubs and the Political Association of Spanish-Speaking Organizations, or PASO.

In the late 1960s, younger activists calling themselves Chicanos and Chicanas joined the fray in Fort Worth and began to speak in less accommodating tones. Many met their elders in G.I. Forum meetings and attempted to cooperate with them. They participated enthusiastically in the United Farm Workers' grape boycotts and invited César Chávez to the city, but they faced an uphill battle locally. At the time of Chávez's visit in November 1969, grape sales were down 33 percent nationwide but had increased 12 percent in Fort Worth.[14] The city's Chicanas and Chicanos also served their communities as social workers through the Community Action Agencies of the War on Poverty. But they observed that they did the grunt work while their elders sat on the board.

By the 1970s, a series of incidents of police brutality and discrimination clarified the distinction between the two groups of activists. After policemen in the western suburb of Lake Worth beat several Mexican wedding guests without provocation, and a grand jury dismissed any charges against the officers, the city's Mexican American elders told the Chicano activists not to organize a protest. Soon after, the *Fort Worth Star-Telegram* asked the Chicanos for their reactions. In the paper's first special edition dedicated to "The Mexican American in Fort Worth," Chicano activists aired their grievances and described persistent abuse by law enforcement, as well as discrimination in housing, employment, and schooling. Although the young white journalism interns assigned to the story hewed to the "culture of poverty" theory, the Chicano social workers believed the articles accurately portrayed the issues confronting Mexican-descended people in the city. By contrast, the elder board members of the Community Action Agency expressed frustration with the paper's use of the term *Chicano* and the "immature" interviewees. "There are at least 40 people who have been successful in business," complained J. P. Zepeda. "They are the ones who should have been contacted, not some social workers."[15] At a meeting of the Worth Heights Barrio Betterment Council of the Community Action Agency, the social workers retorted that "perhaps those who expressed displeasure about the section were unhappy because they were not interviewed."[16] Following these incidents and a near fistfight at another local Mexican American leadership conference, Gilbert Garcia established the Chicano Luncheon to encourage unity among activists.

By the late 1970s, Mexican American and Chicano/a activists in Fort Worth settled into a new paradigm. The nascent radicalism of the *movimiento* years had given way to a system of token representation in which businessmen in the Hispanic Chamber of Commerce allied with Anglo oligarchs downtown to select "responsible" leaders for the only majority-Latinx single-member city council district on the Northside. Latinx peoples on the Southside enjoyed only proxy representation via their coethnics across town.

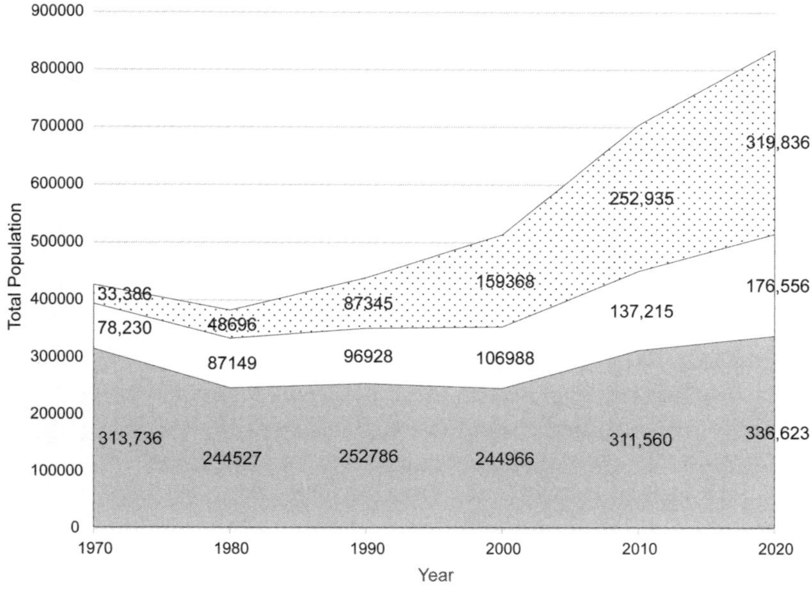

FIGURE 8.1. Fort Worth Population, 1970–2020.

Middle-class Mexican Americans again assumed the mantle of political leadership, attempting to meet the needs of their communities but avoiding actions that might cost them their seats at the table with Fort Worth's white establishment. Other self-appointed Mexican American community leaders kept their focus on education, entrepreneurship, and homeownership. Although it was born of grassroots activism, the Chicano Luncheon became a space for sundry politicians to speak to Mexican American small businessmen, political operatives, and social service providers. The radical critiques of the past were a distant memory. In the early 1980s, Sam Garcia, another veteran and G.I. Forum member, published *Community News and Events*, a newsletter that reached more than ten thousand homes and businesses. It reported on the monthly meetings of various "Hispanic" organizations, the good deeds of local politicians, social issues related to Mexican Americans, local companies' employment needs, and the dates of upcoming elections. Similarly, the Hispanic Directory, a listing of Hispanic-owned businesses in the area created by both Sam Garcia and Gilbert Garcia (no relation), helped support the growing Mexican American middle class by making it legible to the city's white business leaders. Yet neither publication nor any of the

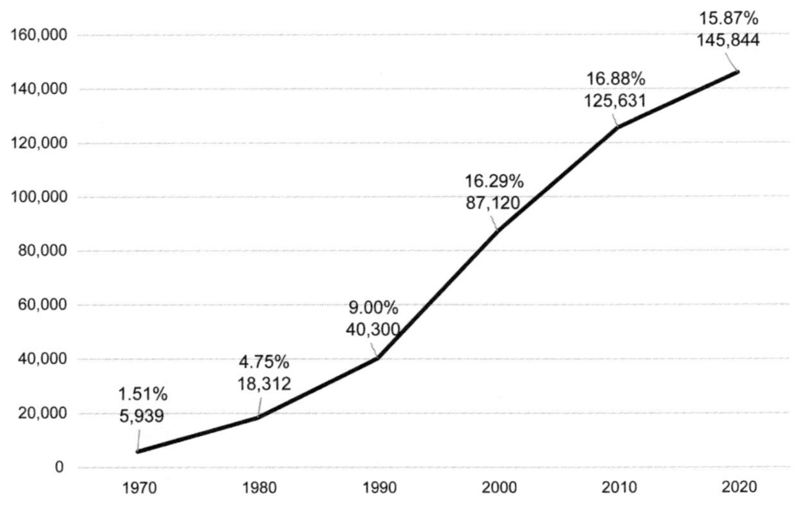

FIGURE 8.2. Foreign-born population (all).

numerous "Hispanic" organizations actually spoke for or to the majority of ordinary Mexican Americans—and increasingly, Mexican immigrants—still struggling in the barrios. Transformative change was no longer on the table, only individual uplift. The new political and economic arrangements proved stable and good for business, even as the vestiges of Juan Crow remained.[17]

Yet in the background a demographic revolution remade the city, setting the stage for new Latinx political formations. As shown in figure 8.1, Latinxs accounted for most of Fort Worth's population growth. Of the city's net gain of more than half a million residents from 1970 to 2020, over 286,000 were of Hispanic heritage, alongside 98,000 Black people and only 13,000 whites. Over those fifty years, Latinxs had grown from less than 9 percent to nearly 35 percent of city residents. Meanwhile, the city's foreign-born population mirrored this growth, rising from 6,000 to 146,000 and from a mere 1.5 percent to 16 percent (fig. 8.2). Among Latinxs, at least 30 percent of city residents were foreign-born.[18] What did these changes mean for the longer-term *colonia* in the city? How did the arrival of these newcomers affect those communities and the city as a whole? And what did it mean that they entered a city with an already-established Latinx population and with preexisting histories of Jim Crow and Juan Crow?

Polytechnic Heights: A Microcosm of Fort Worth

To answer these questions, we turn to Polytechnic Heights, a nearly three-square-mile neighborhood on the city's Eastside, roughly four miles from city hall. In "Poly," as locals call it, much of Fort Worth's urban history can be seen in microcosm, often in exaggerated relief. At the same time, the specific shape of the emerging Latinx community in Poly stemmed from its location away from other, more established barrios, rapid and intense private capital flight, and protracted neglect by City Hall and allied nonprofits, often cloaked as well-intentioned but failed interventions.

From its origins as a slave labor camp built on stolen indigenous lands, Poly experienced several demographic revolutions—from white to Black and, more recently, majority Latinx.[19] Originally a postbellum independent municipality linked to Fort Worth by train, Polytechnic was annexed into the city, serving as a semirural streetcar suburb before the World War II boom and interstate highways pulled the professionals and managers away. By the 1950s, Poly had become known as a heavily white, largely working-class, tough neighborhood shored up by its proximity to downtown and crumbling Jim Crow segregation. Once African Americans effectively challenged the caste system, whites fled.[20]

As seen in figure 8.3, the numerical shifts were dramatic: In 1960, Poly remained 99.8 percent white, with only 18 African Americans appearing in the Census. By 1970, the neighborhood of around 13,000 people was already 10.5 percent Black. White flight then accelerated so rapidly that by 1980, the Black population quintupled to nearly 6,900 people (51 percent), while its Latinx demographic quietly doubled to 1,687 (12.5 percent). Whites accounted for just 35.5 percent of the neighborhood's population.[21]

By 1980, many residents and outside observers held a grim view of daily life in Poly. The *Star-Telegram* linked the neighborhood's present to its frontier past: "Wolves wandered into the front yards when Polytechnic was an independent city, old-timers say. It took some effort, but the early settlers got rid of the animals. In the 1960s, the wolves came back, this time in the clothing of urban blight, baring fangs of crime and deterioration." The subtext was all about racial difference: the "old-timers" and "settlers" were white, while the "wolves" represented not just social ills but also the Black people who perpetrated them. But the (white) "Poly residents again are fighting the wolves, and it's the 'old-timers' who have taken charge," working now in collaboration with "ambitious new residents" and various nonprofits to restore the area to its past glory. As another article put it two years later, "The challenge facing Poly is whether multi-racial organizations can join to keep the community integrated and economically sound."[22]

The neighborhood's lack of resources became its essence. Throughout the 1980s and into the 1990s, Poly became a Rorschach test upon which residents and outsiders projected their fears, hopes, and visions. Regular profiles in the

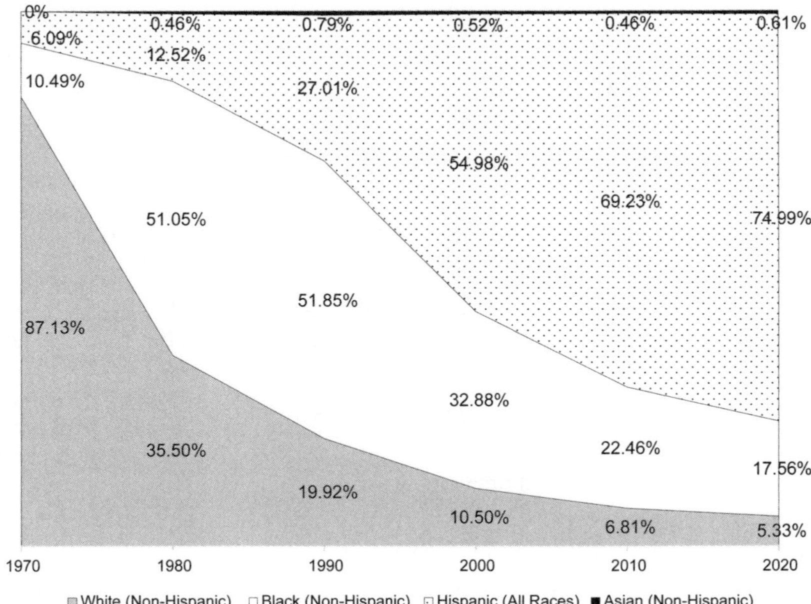

FIGURE 8.3. Polytechnic Heights demographics, 1970–2020 (on 2010 tracts).

Star-Telegram sought to unpack the dizzying kaleidoscope of revitalization, renewal, and uplift efforts while also attempting to portray and garner sympathy for the area's diverse residents. Perhaps most promising was the Black-led Liberation Community Inc., which worked with area residents to rebuild entire blocks, with area residents driving the decision-making processes and contributing much of the labor. Still, these efforts struggled to build enduring relationships with ordinary residents in Poly, especially Latinx newcomers. As one newspaper article put it, "On the streets of Polytechnic, people are largely unaware of the ambitious plans and pronouncements of the downtown bureaucrats and marketeers. . . . They talk of survival and of a neighborhood that is vanishing."[23]

Across the board, "revitalization" efforts remained undercapitalized and ill equipped for the ravages of the free market. The city's Economic Development Corporation, federal Community Development Block Grants, and small private donations spurred less reinvestment than hoped, as commercial banks mostly refrained from investing, and insurers remained skeptical. In contrast, the Fort Worth Police Department did not need to fundraise for its new Weed and Seed program, an expansion of both community-based and broken windows policing centered on Poly that predictably resulted first in a spike in crime statistics and then a much-celebrated and probably meaningless decline.[24] Eventually, even community development advocates lost hope. The newspaper reported in 1989 that "a staggering exodus of blacks and whites" was taking place. Businesses were closing and stood empty, along with hundreds of vacant houses.[25] Still, the efforts of residents and neighborhood advocates did have some effect. The various government and nonprofit groups provided enough low-income loans, educational programs, community empowerment workshops, and other services to staunch the bleeding. In the end, many of the vacant houses were not demolished but acquired by new owners.

Migration and Regeneration in the New Poly

Where government-sponsored efforts failed, ordinary people succeeded. The restrictionist inclinations of Fort Worth's city fathers did not prevent Poly from becoming a leading destination for immigrants from Mexico and Latin America. By 2000, Latinx peoples represented the largest nonwhite group in Poly, where they formed an absolute majority (55 percent). Meanwhile, the share of African Americans dropped to 33 percent. Two decades later, in 2020, Latinx peoples represented fully three-quarters of Poly's population, while roughly one in six neighborhood residents was Black. Only 696 white residents remained—just 5.3 percent.

The neighborhood's economic indicators reflected both the disinvestment wrought by white flight and Black departure and its gradual rebirth thanks to community resiliency and Latinx in-migration. Put simply, decline in the 1980s gave way to rebound in the 1990s. In the first decade, median household income in Poly fell by 16.6 percent (in constant dollars), rent rates grew by 13 percent, the housing vacancy rate skyrocketed, the share of owner-occupied homes fell, and the poverty rate increased substantially. The residents of Poly were indeed "left behind," squeezed to pay higher rent even as incomes fell and housing units stood empty. Then, in the 1990s, median household income in Poly increased by nearly 16 percent, the neighborhood's poverty rate fell to 26 percent, the percentage of owner-occupied households rebounded, and the number of vacant residential units plummeted, at least in part due to demolition.[26]

Who were these new Latinx residents of Poly? Already in 2000, they were mostly immigrants, a new development in the neighborhood's history. In 1970, the Census counted only 78 foreign-born people in Polytechnic Heights.

By 2000, that number had skyrocketed to a whopping 3,992—fully 30 percent of Poly's population. Ninety-five percent of the immigrants hailed from Mexico, and six in ten had immigrated to the United States in the previous decade. Meanwhile, among the over 7,000 Latinx people counted by the Census in Poly (of any nativity and citizenship status), 90 percent identified as of "Mexican" origin, including some from generations-old Tejano Families. In short, the neighborhood's largest ethno-racial group consisted of a blend of very recent arrivals from Mexico, prior groups of Mexican immigrants, Mexican Americans, and old-stock "Hispanic" residents.[27] And half of all Poly respondents over five years of age spoke Spanish at home, with some two-thirds of that subgroup speaking English "less than 'very well.'"[28]

These demographic transitions and boomeranging economic indicators demonstrate that the new Latinx residents of Poly moved into an area defined first by the white exclusion of nonwhites, then white flight following its integration by African Americans, then relative Black dominance and power, and finally Black departure and Latinx in-migration. Each of these shifts proved value-laden. Prior to World War II, Poly's white residents enjoyed new city services, expanding housing stock, and well-regarded educational institutions. In contrast, the post–civil rights period of Black predominance was accompanied by neglect and disinvestment from city hall and private capital alike, along with several halted renewal efforts and enhanced policing. The beginning of Poly's Latinx-led era followed decades of seeming decline and community resiliency.

Oral histories with Latinx newcomers demonstrate how the migrant families carved out space for themselves and contributed to the regeneration of Polytechnic Heights and Fort Worth as a whole. Ramon Romero Sr. and his wife, Maria de Refugio (nicknamed "Cuca"), migrated to Poly from Mexico in 1969. As in other integrating communities across the nation, as Black families moved in, white families rushed to sell their homes, further depressing property values. Romero began purchasing inexpensive homes in the neighborhood in the mid-1970s. His son Ramon Romero Jr. now represents Poly and the rest of District 90 in the Texas House of Representatives, having defeated an eighteen-year incumbent in the 2014 Democratic Primary to become that body's first Latino member from Tarrant County. Ramon Jr. remembers working on his father's rental homes from an early age, along with his siblings. The elder Romero eventually accumulated twelve houses that he made available to other families like his own, immigrants who needed a place to begin their lives in the United States. Without the aid of city services, Romero's labor helped improve the housing conditions of his new community. His business had no name. According to the junior Romero, people in the neighborhood just knew to ask "Don Ramon" and Cuca for help settling in Poly.

While Don Ramon and his children made tangible changes to Poly's landscape, Cuca made spiritual changes to the neighborhood. Although some Northside and Southside parishes conducted masses in Spanish in those barrios, the Catholic churches on the Eastside did not. Cuca worked with Father Hoover at Holy Name of Jesus Catholic Church in Poly to convince him to begin learning Spanish and to establish a branch of the Sociedades Guadalupanas. The local branch of the diasporic society raised money for community needs, helping convince Father Hoover to begin offering a Spanish mass. Holy Name is now one of the city's largest Catholic churches, and all its Sunday masses and most of its newsletters are in Spanish.

The Romeros arrived in the neighborhood early enough to witness the changing demographics of the community. With the decreasing municipal services that paralleled the transition from a white to a Black and eventually a Latinx Poly, Don Ramon and Cuca had invested their money and energy to create spaces that welcomed the newly arriving Latinx immigrants. Ramon Romero Jr. followed their example. Born in 1973, the junior Romero has lived his entire life in Poly. He purchased a home when he was twenty-one and still lives in it today. He described the neighborhood as "one of the most beautiful, overlooked parts of town" and touted its proximity to downtown, parks, and people, as well as the absence of traffic, as some of the reasons he still calls Poly home.[29] Although Romero's memories of his upbringing in Poly are positive, they reflect the city's inattention to the needs of neighborhood youth as well the neighborhood's changing demographics. Romero fondly recalls playing with both Black and Latinx friends on the streets of the neighborhood. He said it was not just one or two kids, but some thirty to forty kids who ran around together, eating from fig and pear trees and picking up and shelling pecans. Romero's group's good, clean fun sometimes resulted in mischief, acts that doubled as quiet defiance of the city's racial and class norms. For example, the kids jumped the fence to gain free entry into the city pool at Sycamore Park. Romero also recalled playing tricks on the campus security guards at Texas Wesleyan College because they would not let their multiracial group of youths walk through the still predominately white and elite campus.

Romero's teenage years in the late 1980s and early 1990s remained tranquil, even as he and his friends ventured into new spaces that opened doors for Black and Latinx youth. He remembered spending Sundays with his siblings, cousins, and friends in Trinity Park near downtown, cruising and playing volleyball on the one day each week on which Latinx peoples from across the city converged. On other days, Romero socialized with African

American kids at Sycamore Park and attended multiracial parties sponsored by K104, the local hip-hop radio station. Although he recalled some violent interactions between white, Black, and Latinx youths, Romero maintained that music and dance blurred racial lines and included all people from the neighborhood. He remembered hanging out and playing video games at Ashburn's Ice Cream Parlor (where he also worked his "first real job") and going to Jolly Time Skating Rink, where he watched his brother win breakdancing competitions featuring Black and Latinx kids. Romero attended Polytechnic ("Poly") High, graduating in 1992 following stints at both North Side and Trimble Tech, two traditional schools for Mexican Americans in the city's main barrios. Romero recalled that the gangs that infiltrated North Side High School made it difficult for a "Mexicano" from the Eastside to safely walk its halls, while, in contrast, he remembered Poly High as a "melting pot . . . probably half Black, half Latino, and a little bit of Anglo." He concluded that Poly High was a safe place with wonderful teachers who loved their students despite occasional fights and their own gangs.[30]

Romero's experiences propelled him into both an occupation and a vocation that continued his parents' more intentional work of revitalizing the community. A few years after graduating, he attended a community meeting at the urging of his mother. He was unaware of its agenda, but he was accustomed to serving as an interpreter for his immigrant parents. As it happened, the gathering centered on the school district's plan to expand Poly High's footprint to accommodate the building of new baseball fields just blocks from his family home on Avenue D. The next thing he knew, the neighbors had elected the young bilingual community college dropout as the leader of what they called the "El Poly Pyramid" Neighborhood Association. Recognizing the need for a collective voice to create change, Romero began his career in public life. At the same time, he launched a pool installation business that grew to employ sixty people by the time he was twenty-five. Romero's business and work in the neighborhood association led him to volunteer for a seat on the city's planning commission, to stage an unsuccessful bid for city council, and finally to gain a seat in the state legislature.[31] Today, Romero is fully aware of the immigrant community that "raised him" and wants to help make them feel safe in their communities.[32] He often reminds other local leaders that just "because they cannot vote does not mean that's not who you are serving."[33]

Much like the Romero family, Toni and Louie Ruiz began buying and renting out properties in Poly shortly after they arrived in the late 1980s. The investment of their limited capital and ample sweat equity contributed to the preservation of the area's housing stock and the Latinization of its daily rhythms. Like the Romeros, the Ruizes recognized the need for more affordable housing and benefited from white flight. In her interview, Toni recalled that Louie got a job with FHA Investments, a private LLC, remodeling homes that the company owned in the neighborhood. While Louie was at work, a well-dressed man in a Cadillac pulled up to one of the boarded-up homes and asked if he was interested in purchasing any of the surrounding houses. Louie said he did not have the money to buy them, but the gentleman replied that he owned Weatherford Bank and would finance the purchase of some of the foreclosed properties that he had just acquired. The mortgages cost them less than eighty dollars a month, so they purchased seven or eight properties, and Louie began remodeling them. This moment reflects the aftereffects of white flight, as a desperate absentee owner canvassed the neighborhood and then provided accessible financing at good terms to an otherwise ineligible buyer—in this case, a Latino contractor with little capital or credit of his own.

The Ruizes had faith that they could recoup their investments and help the neighborhood rebound, and the side hustle soon became their full-time job. They purchased a duplex on Avenue K and made it into their offices. Shortly after, they met a couple of women from Oklahoma who had inherited land in Poly from their parents. The women wanted to sell the land and offered to owner finance it. The Ruizes paid one hundred dollars per month on the mortgage, which bought an astonishing thirty-five lots just behind their offices. In a short period of time, the Ruizes had become owners of a large swath of the crumbling neighborhood. They recognized Poly's potential as a home for both the city's dispossessed African American and new Latinx migrants and made the area's fortunes their own.

As landlords in the transitioning neighborhood, the Ruizes at times negotiated conflicts with their Black neighbors and tenants. Toni recalled that in 1989, Louie met a local pastor named Mr. Lampkins who owned some property on Vaughn Boulevard, the neighborhood's formerly thriving commercial corridor. The preacher offered to sell the property at a cheap price, but he required that the Ruizes be responsible for its tenants. Toni remembered going with her husband to tour the dilapidated home. She recalled telling her husband: "We are not buying this property. This is scary." But Louie replied, "Oh no, this is perfect!" Toni recalled that her husband "made himself at home with the people that were in there. . . . I think it was more like a prostitute and drug house. Everybody was lying around on the floor and the bed, and someone was cooking in the back, and my husband goes, 'Oh, it sure smells good—is breakfast ready?' "[34] Despite this warm reception, the Ruizes soon evicted the tenants and moved their offices into the building, reasoning that if the tenants' illicit business was good on this corner, his property management would succeed too. It was a risky, confrontational strategy—and one that prioritized the family's capital accumulation over his tenants' residential continuity. Indeed, Louie had to arm himself, at times literally, to fight his way into the impoverished community. Still, the Ruizes continued to purchase more rundown homes in Poly. To build positive relationships with their new neighbors, they often hired Black men from the community to repair and maintain the homes. Toni remembered one particular man nicknamed "Cornbread" who worked for Louie for many years. Louie helped him take care of his wheelchair-bound mother and often worked alongside him. Cornbread became the Ruizes' character reference, vouching for them to other skeptical neighborhood residents.

As the Ruizes' real estate business prospered into the new millennium, they also invested in reshaping Poly to welcome the growing number of Latinx immigrants. Louie bought an old bar on Vaughn Boulevard and turned it into a restaurant, since the neighborhood did not yet have many Latinx-oriented businesses. Toni recalled opening Café Campesinos Mexican Restaurant in 2003. Reaching back to their California roots, Toni chose the name and used imagery from the United Farm Workers throughout the restaurant. César Chávez appeared on an outside wall in a mural painted by Poly High School art students, and in 2004, Dolores Huerta came for a visit after the Fort Worth Independent School District named a Northside elementary school in her honor. The Ruizes' passion for honoring and celebrating the farmworkers union went beyond the décor. In 2006, Toni helped start the César Chávez Committee of Tarrant County, which held its meetings at the restaurant. The group organized solidarity walks through the neighborhood and later an annual march and rally in downtown Fort Worth—events that made the city's Latinx migrants visible and connected them with the longer history of Mexicanos in Texas and the Southwest. The Ruizes remember picking grapes and oranges in the summer as kids in California, and the restaurant included photos of their family working the fields back home. Toni hopes that the committee, now an incorporated nonprofit organization, will eventually purchase the old Poly Theater, also on Vaughn Boulevard, for its new headquarters. Although their success as neighborhood real estate tycoons stemmed from white flight and at times resulted in friction with their Black neighbors, the Ruizes' expanding property businesses, restaurant venture, and activism helped regenerate the neighborhood and paved a path for further Latinx immigration.

A third and final example is Geovanni Rojero, a young entrepreneur who arrived from Mexico with his parents as an infant in 2000. His unconventional path to running his own business and owning properties in Poly began with his father's talents in making *cintos de pita*, elaborately decorated hand-stitched belts that were popular among vaqueros in his village near Sombrerete, Zacatecas. His dad was surprised to discover that Texans wanted to buy his cowboy couture, so he also began importing and reselling boots out of his home. Eventually, the family opened up a small store, Botas Rojero, on Vaughn Boulevard. At fifteen years old, Geovanni took over when his mom had grown tired of it and wanted to close its doors. For the next three years, he juggled school at Poly High with his growing western-wear store. With business booming and their parking lot proving too small, Rojero purchased a larger property at the northern edge of Poly, on Ayers Avenue, adjacent to the Texas and Pacific train tracks. His sister, Alejandra, started working with Geovanni and convinced him to experiment with selling women's clothing. The new products flew off the shelves, quickly becoming the majority of their business. Thanks to this flexibility and extensive use of social media and branding, Botas Rojero is doing better than ever. With Geovanni's support, Alejandra is opening up her own boutique in Poly to sell more urbane women's clothing "for going out." Geovanni has also purchased another old building in Poly that he plans to restore into a large entertainment hall for weddings, quinceañeras, and other community celebrations—a venture that, much like Café Campesinos, would also create vital space for the mushrooming Latinx immigrant community.

Geovanni's desire to continue investing in his community stems from his experiences growing up in the neighborhood. At William James Middle School and Polytechnic High School, he saw how Poly residents and youth "were always left behind." He noticed a huge difference when he attended McClung Middle School just on the other side of Interstate 820. "The football team had all the equipment brand new," he recalled. "At William James, we had equipment [that had been] there probably for . . . twenty years, thirty years." Watching the parents of the opposing teams cheer in the stands and the fancy trucks they drove to the games made him keenly aware of all that he and his teammates did not have. His parents worked and could not attend their games, while some of his friends had parents "in jail because of drugs and violence." Rojero remembered that one of his friend's grandparents tried to shield them from their parents' indiscretions and addictions, but the kids always knew what was going on. He attributes the recent decrease in gang violence and the growing economic resurgence in Poly to his classmates' collective determination to take a different path. Rojero remembered the visible presence of police officers in Poly, but he maintained that they had not made any positive difference in the neighborhood. Instead, he said, "I think what makes a difference is [when] people get tired . . . they didn't want to be the new generation of that . . . same violence . . . They don't want to keep doing it . . . [but] not because there are a lot of cops."[35] For change to occur in his neighborhood, he concluded, community members themselves had to act. The Rojero family's success in business thus went hand in glove with deep connections and enduring concern for the entire neighborhood and its residents. Together with the Ruizes and Romeros, they engaged in placemaking, rebuilding Poly's economic foundation and regenerating its culture to become a true home for Latinx migrants. Their labors and investments revitalized from the bottom up a part of Fort Worth that had long been neglected by city fathers. The area continues to experience high poverty rates, but its population has rebounded, and its economy is growing. In Poly, as across the city, Latinx immigrants provided the spark for rebirth—even as politicians downplayed their contributions and sought to exclude them.

Poly High and the Struggle for Immigrant Rights

The disjuncture between city officials and the people who were rebuilding the neighborhood was exemplified in the area's most enduring institution, Polytechnic High School—especially in the ways its students and community activists struggled to create a more welcoming environment for immigrant families and to make local governance responsive to Poly's new residents. Poly High reflected the ebb and flow of the neighborhood's residents and fortunes, including its many demographic shifts, ongoing political marginality, and the resiliency and ingenuity of its people, including the latest *migrantes*. By 2000, the school's Latinx student population neared 50 percent, including an increasing number of foreign-born and second-generation students. They soon made their mark on the Poly High campus: both the boys' and girls' soccer teams garnered coverage in the *Star-Telegram*, and another edition ran a front-page feature on the son of immigrants with only grade school educations who was offered admission by all eight Ivy League schools.[36] But despite these extraordinary accomplishments, Poly High continued to suffer from a lack of resources, compounded by the alleged accountability mechanisms of No Child Left Behind. Between 2005 and 2008, the school received an "unacceptable" rating from the state based on its students' low scores on the Texas Assessment of Knowledge and Skills standardized test. A fifth consecutive failure would have resulted in the state's closure of the school. Yet a double-digit increase in test scores in 2009 provided a stay of execution, leading to a community-wide celebration that spilled into the streets. Tommie Carter, a 1971 graduate, remarked, "I love this . . . It makes my heart proud and glad to be a graduate of Poly High School."[37]

The school's hard-won successes contrasted sharply with its neighborhood's ongoing political marginalization. This proved even clearer when Poly High students joined their counterparts nationwide in demonstrating against HR 4437, the Sensenbrenner Bill, in the spring of 2006. The proposed legislation would have made being an undocumented migrant in the United States punishable as a felony offense, built a new border wall, and imposed harsher sanctions on employers that hired undocumented workers. After hearing about a student-led protest, Reyna Martinez and Judith Balleza decided to organize their classmates, sparking a movement across Fort Worth. The *Star-Telegram*'s Diane Smith reported that Martinez "talked to some friends. They talked to their friends. By lunchtime, a rally was in the works. 'When the bell rings, don't go to sixth period,' students told one another. 'Go to the parking lot.'" About two hundred students headed for the exits and outside, "but school officials ended the rally quickly and sent the teens back to class." The majority of the school's thousand students were Hispanic, mirroring the district as a whole, and many hailed from mixed-status families. "This is not something we can ignore," Martinez told the newspaper. "Most of our parents don't have papers."[38]

The next morning, the Poly students staged another rally outside the school, waving Mexican flags and homemade signs as they marched three miles to downtown Fort Worth. Some called and texted their friends, and the walkouts spread across town. Helpless police officers tried to keep the students on the sidewalk, at one point pulling demonstrators out of the crowd to cite them for jaywalking. Fort Worth Independent School District officials rushed downtown with empty buses to beg the students to return to school. "You've made your point," the deputy superintendent Pat Linares chided them.[39] Yet many lingered for hours, claiming both physical and metaphorical space in the city by occupying, even if for just a day, the normally high-rent, heavily privatized, and overwhelmingly white downtown. They also claimed the "right to be" in Fort Worth and in the United States generally, to keep their families and diasporic communities together in their adopted home. "A family is the most important thing we have," Balleza, the Poly student, said. "If we lose one, it's like losing everybody."[40]

Most adult reactions to the walkouts proved predictably condescending. At a regularly scheduled school board meeting, Superintendent Melody Johnson made her position clear. "We don't condone the walkouts," she said, adding that students would be assigned unexcused absences.[41] *Star-Telegram* columnist Bud Kennedy blasted them as opportunists who took advantage of legitimate grievances to skip class, neophytes who targeted the wrong levels of government, and clueless kids who inexplicably carried Mexican flags while chanting "¡Viva México!"[42] Still, the demonstrations continued in both Fort Worth and Dallas, where as many as a half million people joined the Mega Marcha on April 9.[43]

On May 1, the Day without Immigrants, or El Gran Paro Americano, Poly students joined the nationwide general strike. Several fifth-grade students at T. A. Sims Elementary School, a feeder of Poly High, were surprised by their teacher's reaction the next day. One mother reported that Jan Shannon, a twenty-year veteran educator, had forced her eleven-year-old child and several other students to sit in the sun outside for two hours, even denying them access to a drinking fountain and proper shelter so that they came home with sunburns. Shannon reportedly also refused to accept the students' district-approved makeup assignment and insulted them repeatedly.[44] District officials placed Shannon on administrative leave while they investigated the parents' complaints, but they determined only that she had placed them outside her classroom unsupervised during one hour of instructional time—a practice "that was not out of the ordinary at the school." Investigators further concluded that they "could not prove that Shannon used racial slurs or criticized the students for participating in an immigration demonstration," as parents had alleged. In the end, Shannon rejected the district's proposed suspension and resigned instead. Still, the incident reinforced the parents'—and the neighborhood's—ongoing political exclusion.[45]

The persistence of these issues was on display again more than a decade later, in 2017, when Fort Worth high school students staged two additional rounds of walkouts, first in February in support of another Day without Immigrants and later in September in protest of the Trump administration's rollback of the Deferred Action for Childhood Arrivals (DACA) executive order and the state's passage of SB 4. Although Poly High students did not feature as prominently as in 2006, members of United Fort Worth (UFW) actively supported the September protests, building on the momentum of the mass marches and returning to their home base—most of the cofounders of UFW first came together while students at the neighborhood's Texas Wesleyan University.[46]

The immigrant rights struggle of the twenty-first century made plain the gap between the lived realities of recent arrivals in Fort Worth and their hostile reception by city leaders. Immigrants and allies repeatedly bared their souls, pleading with local government officials to make their city more secure and humane, while politicians waffled between passive neutrality and outright contempt. After the demonstrations of 2017 and the city council's refusal to take action against SB 4, UFW carried the struggle forward in new arenas. They worked to bring migration and other issues specific to Latinx communities to the attention of the City's new Race and Culture Task Force, which had been launched in response to a police beating of Jacqueline Craig, a local Black woman.[47] UFW activists also protested Tarrant County's new 287(g) contract in which the Sheriff's Office offered to help federal Immigration and Customs Enforcement detain and deport undocumented migrants. The pattern from city hall repeated itself at the county Commissioners Court (its legislative governing body): in 2019 and again in 2020, members of ICE Out of Tarrant, a coalition that included UFW leadership, mobilized around one hundred immigrants and allies to demand that the county not renew the 287(g) contract. An all-white majority voted 3–2 to extend it, overwhelming their Black colleagues (no Latinx person had yet served in that capacity).[48]

The persistent deaf ears of elected officials accelerated the entry of UFW and other advocates into the political arena. In 2019 and 2021, UFW endorsed candidates for city council and mayor, organizing expansive get-out-the-vote campaigns that targeted low-propensity Latinx and Black voters. The first campaign in the "majority-minority" District 6 forced a twelve-year incumbent, an Anglo conservative, to campaign and spend at extraordinary levels; the second campaign saw his defeat. The UFW-endorsed candidate in District 8, which includes part of Poly, was a self-declared outsider candidate "for the people" who likewise defeated a long-term proestablishment incumbent (both are Black). Countywide campaigns against the pro-Trump sheriff and reactionary district attorney came up short, but there has been growing momentum for change across the county. Indeed, Deborah Peoples, the two-time progressive candidate for mayor, won the Democratic Party nomination for County Judge (chief executive) in 2022. As these examples demonstrate, Latinx immigrants and their allies had formed deep connections and an enduring partnership with many progressive African American leaders and organizations. Exclusion remains the norm in Fort Worth and Tarrant County politics, but communities of color are building power in unprecedented ways.

Discussion and Implications

The bottom-up, immigrant-led transformations of Poly and Fort Worth invite new interventions and questions in the historiography of metropolitan Latinidad in the U.S.[49] Unlike their counterparts in Los Angeles or elsewhere in the Southwest, Mexican immigrants to Poly and other new barrios in the city remain a "people without history," liminal to Mexican American historiography and yet shaped profoundly by generations of Chicanx experiences.

Despite the long-standing colonia in Fort Worth, as migrants forged a new community in Poly, they were doubly marginalized by the presence of established Latino neighborhoods and the ethnic brokers who assisted the Anglo power structure in containing their ambitions—by the larger palimpsest that was Fort Worth. The 2006 uprisings against the Sensenbrenner Bill and the 2017 revolt against SB4 made plain the need for newer Latinx migrants to have their own seat at the table in local politics rather than representation by diplomats across town. As observers across Texas and the United States continue to speculate about the future of the so-called Latino vote, scholars must scrutinize closely the "walls and mirrors" that emerge within diverse, mixed-status Chicanx/Latinx communities, especially as newcomers redefine metropolitan politics and space.[50]

Put another way, scholars must dig more deeply to understand how the legacies of Juan Crow have shaped the contours of recent immigration and especially the making of new Latinx communities, the revival of older urban spaces, and the experiences of Latinx youth in the twenty-first century. This is an especially important and challenging task for scholars of the U.S. Southwest, where the standard generational approach to Chicanx history has not yet yielded new theoretical frameworks that center the relational experiences of Mexican-origin people, both native and foreign-born, in urban Aztlán over the past half century—that is, in the post-*movimiento* years. Instead, Chicanx historiography remains rooted in a fixed timeline that begins with conquest and ends with the Chicano movement, even though the mass migration of the past half century dwarfs quantitatively all the previous waves combined, and despite the fact that qualitatively the newcomers have remade the nation's cities and politics in unprecedented fashion.[51]

The palimpsest of Fort Worth Latinx history also underscores the urgent need to problematize what it means when new, predominantly immigrant Latinx communities take shape in the former Jim Crow South. Scholars of urban America have begun exploring the experiences of Latinx newcomers in neighborhoods divided between white and Black people, places of double transitions in which the newest migrants are understood within a framework of foundational anti-Blackness.[52] The Southern caste system, paired with Sunbelt boosterism and neoliberalism, often rendered the Latinx migrants who arrived in these kinds of urban spaces even more powerless and all but invisible.

The present and future of Latinx Fort Worth remains uncertain. After decades of struggle, the city council was expanded by two seats prior to the municipal elections of 2023. The redistricting process produced a map that includes one new Latinx opportunity district, but only just so—the demographic majority is far slighter than is typical for encouraging minority representation. For many Latinx residents, progress came at a hefty price: lawmakers again split Poly, halving it straight down the street in front of United Fort Worth's Community Justice Center, and they chopped apart another barrio, Rosemont, to draw a cartoonish horseshoe shape for the new District 11 that simultaneously cracked the natural constituencies of other potential Latino challengers to the status quo. While the map did end up producing a second Latinx council member as intended, it tears both neighborhoods asunder, ignoring their "communities of interest" in favor of far-flung, extreme gerrymandering.[53] Regardless, history suggests that descriptive representation alone won't be enough to alter City Hall.[54] Indeed, the best-laid plans of city planners, nonprofit agencies, and even allied ethnic politicians all failed to revitalize Poly, largely because they ignored the bottom-up regeneration being wrought by recent Latinx immigrants. Rather than embrace the newest arrivals as engines of economic growth and cultural heterogeneity, Fort Worth's Anglo-led establishment persists in demonizing and excluding them. The latest gerrymandering is but the most recent example of the city's politics of exclusion. New Latinx immigrant communities will thus continue the struggle to make their voices heard in local politics—even as they inexorably transform their neighborhoods and the city's built environment from the ground up.

9

"Gastronomical Gallivanting in Foreign Fields": Mexican Restaurants and Cultural Exchange in Interwar Chicago

MICHAEL D. INNIS-JIMÉNEZ
University of Alabama

An October 1926 editorial in Chicago's *Correo Mexicano* newspaper described the Mexican Inn Restaurant at 442 North Clark Street as "yet another piece of our country," one that is "flirtatiously elegant" and features curtains in the "purest national style." Upon entering the restaurant, the writer declared, patrons will "breathe in an authentic home-like atmosphere that will make one feel as if they were in Mexico" in a space "reminiscent of family dining rooms." With its detailed description of the establishment yet curiously without a mention of the quality of the food served, the editorial depicted the Mexican Inn as a place designed to figuratively transport people to their hometowns and provide them with a dining experience that reminds them of Mexico. The familiar curtains and homelike atmosphere described in the editorial suggest that the restaurant created a warm, elegant, and welcoming environment for its patrons as it appealed to the Mexican community's sense of nostalgia and desire for a culturally rich dining experience.[1]

That same year, Manuel Gamio visited Mexico Bello, a Mexican restaurant in the heart of the Near West Side, Chicago's largest Mexican neighborhood. Gamio, a titan in Mexican anthropology and archeology, was best known for his work on indigenous Mexican communities' history, culture, and social organization. But he also wrote extensively on Mexican immigrants in the United States. He was back in Chicago—having received his doctorate nine years earlier from the University of Chicago—researching the Mexican communities in the area. Gamio described Mexico Bello's decor as consisting of portraits of Mexican national heroes Benito Juárez and Miguel Hidalgo and a clay bust of dictator Porfirio Díaz. After mentioning that Mexico Bello served Mexican national dishes, Gamio went on to describe ceramic pieces from Guadalajara as cheap and in bad taste. To further emphasize the lack of

MEXICO BELLO

RESTAURANT MEXICANO

— Servimos platillos netamente mexicanos. —

VENGA USTED Y TRAIGA A SU FAMILIA

Esmero y Prontitud en el Servicio

735 WEST TAYLOR STREET CHICAGO, ILL.

Heràclio Alemàn, Prop. Telèfono Monroe 5158

FIGURE 9.1. Mexico Bello advertisement, *Correo Mexicano* (Chicago), October 24, 1926, 4.

genuine ambience, he also noted the presence of a self-playing piano grinding out "dated provincial music." Notably, Mexico Bello (fig. 9.1) had been open for fewer than two years at the time of Gamio's visit and was owned by a longtime Chicago resident from Zacatecas who first came to the United States in 1913 to work as a laborer and moved to Chicago between 1917 and 1919.[2]

Gamio's unflattering description of the popular neighborhood restaurant should not be surprising since it came from an upper-class, city-dwelling Mexican who anticipated the sights and sounds of a neighborhood restaurant in Mexico itself. His expectations were not necessarily the same as those of Chicago's working-class immigrants. Aside from Gamio's emphasis on what he considered garish—he never evaluated the taste of the food—his comments were anything but random. By mentioning the depictions of Hidalgo and Juárez, Gamio emphasized Mexico Bello's standing as a restaurant for working-class customers, as these decorations were consistent with "common" Mexicans' emphasis on nostalgia for their national heroes. Gamio's mention of Porfirio Díaz's bust also goes beyond its gaudiness in a restaurant. Díaz, Mexico's dictator for over thirty years, was overthrown at the start of the Mexican Revolution, a conflict that eventually seated a government that placed strict limits on the Catholic Church. His likeness was an unmistakable indication of the restaurant owner's "pro-Catholic" stance during the Cristero Rebellion that was getting underway in central Mexico. Together, Gamio's emphasis on the restaurant's sights and sounds illustrates the importance he placed on restaurants in local Mexican life. As with Gamio, the *Correo Mexicano*'s assertions of the Mexican Inn's authentic representations of spaces that Mexicans left behind—again without discussion or even mention of the eatery's menu—further demonstrated the importance of Mexican restaurants, the spaces they occupy, the people who frequent them, and their representation of the *patria* for those *de afuera*. The newspaper's description, after all, urged the local Mexican community to visit the Mexican Inn to feel like they were in the homes they had left behind.[3]

These accounts from a newspaper article and a scholar's field notes are relatively brief. Still, they have much to tell us about everyday life in Mexican Chicago in 1926. From the standpoint of urban history, scholarly accounts of ethnic restaurants are just one excellent example of a historiography that uses small but very common urban establishments as a means of pursuing the social and cultural history of cities. These include histories of brothels penned by Tim Gilfoyle and Sharon Wood; of amusement parks from John F. Kasson and Kathy Peiss; of department stores from William Leach and Susan Porter Benson; of drinking establishments from Madelon Powers and David W. Conroy; of restaurants by Rebecca Spang and Cindy Lobel; and of boardinghouses from Wendy Gamber and Thomas Gunn. These establishments often reflected the values, tastes, and needs of the people who frequented them, and they can provide insight into the larger historical context in which they operated.

The history of restaurants can reveal a great deal. The historian Hasia Diner argues that to understand any society, one must "look at what the women and men in it have eaten, how they got it, with whom they ate it, who prepared it, and what it meant to them." Diner's statement highlights the particular importance of food and dining in understanding a community. By examining ethnic restaurants in particular and their meaning to local communities in America, we can gain a deeper understanding of the complex social, economic, and political forces that shaped the ethnic community, its neighborhood, and the larger city. Studying the history of restaurants and other food-related establishments can therefore be a rich and revealing way to pursue urban history.

Moreover, texts like these can be crucial in constructing a clearer picture of what would become one of America's most important immigrant settlements when it was less than a decade old. Scholars of the Mexican and Mexican American experience in the United States have for some years pondered the significance of restaurants, with newer advances in the scholarship highlighting how much we can learn when we prioritize the investigation of Mexican restaurants and the immigrant and domestic communities they served.[4] Anyone who studies the historical role of Mexican food in society is familiar with the work of historian Jeffrey Pilcher and literary scholar Meredith Abarca. Although they have approached their subject by focusing on very different focal points using different disciplinary methodologies, their works are in many ways foundational to Mexican and Mexican American food studies in the United States. One of many notable contributions by Abarca is her 2007 article "Charlas Culinarias: Mexican Women Speak from Their Public Kitchens." In it, she explores the transformation of working-class Mexican women's home cooking skills into an economic resource to support their family and community. Abarca highlights a concept she calls familial wealth as a way to recognize the social, cultural, personal, and ideological benefits of food-related business ownership for women and the communities they support.[5] Jeffrey Pilcher's extensive body of work includes the monograph *Planet Taco* (2012), which offers a global perspective on the influence of Mexican food, transcending borders and showcasing its impact on Mexican American society. Pilcher's earlier *Food and Foodways* article, "Who Chased Out the 'Chili Queens'? Gender, Race, and Urban Reform in San Antonio, Texas, 1880–1943," examines ethnic Mexican "chili queens" and their significant role in the city's culinary, social, and political landscape while exploring the intersections of race, class, gender, and food in San Antonio's evolving urban landscape.[6]

Most recently, Lori Flores has analyzed the placemaking role of ethnic Mexican restaurants, the food they served, and those who were responsible for their popularity. Her article in *Food, Culture and Society* on Chef Zarela Martinez's trailblazing role in popularizing haute Mexican food in New York City and complicating people's understandings of Mexican cuisine as much more than its simple, fast, and cheap stereotype. Flores explains the role of Mexican immigrants in the New York City area in the late twentieth century in the creation of a new and thriving Mexican food scene that included everything from taco trucks to high-end Mexican restaurants. In examining Martinez's role as chef, business owner, and cultural trailblazer, Lori Flores helps historicize the role of women restaurant owners not only as placemakers for the Mexican and Mexican American community but also as mediators between cultures.[7]

As Flores notes, ethnic food has often functioned as a way for immigrants to share their culture with the broader American public, introducing new and exotic flavors and culinary traditions. With that in mind, and acknowledging that Mexican restaurants are—at their core—particular to their location and moment in time, examining them along with related clienteles, interactions, and material culture provides alluring case studies of their importance to the physical and cultural growth and development of urban Mexican communities. This chapter illustrates the importance and urgency of research on urban Mexican restaurants as essential for learning about and archiving the cultural production and everyday life of these influential spaces. I begin by highlighting the work of Natalia Molina, focusing on one mid-twentieth-century Los Angeles restaurant, and juxtaposing it with my current research on a Chicago restaurant during the interwar period. While they depend on different primary sources, both studies demonstrate the social importance and intellectual promise of research on urban Mexican restaurants in the United States and the concurrent creation and organization of new archival materials. In the process, they address Molina's clear and poetic question: "What is at stake if we do not begin to capture these stories?"[8]

Natalia Molina's *A Place at the Nayarit* is the story of a Los Angeles establishment where immigrant employees and patrons could be themselves. Molina explains how the Nayarit provided what she calls "uncontested public space" in a city whose white majority usually wasn't keen on sharing the public realm.[9] The Nayarit provided what was needed to allow "working people to assume full identities that went beyond who they were as laborers." At the restaurant, "immigrants might not feel any more American (nor was that necessarily their goal), but they were insiders." The Nayarit was therefore an essential community institution where "immigrants lived out values of mutuality, public sociability, and collectivity." It and similar restaurants were safe spaces that provided those who entered "the familiarity of home and a ready-made social network, offering local history, introductions, and information about how to navigate the system."[10]

The Nayarit was inseparable from its creator, a woman with a compelling personal history. Natalia Barraza came to the United States on her own, and by opening several restaurants, she became a vital placemaker: someone who appropriated specific spaces and turned them into places with meanings for themselves and the community. Doña Natalia—she was always respectfully addressed with the Spanish-language honorific—created indispensable community institutions where "ethnic Mexicans who worked and ate [there] were not just putting food on the table or into their mouths." By being there, they created "meaning, establishing links with one another, and tending to roots both old and new."[11] At the Nayarit and at similar restaurants across the country, Mexican immigrant employees and patrons "assert[ed] their place in a nation that often seemed intent on pushing them to the margins."[12] Doña Natalia's influence extended beyond her restaurants and throughout Los Angeles because she "encouraged her workers to be both placemakers and place-takers"—to claim their place in their neighborhood, workplace, and city.[13]

In studying Natalia Barraza's life in California and the significance of the restaurant she named after her home state, Molina emphasizes "urban anchors"—her term for "spaces that marginalized and racialized placemakers have cultivated—including restaurants, bars, jazz clubs, music stores, and performance spaces."[14] Molina differentiates *urban anchors* from *anchor institutions*, an urban-planning term usually referring to large institutions such as hospitals, libraries, and schools.[15] Although some establishments might fall under both categories in rare cases, Molina points out that urban anchors are usually smaller institutions. Scholars should prioritize the study of these Mexican community urban anchors because, as Molina points out, "we can broaden our conceptions of who creates meaningful public places, what those places look like, and how community dynamics take shape."[16] Molina's story of the Nayarit and the people who occupied its space is just a preview or glimpse into the lives of restaurant owners, employees, and patrons in the spaces that anchored and sheltered them.

Molina, however, expands the conceptual framework of urban anchor beyond any individual restaurant. She explains how urban anchors helped immigrants establish and maintain transnational—more accurately defined by Molina as translocal—ties that assisted immigrants in adapting and creating community in their new city while also binding them to their Mexican hometowns: they facilitated new immigration and on occasion transformed culture and political economy back home. These transformations occurred through constant and circular migration, along with remittances and letters like those that bound communities in Nayarit with those in Los Angeles.[17]

By gathering research for *A Place at the Nayarit* and conducting a trove of oral histories, Molina does the important work of creating an archive. She adds to the dismally thin written record of working-class Mexican and Mexican American women and their histories in the United States. These missing histories, she explains, reveal "young Mexican and Mexican American women [who] faced immense difficulties, including educators who underestimated them, social workers who wished them to abandon their culture, and police who criminalized them. At home, these women also experienced tensions with their parents, nearly all of whom lamented in one way or another how much their children changed in this new land and worried about their daughters adopting American ways and abandoning their culture, and perhaps their morals."[18] Too many of these histories have been lost to institutional indifference and the passage of time, and Molina makes clear the urgency of this kind of collection and archiving.

The Nayarit was a very distinctive type of Mexican restaurant that Doña Natalia positioned in very specific ways regarding clientele and authenticity. She chose to open the restaurant outside of a Mexican neighborhood or tourist district in favor of a major thoroughfare in a multiethnic neighborhood at the crossroads of many different cultures. Barraza's restaurant was primarily dedicated to attracting working-class Mexican immigrant patrons from throughout Los Angeles, but it did bring in the occasional Anglo diner. The exact reasons Mexican immigrants favored one Mexican restaurant over another varied. It took more than the name to attract newcomers from the Mexican state of Nayarit to Doña Natalia's restaurant. Molina explains several reasons the restaurant became an urban anchor for the Nayarit community in Los Angeles. For some, it was proximity to home, work, or church. For others, it was the name and reputation that got them through the door, but the employees and Doña Natalia kept them coming back and feeling safe within its walls. For many Nayaritans, the restaurant served as a representation of home. Another reason they came back might have been its fare. Molina documents Doña Natalia's unwillingness to compromise on the Nayarit's menu. With minor exceptions, Barraza refused to add anything she did not consider from Mexico or her home state in order to attract paying non-Mexican customers. While other Mexican restaurants changed recipes or added items likely to attract non-Mexican diners to their eatery, Barraza limited the Nayarit's menu to what she and fellow Nayaritans would recognize as "authentic" to their *patria chica*.[19]

At one point, Molina recounts a 1949 visit to the Nayarit by Paul Coates, a newspaper reporter for the local *Mirror News*. Claiming to know only a bit of Spanish, he brought a local Spanish-speaking guide. This guide, Molina posits, was a Mexican American who grew up in another part of the city and was most likely there to help Coates navigate the menu and suggest standard dishes. In writing about his time at the Nayarit, Coates focused on the danger and exoticism that lurked within the menu. He warned his readers that the usual hot sauces and dishes were much spicier than what his palate considered normal and were therefore meant to be consumed only by the "more 'experienced diner.'" Although Doña Natalia focused on providing familiar food and a friendly space for Mexican immigrants and Mexican Americans, the Nayarit also functioned as a place of cultural interchange. It was a public-facing institution created by Mexicans and primarily for Mexicans, but it was located both physically and metaphorically at the crossroads of cultures.[20]

Nineteen years earlier and just over two thousand miles away, a different local reporter visited a neighborhood Mexican restaurant. In that case the reporter was John Drury, a native Chicagoan working for the *Chicago Daily News* who just happened to have started his career at a Los Angeles daily newspaper. In March 1930, Drury visited El Puerto de Veracruz Restaurant, located at 811 South Halsted Street in Chicago's Near West Side. Local Spanish-language newspaper advertisements and editorial articles confirm that Juan Malpica had opened El Puerto de Veracruz in 1926 in the heart of Chicago's largest Mexican community. It was just down the block from the Mexico Bello restaurant that Manuel Gamio had written about four years earlier. Malpica was born in 1884 in the village of San Juan, Veracruz, and arrived in Chicago in 1919 to work as a laborer, part of the first large wave of Mexican migration to the city. In 1922, he lived at 735 West Fourteenth Place, a short ten blocks from the location of his future restaurant located across from Hull House.

According to the 1930 census, Malpica was renting an apartment above the restaurant. He lived there with his wife, who worked as a cook in the restaurant, his widowed sister-in-law, who was a waitress, and two young nephews. It was not unusual to find family members, including women, working in small Mexican restaurants in Chicago. For example, Mexico Bello's owner, Heraclio Aleman, depended on his seventeen-year-old daughter to work as a cashier and his sixteen-year-old son as a waiter.[21] While advertisements may not have explicitly highlighted women's roles in these restaurants, their repeated promises of superior service and a comforting, homelike environment underscored the cultural significance of women's labor. Phrases in the advertisements, such as *servicio esmerado* and *prontitud y limpieza* were deeply associated with femininity in Mexican culture. Thus, when a Mexican restaurateur marketed an "authentic homelike atmosphere" reminiscent of family dining rooms, this evoked a domestic ideal intrinsically tied to women's work in the kitchen and at home. This emphasized the pivotal role of women's labor in shaping both the culinary experience and the cultural identity of these establishments.

According to local Spanish-language newspapers, Mexican women also owned restaurants in Chicago. The Zacatecas native Flora Miranda owned at least three, though not necessarily at the same time. The earliest record of her owning a restaurant was in January 1927, when she placed an advertisement for El Foco Rojo at 846 South Halsted Street, just down the block from El Puerto de Veracruz. The sources are ambiguous but show that the restaurant was in her hands at least between 1927 and 1930. In October 1927, Miranda placed an ad for El Porvenir Restaurant, located less than a mile from El Foco Rojo, at 1342 S. Sangamon Street. And by 1932, Miranda owned the Venus Restaurant at 720 South Halsted Street.[22]

What can El Puerto de Veracruz, Mexico Bello, and El Foco Rojo tell us about this time, this place, and this community? The way the restaurants functioned at this major cultural crossroads was the result of various factors. These included the owners' intentions for the restaurant, their geographic location in the heart of Mexican Chicago, the local Mexican community's preferences and practices, and the expectations of the city's non-Mexican population. The available historical evidence is different from what Natalia Molina uses to document the Nayarit, but the sources offer us a detailed look nonetheless.

The Near West Side, home to all these restaurants, was one of Chicago's seventy-five officially recognized "community areas" at the time. The establishments were situated on a stretch of South Halsted Street dubbed Mexican Boulevard, in the section of the neighborhood Mexicans referred to as *la colonia Hull House* and others called Little Mexico. *Colonia Hull House* was the oldest and largest of Chicago's three distinct Mexican enclaves during this period. Another concentration of Mexicans was located in and adjacent to the neighborhood of South Chicago, concentrated near and around the gates of the steel mills that dotted the landscape. The third concentration was in the Back of the Yards neighborhood. This was the "Jungle" made famous by Upton Sinclair's 1906 book, located just south of the infamous slaughterhouses of the massive Chicago Stockyards. In addition, smaller groups of Mexicans lived in "boxcar camps" provided by railroad companies to Mexican maintenance-of-way workers and located adjacent to the numerous railyards and roundhouses throughout the Chicago area.[23]

La colonia Hull House served as the Mexican cultural and commercial hub for the greater Chicago area. It was the most popular colonia among Mexicans, tourists, journalists, and others seeking an authentic Mexican experience. By defining this area as Little Mexico or *la colonia Hull House* and describing its centrality to the development of a greater Mexican Chicago then and now, I risk romanticizing this area. Although the descriptions and memories of the restaurants and other establishments along this stretch of South Halsted Street evoke home for Mexicans and were visitors' portals into the foreign and exotic, this was a gray, deteriorating neighborhood with decaying housing long reserved for the newest and poorest immigrant to Chicago. In his 1920 book, Robert Shackleton described the area as one of "drab despair, especially from debris and litter and mud," with "here and there a tottering wooden house on rotting wooden foundations" visible as soon as one stepped off South Halsted or any other main thoroughfare. It was these poor conditions, however, that made it affordable for Chicago's newest immigrants. Others described the area as defined by the traffic noise of Halsted Street, the crowds and noise of the adjacent Maxwell Market, and the "treeless back streets," with "dilapidated two and three-story houses" that "elbow each other for room and struggle to give shelter to the many families who overcrowd their interiors." Despite being the cultural hub of Mexican Chicago and home to America's first settlement house, Shackleton makes clear that those living in this neighborhood did so not because it was the most

FIGURE 9.2. El Puerto de Veracruz business card (1930), Drury-Neville Collection, Newberry Library, Chicago.

comfortable Mexican enclave, but because it was the least bad or perhaps the only option available to them.[24]

Malpica initially focused on serving the local community. The first extant newspaper advertising for El Puerto de Veracruz appeared in the local *Noticia Mundial* and *El México* newspapers on September 16, 1927. The ad, published on Mexican Independence Day, emphasized *platillos nacionales*, family-size tables, and *servicio esmerado*. A business card for the restaurant (fig. 9.2), also in Spanish, called it "the favorite place of Mexicans," centering Malpica's main intended clientele. It also advertised *Exquisitos Platillos Nacionales*, emphasizing Mexican nationalism, then in high vogue, in its appeal. It also promised *Prontitud y Limpieza*, prompt service and a clean establishment.[25]

Malpica was apparently successful in his appeals because El Puerto de Veracruz was popular with members of the local Mexican community. This popularity was evident in the local Spanish-language newspaper coverage as well as that of San Antonio–based *La Prensa*. Thanks to Ignacio E. Lozano, *La Prensa* is another unlikely link between the Nayarit in Los Angeles and El Puerto de Veracruz in Chicago. Lozano, a Nayaritan living in Los Angeles and a patron at the Nayarit restaurant, founded and ran *La Opinión*, the prominent newspaper cited by Molina. Before moving to Los Angeles, Lozano founded and developed what became the largest Spanish-language U.S. newspaper with a national readership, *La Prensa*. Mexicans in Chicago commonly read *La Prensa* as it was available in numerous newsstands, ran a regular Chicago column, and had a Chicago-based reporter. By analyzing *La Prensa*'s accounts of El Puerto de Veracruz along with those of Chicago's

Mexican newspapers, we can get a better picture of what community members thought about the restaurant. On more than a handful of occasions, Lozano's paper reported on community events at El Puerto de Veracruz or its popularity and positive reputation in the community. A 1932 article noted that "every day a plethora of citizens of this country can be seen at the only establishment which our colony in Chicago can count on," emphasizing that El Puerto de Veracruz was, "we repeat, the gathering place for decent people." On another occasion, a *La Prensa* article mentioned in passing that El Puerto de Veracruz was the community's *centro favorito*.[26]

English-language sources agreed. In his writing, Drury listed local Mexican celebrities and officials who frequented El Puerto de Veracruz. In *Dining in Chicago*, his renowned 1931 guide to eating out, Drury described El Puerto de Veracruz—which notably was the only Mexican restaurant in the book—as a "little unpretentious Mexican restaurant" across from Hull House, where consuls, caricature artists, opera singers, residents of Hull House, newspapermen, students, and gourmets came to "indulge their fondness for 'hot' dishes." Drury's emphasis on the dining choices of prominent members of the Mexican community served as a "seal of approval," giving a tacit endorsement of the restaurant's Mexican authenticity. Drury's notes on Mexican Boulevard, presumably written while visiting the neighborhood and before his visit to El Puerto de Veracruz, recorded that it was the "restaurant for opera stars" and important Mexican visitors such as José Vasconcelos. Vasconcelos, the Mexican philosopher, writer, and politician who is best known for his 1925 book *La raza cósmica*, had visited the area the previous year as a candidate for the Mexican presidency. Similarly, Bruce Grant, a *Chicago Sunday Times* reporter, singled out El Puerto the Veracruz as "the gathering place [of] the young artistic group of Mexicans."[27] The restaurant was, in fact, popular with community leaders, entrepreneurs, newspaper owners, merchants, and artists from within the Mexican community, as well as Latin American consular officials.[28]

Its location directly across from Hull House, one of the most popular cultural tourist attractions in the area, provided Malpica and El Puerto de Veracruz an opportunity to benefit financially from cultural and culinary interest and curiosity about Mexican culture by non-Mexican visitors to Hull House and Mexican Boulevard. In fact, many interwar-era cultural tours into the area included a stop at El Puerto de Veracruz. One of these was an advertised nine-hour tour that occurred a month before Drury's visit. Titled "Our Mexican Neighbors," it included talks by academics, Mexican community leaders, and the Mexican consul at two separate settlement houses, as well as dinner at El Puerto de Veracruz. The dinner was to include a "complete Mexican

Cuisine; tamales, chili, sopa, torillas [*sic*], [and] frijoles." After-dinner activities included a "saunter" down Mexican Boulevard and a *fiesta típica mexicana*. The bill described the *fiesta típica* as including folk dancing and performances and "native young women, in costume," selling "Mexican delicacies." The tour flyer assured participants that they would participate in an authentic cultural experience. Although we know the Works Progress Administration sponsored cultural tours during the Great Depression, most details of the itineraries have been lost. This cultural tour is known to us today only because Drury saved a copy of this flyer with his notes, which he donated with his personal records to the Newberry Library.[29]

Malpica's success in publicizing his restaurant was so great that El Puerto de Veracruz became the preeminent Mexican restaurant featured in the English-language press, where it symbolized the place of Mexican fare among Chicago's many cosmopolitan cuisines. In *Dining in Chicago*, Drury called the Windy City a "bubbling melting-pot of practically all the principal races in the world" that offered "splendid opportunities for gastronomical gallivanting in foreign fields" without having to leave the city's borders. He touted German and Swedish districts on the North Side, Polish and Russian "quarters" along Milwaukee Avenue on the Northwest Side, the Near South Side's "Chinese, Arab, and Japanese neighborhoods," English chop houses in the Loop, and a couple of Filipino and French restaurants just north of the Loop. He reserved most of his excitement for the West Side, home to "most of the foreign quarters." This was where Mexicans resided, along with Greek, Italian, Jewish, Romanian, and Bohemian communities. The area was home to the largest number of immigrants. Drury envisioned his city as a miniature smorgasbord of countries where residents thrived in national communities with culinary open borders that people of all nationalities frequently crisscrossed. Along with out-of-town tourists, locals could cross these imaginary—and sometimes not so imaginary—boundaries to enter a new land where they could immerse themselves in foreign and exotic sounds, sights, smells, and tastes within their own city.[30]

The way each of these constituencies interacted with the other was an important determinant of how they understood each other. And notably, writers like Drury were an important part of this process of self-fashioning and public representation. When he visited Mexican restaurants, Drury anticipated experiencing Mexican food and entertainment that reflected his interpretation of the local Mexican community and Mexico itself. He expected to hear, feel, smell, and taste some small part of "traditional" Mexico and, in a sense, be transported there by its food and the rich cultural content that physically surrounded him. Drury expected the restaurant to be a slice of Mexico, or at least a slice of what he envisioned Mexico to be. Like Coates and the Nayarit, Drury wrote about an institution that served as a cultural crossroads, a place where "authenticity" met the expectations of diners.

This sense of authenticity was not purely fictitious: it was often built on actual Mexican patronage. By listing prominent Mexicans as frequent patrons of El Puerto de Veracruz, Drury played into the idea that culinary tourists looked to the perceived ethnicity of diners—not to mention staff members—to evaluate an ethnic restaurant's authenticity. This is in direct contrast to Natalia Molina's analysis of the Nayarit. Although Molina mentions several celebrity patrons, she focuses on the restaurant's approval by the community through the eyes, mouths, and stomachs of primarily Mexican immigrant working-class staff and patrons. It is through the support of immigrant, working-class patrons that the Nayarit survived financially and earned its badge of authenticity. Molina's collection and deft analysis of oral histories provide scholars with a rare insider's panoramic view of the importance of these voices in understanding the importance of a restaurant to the community. I argue that El Puerto de Veracruz was also important to the community's history and culture, but I must make that argument using the notes and reports of Mexican and Anglo journalists and scholars.

Studying urban Mexican restaurants like El Puerto de Veracruz, which catered to tourists as well as members of the community, gives us an entry into understanding how perceptions of the local Mexican community were shaped. El Puerto de Veracruz's importance goes far beyond its popularity for cultural and culinary tourists; it served as an essential ambassador of public perception for local Mexican food and culture. The shared identity of the Mexican community of Chicago evolved through competing self-representations based on interactions between members and those outside of the community. In many cases, these interactions revolved around Mexican food and foodways available in the area. Mexicans in Chicago accepted—and even promoted—stark contrasts in public self-representations for the financial and political benefit of the community. These contrasts included the representation of Mexicans as dark-skinned, uneducated, hardworking people who cherished an exotic folk culture and simple yet alluring food traditions. Naturally, these exotic representations of food, distinctively gendered "native costumes," and the Mexican people themselves benefited restaurants and other Mexican-owned businesses. Some contrasts and contradictions come, as Vicki Ruiz argues, when these racial and ethnic foodways become markers of belonging and difference set within a larger frame of inequality while negotiating what it means to be American. The Mexican community of Chicago, and local Mexican culture as a whole, benefited from this food-based cultural tourism while at the same time perpetuating the idea that Mexican immigrants and food culture were exotic and, in many ways, inferior to Americans.[31]

Many of these safe spaces and the Mexican communities they served are now gone or in the process of erasure. Natalia Molina laments the displacement of Echo Park's Mexican residents through a painful process of gentrification and forms of urban renewal, including the construction of Dodger Stadium. On Chicago's Near West Side, all that remains of *colonia Hull House* is Halsted Street itself, some of the cross streets, and two buildings from Hull House's thirteen-building complex. In the early 1960s, Mayor Richard J. Daley and the City of Chicago chose the location for what is now the University of Illinois Chicago. In the name of urban renewal, Daley displaced the entire Little Mexico community.

What happened to the communities that supported the Nayarit and El Puerto de Veracruz are just two of many examples of, as Molina describes, "how even when Latinx residents are placemakers, their communities remain vulnerable to the powers that be."[32] In a 1990 poem, "Requiem for a Street," the Chicagoan Carlos Cortez grieves the destruction of Mexican Boulevard while recalling a "street once lined with an endless array of small shops, bistros and hole-in-the-wall restaurants." The street was one "where one could bask in the culinary delights of faraway places, where one could walk by small music stores and hear strange music that somehow was not strange at all," as Mexican culture was just one of many on this street that was home to immigrants for a hundred years. Cortez remembered this stretch of Halsted as a place where "the sidewalk passerby would be constantly beset by sidewalk pitchmen and Gypsy fortune tellers" and where you could hear "Spanish with a Yiddish accent." This street was, Cortez wrote, "a small united nations that somehow wasn't completely united, and somehow it didn't make too much difference."[33]

Yes, many established urban ethnic restaurants disappeared during this period because of rising rents caused by gentrification, urban renewal, or everyday economic reasons and continue to do so. Yes, many of these closed eateries were community and cultural hubs for immigrants and need to be remembered in the archive if at all possible. Yet—at the risk of sounding brash and stating the obvious—this does not spell doom for the ethnic Mexican restaurant in the United States. Even as they continue to close, urban, ethnic Mexican restaurants are more plentiful today than during the twentieth century. As historians, we must keep that in mind and not ignore our neighborhood ethnic Mexican restaurants that currently serve as cultural and community hubs for twenty-first-century immigrant communities.

Why study individual ethnic restaurants? As historians, we bear the responsibility of finding the stories of yesterday and making them speak to the present. We might learn these stories by digging through archives, reading old newspapers, or scanning government records. If we haven't waited too long, we might seek out and listen to the people who have been part of the story. Through these restaurants, we can learn much more than what they served or who their patrons were. The histories of the Nayarit and El Puerto de Veracruz make that abundantly clear. These restaurants can be entry points into the examination of culture, be it the portrayal of Mexicanness facing outward or within the community, or the influence of non-Mexican culture. They can also provide us the opportunity to understand better local food and foodways, community politics, *México de afuera*, Mexican hometowns, translocal links, the employees, the owners, and the power dynamics within the restaurant, the neighborhood, and perhaps even the city. This one type of small institution is vital to learning histories, be they personal, business, cultural, social, or political. As several historians have already made clear, by studying the histories of urban ethnic restaurants, we can better understand immigrants' lives, along with the views of outsiders.

In my analysis of ethnic Mexican restaurants on the Near West Side of Chicago, I focus on these establishments as places of mediation between Mexican and non-Mexican cultures while also emphasizing their role in supporting the local Mexican community. In *A Place at the Nayarit*, Natalia Molina concentrates on restaurants that served primarily as anchors, with all the benefits, pressures, and responsibilities of such establishments. The contrast between my interpretive emphasis and Molina's highlights the various perspectives that scholars can bring to the discussion, emphasizing the role that restaurants play in creating community while bridging cultural differences and facilitating cultural exchange. Individually and together, these approaches provide a more nuanced and comprehensive understanding of the role that ethnic Mexican restaurants played in making urban places.

In shaping local Mexican culture, restaurant owners and employees constructed establishments that not only influenced local identity but also served as spaces that financially, physically, and emotionally helped Mexicans in essentially unfriendly cities. Restaurateurs and their employees did this while shaping and creating local Mexican foodways that evolved around some combination of the Mexican migrants' culinary nostalgia, community expectations, the availability of and experience with foods from neighboring ethnic groups, and the tourist expectations of non-Mexicans. Doña Natalia could stay true to her vision of a Nayarit restaurant uncompromisingly authentic to Nayaritans, but other urban Mexican restaurants catering to the Mexican community survived by choosing to leverage stereotypes to attract culinary and cultural tourists. The survival of a Mexican restaurant in a tourist destination such as Chicago's Mexican Boulevard or Los Angeles's Olvera Street depended on how the restaurateur approached questions of authenticity "of the other" posed by tourists and the authenticity "of the familiar" posed by local Mexicans. El Puerto de Veracruz was a relatively rare example of a restaurant that could serve the Mexican immigrant community while getting the word out that tourists could visit to experience a little slice of Mexico in an American city.

At first glance, the historical study of restaurateurs as placemakers and the role of culinary tourism to these ethnic restaurants help us better understand city life. They do that, and much more. Placemaking studies including *A Place at the Nayarit* and my next book *Made in Chicago* offer important lenses through which we can better understand the dynamics of ethnic Mexican urban environments and help underscore the significance of restaurants and their role in creating and maintaining community. These lenses not only begin to uncover the layers of cultural, social, and economic significance of these communities and sites within cities but also contribute to ethnic studies and Latinx urban history. These scholarly approaches illuminate the intricate ways in which culture, identity, memories of home, cultural expectations by others and the tourist gaze preserved and transformed Mexican space. By expanding our use of these lenses, we can only gain a richer understanding of the diverse tapestry of urban life, ethnic identities, and Latinx urban history.

Cultural and community mediation between Mexican and non-Mexican urban communities and cultures can occur in a variety of spaces beyond restaurants. Other examples of places of mediation in cities include community centers and parks frequented by multiple ethnicities. These spaces facilitated interactions between different groups, playing a crucial role in the process of cultural mediation in cities. We need to continue creating archives documenting the history of specific urban institutions, including their owners, managers, employees, customers, and atmosphere. With these histories, we can become better attuned to the broader cultural and historical contexts in which these ethnic Mexican establishments operated in U.S. cities, thereby making it part of the more expansive panorama of metropolitan Latinidad in America.[34]

Hemisphere

10

LatinX Metropolitan Pasts: A Hemispheric and Speculative Approach

EDUARDO CONTRERAS
Hunter College–CUNY

Mr. X and Jose Mendes probably never met, although they surely encountered each other's counterparts as they traversed metropolitan orbits of the early twentieth century. These men's lives began in Colombia and Costa Rica, respectively, but much of their existence unfolded elsewhere: in other nations, in imperial satellites and metropoles, on the margins, and in sites of possibility and insurgency. X left Colombia at a young age. He engaged in seasonal work in various Central American countries and found stable employment in U.S.-occupied Managua. Manual labor on steamers owned by the United Fruit Company often took X to New Orleans and San Francisco, where he witnessed "the modern progress of American cities." He opted to settle in San Francisco by 1925, a year after Mendes arrived in the city. Neither U.S. employers nor metropolitan authority proved new to Mendes. He had toiled in the Panama Canal Zone for almost a decade before a brief stint on a cargo liner led him to San Francisco. Settling in the metropolis on a semipermanent basis, he joined other Latines who trekked north to Alaska fisheries and east to agricultural fields in pursuit of enhanced economic prospects.[1] Circulation, experimentation, and marginalization within and across metropoles clearly shaped these men's lives.

An excavation of LatinX metropolitan pasts demands that historians attend to such lived experiences and situate LatinX bodies, labors, landscapes, and developments in the metropolitan arenas of the nineteenth and early twentieth centuries.[2] X's and Mendes's labors and crossings fit within large processes linked to the expansion and maintenance of metropolitan and imperial agendas. As such, their trajectories raise vital questions for historians of Latines and metropolitan worlds.[3] Should we approach their work and contributions as the building blocks (or early manifestations) of a LatinX metropolitanism? Could LatinX conditions have started in a Latin American city under U.S. occupation, at the Panama Canal Zone, or aboard United Fruit's ships? Most important, how might we capaciously assess, rethink, and unearth LatinX metropolitan pasts?

It behooves historians to wrestle with the pressing matters just mentioned. LatinX continues to proliferate and expand its currency in Latino/a/X studies. Scholars who study the present understandably focus on the ethnographic and cultural dimensions of LatinX in the contemporary moment.[4] Numerous intellectuals have also reflected on LatinX's "futurist implications" and "Latino/a/X futures." They have weighed potential directions for the academic field and prospective realities for people identified as Latina/e/o/x. What we deem possible or "conceivable" in Latino/a/X studies, stresses the anthropologist Nicholas De Genova, "is palpably reconfigured by the unforeseen futures and hitherto unfathomable futurities of an ever more heterogeneous and variegated spectrum of illegalized and criminalized Latino/a/Xs."[5] Unanticipated situations and ungraspable states of being may indeed lie ahead; they might also be uncovered in what is now behind us. The unexpected, the unknown, and multiple forms of unrecognizability point us to a LatinX future and a LatinX past. "LatinX sounds like the future," affirms the theorist Claudia Milian. "But it also holds the past and present."[6]

Building on recent paradigm-shifting insights by theorists and social critics, this think piece speculates that LatinX—as a tool and approach for inquiry—offers historians a potent means to augment our perspectives on urbanism and metropolitanism inflected by Latinness: temporally, geographically, conceptually, and hemispherically. It is a flexible method for delving into Latin—and Latinized—environments and situations, including ones traditionally absent from Latino/a urban histories. LatinX, as a concept, probes how Latinness colored sociohistorical terrains. It orients us in and/or to a multiplicity of directions, locations, and experiences that intersected with Latin but did not necessarily result in Latina/e/o/x embodiment. Moving beyond identity and demographic impulses to assess who counted or regarded themselves as Latina/e/o/x, LatinX functions as an instrument to tease out the manifestations, erasures, and significance of Latinness. A construct rooted in its Latin signifier, Latinness has been commonly deployed to represent or accentuate non-Anglo cultural practices and worldviews; ethnoracial mixture, in-betweenness, and ambiguity; excess, passion, underdevelopment, and disposability; and inferior status in a racial and imperial order.[7] Our task in examining the workings and "tropes of 'Latinness,'" as the literary scholar Kirsten Silva Gruesz instructs us, is not to determine "whether they are authentic or stereotypical, but how they locate this representational quality in time and space."[8] Attuned to temporality and spatiality, historians are well poised to examine how Latinness molded, altered, made possible, and closed off relations and formations in a host of settings, including metropolitan ones.

The metropolis as a site of analysis has captivated historians for generations. Over the past quarter century, postwar metropolitan history has deepened our understanding of the relationships and tensions between cities and suburbs and the regional outgrowths generated by city-suburb dynamics. A limitation of this orientation, as Andrew Needham and Allen Dieterich-Ward explain, has been its inattention to hinterlands beyond suburbs. These historians advance a more encompassing framework, one that addresses the "interconnections between metropolitan regional communities as well as the role of hinterland actors in shaping metropolitan growth."[9] We must certainly take up that call and also approach U.S. metropoles as imperial centers. In doing so, it is imperative to build on the insights of Latin American historians who have long recognized the entangled histories of U.S. empire, capitalism, and metropolitan power.[10]

It is crucial to interrogate how imperial logics and ventures facilitated and sustained metropolitan developments in the hemisphere. U.S.-centered urban historians have been slow to incorporate the metropolitan-imperial relationship into their modes of analysis. Treatments of fringe regions and transnational zones that exceed contiguous land areas promise to enrich our investigations and spur us to concretize the linkages between metropolitanization, transnational flows of capital and labor, and imperialism. "Situating 'empire' within an expanded spatial and temporal landscape," as Fernando Coronil avers, "makes it easier to overview its varied historical forms" and consequences. In a related vein, Thomas Bender has challenged U.S. historians to move beyond "the domesticity of our approach to urban history" and trace the imprints of imperial connections on "the social, economic, and even cultural history of the metropole."[11] This volume's invitation to chart the locations and formations of what may be labeled *metropoLatinX* demands that we contend with how metropoles and metropolitan expansion activated or reframed LatinX practices and circumstances, and vice versa. At the same time, LatinX as an approach urges us to consider speculative or unconventional ways to access and evaluate metropolitan lives and arenas.

With these points of departure, I propose we apply *LatinX* as a framework to assist us in examining and reckoning with urban and metropolitan pasts preceding the mid-twentieth century, extending beyond the United States, and involving historical actors not immediately or neatly perceived as Latina/e/o/x. Used as an adjective, *LatinX* at times denotes or qualifies what is and/or was unknown, ambiguous, peculiar, disorienting, and uncategorizable. We should be careful not to treat it as a prescriptive or static modifier. The capitalized *X*, after all, foregrounds indeterminacy. *LatinX* in this sense gestures to what is and/or was imprecisely defined or fixed, unbounded, and perhaps paradoxical. Indefinite in meaning, *LatinX* as applied in these pages does not correspond with individual, communal, or structural modes of identification. Rather than treating LatinX as an identity, a consciousness, or political category, it serves as an interpretive resource or method for working through historical experiences, processes, and trajectories marked by Latinness. Milian's insight is essential here. "LatinX, it seems to me, rearranges our Latino/a dictionary—our largely U.S.-situated lexicon," she asserts, "and moves to other conceptual histories, spaces, and perspectives."[12] This proposition should propel us to undertake bolder investigations and utilize LatinX as a springboard for delving into temporalities, geographies, conditions, and episodes not typically registered in urban and metropolitan histories. Doing so has the potential to reveal more nuanced and muddled pasts, to challenge us intellectually, and to locate LatinX subjects in places and occurrences that we have not yet explored or imagined. As De Genova reminds us, "Work in our field has always been most compelling and relevant when it can illuminate something about the historically specific relationalities that situate Latino/a/Xs at the center of larger processes of social and political transformation."[13]

In the age of revolutions, a rarely acknowledged set of historical actors—LatinX ones—played seminal roles in growing and sustaining a LatinX city in transition, as a French colonial regime gave way to Anglo-American control. Some fifteen thousand refugees from Saint-Domingue (Haiti after 1804) entered New Orleans between 1791 and 1810. Approximately two-thirds of these migrants had lived in and later been expelled from Cuba; a similar number arrived either as free people of color or as slaves. Some left Saint-Domingue to escape the political and economic turmoil engendered by the Haitian Revolution; others moved as their enslavers ordered; still others fled as France attempted to reimpose its might and restore slavery.[14] Their arrival in New Orleans further Latinized that urban milieu—or, more precisely, Latinized it with people of African descent—as it adjusted to Anglo-American domination. Including people from Saint-Domingue here is neither a claim that they imagined themselves as Latinx nor a move to assign a present-day ethnoracial category onto them. Rather, the aim is to scrutinize how their distinctive Latinness molded their experiences and enmeshed them in the evolution of this early nucleus of LatinX urbanism.[15]

Early nineteenth-century New Orleans may well represent the first LatinX city—and nascent LatinXness—in the United States. This speculation should prompt us to pause and ruminate as it upends how we map and what we traditionally assume about urban pasts colored and altered by LatinX bodies and developments. Ceded to the United States decades before San Antonio and Santa Fe, in 1803, New Orleans owed its metamorphosis and growth to LatinX circumstances. Its excision from Latin European control resulted in its incorporation into a young republic-cum-empire; its Latin population had to contend with Anglo-American hegemony. The number of migrants from Saint-Domingue entering New Orleans grew precisely at this imperial juncture. They departed Latin-Caribbean locales marked by revolution, insecurity, and expulsion—presaging the fate of thousands of Latin American and Caribbean migrants later in the nineteenth century and millions of them in the twentieth. Once in New Orleans, the Saint-Domingue refugees and their offspring replenished the city with their labors and culture, even as Anglo Americans questioned their presence and value.

Appraising New Orleans as a locus of LatinX metropolitanism-in-the-making demands that we weigh issues involving demography, cultural life, Anglo-American reaction, and labor. Seven years after its transfer to the United States, the city had become the seventh most populous "urban place" in the nation; by 1820, it ranked as the fifth largest. The Saint-Domingue diaspora fueled much of the increase in population as approximately ten thousand migrants arrived in 1809–1810 alone.[16] What census enumerators did not tease out leaves much open for exploration: an overwhelmingly non-Anglo population—linguistically dominant in French, Spanish, and/or Creole languages; considered foreign or peculiar; and shaped by crossings and experiences in the circum-Caribbean—recast New Orleans as LatinX in composition. The city's Spanish architecture and an imposing central plaza, among other components of spatial configuration, further befuddled Anglo Americans; this urban landscape appeared "strange to [their] eyes." "But, most importantly, it was the city's people," as Jennifer Spear emphasizes, "who struck visitors as 'a sight wholly new even.'" The range of colors and phenotypes, including "all hues of brown," evinced diversity, mixture, unfamiliarity, and oddness—in effect, a LatinXness.[17] Bolstering this phenomenon, the migrants from Saint-Domingue reinforced and amplified the French language, Catholicism, and other components of "Gallic culture."[18] Most migrants, especially those of African descent, did not transport a traditional or static French culture; they brought languages, religious practices, and folklore produced by creolization. Paralleling the syncretism in the Spanish-speaking Caribbean, much of the Saint-Domingue culture found itself infused with African traditions and influences. More fusion occurred once migrants settled in New Orleans.

The migratory flows and interactions between people resistant to Americanization both reproduced and modified the city's Latinness. Anglo Americans intent on asserting their authority found this course of events troubling. At the crest of the wave of Saint-Domingue refugees, the Louisiana governor William Claiborne noted, "Many good Americans are dissatisfied with so great an influx of foreigners."[19] Their discontent and alarm grew out of multiple assessments. French-speaking, and sometimes Spanish-speaking, Catholic migrants resisted the project of Americanization; refugee slaves might foment rebellion among the domestic slave population; free people of color challenged the racial project equating African origin with enslavement. Ire or suspicion involving culture and politics in no way overrode the workings of the market. More specifically, the labors of the enslaved and free people of color sustained and aggrandized urban infrastructure, port operations, affluent households, and the burgeoning complex of sugar and cotton plantations nearby. Latinized, African-origin workers buttressed New Orleans's metropolitan ambitions well into the antebellum era. Third only to New York and Baltimore by 1840, New Orleans stood as an economic capital in the slaveholding republic and the proto-metropole of the circum-Caribbean. Vestiges of a Latin heritage, profits based on exploitation and abjection, and the city's location as a "liminal zone between the Anglo and Latin worlds" intertwined and positioned New Orleans on the cusp of becoming a LatinX metropolis.[20]

Anglo America and Latin America found themselves on a collision course in the mid-nineteenth century—one provoked by the United States and its commitment to white supremacy and empire building. Expansionism and war resulted in displacement, subjugation, and disorientation, as illustrated by the state of affairs in the city of Granada, Nicaragua, in the mid-1850s. A cosmopolitan capital with long-standing ties to North Atlantic economies, Granada found itself occupied by William Walker and his filibusters in 1855. The Anglo American and his mercenary force had actually been "invited," as Michel Gobat has shown, by an elite faction seeking to Americanize Nicaragua, augment capitalist enterprises, and topple their political rivals. While the experiment did not pan out as these elites had envisioned, Walker's rule and the arrival of thousands of settler colonists from the United States generated a set of LatinX relations and realities. Granada and its metropolitan region became the epicenter of a "filibuster state" and a place in suspension—*more and other* than Nicaraguan while under the grip of U.S. citizens who did not answer to the U.S. government. Its residents lived under perplexing conditions and confronted an ethnocentrism and "development project" manufactured in the United States. Undergirded by Manifest Destiny, Walker's Granada resembled a cauldron of an imperialist enterprise bent on modernizing what most Anglo Americans perceived as an undeveloped, tropical society.[21]

A realignment of power and governance, an altered set of social relations, and attempts to redesign Granada's urban form exposed a LatinX metropolitan order in progress. Walker's state depended on military force, although Nicaraguan "collaborators" and pro-Walker government officials legitimized the Americanization agenda. Some local allies went further and propagated ideas about a Latin public in need of regeneration and civilization.[22] A reform impulse imbued with racism and Protestantism guided the official modernization program and the vision of many newcomers, most of whom settled in or around Granada. Anglo Americans' sense of superiority and contempt for "the inferiorly developed Indian, [and] half-breed of Central America," as the regime's *El Nicaragüense* described the native population, cast the masses as deficient and abject beings while simultaneously circumscribing social relations.[23] Here lay ideological cornerstones for a dominant and perverse version of nineteenth-century LatinX metropolitanism: the metropole's strength and success rested on Anglo control and Latin subservience and dependence. The metropole's physical contours, too, became targets for reform. Initiatives to revamp public infrastructure and urban layout—modeled after American and European cities—alongside colonists' entrepreneurial activities would supposedly spawn a "new Granada." Most public works never materialized, as a Central American army mobilized against Walker's regime and overthrew it in 1857. The short-lived imperial venture centered in Granada nevertheless presaged metamorphoses that could occur when and if Anglo Americans occupied and took control of Latin American environments.

Great transitions in Granada, and Central America more broadly, began before Walker's arrival and overlapped with the emergence of a Pacific coast hub with a motley Latine population and permeated by Latinness: San Francisco. Circumstances in post-1848 San Francisco begot consequential forms of LatinX metropolitanism in the continental United States. The golden city's accelerated course from "mission to metropolis" relied on and collided with Latinness; it simultaneously benefited from and shunned Latin bodies and practices.[24] These opposing inclinations defined the lives and challenges of Latines in this city-cum-metropole well into the twentieth century.

LatinXness proved foundational to San Francisco's phenomenal growth. The gold rush, the displacement of Native and Californio/x populations, and the arrival of gold-seeking migrants and transients all evinced LatinX processes at work. They unleashed unprecedented, disorienting, and exploitative conditions as they closed, opened, and blocked opportunities for Latines. Historical actors implicated in these developments assigned divergent values, X values if one will, to Latinness. Negative appraisals proliferated even as the city and region relied on the labor and contributions of Latines. Edward D. Melillo's investigation of Chileans offers a seminal case in point. "Chileans helped build the commercial world of nineteenth-century California," underscores Melillo. "Some of these women and men labored as bricklayers, shopkeepers, and sex workers in San Francisco, while others taught Yankees how to mine gold in the Sierra Nevada or extracted precious mercury ore in the Santa Clara Valley." Ethnic Mexicans, Peruvians, and other Latin Americans joined Chileans in these endeavors; they participated in the construction and expansion of the mid-nineteenth-century metropolitan region, with their hands, know-how, and fortitude. Some Latin contributions undergirded San Francisco's capitalist structure at the most literal level. In the 1850s, "scores of abandoned Chilean ships provided much of the wooden scaffolding on which San Francisco's developers expanded the city's waterfront real estate."[25] The groundwork for metropolitan ascension depended on, among other components, Latin resources and capitalist shrewdness.

Economic fortunes and misfortunes intensified alongside racism here, as they did in many settings; so doing, they fueled additional LatinX situations. The drive to subdue, expel, and literally X out Latines from the city and region proceeded swiftly and relentlessly. The form and scale of this social world—composed of an emergent metropole, small towns, mining camps, and Native hinterlands—undoubtedly differed from its mid-twentieth-century successors spurred on by a "second gold rush" and analyzed by various scholars.[26] Still, both metropolitan worlds revolved around capital accumulation, a valorization of property over humanity, and white entitlement. Nativism, economic competition, and cultural chauvinism bred racial violence and expulsion campaigns that targeted Latines and other nonwhite peoples in San Francisco and the mining camps. The consequences for Latines ranged from loss of livelihoods and banishment to lynching or, as Melillo chillingly puts it, confronting "Manifest Destiny at the end of a rope."[27] Manifest Destiny fed off nationalist and racist notions of exceptionalism. The ideology permeated the gold rush and the metropolitan order it engendered. The processes themselves exhibited extraordinariness, aberrance, familiarity, racism, and LatinXness.

As San Francisco marginalized its Latinness and secured its role as "the metropole for U.S. Pacific imperial interests," New Orleans continued its

LatinX evolution and cemented its influence over Central America and the circum-Caribbean region.[28] Its role as a nexus for commerce and cultural exchange between the United States and its southern neighbors swelled in the decades after the Civil War. By the late nineteenth century, "the economic and political worlds of Louisiana and Central America seemed to blur"; much of this ambiguity flourished and ran through New Orleans.[29] One Latin product—tropical, sexualized, and born of exploitation—accounted for these developments: bananas. The bulk of bananas bound for the United States passed through New Orleans, where two of the three major banana corporations had their headquarters. The fruit's cultivation entailed more than profits and markets; it involved labor and migration. All these elements coalesced in New Orleans. As bananas bolstered the city's economic dynamism, the fruit also fomented the circulation and settlement of Latin bodies, including ones not counted or seen as Latin American or Latina/e/o/x.

Banana profits and migrants from the banana zones solidified New Orleans's ascension to and status as a LatinX metropole. Latinness had a long presence here, as discussed earlier. In the late nineteenth century, small cadres of intellectuals and exiles from in/dependent Latin America, especially Cubans, passed through or lived in the city for some time.[30] More migrants from the Western Hemisphere did so in the twentieth century's early decades; many had ties to the banana zones in Central America. Decades later, the *Times-Picayune* acknowledged the linkage between the banana industry and migration. The newspaper reported that working for and forging connections with fruit companies "brought thousands of Hondurans to New Orleans, forming the core of the city's largest Latin population."[31] Notably, many of these migrants did not view themselves exclusively or primarily as Honduran or Central American; they or their parents also identified as West Indian. "Central American immigrants have been invisible [in New Orleans]," observes Glenn A. Chambers, "in part because most did not fit the stereotypical profile of a Latino in the North American sense. They were of African descent, had English surnames, and in some cases held British passports." Their multidimensional existence fell prey to racism in Central America, the edifice of Jim Crow, and popular imaginaries involving Latines, which worked in tandem to ignore or call into question their "complex experiences."[32]

Imperial, racist, and personal histories led migrants to the metropolitan center made richer by trade and investment in, quite literally, the fruits of their labor. Here, they encountered a society that celebrated its "Franco-Spanish atmosphere and strong Catholic influence" while also being committed to Jim Crow.[33] Infused with a Latinness that praised European heritage and Romance languages, New Orleans left little latitude for Black Latinness and Afro-descended Latines. These social conditions betrayed LatinXness: they exalted some versions of Latinness and left others unacknowledged; they recognized some Latin bodies while marginalizing and crossing out others.

A continental crossroads "*donde comienza la America Hispana* / where Hispanic America begins," as *La Voz Latina* advertised it in the 1930s, New Orleans functioned as a LatinX metropolis for multiple reasons. First, as implied by the tagline above, some New Orleanians branded the metropolis as an extension of or "the gateway to" Latin America.[34] The slogan involved a good deal of boosterism, to be sure; yet it recognized New Orleans's position: simultaneously in the United States and an integral part of Latin America. Cultural linkages notwithstanding, the metropole's might in the early twentieth century largely revolved around "the business of empire," which hinged on the exploitation of natural and human resources beyond U.S. borders. Whether it involved bananas, lumber, or precious minerals, "the establishment of North American industrial enterprises in Central America," as a preeminent example, fostered "the economic and political dependence" of the region.[35] Political economies in the isthmus found themselves circumscribed by an imperial agenda radiating from New Orleans—with support from Washington as well as Central American elites—which touched people's daily lives even if they never ventured to Louisiana. In this way, the metropolis exerted much influence at a distance while relying on Latin/Latinized bodies to "make the empire work."[36] That is exactly what Central American and West Indian laborers did in the banana zones and once they migrated to the metropole.

Multiple migratory streams converged in New Orleans in the 1910s and 1920s, which set in motion unsurprising and unexpected crossings. The settlement or sojourn of laboring peoples from the banana zones coincided with the arrival of Mexican migrants in the wake of upheaval and revolutionary change. Historical studies to date do not reveal prolonged or meaningful interactions between these groups. "With the exception of a small pocket of Hondurans living in close proximity to each other, most Latin Americans chose to live among other (particularly white) New Orleanians," details Chambers. Middle-class occupations and educational pursuits, notes this historian, allowed many Latines to "transition into whiteness."[37] In a related move, Mexicans relied on cultural strategies grounded in nationalism and an elision (an X-ing) of race, according to Julie Weise, to assimilate into whiteness and gain "acceptance as whites."[38] Their passages occurred as Central Americans of West Indian descent blended into and "augment[ed]" African American life. The work of Jim Crow seemingly subsumed Latinness under a Black-white binary that negated and skirted around brownness, mixture, and ambiguity.

Social realities and lived experience, however, could not be contained by law; some “racially ambiguous Latin Americans” either could not melt into whiteness or resisted doing so.[39] The X of Latin pointed in various directions. It could signal an absorption into African America, a crossover into white America, or an existence in another ground—in a messy, ill-defined elsewhere.

Some 650 miles east of New Orleans, in Tampa, a distinct type of LatinX metropolitanism took hold. Urbanization and immigration fed off each other in the Florida city; the interdependence was neither novel nor exceptional in the early twentieth century. Still, Tampa’s trajectory significantly diverged from other locales because Latin bodies undergirded both large-scale processes. “Tampa’s urban-ecological portrait differed sharply from the metropolitan growth of the Northeast and Midwest,” stress Gary R. Mormino and George E. Pozzetta in their classic study of Ybor City, a company town absorbed by Tampa in 1887. The immediately identifiable differences rested on industrial output and the labor force: factories overwhelmingly manufactured cigars, and the workers at the center of production were Cubans, Spaniards, and Italians. “Drawn to the city by work in the cigar industry between the late 1880s and 1920s,” writes Sarah McNamara, “these Latinas and Latinos built the Tampa economy and established Ybor and Tampa as the cigar capital of the world.”[40] As they did so, they created and moved through a LatinX environment characterized by unconventional social dynamics, a pastiche landscape, and cosmopolitan sensibilities. These components revealed the contours of a unique LatinX metropolitanism in the U.S. South.

Residents of Tampa racialized as Latins pieced together, accessed, and navigated “geographies of Latinness.”[41] These social terrains exhibited features and arrangements evoking familiarity and novelty on one hand while provoking exchange, experimentation, interrogation, and friction on the other. Latinized peoples from the Old and New Worlds encountered one another in workplaces, residential zones, and an array of communal institutions. Their labor guaranteed cigar magnates’ wealth, even as their political work challenged the capitalist order and inspired a formidable degree of collaboration and unity. The connections forged in Tampa contrasted with the antagonism between Italians and Puerto Ricans in 1920s New York City—another setting where these populations met—owing to conflicts over turf and race.[42] Color and race certainly mattered in Tampa; Afro-Cubans and African Americans consistently endured varying forms of prejudice. Yet “Tampa faced no simple black-and-white equation in race relations,” according to Mormino and Pozzetta. “Instead the cigar city confronted an array of possible configurations in its social structure and cultural framework.”[43]

The indeterminacy of racial locations and the myriad sociocultural experiences gestured toward LatinXness as well as social relations that muddled Jim Crow. If Latinness found itself largely subsumed by the Black-white binary in New Orleans, it appeared to operate outside or in between the binary in Tampa. The case of Afro-Cubans, for example, suggested some intermediateness and malleability. While "living and working in [this] immigrant community," maintains Nancy Raquel Mirabal, Afro-Cubans "occupied a fluid, in-between position where they were neither white nor necessarily black."[44] To be sure, governmental authorities and Anglo Tampans regarded them as Black. Some Anglos concurrently questioned Italians' and Spaniards' whiteness and "claim[ed] that Latins were not members of the 'white race.'" Distinguishing Southern Europeans and all Latins from Anglo-Saxon Americans—as "inbetween peoples" in a racialized state between white and Black—proved common in the United States at this time.[45] The phenomenon conveyed much about the mapping of Latinness on ethnoracial landscapes such as Tampa's. Here, Latinness equaled Xness: in-betweenness, perplexity, and unsettlement.

Tampa's Latin laborers regularly joined forces to unsettle capitalist prerogatives and to demand rights and autonomy in the workplace. Their activism and mobilizations drew strength from socialist and anarchist agendas, which linked them to global networks even as local power brokers set out to extinguish them. Business owners, government officials, and the Anglo public responded by turning to the then-standard arsenal for suppressing labor: capitalist intransigence, harassment, repression, nativism, and, at times, vigilante terrorism. Workers' solidarity amid unrest and repression "helped transform clusters of Italians, Spaniards, and Cubans into a distinctive 'Latin' community," observe Mormino and Pozzetta. These peoples' "struggle to persist" and to envision a radical reordering of work and power "produced something of a 'we-ness.'"[46]

It might be tempting to historicize this we-ness as a proto-latinidad; however, it is best to approach it as a LatinX phenomenon: intersectional, open, and indeterminate. Spaniards and Italians have generally stood outside the construction of latinidad, an ideology and political project with a Latin American foundation.[47] The consideration before us is neither to make them fit nor to keep them out, but rather to move beyond it. Circumstances in Tampa demonstrated that class standing and Latinness overlapped, and promoted affinity and a sense of unity. The evolution of Tampa's Latin collective and related experiments among peoples who traced their ancestry to Latin terrains in both hemispheres deserve more investigation. Other cities certainly housed diverse Latin populations at this time; if Tampa exhibited a singular course, then, we might also label this LatinX development as exceptional. Cigar workers surely did not see themselves as special or uncommon; rather, they linked their struggles and visions with those of working people well beyond the United States. The possibilities of "international brotherhood" captivated their imagination as they infused their politics with internationalism. Although they lived in the U.S. South, they immersed themselves in a capacious and worldly arena, at once transnational and cosmopolitan. "In the 'Cigar City,'" McNamara reminds us, "politics and personal relationships were transnational."[48]

Tampa's Latin proletariat embedded their cosmopolitan sensibilities and transnational perspectives in the built environment and urban areas. In contrast to Latino landscapes, as recently analyzed by A. K. Sandoval-Strausz, early twentieth-century Tampa witnessed the emergence of LatinX formations. Sandoval-Strausz explains that Latinos in the late twentieth century "occupied and produced" spaces that drew on "distinctive forms of urbanism from the cultural hearths" in Latin America.[49] The landscapes in Tampa certainly engaged in dialogue with Latin America and the Caribbean, but also with Latin Europe and the Arab world. Buildings big and small exhibited an array of cultural influences and references. Take, for example, the edifices for L'Unione Italiana and El Centro Español. The former "embodies elements of classical and Mediterranean architecture"; the latter includes "wrought-iron balconies with Spanish motifs, [a] decorative Moorish entrance arch with cast-iron trim, and eyebrow windows with white stone trim and decorative stonework."[50] Beauty and awe notwithstanding, grand brick-and-mortar structures such as these housed community organizations—not museums or government agencies—that served multiple functions (e.g., mutual aid, political debate, entertainment) and often catered to mixed clienteles. The public culture nurtured in these sites allowed for regular exchange, deliberation, and art forms (e.g., community-centered theater) in decline—or perhaps, on their way to becoming extinct—in other parts of the country.

Working people encountered one critical art form—*la lectura* (reading)—in Tampa's preeminent LatinX space: the cigar factory itself. An everyday meeting ground for Latin laborers, the cigar factory functioned as workplace, locus of political organizing, educational center, and hub of cultural life. Much of the non-work-related activities and significance hinged on *la lectura* and its lectors—a cultural practice transported from Cuba and made accessible to cigar workers of all backgrounds. Readings throughout the workday taught lessons in everything from literature to political economy, entertained laborers, politicized them, and served as a means for Italians to learn Spanish.

"Workers controlled *la lectura*," underscores Mormino; guarding and maintaining the tradition proved essential to their laborite agenda.[51] Together with the lectors, they transformed the cigar factory into much more than an area of production; it became, figuratively speaking, a school, a theater, and community center. The work arena thus had multiple meanings and dimensions, including unintended ones as employers discovered. It epitomized the grounds in which to acquire or sharpen the tools for advancement and liberation—a realm in which to imagine a world of possibilities beyond the materiality required by the factory. "A LatinX space may demand," posits Milian while drawing on philosopher Henri Lefebvre's insight, "'x-dimensional spaces . . . spaces of configuration, abstract spaces, spaces defined by deformation and transformation.'"[52] Altered by a practice managed by workers themselves, the cigar factory operated as just that: a LatinX terrain.

In our present day, the National Park Service recognizes Ybor City and the Vieux Carré (French Quarter) in New Orleans as historic districts and national landmarks. These sites presumably evoke and assist in "tell[ing] the breadth of the Latino heritage story."[53] My discussion in the preceding pages suggests that these districts and the cities in which they grew can tell us much more, possibly disorient what is contained under Latino heritage or urban Latino/a history, and propel us into the unknown or unexplored—into X spaces and conditions. The cities surveyed here nurtured and witnessed early manifestations of LatinX metropolitanism: urban experiences and developments imbued with Latinness and intertwined with imperial and transnational processes. Focusing on labor and the people who built these metropoles, I have centered on the bodies, practices, and social relations permeating these settings, as these are often crossed out (X-ed out) by popular fascination with historic buildings and physical landscapes. The National Park Service's online introduction to the Vieux Carré, as an example, does not reference working people at all, as if New Orleans's grandeur and economic preeminence could have been possible without laborers in its metropolitan orbit.[54]

The *X* in *LatinX* should encourage us to undertake investigations that orient us in multiple and novel directions: temporally, geographically, conceptually, and hemispherically. The case studies sketched here offer examples of how we might do so; they are neither exhaustive nor exceptional. Although this discussion treats only the nineteenth and early twentieth centuries, one can certainly envision seventeenth-century Santa Fe as another starting point. Attention to Granada could occur alongside an examination of the state of affairs in Havana, Panama City, or Manila, among many others. The lives of Filipina/e/o/xs and French Canadians in various U.S. cities, too, might elucidate LatinX processes and states of being. In short, the imprints of LatinX metropolitan pasts can be found in X times and places. What we deem revelatory might prove more expansive if we probe beyond what is readily apparent. LatinX as a concept and method, after all, affords us the flexibility to contemplate and tackle our subject matter in an untraditional and multidimensional manner, upending or displacing our historical optic along the way.

11

"In the Grips of the Monster That Forced Us to Flee": How the Cold War Made Our Latino Cities

MAURICIO CASTRO
Centre College

The March 23, 1963, issue of *Zig-Zag Libre*, a Miami Cuban exile humor tabloid, featured a cover illustration of the attack by forces opposed to Fidel Castro's revolutionary government on the Soviet freighter *Baku*.[1] The predawn raid by fast boats had taken place on March 17 and was part of a series of assaults carried out by paramilitary exile groups against ships conducting trade with Cuba. These attacks led to denunciation by the Soviet Union, to a statement by the Departments of State and Justice declaring that they neither supported nor condoned them, and to the April arrest of a Miami-based raiding party by British authorities in Bahamian waters as the group prepared to attack a Soviet tanker off the coast of Cuba.[2]

The art on the cover of *Zig-Zag* did not, however, convey the diplomatic firestorms these raiding parties ignited with their attacks. Instead, the illustration showed a small boat with a large Cuban flag firing upon the much larger freighter emblazoned with the hammer and sickle with the headline "¡ARMAS, SI! ¡ISLITAS, NO!" The headline both approved the use of armaments against the revolutionary government and decried the recent suggestion by former Florida governor LeRoy Collins that the Cuban refugee population in the state be relocated to a small island in the West Indies to found a "new Cuba" allied with the United States.[3]

Inside the periodical, readers also found a recurring segment entitled "Cosas de nuestro exilio" (Stuff from Our Exile), in which the cartoonist Silvio illustrated snapshots of the Miami exile experience. These included a man with a weathervane on his head and the caption "Para aprenderse la ciudad" (To learn your way around the city); a woman hiding five children under her skirt as she applied for a rental property, claiming "Somos tres nada más . . ." (It's just three of us); and a man drenched in seawater, carrying a boat over his head being greeted by a friend who asked "¿Llegaste ahora?" (Did you just get in?)[4] The readers of *Zig-Zag Libre* in Miami would have understood both of these segments as part of the reality of exile, as part of an experience that was both local and tied to the global struggle of the Cold War. For many of Miami's Cuban refugees, the trials and tribulations of paramilitary exiles engaged in a campaign against Castro's government were no less real than the everyday challenges of arriving in South Florida, of navigating the city's unfamiliar streets, and of finding accommodations in an overcrowded housing market. They might not have been active participants in the armed raids against Cuba's government, but life in Miami was part of the same broad struggle.

The continuity between life in an American city and the ongoing struggle against communism that many of Miami's Cubans felt engaged in, as alluded to by the writers and illustrators of *Zig-Zag Libre*, suggests an underexplored phenomenon in Latino urban history. The exciting and important work being done by scholars in this field has tackled significant questions. Important among them are the conditions that drove Latin American migration to cities, the ways they were racialized, the process by which they Latinized their adopted cities, and the effects of government policy on population movements and the lives of migrants in their new communities. As the practitioners in this volume and elsewhere seek to explain this historical evolution, however, we should build on the work of historians of migration and the Latino experience who have engaged the impact of the Cold War; in so doing, we can create histories that center that global conflict in the Latinization of American cities, fitting it within broader patterns of empire and imperial migration but focusing on how it shaped urban spaces, economies, and polities.

Existing histories of the Latinization of American cities have been revelatory and provide essential interpretive frameworks that can be enriched by interpreting the Cold War more broadly: not only as a driver of migration but also as a conflict that defined the way many newcomers understood their new homes, forged their communities, and ultimately transformed entire metropolitan areas. The subfield's leading scholars have taken a perspective on the American city that looks far beyond the nation's borders, especially by examining the actions of U.S. governments and corporations and the broader influence of American empire. In *Brown in the Windy City: Mexicans and Puerto Ricans in Postwar Chicago*, Lilia Fernández notes that the migrations of these groups to the U.S. mainland were in part the result of "the economic, social, and political dislocations" created by American imperialism.[5] These dislocations set the stage for migrants from Mexico and Puerto Rico to become "subjects of state-sponsored mass labor importation programs in the

United States," specifically the Bracero Program for Mexican laborers and the labor migrations as part of the Operation Bootstrap for Puerto Ricans coming to the U.S. mainland. Fernández shows how these populations, which had already been racialized within U.S. colonialism, were reracialized and made vulnerable to exploitation, whether as agricultural laborers or after they converged in the factories of the Midwest.[6]

Other scholars have expanded on the conditions that drove migration. Llana Barber has emphasized the way in which American imperialism created push factors for immigration. Why, she asks in *Latino City: Immigration and Urban Crisis in Lawrence, Massachusetts, 1945–2000*, would "tens of thousands of Latinos settle in a small, obscure city with a resistant white population and a troubled economy?"[7] Even more than Fernández before her, Barber points to the dislocations in migrants' homelands created by American empire. She draws on Juan González's concept of Latin American migration to the United States as the "harvest of empire" to foreground more than a century of American interventions and invasions. Beyond the "pull" factors offered by better wages, "the U.S. also helped 'push' migrants out of their home countries by foreclosing economic opportunities and eroding dreams of a better life at home."[8] As such, Barber contends, U.S. imperial interventions in Latin America are central to our understanding of the Latinization of American cities.

To get a full picture of these transformations, scholars of Latino urban history have also contended with government policies both foreign and domestic that have shaped not only the arrival of migrant communities but also their relationship to cities. For example, A. K. Sandoval-Strausz's *Barrio America: How Latino Immigrants Saved the American City* argues that various Latin American governments responded to U.S. economic coercion with industrialization policies that drove their populations into cities, connecting them with a "pan-American urban system" that fostered their subsequent emigration. He also focuses on the undocumented status of some among these immigrant groups, drawing on the work of Mae Ngai to foreground the way that the Immigration and Nationality Act of 1965 (also called the Hart-Celler Act), shaped by the racism of key opponents in Congress, imposed "unprecedented limits on Latin American immigration in a way that would place the stigma and burden of illegality on millions of Hispanics for decades to come."[9] Further federal actions, like the Immigration Reform and Control Act of 1986, propelled Latino migrants into cities and helped them revitalize their neighborhoods: its militarization of the border created incentives for migrants to remain in the United States year-round and to seek higher-paying urban jobs rather than engaging in seasonal labor migration; the law also made almost three million undocumented people into legal residents more willing to make long-term investments in their adopted city neighborhoods.[10]

Historians working outside Latino urban history, particularly in the broader fields of immigration and Latino history, have created frameworks that help us understand broader imperial migration structures and the impact of the Cold War on immigration after the spatial and transnational turns. Paul Kramer has argued for an understanding of migration using the concept of the geopolitics of mobility, "the ways in which global structures and processes have shaped large-scale population movements and the roles that migration has played in states' attempts to secure and organize power in a globalized arena." Kramer explains that the restrictive state, which prevented the crossing of boundaries, is entwined with the magnetic state, which streamlined the migration interests of state and corporate power.[11] Jesse Hoffnung-Garskof has similarly urged historians to understand migration "as a consequence of relationships between the United States and particular other parts of the world, and as a constituent part of some of those relationships," and has argued that most of the societies that "most prolifically sent immigrants to the United States after mid-century not only had deep and intimate ties with the United States; they were primary targets or principal adversaries of U.S. imperial power" during the Cold War.[12] These scholars, and others working on subsets of migration categories or national origins, have demonstrated that the broader struggle of the Cold War shaped midcentury immigration to a significant degree.[13] Indeed, the broader field of Latino history has often taken the Cold War as a useful avenue of analysis that provides a broader understanding of how the conflict affected relations between the United States and Latin America and how it influenced movements on both sides of the border.[14]

As foundational as these and many other works in the field are, a fuller understanding of these patterns should include direct engagement with the impact of the Cold War and how it created new patterns of Latinization in U.S. cities while also reshaping older patterns.[15] The Cold War was at the core of the experience of multiple groups of Latino immigrants who came to the United States because of the structures of ideological violence and upheaval unleashed by the broader conflict and sometimes directly by American action. Migration to the United States and conglomeration in American cities, sometimes with the encouragement of the U.S. government but often without, became a key avenue for the Latinization of urban spaces that is too often glossed over or treated as an outlier. This chapter seeks to frame the importance of the Cold War to the field of Latino urban history by showing how the conflict brought Latino migrant groups and significant changes to

American cities starting before the 1960s but lasting for decades to follow. It also shifts the center of historiographical weight back several years to before the Hart-Celler Act and the mass migrations that followed by showing how key developments from 1959 to 1965 bore consequences that long outlasted the conflict that originated them.

This chapter's primary case study is the arrival of the Cuban community in Miami, a significant influx that led to what might be the most thoroughgoing Latinization of any American city but one that is often viewed by various literatures as an exception because of the Cold War context in which it occurred. Instead, the case of Miami must be understood as the clearest example of a broader and understudied trend in Latino urban history—and one that has connections to other subliteratures in American urban history as well. The case study of Miami illustrates three main points in how the Cold War shaped our Latino cities. First, while patterns of American empire had driven migration from Latin America to U.S. cities for decades before the start of the Cold War, this ideological struggle was key to the destabilization of the migrants' countries of origin—and to how the federal government understood the newcomers as potential diplomatic assets or liabilities in the broader conflict. Second, the Cold War–inflected understanding shaped the lives of the migrants and their relationship to the cities around them, as the beliefs of powerful officials led directly to federal action intended to shape the flow of migrants and to either discourage their settlement or ease their transition into life in the United States. Third, these policy decisions resulted in contingent actions within these urban contexts, reshaping these environments and leading to their use by the migrants as places in which to continue the struggle that had driven them from their homes. To illustrate Miami's place within a broader pattern, the case of the Cubans in Miami is followed by briefer connections of these patterns in New York's Dominican population and in the Central American communities of Washington, DC. Finally, this Cold War–inflected Latinization will be put into conversation with the literature on the impact of this conflict and the policy decisions it drove in other areas, suggesting further connections between Latino urban history and other subfields in urban and metropolitan history.

When Fulgencio Batista fled Cuba on New Year's Eve 1958, Miami did not appear poised to become an economic juggernaut and, despite the best efforts of city boosters to connect it to the Caribbean, had fallen well short of any attempts to turn it into a gateway to the Americas. The Miami metropolitan area, which comprised the city of Miami, twenty-five suburban municipalities, and an expanding unincorporated area, was not a model of economic growth. The central city was growing at a much slower rate than the periphery as the suburban municipalities competed with the city for commercial and industrial establishments.[16] Urban renewal schemes, combined with "seeming successes" in Black suburbanization in areas like Liberty City, Richmond Heights, and Brownsville, further drove the depopulation of the central city as African Americans either chose to leave the area or were forced out by eminent domain evictions.[17] While Miami had an established garment industry and served as a tourist destination, unemployment was a noted problem on the eve of the Cuban influx.[18] Even some of the noted tourist areas had fallen into disrepair: neighboring Miami Beach increasingly took on the character of a retiree community in the 1950s with "its art deco hotels decaying in unison with its inhabitants."[19]

The Cold War's influence on Miami was shaped by the interactions between the federal government, the city of Miami, and the Cuban migrants who arrived in the aftermath of the revolution. While these categories were never completely discrete, particularly as the Cuban population settled into the city, the context and resultant policy choices created an environment for historical actors to make politically contingent decisions based on how circumstances in the city fit with the influx of Cubans and the broader Cold War. In Washington, growing distrust and opposition to Cuba's revolutionary government shaped the way policymakers and the public understood, or were told to understand, the influx of refugees into South Florida. From January of 1959, U.S. policymakers had been concerned about communism being the driving force behind the Cuban Revolution.[20] As the property of U.S. investors and firms was nationalized (leading to the largest uncompensated nationalization in U.S. history), these fears were reinforced by the furious demands by those same individuals and entities that the federal government intercede on their behalf.[21]

President Dwight D. Eisenhower was committed to the removal of Fidel Castro from power and laid the groundwork for the disastrous Bay of Pigs Invasion, an operation conducted with such a lack of secrecy that Cuban intelligence had produced reports on the training of Cuban exiles by U.S. nationals some eight months before the attempted action.[22] Even before the plans fell apart, however, the federal government had already turned its attention to the growing number of Cubans choosing to leave their homeland in the aftermath of the revolution's victory. As Castro solidified his hold on power, this migration, initially defined by a heavy component of people associated with Batista's regime, came to include a greater proportion of other members of Cuba's upper and middle classes. These opponents of the revolution, or of the turn the revolution had taken since Batista's fall, could be useful by virtue of their image and class status in the fight to portray Castro as a destructive and destabilizing influence even before the federal government took an official oppositional stance. As such, the Eisenhower administration established an open-door policy for Cubans migrating to the United States with the hope that a heavy flow of temporary refugees would discredit the new regime in the eyes of the world.[23]

This understanding of the Cubans seeking to leave their homeland as products and potential co-belligerents of the broader struggle with Marxism led to the adoption of policies that facilitated the entry of Cubans into the United States and would then boost their fortunes to significant effect on Miami's metropolitan area. An early version of this took the form of benign neglect. Until January 1961, while the United States and Cuba maintained normal diplomatic relations, Cuban citizens were able to apply for a visa or a nonimmigrant visa—a visa with an expiration date, as for tourists or students—to the United States. Cubans could travel to the United States with either form of visa, but the U.S. government allowed individuals who stayed past the period allowed by their visa to remain in the country rather than return to their homeland if they claimed they could not return so long as the Castro government was in control of the island. After January 1961, Cuban citizens could apply for a "visa waiver" that would waive visa requirements to enter the country.[24] As the political scientist María de los Angeles Torres has argued, "For the U.S. government Cuban émigrés provided the rationale for continuing a foreign policy aimed at containing communism and expanding the forces needed for battle."[25] The Cold War concerns over Cuba overruled traditional administrative requirements and restrictionist impulses.

This allowed for the Cubans coming to the United States to move outside of the reach of the government they opposed without claiming official status as opponents of the regime. Few Cubans were eager yet to embrace the label of refugee for fear of consequences for friends and family back home, and a significant segment of the new arrivals traveled to Miami, a popular shopping destination for middle- and upper-class Cubans, on tourist visas and simply overstayed them. Between Batista's flight from power on New Year's Eve in 1958 and the Cuban Missile Crisis in October 1962, approximately 248,070 Cubans emigrated to the United States while the federal government turned a blind eye to visa overstays.[26] The influx of Cubans was heaviest in South Florida and by January 1961, officials estimated that 33,000 Cuban refugees were living in the Miami area with few resources, little access to aid, and an inelastic job market ill prepared for the new arrivals.[27]

For local elites, gaining the resources they needed to deal with this crisis meant embracing its Cold War nature. The city's leaders could see that Miami had become a battlefield in a worldwide struggle, and they sought to make federal policymakers share this vision in ways that would benefit the city economically.[28] Miami Mayor Robert King High declared in 1960 that his city was a "bastion against communism" as part of a campaign to involve the federal government and its resources in dealing with the growing Cuban population.[29] City religious and civic leaders understood the nature of the problem they faced, as when Dr. Franklin Williams, the president of the Welfare Planning Council, noted that this influx, which was deeply affecting the Miami metropolitan area, was not a local issue but rather "a cold war problem."[30] The Eisenhower White House responded to pressure from Florida with meetings and a special envoy, but the selling of Miami as a front in the Cold War significantly influenced the longer-term federal response and the creation of the Cuban Refugee Program in February 1961. This federal response, aimed at more than a propaganda victory, would in turn have a deep impact on the broader development of South Florida.[31]

As Eisenhower left office and John F. Kennedy assumed the presidency, the federal government shifted into a more active stance that embraced the Cuban arrivals and solidified their status as refugees. The Kennedy administration established the Cuban Refugee Program (CRP), a government entity that paired Cold War strategy with robust welfare programs. Starting in 1962, this program operated out of the former *Miami News* building, redubbed the Cuban Refugee Center or, more commonly, the Freedom Tower, and processed approximately 450,000 Cubans seeking assistance in the twelve years in which the program was headquartered there.[32] While the CRP's aid was conditional and often coercively tied to refugees accepting reasonable offers of resettlement, this was unlike even previous resettlement programs for Cold War migrants. The refugees from the Soviet crackdown on Hungary in 1956 came to the United States through a single point of entry, the Camp Kilmer army base in New Jersey, and were processed and immediately resettled without being given the option of clustering in a single location.[33] This opportunity to create a critical mass for a community in South Florida, combined with an unprecedented level of aid for any group coming from Latin America, made the transition into Miami far easier for the thousands who applied for assistance in the form of direct aid, English classes, vocational training, and a slew of other services. This, in turn, fundamentally changed Miami's economy as it empowered these refugees to pursue old careers or new opportunities, fostering entrepreneurial impulses through benefits unheard of for other immigrant groups or by people of color born in the United States. Cold War policymakers had ambitious and secretive plans for these early waves of Cubans, but the long-term effects of their ambition can be widely understood in terms of a Cold War investment with wide-ranging consequences.[34] By economically empowering a growing Cuban community in the city, the federal government drove the Latinization of Miami and its economy, deepening the connections of the city to Latin America and the Caribbean.

Although the literature on Latino urban history has shown the extent to which Latino immigrant groups were able to repopulate and revitalize the economic landscapes of cities deeply affected by the urban crisis, the case of Miami illustrates how the Cold War context and policy decisions could establish fundamental conditions by which Cuban individuals and groups could remake Miami's economy and relationship to Latin America. As Fernández points out, much of what drew Latino groups to American cities was the demand for cheap labor in agriculture and industry occasioned by the upheavals of American imperial action. In Miami, the choice of policymakers to foster the migration of a group that was largely middle class, largely entrepreneurial, and which could serve U.S. Cold War needs on American soil, combined with unprecedented financial assistance and access to citizenship, gave these newcomers opportunities unheard of by other migrant groups. Those who provided sought-after labor for growing local industries could do so without the vulnerabilities experienced by other immigrant groups. Professionals were given the training and support to pursue their careers in the United States. And entrepreneurs received encouragement and financial support in creating businesses at such a rapid pace that by the 1970s, the city's economy had shifted significantly from its dependence on seasonal tourism at the end of the 1950s. CRP expenditures, along with access to other government programs once Cuban migrants had naturalized through the path laid out by the Adjustment Act, helped reshape Miami's economy. Cuban-owned businesses were estimated at two thousand by 1966 and at six thousand by 1971.[35]

This growing economic power of South Florida's Cuban community, and the political clout that developed alongside it, made Miami a space in which the Cuban refugees could continue the struggle of the Cold War. While South Florida served as home base to many of the paramilitary outfits conducting raids like the one on the Soviet freighter *Baku*, who vowed to keep fighting despite the U.S. crackdown on raiding parties, Miami is more important to this history as the environment in which Cuban civilian organizations organized new forms of struggle.[36] Even as the refugee population was embracing the opportunities presented by the CRP and reshaping Miami's economy as workers and new business owners, they were establishing a base of political and economic power aimed at bringing about regime change in Cuba. While these efforts would be formalized with the creation of advocacy and lobbying organizations during the 1970s and 1980s, many Miami Cubans understood their place in the city as ultimately temporary. Miami was a platform from which to determine the future of Cuba. They could build lives, businesses, and organizations in Miami, contributing to the city—but they expected that changes in Cuba would make their lives in the city transitory.

When the cofounder of the anticommunist Truth about Cuba Committee, Luis V. Manrara, donated the organization's records to the University of Miami in 1988, twenty-seven years after the committee incorporated, he made it clear that the donation was temporary. Manrara's agreement with the university stipulated that once Cuba had regained "independence" from the Soviet Union and had established a democratic government with free elections for five consecutive years, the university would thereupon make the records available to the new Republic of Cuba.[37] Those increasingly bothered by the prominence of Cubans in Miami, however, called into question whether their actions in the city could really shape the wider conflict. By 1963, the *Miami Herald*, the city's largest newspaper and increasingly an adversary of the Cuban community, was grousing that Cuba's future would be decided on the island, not in Washington or Miami.[38] The piece's author, Max Freedman, urged U.S. policymakers and the Cuban refugee community to support anti-Castro forces in Cuba rather than attempting to take on the task of regime change themselves. While trying to question the effectiveness of Miami's Cubans to bring about change on the island, however, Freedman was tacitly acknowledging how the city had become a battleground in the continued struggle over the future of their homeland. What Freedman did not yet see, only a few years into the Cuban influx into the city, was that this continued struggle and the politics around it would become a defining characteristic of public life in Miami.

Miami was not, however, the only American city shaped by Cold War struggles, political maneuverings, and conflict-driven migration and migratory policy. Some of the changes brought about in other cities involved extensions of the same conflict that shifted South Florida's urban environment. By the early 1960s, Fidel Castro's government had already begun projecting its revolution outward, including an attempt to bring about regime change in the Dominican Republic. Dominican dictator Rafael Trujillo's repressive regime made the Eisenhower administration concerned about a Cuba-style revolution in the Dominican Republic, and by 1961, the Central Intelligence Agency backed his assassination.[39] The Kennedy administration, frustrated by the failure to overthrow Castro at the Bay of Pigs, sought to shape the new Dominican Republic. Ultimately, the populist democrat Juan Bosch came to power after an election in 1962, but the following year, after being denounced as a communist by the country's business sector and church, he was overthrown and replaced by a military junta. After an attempted return by Bosch and a rebellion driven by the political disaffection of some in the political classes and the desperate economic conditions facing the urban poor, the Johnson administration invaded Santo Domingo in April 1965. This intervention came from both an overestimation of the influence of communists in the rebellion and from a desire to project strength in the Cold War in domestic politics, with the president declaring that he had "just taken action that will prove that Democratic presidents can deal with Communists as strongly as Republicans." This confluence of domestic and foreign policy concerns ultimately led to the extended tenure of Joaquín Balaguer.[40]

Cold War geopolitics in the Dominican Republic created the push factor that drove tens of thousands of Dominicans to leave the country, with the Dominican-born population in the United States going from under 10,000 in 1960 to 170,817 by 1980.[41] Furthermore, the U.S. government also sought to use migration to influence the country's direction: it ordered the issuance of increasing quantities of passports under the assumption that this would help "push troublesome actors out of the country."[42] This, paired with riots and demonstrations that fueled the U.S. embassy's fear of unrest and led to an increase in visas issued, helped drive the influx of Dominicans into the United States.[43] American policymakers not only drove Dominicans away from their homeland; in the service of anticommunism, they directly funneled migration into the United States. This was not an "elite" migration, as policymakers had framed the Cuban arrivals, nor was it received with the same largesse, but the use of immigration policy as a tool in Cold War foreign policy creates significant parallels between the Dominican and Cuban cases.

This migration led to significant changes in New York City. As the Dominican *colonia* in the city grew into the largest Dominican population in the United States, the presence of these newcomers did not go unnoticed. The year after the U.S. invasion, the *New York Times* noted the significant influx of Spanish speakers to the city, the changes it was bringing about, and the tensions that came along with the new arrivals. While the piece mostly focused on the city's new Puerto Rican residents, it also noted that, as of January of 1966, 28,950 Dominicans had registered as resident aliens in the city—although the consulate estimated the correct number of Dominicans in the city to be closer to 65,000.[44] Just five years later that number was estimated to be between 100,000 and 200,000.[45]

As they arrived in the city and began to settle in neighborhoods like Corona in Queens and Washington Heights in Manhattan, the new Dominican arrivals were clear on what had brought them to the city. One supporter of the Bosch's Partido Revolucionario Dominicano made clear to the *Times* that his community had come to the city because of the chaos and privation unleashed by U.S. intervention. "Because of our economic misery," a twenty-eight-year-old student named Winston Arnaud told the newspaper, "we have been forced to come to the United States and place ourselves in the grips of the monster that forced us to flee."[46]

While the numbers of self-identified exiles and their political leanings were different among the Dominicans in New York from those of the Cubans in Miami, New York also presented a space in which to continue to support their side in the ideological conflict at home. Jesse Hoffnung-Garskof argues in *A Tale of Two Cities: Santo Domingo and New York after 1950* that "the experience of exile, though numerically small, had a profound influence on the way Dominicans expressed their national identity in New York."[47] Much of the city's Dominican *colonia* engaged in opposition to the Balaguer regime through an embrace of the Partido Revolucionario Dominicano, including an annual parade through Washington Heights that performed "an active resistance against Joaquín Balaguer and against Yankee imperialism, only temporarily displaced to the 'belly of the beast.' "[48] The presence of foreign dignitaries at the United Nations also made New York City a prime site of struggle as it allowed exiles a space to exert pressure on the Dominican government. In 1975, exiles and members of the Puerto Rican Socialist Party picketed Dominican officials at the Statler Hotel over the imprisonment of three Puerto Rican socialists accused of bringing guerilla leaders into the Dominican Republic.[49] Dominican Americans would gain importance in the city's politics, and by 2004, the Dominican American population in New York City had become a transnational electoral bloc, voting in both U.S. elections and, after an eight-year push in the Dominican Republic, becoming almost half of the population nationwide that was able to participate in Dominican elections from polling places on U.S. soil.[50] With the election of the first Dominican American U.S. Representative, Adriano Espaillat of New York's 13th Congressional District, and the growing number of elected Dominican Americans in the city, the long-term impact of this Cold War–inflected migration was ongoing both in New York City and in the Dominican Republic.[51]

Cuba and the Cold War in the Caribbean remained at the center of the U.S. imagination as Jimmy Carter's administration attempted to prevent another "loss" of a Latin American country in El Salvador. A coalition of the urban members of the Christian Democratic Party and of members of the Catholic Church who organized peasants in rural areas became the base of political opposition to the oligarchy in power. The appearance of a leftist guerilla movement brought about new forms of repression, but the support of the Salvadoran people in the United States led to pressure from the Carter administration to press for ending the use of death squads by the Salvadoran government.[52] Ronald Reagan further escalated the conflicts in Central America, justifying nearly $45 million in aid to the Salvadoran government by claiming involvement there of Cuba and the Soviet Union.[53]

Central American migrants displaced by the conflicts of the 1970s and 1980s came to the United States as other Cold War migrants had; many of them congregated in Washington, DC, and its suburbs. Central American migrants began arriving in the area in the 1960s and 1970s in significant numbers "when U.S. and home country diplomats, government employees, and international agency personnel" sponsored Central American women as domestic workers and childcare providers.[54] Migrants often cited this earlier presence as the reason they selected the DC metropolitan area, with one woman noting that by the time her family fled the civil war, the people from her area of El Salvador were in DC, Northern Virginia, or Silver Spring, Maryland, including two of her father's brothers.[55] By the end of the 1980s, the concentration of El Salvadorans in the Washington area was so pronounced that refugee aid workers in Miami had begun to funnel new El Salvadoran arrivals to the area as a natural destination.[56] The historian Andrew Friedman has a different conception of the migration to DC and its suburbs, which is useful in this context. In *Covert Capital: Landscapes of Denial and the Making of U.S. Empire in the Suburbs of Northern Virginia*, Friedman describes the growth of the Salvadoran community and of other Central American communities in Edge City, Virginia, as the "return of the oppressed." Edge City's place as the second-largest Salvadoran community by 1987 was largely a product of the decisions made by the very Cold Warriors who had engaged in a new round of destabilizing overt and covert actions in Central America and who worked and resided in the DC suburb. As Friedman notes, these very Cold Warriors described the influx of Central American refugees as a crisis, framing it in apocalyptic terms. While testifying before Congress in 1987, Oliver North warned that the instability in Central America might lead to "the construction of a Berlin-type wall along the Rio Grande to keep people out."[57] North, however, depicted the scenario as democracy perishing from the rest of Central America rather than from the continued chaos he had helped create.

Much as Winston Arnaud and other Dominicans understood their presence in New York as a function of U.S. action, many politically active Salvadorans understood their presence in the DC suburbs in the same way. Even as Salvadorans and other Central American migrants moved into older housing once built for defense and intelligence workers and provided a source of cheap labor for area restaurants and other small businesses, activists in their communities sought to bring attention to the causes of their migration. When interviewed by a reporter, one activist denied that Salvadorans had come to the area seeking economic gain, instead saying, "We are a direct product of the war in El Salvador." Central Americans attempted to use protest actions to bring attention to the Cold War conflict that had brought them to northern Virginia. They also did so through artistic expressions ranging from plays that likened the sanctuary movement for Central American refugees to the Underground Railroad to stories about the chaos unleashed on their countries by Central Intelligence Agency officers who then happily went home to suburban Virginia.[58] The ways in which ordinary Salvadorans and other Central Americans reshaped the DC suburbs should be further explored, building on Friedman's "return of the oppressed" framework, moving beyond those most politically engaged and finding the Cold War implications of everyday action by the region's migrants.

Likewise, we should further explore the lines of demarcation between permanent effects and those circumstances that may have changed for certain migrants as the Cold War ebbed and patterns old and new asserted themselves in its place. In his study of the lives of Salvadorans in the town of Intipucá and in Washington, DC, David Pedersen tells the story of a migrant he calls Manuel, whom he had known in the 1980s in Washington. Manuel would tell Pedersen of his hometown of Intipucá, from which he had been displaced by the ongoing civil war, encouraging him to visit even though Manuel believed that he himself would never be able to return. Pederson goes on to note his surprise upon encountering Manuel in 1993, after the end of the civil war, in a pool hall in Intipucá where his Salvadoran acquaintance observed that the Mount Pleasant neighborhood in the 1980s had not been a good place for him and that he seemed quite happy to have returned to work his family's small plot of land.[59] Manuel was able to do what Luis Manrara never could with his native Cuba: return upon the end of the Cold War. As El Salvador transitioned into an apparent "neoliberal success story," Manuel and other returnees navigated a complex landscape where many of the conditions that drove the conflict remained and the imperial relationship with the United States was shifting into a new form, but the passing of the Cold War had nonetheless changed things. A renewed focus on the impact of the Cold War on the Latinization of cities like Washington should also extend to studying cities and home countries in the post–Cold War period, with migrants' changing calculus of whether to live "here" or "there."

Recognizing the distinctive impact of the Cold War in the Latinization of U.S. cities should shape our understanding of postwar metropolitan history: scholars should recognize that there are also largely unexplored connections between Latino urban history and histories of the Cold War's influence on American cities that could prove revelatory to both subfields. In *From Warfare to Welfare: Defense Intellectuals and Urban Problems in Cold War America*, Jennifer S. Light has brought attention to how various entities sought to address the problems of the escalating urban crisis by treating them as strategic challenges to be met by defense intellectuals employing the tools and techniques that they utilized to pursue the Cold War. At the time of Light's writing, she was issuing a corrective to how urban historians had largely "overlooked how two of the era's defining features, the cold war and the growth of the military-industrial complex, intersected with approaches that federal and local leaders chose to address the complex problems they identified in the postwar period."[60] While the Cold War policies that drove the Latinization of American cities were not intended as solutions to the urban crisis, they functioned as a point of articulation between the broader conflict and the pathway to resurgence for these metropolitan areas, with Miami, the Cuban migrants, and the CRP serving as only the most salient example of a much broader trend.

There are Cold War connections to stories of Latinization that are not as explicitly geopolitically inflected as the ones discussed in this article. One way to illustrate this is to draw connections between the insights of Margaret Pugh O'Mara and the processes of Latinization described by A. K. Sandoval-Strausz. In *Cities of Knowledge: Cold War Science and the Search for the Next Silicon Valley*, O'Mara discusses the processes by which Cold War spending patterns fostered the urbanization of American suburbs as sites of knowledge creation and high technology. Several factors drove the movement of technology industries and research centers to these suburban areas, including civil defense concerns. "Concern about the vulnerability of central business districts during nuclear attack," O'Mara writes, "prompted officials to build in a number of powerful incentives into federal defense contracting policy that encouraged contractors to choose suburban locations over urban ones." These "industrial dispersion" policies worked similarly and in conjunction with other federal mechanisms that indirectly drove postwar decentralization.[61] O'Mara shows how these civil defense concerns eased over time and how they were part of a broader set of forces that pulled jobs and population out of American cities, but Cold War strategy played a key role in driving one some of the most significant forms of postwar urban investment away from central cities. As such, Cold War–era government spending that pushed investment and population to urban peripheries had a significant role in emptying the industrial and residential parts of cities that Latino migrants would subsequently repopulate and revitalize. If we can recognize that Cold War strategic spending moved mostly white, educated, and affluent people to the suburbs as the central cities were diversifying, we must also note how many Latino immigrant populations that were not directly pushed from their homelands by the conflict had the confines of their areas of urban settlement in the United States defined by the driving force of American foreign policy. Making this connection can also help clarify why metropolitan regions like Silicon Valley and Boston, which were simultaneously becoming technological hubs and Latinizing, developed sharp class and racial segregation and dramatic economic inequality.

At the core of the intersection between Cold War and Latino urban histories is the causal relationship between destruction and transformation, between ideological violence on a global scale and its impact on the development of urban communities on a local scale. Patrick Vitale's *Nuclear Suburbs: Cold War Technoscience and the Pittsburgh Renaissance* makes the claim that the politics of technology, science, and the Cold War were embedded into everyday life in western Pennsylvania. He goes on to argue that exploring the creation of Cold War–era suburban bubbles "helps us understand how, as many geographers and others have argued, war and violence are not exceptional but are foundational to capitalist economies, the state, and the production of space."[62] Vitale calls for a broader understanding of how violence shapes our environments even in moments of nominal peace. Older urban populations often did not see or choose a willful ignorance about the violence that had pushed Cold War Latino migrants from their homes, as when Anglo Miamians decried the changes to their city with complaints that the "Cold War allies" justification for the Cuban presence was wearing thin. Our scholarly understanding of cities has sometimes ignored this dimension as well. A Latino urban history that carefully considers the Cold War can serve to connect familiar forces that shaped cities, including racial segregation, disinvestment, and the struggle for resources, with a longer history of state-sponsored violence that is less obvious to those outside migrant communities but that has fundamentally shaped their new neighborhoods and cities.

Cold War migrants like Winston Arnaud were sometimes explicit in making the connection between American Cold War policy and the military-grade violence that destroyed their homes and drove them from their countries. What became clear only with time was that once ensconced in the clutches of the monster that forced them to flee, Cold War migrants would seek to rebuild their communities and influence the conflicts that brought them to U.S. cities—and in doing so profoundly reshape these urban landscapes. American policymakers attempted to shape the outcome of a global conflict. They sought to influence foreign nations in service of their own. American cities were in many cases reconfigured by these actions and by the collisions they set into motion between global and local forces.

12

Navigating Space and Race: Afro-Cubans in Miami and Los Angeles

MONIKA GOSIN

University of California, San Diego

Ramón arrived in Miami during the Mariel boatlift of 1980, joining approximately 125,000 Cubans who also fled the island in the sudden exodus. Before leaving Havana at the age of thirty-one, he thought he was prepared to "be an American" because he was, in his words, "very McDonaldizado," a lover of all things American. But things changed as he settled into life in his new city and found his prior fascination dwindling. "I became nostalgic and longed for Cuba," he explained in a 2007 interview. Miami's appeal increasingly consisted in its similarities with the city he left behind, rather than its being part of the America he had imagined. Nevertheless, Ramón chose to put down roots, including marrying a Cuban American woman with whom he went on to enjoy a family life filled with her extended relatives and their grandchildren.

Manny came to Miami on a B-2 visitor visa in 2007, after months of living in fear that his employers in Cuba would learn that he was trying to leave the country. He explained that had they known his plans, they would have fired him, so he stayed silent, quitting his job only on the day he left. His wife, Lila, added that the decision to leave had been made with a lot of heartache "because it is desperation that every Cuban family lives and goes through." Manny and Lila had been in the United States for just a few months and were hopeful about their new life in Miami. They were ambivalent about having left Cuba, however, and acknowledged the sadness that they claimed touches every Cuban family, "with the 'leaving' at the center of their drama."

Luis arrived as an adult during Mariel, but rather than remaining in Miami, he eventually established himself on the other side of the county. Like many other single Black men who came at the time, he was unable to find a sponsor. Luis was first sent to a resettlement camp in Fort Indiantown Gap in Pennsylvania, later transferred to Fort Chaffee, Arkansas, and eventually settled into a halfway house in Seattle, Washington, in 1987. Drawn by the Cuban music scene and the availability of work, he decided in 1991 to relocate to Los Angeles, where he taught Afro-Cuban dance classes and played music professionally.

Lucy, who arrived in 1996 at the age of thirty-three, had quite a different story in that she came to reunite her family. Her then husband arranged for her and her son to come to the United States. "He sent for us," she recounted. "He came here as a Cuban national via Mexico, through his job as a musician [in a band that performed in Mexico]. He got here and petitioned for political asylum, and within three years he sent for us, and we were able to come over." Lucy also settled in Los Angeles and described herself as "professional in every way. I came here with my degree from a university in Cuba and am a librarian."

Stories like these, drawn from my in-depth interviews with Afro-Cuban immigrants who arrived in Miami and Los Angeles between 1980 and 2010, provide insight into their changing perspectives, especially how they fared over time as they settled into these two metropolitan areas. While some aspects of these journeys were similar to those of their non-Black compatriots, over time interviewees would learn that the paths of white and Black Cubans would diverge because of the particular ways Blackness mattered in the United States. They would, for example, find that a key dynamic of life in both cities was that they were constantly obliged to respond to people who were confused about the combination of their dark skin (or Blackness) and Spanish accents. They were repeatedly denied full inclusion in the groups they "should" belong to, such as Cuban, Black, or Latinx. As a result, adjusting to life in the United States also meant negotiating a U.S. racial climate in which they would have to work to make their multidimensional identities legible—not only to non-Latinx Americans but also to non-Black Latinxs who viewed Blackness and Latinidad as incongruent.[1]

This chapter analyzes how the perspectives of Afro-Cuban immigrants developed as they navigated the ethno-racial contexts of Miami and Los Angeles, and it explores the operations of complex race relations in areas of the country with large Latinx populations. Since the dramatic growth of the Latinx population since the 1960s, U.S. cities have become the largest settlement sites, with sizable proportions of Latinxs among whom diversity also continues to increase over time. Immigration scholars have long emphasized the context of reception, or the treatment and acceptance of immigrants by members of the host society, as key in facilitating or hindering immigrant advancement. Perhaps counterintuitively, this scholarship has been relatively silent on "majority-minority" areas, most often characterizing the United States as a host society wherein new immigrants negotiate economic and social advancement primarily in relation to whites. This characterization of the nation has become less and less relevant, as seen especially in places like Miami and Los Angeles, early harbingers of a new ethno-racial order that has emerged in several other metropolitan areas. The widespread growth of exceptionally diverse areas demands we reconceptualize the U.S. context to account for demographic shifts while focusing research on the complex operations of race seen in interactions not "between immigrants and some core group of white Americans but between immigrants and native-minorities."[2]

Exploring Afro-Cuban experiences with race over historical time gives us an unparalleled opportunity to examine the issue of racial differences in these diverse areas and to delve deeper into how race and Latinidad have operated situationally. Through close examination of these immigrants' stories, this chapter examines their day-to-day interactions with those they were most likely to encounter—other Cubans in Miami and people of Mexican descent in Los Angeles. While most studies examining racial dynamics have focused on institutional actors, the chapter explores the everyday mechanics of race making as Afro-Cubans encountered the policing of their identities. Focusing specifically on Afro-Cuban immigrants both inside and outside the urban enclave, the study sheds light on three factors: their positioning vis-à-vis white Cuban immigrants, other Latinxs' limited views about who qualifies as "Latinx," and the specific intervention of place in the lives of Afro-Cuban immigrants. The chapter offers a window into the daily operation of anti-Black racism and of complex intra-Latinx power relations within majority or near-majority Latinx metropolitan regions.

Background

The history of Afro-Cuban immigration to the United States extends further into the past than popular perception would suggest. Afro-Cubans began arriving in small numbers in the nineteenth century, often settling in places like New York and New Jersey as they sought to avoid the Jim Crow South.[3] Having arrived after 1980, the interviewees in this study, however, entered a very different ethno-racial terrain. A combination of 1960s Latin American economic and political crises and ongoing U.S. interventions had set off waves of migration from the region, and in the 1980s, Salvadorans and other Central Americans arrived in large numbers. Due to the tremendous growth of the Latinx population in the United States, Afro-Cubans who arrived after 1980 would negotiate their placement in U.S. society not only in relation to "white"

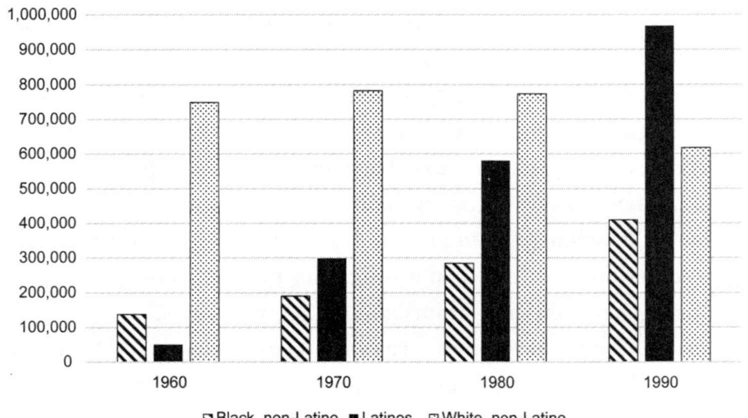

FIGURE 12.1. Comparison of Miami-Dade population by race/ethnicity, 1960–1990. Metro-Dade Planning Department.

and "Black" but also in relation to other Latinxs and the "Latino/a/e/x" label itself.[4] Moreover, by 1980, Miami had fully transformed into the "Cuban capital of the U.S." Before 1959, when Cubans began to come to Miami in large numbers, the area was a southern town with stark divisions between Blacks and white Anglos (fig. 12.1). Before the Cuban Revolution, there were just twenty thousand Cubans in Miami. However, by the early 1980s, the number of Cubans had risen exponentially to six hundred thousand. White Anglos fled the city in the 1970s, and the city became "majority-minority," with the Latinx population twice as large as the Black population by 1990.[5]

Other metropolitan areas, such as Los Angeles, also saw a tremendous demographic shift. For instance, in 1980, Latinx people were 28 percent of the population, which rose to 39 percent in 1990. By 2010, Latinxs composed 48 percent of the population of the Los Angeles metro area, with 28 percent white non-Hispanic, 14 percent Asian American, and 9 percent Black. Thus, Latinx people became a large proportion of the total population in these areas, and similar shifts across the country meant that Afro-Cuban immigrants could end up in areas requiring substantially different strategies for "becoming American" than those needed in places with white Anglo majorities.[6]

Miami would seem to be the place where Cuban immigrants would prefer to live because of its characterization as a "little Havana." Indeed, researchers studying the experiences of Afro-Cubans in places like New Mexico have postulated that the Florida context would be more favorable for them because of the large presence of Cubans and Black immigrants. However, studies focused specifically on Afro-Cubans in Miami have found this has often not been the case. There are few studies on post-1959 Black Cuban immigrants, especially in contrast to the plethora of studies focused on the mostly white Cubans who came to the United States in the 1960s and 1970s. However, the studies that do exist have found that Miami has not been a fully welcoming place for Black Cubans, who have instead met rejection from some white Cubans who were racist against Blacks. Moreover, those who arrived during Mariel in 1980 were twice stigmatized—because they were Black and because the so-called Marielitos were characterized as criminals in the Cuban and U.S. press.[7]

The Afro-Cuban immigrant experience has been unique because of the way cohort effects created a racial divide within Cubans who live in the United States. The majority of Cubans who arrived between 1959 and 1980 were white, and few Blacks arrived from Cuba before the migration waves of the 1980s and 1990s. The Cubans who arrived between 1960 and 1980 and settled in Miami were highly successful and amassed social, economic, and political power in the area, gaining "implicit white privilege" as U.S. officials and media praised their exceptionality. They benefited from U.S. efforts to make a statement to the world about its strong anticommunist stance by opening the door with the Cuban Adjustment Act of 1966 and from the U.S. government's provision of unparalleled resettlement aid to Cuban refugees. Scholars have pointed out that for this group, part of its efforts to maintain this favored status over time entailed distancing themselves from Blackness to consolidate power and further assimilate into the context of the United States. Given this racial differential wherein previous Cuban immigration cohorts were "whitened" while newer Cuban immigration cohorts were stigmatized, examining Black Cuban relations with white Cubans in Miami allows for an engagement in a critical Latino whiteness study that interrogates intra-Latinx anti-Blackness.[8]

Afro-Cubans settled all over the country post-1980, their destinations not always a matter of choice due to refugee resettlement program regulations. In this study, I focused on a sample of Black Cubans who settled in Los Angeles, because the area has epitomized the striking diversity of the "new" America both historically and currently. Examining the historical experiences of Afro-Cubans in Los Angeles, where the Latinx population is also numerically predominant but has not amassed as much power as Cubans in Miami, provides a comparison that reveals how differential configurations of power have shaped intra-Latinx relations. Moreover, examining how Afro-Cubans encountered anti-Black sentiments from a different Latinx group—people of Mexican origin—further underscores the need to understand and challenge anti-Blackness among Latinxs. Unlike Miami, which attributes much of its diversity to Latin America and the Caribbean, Los Angeles can be viewed as a microcosm of U.S. ethno-racial diversity on a global scale, with residents from

Mexico and Latin America and a large proportion of people from Asia and the Middle East, intermingled with native-born Blacks and whites. Moreover, Los Angeles has been the subject of much scholarly inquiry about race and race relations. Likely because of the small numbers of Cubans there, however, published scholarship on Cubans who migrated to the Los Angeles area is sparse. Examining the experiences of Afro-Cubans living in Los Angeles allows for an analysis of what they may experience in an ethnically diverse gateway city where Cubans are a much smaller proportion of the population and Latinx identity is defined as distinct from their own. Although in 2010 California had the second-largest Cuban population in the United States by a small margin (edging out New Jersey), the number of Cubans in Los Angeles was, and continues to be, quite small. In 2010, there were only about fifty-five thousand Cubans in Los Angeles, or less than 1 percent of the city's population. Of the population of Latinxs in Los Angeles County in 2010, about 80 percent were of Mexican origin. With the high percentage of people of Mexican origin in Los Angeles, Afro-Cubans in the area negotiated their Latinidad with people of Mexican origin as their primary reference group. By allowing a comparison between Afro-Cuban experiences navigating space and race among Cubans in Miami and among Mexicans in Los Angeles, the current research provides a broader view of intra-Latinx relations.[9]

Studies focused on intra-Latinx relations have been growing, and this area of research is foundational to thinking about the country's demographic shifts. Examining intra-Latinx relations intervenes in Latinx studies by casting doubt upon a static, unified identity that is presumed to be inherent in the category "Latino/a/e/x." Existing intra-Latinx relations research has identified efforts by native-born Latinxs to dissociate from newer immigrants, whom they perceived to be not "American enough," as they worked to escape what some researchers call the "immigrant shadow." Such research areas capture the evolution of Latinx identity and the complexities that may influence levels of coalition building and political behavior.[10]

On the subject of race, Afro-Latinx scholarship has further highlighted that phenotypically Black Latinxs can encounter acts of exclusion from the category "Latinx" because others fail to perceive them as such or actively choose to reject their Blackness. This scholarship brings to light ways in which the pan-ethnic terms *Hispanic* or *Latino/a/e/x* erroneously assume a heterogeneity that is inclusive of racial difference. Early Latinx studies scholarship made a key intervention by emphasizing how people of Latin American descent in the United States have resisted imposed binaries of race, gender, or national origin by broadening their sense of identity into a collective one, utilizing pan-ethnic terms to affirm their multiple hybrid identities.

However, Afro-Latinx studies scholars point out that Latinx studies scholarship often neglects the issue of Blackness and the specificity of Black Latinx daily experiences with the workings of race. The supposed exaltation of Latinx heterogeneity within Latinx studies can work inadvertently to affirm problematic racial democracy discourses that pervade some Latin American countries with substantial Black and indigenous populations. When they issue official declarations of racial democracy, these nations make the case that extensive racial mixing within the population means that racial difference no longer matters because class, rather than race, is the basis for social stratification. These discourses have been effusively criticized by scholars who point out that in Latin American countries with significant Afro-descendent and indigenous populations, these groups have been relegated to the bottom of the social structure. These scholars point out that in the United States, the racism that can be seen in Latin America, persisting despite the glorification of *mestizaje*, intersects with the racial notions of the United States. These convergent racisms work to differentially affect the lives of Afro-Latinx immigrants like the Afro-Cubans in this study, mediating in their incorporation experiences. As Afro-Latinxs, Afro-Cubans' positionality complicates how we understand Black and Latinx identities in the United States; accordingly, it also undermines dominant assumptions about whether various racial identities can coexist.[11]

Intra-Latinx Contexts of Reception

MIAMI

To examine such dynamics in the full context of concrete experience, we turn to the stories told by interviewees in Miami, reflecting on how they were received by the Cubans living there. Gladys, a Black woman who came to Miami from Cuba in 1980 during Mariel along with several family members, was quick to talk about the cold reception she and the rest of her family members experienced when they first arrived. She emphasized that those rejecting them were Cubans, like them, but white. Her family faced many instances of discrimination as they tried to establish themselves economically in the city. She told the story of a particular instance experienced by her brother. One day he went to an appointment for a job interview, and as she recounted: "He kept his appointment and when he got there, told [the receptionist] 'I have an appointment for 10 a.m. and my name is Carlos Mendez.' The woman gave him a look and looked in her records and told him, 'We already have an appointment at 10 a.m. for Carlos Mendez.' He replied, 'Yes, I am Carlos

Mendez.' The woman looked again and told him, 'We have another Carlos Mendez here.' Since everything was done over the phone, they thought he was White. Understand?" In her narrative, Gladys did not specify whether the receptionist was Anglo or Latinx white, but given the demographics in Miami at that time, it was more likely the latter. It is also not clear whether the conversation on the phone was conducted in English or in Spanish, but what is clear is that in whichever language, the receptionist had been unable to identify Mendez as Black on the basis of his speech. What was evident regardless was that since they had foreknowledge of his clearly Hispanic first and last names, the basis for the discrimination was not because he was Latinx but because he was Black. In the mind of the receptionist, his Blackness served to erase him completely from a "proper" Latinx identity. Even though he was still Carlos Mendez, the identity conveyed by his name had been reduced to a title that could be withheld from someone who looked like him.

The Afro-Cuban migrants to Miami whom I interviewed offered many such examples of anti-Black discrimination. Their prevailing evaluation was negative: more than half of respondents offered harsh critiques based on their direct experiences. The established Cubanness of Miami had offered comfort for some, who described it as "another Havana," citing a familiarity around Cuban culture, food, and identity worth celebrating. In fact, two respondents cited help they received on arrival, insisting that the (white) exile community cannot be painted with a broad brush. But as Gladys and others capture, in a space where Cubans held power as business owners and employers, the problem of white Cuban racism meant economic exclusions like job discrimination and unequal access to gainful employment. This led to material privation: as Eugenio Rothe and Andrés Pumariega noted, in 2007, only 13 percent of white Cubans but 23 percent of *mulato* Cubans and 35 percent of Black Cubans lived below the poverty line. This data brings to bear what other researchers have asserted in their work on other Black immigrants, which is that being identified as Black or associated with African Americans has carried negative social, economic, and political consequences.[12]

These interactions, which Afro-Cuban migrants to Miami often described as unexpected, challenge scholarly assumptions about the intrinsically protective potential of enclaves based on national origin, highlighting how different race, class, and political identities can instead cause contention. Researchers have argued that ethnic enclaves such as Miami have been particularly beneficial to newcomers because coethnics help newcomers find resources such as jobs and other forms of social support. Such benefits can have an insulating effect for newer immigrants. This cohort effect was often apparent with white Cubans arriving in Miami, but my research and that of others indicate that this was far less evident with Black Cubans.[13]

While these economic barriers were more measurably consequential for immigrant upward mobility, Black Cubans in Miami put even more emphasis on the impact of their social exclusion from the categories "Latinx" and "Cuban." Interviewees were most upset by everyday experiences of not being accepted as Cuban because of their Blackness and of being viewed as an exception when they did not fit a Black stereotype. For instance, Caridad, a thirty-six-year-old Miamian who came to the United States in 1980, explained that she has few Cuban friends because she was so turned off by the way white Cubans have treated her. She explained that they often masked their racism in the form of backhanded compliments: "'Oh, you're pretty enough to be Cuban,' 'You sound, God, you sound white on the telephone!' 'Yeah, you're Black but you know, your heart is gold.' Things like that. It's just, for me it's frustrating when people are saying comments like that, you know? You're Black, but. . . . What do you mean 'but,' where's the 'but'?" These attitudes and the denial of Blackness on the part of some Cuban exiles were inexplicable to those Blacks who had recently arrived from Cuba, where Blacks and *mulatos* are highly visible in the population.[14]

The anti-Black stance of some white Cubans in Miami extended beyond Afro-Cubans to encompass the conflictive relations and understandings they often had with African Americans. As Antonio López has explained, white Cuban American attitudes were solidified in the context of a historically segregated South, against the backdrop of white Anglos' denigration of African Americans. Post-1959 Miami Cuban Americans established the worth of their whiteness through social and economic dominance and the embrace of U.S. capitalist values in contestation of Castro and communism. They subsequently preserved this status by distancing themselves from island Afro-Cubans. Based on this argument, we can make the case that scarcity-based competition was not a primary factor in the conflict over social membership; rather, such conflict reflects a jockeying for advantaged racial positioning in the United States.[15]

Race relations among Miami's Cuban immigrants also extended into a transnational phenomenon, however. Thus, our observations cannot be complete without taking into account how race operated in Cuba and understanding the resultant position of white Cubans in the United States. Cuba had its own long history of slavery and the related social structures that permitted whites to maintain their power. Blacks continued to experience institutional discrimination stemming from this legacy. They also experienced interpersonal discrimination in many forms, including anti-Black sentiments that came through in sayings and jokes. For example, Luis, who arrived in the United States during Mariel, discussed how some white families, like that of his ex-wife, disapproved of their daughters marrying Black men. He emphasized this point by capturing how the white family equated his joining their family as a form of pollution: "They say, 'A fly fell into the milk.'" In Cuba, a woman may also be told she is *una negra blanca o una negra rubia* (a white or a blond Black person) because she is polite or viewed as being intelligent or well educated, insinuating that these characteristics are associated with whiteness and not with Blackness. These biases have persisted despite the fact that antiracist discourses celebrating the ideas of pluralism and equality of the races had been central to the national discourse on the identity of the nation in Cuba historically, from the nineteenth-century anticolonial struggles against the Spanish to the Fidel Castro revolution.[16]

Racial politics framed the early years of the Castro revolution, playing a central role in the divisions that formed between Cuba's new government and those who fled to the United States as exiles. As Devyn Spence Benson points out, the story about these divisions is often told only in terms of economic and ideological concerns. Yet as she notes, Cuba's new government and the exiles engaged in "a moral battle over the ownership of a revolutionary vision of Cuba" and racialized the conflict between them. For instance, revolutionary leaders called those who left for the U.S. "racist," since some who expressed dissent against the new Cuban government indeed were anxious about the racial integration that Castro had promised, fearful especially that it would lead to interracial intimacy. Revolutionary leaders sought to discredit the exiles and garner the support of Afro-Cubans on the island. In response, Miami exiles accused Castro of inventing racial and class tensions, which they argued were previously nonexistent, in a quest to secure his power. The result of this transnational struggle over race and Cuba's revolutionary future was a widening of the schism between Miami and Havana.[17]

The context of this transnational struggle and the legacy of anti-Black racism in Cuba continued to play a role in dynamics between Black and white Cuban migrants after 1980—however, interviewees also believed that anti-Black sentiments and actions had intensified among white Cubans in the United States. They asserted that their former compatriots fell under the influence of the society into which they had assimilated, where upward mobility was measured by how closely one could approximate middle-class whiteness. Several respondents lamented what they believed to be the Miami Cubans' less friendly and family-oriented nature, clouded by an obsession with U.S.-Cuba politics and materialism. For instance, Caridad explains, "These are the people who left in 1959, 1960. They view things a little bit more superficial . . . whereas the Cubans who come recently, you can see that they're more into family, their sense of family, friendship . . . closer to how we live in Cuba. Once people have been here for a while, we call it—they become Americanized, more concerned about the car, more concerned about, you know, you earn $50,000, owning a home." Magaly, who arrived in the United States in 1997, argued that the preoccupation with materialism and anti–Fidel Castro politics had also made Miami Cubans biased in their view of Cuba and less empathetic about the plight of people who lived on the island. She argued: "They don't really want to talk about Cuba, I mean, they don't say a lot of *good* things about Cuba. The first thing they want to talk about is Fidel. And then some of the people they say, well, I'm not going to send any money until Fidel dies. And I'm saying, well, your family is going to be starving, you know? They need money, so I don't think like that. For me, my family is my family. So even if Fidel, even if Bush, even Chavez—I don't care who is the president, but my family for me is priority." As Alejandro Portes and Alex Stepick argue, Miami Cuban exiles created an exile politics that unified the community in its polarity, dividing its fierce devotion between loving the Republican Party and hating Castro with equal dedication. Hence, membership in their community was not simply about being from Cuba but also about the subscription to and promotion of particular political ideals. Interviewees expressed that they indeed felt they would be ostracized if they demonstrated less preoccupation with U.S.-Cuba relations than their counterparts who had arrived in earlier years. Although interviewees were not necessarily supportive of the Castro government, they understood that an apolitical stance could be interpreted as equivalent to support. Further assumptions made by members of the earlier Cuban migration cohorts followed the line of reasoning that because so few Blacks came to the United States immediately after Castro came to power, they could not help but support him since they had lived all their lives under his influence. Clearly, in the case of intra-Cuban tensions, it was difficult in practice to fully separate the issue of politics from that of race.[18]

To combat the exclusions they encountered, respondents deployed several strategies, including staking a claim to Cuban identity by emphasizing their greater connection to the island than Cubans who left the island many years ago. For instance, Antonio contended that he is more Cuban than the Cuban Americans who called him what he saw as a pejorative, "un Marielito," when he first arrived in 1980. He explained: "It's a matter of generations. In my town I am the fourth generation from that place—the same town. . . . Everyone knows us from there, from Matanzas. Why? Because we are four generations: my great-grandfather, grandfather, father, and me." By emphasizing how far back his connections go in one town in Cuba, Antonio offers a contrast between himself and the Cubans in Miami who may have little connection to the country yet ironically place themselves is a position of authority on who is more Cuban than whom. Lucas similarly drew upon his more recent Cuban connections, this time to "one-up" Cuban Americans who displayed racist sentiments. Referencing the fact that in Cuba, Blacks and whites commonly associate together and that Black people are very visible on the island, he says, "But like me, I'm born in Cuba, so to me Black, white, whatever, I don't care, you know. It's like they're all the same . . . when you are in a place where you already were born [being used to this type of diversity], you don't see a difference." Thus, while the daily need to respond to people who did not view them as fully Cuban because they came to the United States during Mariel or because they were Black was frustrating to several interviewees, they also held strongly to and asserted pride in their Cuban identity.

As we can see from the case of Afro-Cuban experiences with race in Miami, simply residing among other Latinxs in the United States, if several members of the dominant Latinx group emulate the white dominant society, is not necessarily protective. Here we have discussed Afro-Cuban relations with white Cubans, who remain the largest proportion of Latinxs in Miami. However, the Latinx population has continued to diversify. As Alan Aja and Elizabeth Aranda and colleagues point out, today there is a more layered social order in Miami, wherein Latinxs from Cuba and South America who tend to self-identify as white are faring better than Blacks, regardless of immigrant or native-born status. Thus, race continues to structure social relations in this space, persisting despite shifting demographic variables: from white Anglo versus Black American to foreign-born whites versus foreign-born Black people. The Miami case is unique in that a larger proportion of the Latinx population there tends to be politically and fiscally conservative than in other cities. This distinction means members of these groups may appear to be more "anti-Black" than are members of other groups because they are less likely to vote for policies that have benefited Black people in the United States. Still, Miami presents itself as a cautionary tale against making the assumption that "diversity" is always a protective factor, and it provides insights for further analyses of the complex future of race and power in the United States.[19]

LOS ANGELES

While Miami was attractive to some Cuban immigrants because it reminded them of home, other Black Cubans avoided the city because they did not feel fully accepted there. Moreover, some did not find the job opportunities they hoped they would in Miami. One metro area to which they relocated was Los Angeles. "My dad's experience was hard when he came to this country," remembered Regla, whose father, Eladio, arrived in the United States during Mariel in 1980. "He started out in Miami, with hardly no job, no nothing, no English, so he had to move out of Miami and got out to New York. Which it was worse, you know, bigger, [too] many people. He knew people, he had family but none would help . . . 'cause they struggle a lot too. So after that he moved to Los Angeles, right here. He got a good job, [and] this is where he met my mom, you know?" The Los Angeles area provided Eladio a job he liked, and upon settling in, he met Regla's mother, who had immigrated to the area from El Salvador. As was the case with Eladio, the greater demographic diversity and the metropolitan geography of LA placed the Afro-Cubans who moved there in a position where they had fewer opportunities to meet other Cubans. They thus became adept at building relationships with people from diverse backgrounds.[20]

While respondents reported that they generally enjoyed LA because of its ethno-racial diversity, this diversity did not manifest as seamless integration. For instance, clear residential segregation has endured throughout Los Angeles. Juan, who came to the United States in 1994 at thirty years old to be with his Mexican American wife, highlighted this contrast between belonging in the United States and in Cuba: "In general I feel that I don't fit in any community. I mean, for me it was hard to understand why the Chinese live here [gesturing to one side] and the Blacks have to live here [gesturing to the other]." Although he acknowledged feeling out of place in the United States, he also contended that being from Cuba allowed him to be more comfortable with the crossing of racial boundaries necessary in Los Angeles.

One notable result of engaging with this new urban context was that Afro-Cubans' experience of race and place evolved very differently from Miami, where one could enjoy the familiarity of being around Cuban culture at all times. Lucy, who came to the United States in the early 1990s, observed: "Really, on a daily basis, to go out and find Cubans—no luck. Miami is one of the places that has the most Cubans. Here you can run into them, and there are days that you can go to a pharmacy, to market, and a grocery store, and you can say to yourself, 'Oh, that voice sounds Cuban.' But, no, you can't find them on a daily basis." Because respondents rarely encountered other Cubans in LA randomly, they actively sought them out. As Carla recalled, "we would like to have more contact with other Cubans in order to feel more at home. We are out of familiar territory, not able to feel at home in our own backyard." While there is no one single city where all the Cubans live, Fermín explained at the time of the interview that, if one looked for them, they could be found dispersed throughout places in Los Angeles County, such as Downey and Culver City. Instead of searching for large areas of Cuban people, Regla offered that one way to find other Cubans in LA was to patronize Cuban restaurants and build relationships with the owners. Musical events were also key places to make connections with other Cubans, reinforcing the architecture of community that supersedes physical limitations of a city. As Yenifer pointed out, "A lot of the [newly arrived] Cuban people, that's the reason why they go to the Cuban festival, to see other Cubans." For many of the respondents, music is the heart of Cuban life. As Juan summed up, "That's one thing that unites all the Cubans—dancing and music."[21]

In contrast to the intra-Cuban divisions one might find in the context of Miami, the respondents' descriptions of the LA context seemed to indicate relatively few. Silverio, a club DJ specializing in Cuban music, made a point of differentiating "old white guy" Cubans in Miami from his friends in LA. He maintained that Cubans in Miami were more interested in money and prestige and that they perpetuated the social divisions between Black and white in Cuba. He explained that there, white Cubans demonstrated a racist way of thinking by, for instance, favoring "European" salon dances over rumba-style dances of African origin. By contrast, he contended that in Los Angeles, white Cubans are more "calmed down" or "down to earth" in regard to race. In general, Silverio projected an idea seemingly shared by other Afro-Cubans in the city that LA white Cubans were less complicit in U.S. racism than Miami Cubans. Hence, intra-Cuban tensions were less of a daily concern for Afro-Cubans in Los Angeles.

For many Afro-Cuban immigrants in LA, their most frequent interactions were with ethnic Mexicans. Respondents often found themselves challenging barriers as these two cultures intersected, with varying degrees of success. Alejandro, who arrived in the area with his wife almost twenty years ago (in 2005), was optimistic: "Sometimes, you run into Latins that do not understand your way of thinking [but] those are exceptions. Sometime ago, a Mexican family invited us on a Sunday to their home to try Mexican food. And we shared a good meal, and they were really beautiful people." His wife, Carla, interjected, "They called me back two days ago, telling me that they want to get to know Cuban cuisine and get together." Alejandro concluded: "Yes. That's the way things begin."[22]

While Alejandro and his wife felt that negative interactions with Mexicans were the exception, more of the interviewees in this study consistently experienced rejection by Mexicans—findings that are consistent with accounts from Afro-Cubans in other cities.[23] In some ways, these rejections mirrored those in Miami—they often sprang from other people's surprise at Black people speaking fluent Spanish—but Los Angeles's distinct demographics led to a very different ethno-racial dynamic. Non-Black Latinxs almost always know that there are prominent Afro-Latinxs in the realms of entertainment, popular culture, and sports. For instance, Black Antillean artists and artistic productions have been central to Mexican popular culture since the 1880s. Black Cuban boxers and baseball players have met worldwide fame and are thus also likely known to many Mexicans and Mexican Americans. However, because in the Los Angeles context the meaning of Blackness is so strongly tied to being African American, Cuban and other Afro-Latinx Blackness still sparks cognitive dissonance and subsequent rejection. Afro-Cubans, for example, were subject to comments they believed were influenced by anti-Black racism among Mexicans. For example, Lena captured encountering such rejection of Blackness from Mexicans who insinuated that being labeled "Black" is an insult: "It is hard for them to talk about my skin color and believe that I speak Spanish. And, so I tell them, 'There are Blacks in Cuba.' They'll reply, 'Oh, but you're not Black!' So, they'll try to put things in other terms . . . Mexicans will say, 'Oh, but you're not Black' and use another term for the 'dark-skinned' in their group. Something like that."

Afro-Cubans felt frustration and anger when their interactions with Mexicans followed a pattern in which they were treated as "less than." Pedro, who arrived in the United States during the Balsero crisis in 1994, expressed his irritation with Mexicans who assumed he was African American and made derogatory comments. In response, he worked to even the score: "For example, I go to the place where there's a whole bunch of Mexicans . . . and I go there and I ask the question in the best Spanish I can speak. And they do not understand me most of the time. . . . So when they see this Black guy speaking that perfect Spanish, they totally get scared. I mean, I've seen that many, many times." This and other examples illustrated how angry he and other Afro-Cubans became with the constant presumption by other Latinxs that they could not speak Spanish, and their attempts to reclaim their positionality as Latinxs with "perfectly" spoken Spanish.[24]

The fact that the Latinx majority in Los Angeles was Mexican involved an even more complex racial dynamic, however. Fermín provided a revealing example when he described an incident at a doughnut shop when the Spanish-speaking workers made derogatory comments toward him, assuming he could not possibly understand them:

> I went to a doughnut shop and there was a Mexican guy there working inside, and there was another one outside, I guess he was buying. But I guess they

> knew each other, they were talking, and I guess the guy on the outside, he was kinda drunk . . . he was talking Spanish to the other guy, so he goes, "Oh, we got *otro loco* coming in," you know, like another crazy guy comin' in. So I kinda stood quiet for a little bit, and I said [to myself], should I let him keep talkin', or should I say something right now? So I said [to myself], You know what, before they get out of hand, I'd better say something right now, 'cause I might, you know, end up doing something. So I go [in Spanish], "No, the only crazy guy here is you," like that. So he kinda tripped out—he goes "Oh," and the other guy that works there, he's like "Oh, I didn't know you spoke Spanish, I thought we only spoke Spanish." And I told him "Oh, that's because you think only the Indians speak Spanish," I told him, just like that. "Not only the Indians speak Spanish."

Fermín's comment indicated that in LA, Latinx identity hinged not on cultural practices like speaking Spanish but on stereotypical looks. In particular, this "Latin look," as Fermín observed, was connected to indigenous ancestry. This issue of what constitutes a "Latin look" has complicated the way many Latinxs have navigated race and place and held particular significance among the ethnic Mexican supermajority of Latinxs in Los Angeles.[25]

Anti-Black racism among people of Mexican origin in the United States stems from a complex interplay of ideas held by people in Mexico about Black populations, ideas held by Mexican Americans living in the United States about African Americans (some of which newer Mexican immigrants may have learned even before immigrating), and ideas encouraged within the climate of the United States. Until relatively recently, when they gave the presence of Africans in Mexico official recognition, Mexico had obscured the presence of its own Black population. Thus, it is possible that the views of recently arrived Mexican immigrants on Blackness were influenced by the way it had long been viewed in Mexico.[26]

However, there were also U.S.-specific factors involved. Afro-Cuban interviewees mentioned that people of Mexican origin often perceived them to be *African American*. As scholars have pointed out, given the historical positioning of African Americans as inferior by U.S. whites, immigrants often learn to view them similarly; avoiding association with African Americans is viewed as advantageous for advancement in U.S. society. Moreover, although it cannot be definitively determined from the interviews, for both recently arrived Mexicans and native-born Mexican Americans, the climate of anti-immigrant sentiment and policing of undocumented immigrants—which primarily targeted people with the stereotypical Euro-Indigenous or mestizo "Latin look"—may have also played a role in their disparagement of Blackness in the U.S. context. Some people of Mexican origin may have sought to obscure their own stigmatization in U.S. society by elevating themselves above another marginalized group.[27]

Afro-Cubans in Los Angeles revealed that the persistent climate of anti-immigrant sentiment and policing placed them in a complicated position vis-à-vis people of Mexican origin because being perceived as "Latinx" or Mexican could be viewed as an even greater stigma than being identified as Black. Newby and Dowling have discussed this issue in their findings that Afro-Cubans in Albuquerque and Austin took note of the social structure there and Mexicans' positioning in lower-level manual or service jobs, and thus sought to dissociate from them. After all, even many native-born Latinxs tried to dissociate themselves from more newly arrived Latinxs whom they deemed not properly assimilated.[28]

The interviewees for this study varied considerably in the type of occupations they held: some were in part-time and paraprofessional fields, others were in the performing arts, and still others were training in vocational programs. While several interviewees were still struggling to achieve the upward mobility they desired, the majority were fairly well educated, having completed high school level or greater in Cuba or the United States. Thus, some Afro-Cuban respondents positioned themselves above Mexicans because of their supposed higher educational attainment, class status, and the less questionable immigration status of Cubans (regardless of race). Consistent with the findings of other studies, a small number of respondents living in Los Angeles made disparaging comments about Mexicans (although such a point of view was by no means a majority opinion). Luis, who arrived in the United States in 1980 during Mariel, criticized Mexican friends who were, for example, unfamiliar with world geography and knew very little about Cuba. He derided Mexicans who were racist toward Black people yet continually siphoned Black culture. Similarly, Pedro, in response to Mexicans who were surprised to encounter a Black person speaking perfect Spanish, explained: "Because why—because they are really, really low, low, low-class people. They don't have education." (Notably, these references to "ignorance" are in line with classical prejudice models). In this explanation, while perpetuating problematic stereotypes about Mexicans, Pedro engaged in what I have called "a bitter diversion," a strategic use of wry humor or intense emotion to challenge people who place themselves in a superior position to him. While such strategies may not have made lasting change, they allowed one to gain small victories at the site of everyday life.[29]

What is important to note, though, is that because people of Mexican origin did not pose a power threat to Afro-Cubans in Los Angeles, Mexican rejections of Afro-Cubans were not considered consequential. Mexican attitudes about Blackness were less of a problem in terms of advancement in U.S. society since Afro-Cubans perceived being associated with a lower class or "illegal" to be more disadvantageous. Thus, the adoption of dominant views about Mexicans could be used by Afro-Cubans to align themselves with upward mobility and away from a stigmatized identity. In a society that continuously questions Latinx belonging, they, like other marginalized groups, may feel compelled to prove their moral worthiness by setting themselves apart, portraying their group as more educated, hardworking, self-reliant, law abiding, or patriotic.[30]

These dynamics underscore that when analyzing intra-Latinx relations, along with the question of race, we need to examine the issue of power—how groups seek to negotiate a place of relative power for themselves in U.S. society, even when they do not have an abundance of political, financial, or other forms of power. In the case of the conflicts and misunderstandings between Afro-Cubans and Mexicans described by the interviewees in this study, it is salient that neither group held power over the other, and both faced relative disadvantages in society. Thus, the conflict had little to do with competition over resources but rather was related to the need for both marginalized groups to "defend their honor" in a society that taught them that their race or ethnicity made them inferior. Such interactions speak to the need for more scholarship that gives focused attention to the metropolitan contexts that have framed intra-Latinx relations and the antagonisms that exist between these groups without losing sight of how all Latinx groups are subject to particular forms of policing within the dominant racial order.[31]

Conclusion

Shifting U.S. demographics require more scholarly attention to the dynamics of intra-Latinx relations. This investigation of the scenarios recounted by Afro-Cuban immigrants of their interactions with established Miami Cubans and people of Mexican origin in Los Angeles point to the need to consider the sociopolitical contexts that frame intragroup and interminority conflict. The respondents in this study were more apt to discuss negative treatment by established, white Cubans who held stereotypical views of Blacks and did not equate Cubanness with Blackness. But by contrasting the United States and Cuba on the issue of racism, the interviewees implicated the United States and the transition to the United States in their explanation of the discrimination they experienced by established exiles. In other words, it is not just that Cuban exiles are "white"; it is that they are adhering to a U.S. system of racial oppression.

In Los Angeles, as noted in previous studies, Afro-Cubans also found that many Mexicans resisted or refused the association of a Latinx identity with Blackness. Some of the interviewees responded to this refusal with anger and by referring to the Mexicans as "low class" or "ignorant." The findings point to the need to understand the differential experiences of Latinxs, noting that class, race, and region affect prejudice and discrimination as well as interethnic relations in the United States. Furthermore, a climate of anti-immigrant sentiment and surveillance contributes to feelings of vulnerability among people of Mexican origin; in such a climate, some, recognizing the prevalence of institutionalized anti-Black attitudes and practices in the United States, may adopt a negative stance toward U.S. African Americans and any others they assume to be African American. By analyzing the dynamics of Afro-Cubans' interaction with other Latinxs in the specific sociohistorical contexts of Miami and Los Angeles, we are able to obtain a view into the nature and complexity of intra-Latinx relations within metro areas with significant Latinx populations.[32]

The sociopolitical concerns of the Cuban exiles in Miami and populations of Mexican origin in Los Angeles discussed in this chapter are very specific to the areas studied and are surmised from the scenarios discussed by the interviewees. Future research concentrating on the other participants in the interaction could provide more perspective on the direct motivations of all involved. Because interminority relations may vary considerably depending on the actors involved and regional context, larger-scale studies comparing different locales would allow for a comparative view into how race, power, and politics intersect in relations between established Latinx residents and newer Latinx immigrants. However, in this investigation, we gain an important perspective about the U.S. racial climate from the point of view of Afro-Cubans, a uniquely situated group, as they negotiated being Black, Cuban, and Latinx in the Miami Cuban enclave, and in LA, an environment where Latinx people are largely defined as being from a culture other than their own. The two receiving contexts differ in terms of the actors involved and the specific sociopolitical contexts framing interactions. However, in both contexts, a primary reason Afro-Cubans did not feel accepted was that in face-to-face interactions, their Blackness was often rejected. In the shifting demographic context wherein newer immigrants in some areas will be less likely to interact with white Americans in their daily lives, we must continue to investigate how the racial notions immigrants bring with them intersect with previous U.S.-based white-Black binary and racist power structures. We must examine how these intersections and the quest for relative power frame the dynamics of new interactions, particularly between diverse Latinx groups.

Acknowledgments

This volume is the work of many hands, from its contributors and editors to the administrators and staff who provided essential funding, logistical support, and everyday kindness and good humor.

Metropolitan Latinidad grew out of a conference and associated workshops entitled "MetropoLatinx: The Significance of *Latinidad* in Urban History" that were initially scheduled at Penn State's University Park campus for the fall of 2020. The arrival of a global pandemic in the spring of that year made it impossible to hold in-person events, so everything was postponed for more than a year as more than one million people in the United States and millions more around the world lost their lives to COVID-19.

When "MetropoLatinx" finally convened, it enjoyed the indispensable support of Penn State University's College of the Liberal Arts, its Equal Opportunity Planning Committee, its Department of History, and its Latina/o Studies Program. Nothing gets done at any university without the essential work of dedicated administrative staff, and so we'd like to thank Amber Thomas, Lynn Monoski, Keshia Kennelley, Jennifer Contreras, Lynn Carey, and Kristi Brinker for all their logistical work, from transportation to room reservations to catering to publicity. Without all this institutional backing from Penn State, we could never have produced the scholarship represented in this book.

Throughout our extended journey together, the contributors to this volume consistently exceeded my already grandiose expectations. They turned in superb initial drafts of their papers, enthusiastically launched into first-rate discussions and critiques of each other's work, responded positively to constructive criticism, and showed tremendous patience with my heavily marked-up revision pages and subsequent cuts for length. They also turned in extraordinary performances at the public presentations of our work at annual meetings of the Urban History Association and the Society for American City and Regional Planning History. Thanks also to Gerry Cadava and Johana Londoño, who were part of our original line-up but whom circumstances (in both cases happy ones, to be sure!) prevented from contributing to this collection.

At the University of Chicago Press, executive editor Tim Mennel and series editor Lilia Fernández were an absolute dynamic duo of editorial excellence. They lined up the best readers imaginable, gently alerted us to yawning historiographical omissions, provided crucial input on the structure of the collection and the logical flow between essays and sections—and they did it all with the ideal combination of encouragement and exactitude. As a result, this collection is far and away better than before. Andrea Blatz, Katherine Faydash, and Lindsy Rice guided us through the complex production process with efficiency and grace, making what could have been a fourteen-author pileup into a proper parade. And designer Annie Leue created a cover that beautifully illustrates some of the main themes of the book.

The Penn State University College of the Liberal Arts provided subvention support for this collection, for which we are sincerely grateful.

Finally and most importantly, your humble editor would like to thank his family. Cathleen, after more than a quarter century together I am still dazzled every time you come through the door and profoundly thankful that I can seek your advice on anything and everything. Cecilia, you are so justifiably in charge, just as the eldest daughter of an eldest daughter of an eldest daughter of an eldest daughter should be; and I remain in awe of your impeccable style. Lincoln, hats off to you for your quick wit, comic timing, ability to make yourself at home anywhere in the world, and keen sense of what is best in life. I am so proud *at* both of you! Oh, and Piña, even though you can't read, your humans all want you to know that you are a very, very, *very* good dog.

Notes

Introduction

1. U.S. Bureau of the Census, Census of Population: 1970, Series PHC-1, "Census Tracts," pt. 14, New York, NY SMSA (Washington, DC: U.S. Government Printing Office, 1973), table P-1; U. S. Bureau of the Census, 1980 Census of Population and Housing, Census Tracts, New York, NY-NJ (Washington, DC: U.S. Government Printing Office, 1983), table 16; U.S. Bureau of the Census, 1990 Census of Population, General Population Characteristics, New York (Washington, DC: U.S. Government Printing Office, 1973), table 3; Campbell Gibson and Kay Jung, "Historical Census Statistics on the Foreign-Born Population of the United States: 1850 to 2000" (Working Paper No. 81, Population Division, U.S. Census Bureau, February 2006), https://www.census.gov/content/dam/Census/library/working-papers/2006/demo/POP-twps0081.pdf.

2. Frank Guridy, *Forging Diaspora: Afro-Cubans and African Americans in a World of Empire and Jim Crow* (Chapel Hill: University of North Carolina Press, 2010); Jesse Hoffnung-Garskof, *Racial Migrations: New York City and the Revolutionary Politics of the Spanish Caribbean* (Princeton, NJ: Princeton University Press, 2019); Carmen Teresa Whalen and Victor Vázquez-Hernández, *The Puerto Rican Diaspora* (Philadelphia: Temple University Press, 2006); Ada Ferrer, *Cuba: An American History* (New York: Scribner's, 2021); Nancy Raquel Mirabal, *Suspect Freedoms: The Racial and Sexual Politics of Cubanidad in New York, 1823–1957* (New York: NYU Press, 2017); Lisandro Pérez, *Sugar, Cigars, and Revolution: The Making of Cuban New York* (New York: NYU Press, 2018). Enumerated on a metropolitan-area level, greater Los Angeles has admittedly been home to an even larger number of Latinos, predominantly Mexican Americans.

3. At that time, *Latin* was very common usage in English, much like *hispano* in Spanish. This is illustrated, for example, in the motion picture *Internal Affairs* (1990), especially by Andy García's character Raymond Avila. Note also that the Latin Grammy Awards were organized in 1989 and gave their first awards in 2000: Jon Pareles, "Critic's Notebook: Latin Faces Light Up TV Courtesy of the Grammys," *New York Times*, September 16, 2000.

4. Virginia Sánchez Korrol, *From Colonia to Community: The History of Puerto Ricans in New York City* (New York: Greenwood Press, 1983).

5. Stow Persons, *Ethnic Studies at Chicago, 1905–1945* (Urbana: University of Illinois Press, 1987); Robert Redfield, "The Mexicans in Chicago-Journal" (1924–1925), Robert Redfield Papers, Department of Special Collections, University of Chicago Library; Timothy Ready and Allen Brown-Gort, "This Is Home Now: The State of Latino Chicago," (South Bend, IN: Institute for

Latino Studies, University of Notre Dame, 2005); Brigid Sweeney (text) and Manuel Martinez (photos), "Little Village, Big Business," *Crain's Chicago Business*, September 25, 2015, http://www.chicagobusiness.com/section/little-village.

6. St. Clair Drake and Horace Cayton Jr., *Black Metropolis* (New York: Harcourt, Brace & World, 1945); Arnold R. Hirsch, *Making the Second Ghetto: Race and Housing in Chicago, 1940–1960* (New York: Cambridge University Press, 1983); James R. Grossman, *Land of Hope: Chicago, Black Southerners, and the Great Migration* (Chicago: University of Chicago Press, 1989); Félix M. Padilla, *Latino Ethnic Consciousness: The Case of Mexican Americans and Puerto Ricans in Chicago* (South Bend, IN: University of Notre Dame Press, 1995); Rebeca Raijman and Marta Tienda, "Immigrants' Pathways to Business Ownership: A Comparative Ethnic Perspective," *International Migration Review* 34 (2000): 682–706; Marta Tienda and Rebecca Raijman, "Promoting Hispanic Immigrant Entrepreneurship in Chicago," *Journal of Developmental Entrepreneurship* 9 (2004): 1–21; Rebecca Raijman and Marta Tienda, "Training Functions of Ethnic Economies: Mexican Entrepreneurs in Chicago," *Sociological Perspectives* 43 (2000): 439–56; Eric Klinenberg, *Heat Wave: A Social Autopsy of Disaster in Chicago* (Chicago: University of Chicago Press, 2002); Nicholas De Genova, *Working the Boundaries: Race, Space, and "Illegality" in Mexican Chicago* (Durham, NC: Duke University Press, 2005).

7. James Rojas, "The Enacted Environment: The Creation of 'Place' by Mexicans and Mexican Americans in Los Angeles" (master's thesis, Massachusetts Institute of Technology, 1991); Gustavo Leclerc, Raúl Villa, and Michael J. Dear, eds., *Latino Urban Cultures: La vida latina en LA* (Thousand Oaks, CA: SAGE Publications, 1999); Victor M. Valle and Rodolfo D. Torres, *Latino Metropolis* (Minneapolis: University of Minnesota Press, 2000); Mike Davis, *Magical Urbanism: Latinos Reinvent the U.S. Big City* (London: Verso, 2000); David R. Díaz, *Barrio Urbanism: Chicanos, Planning, and American Cities* (New York: Routledge, 2005); Michael Mendez, "Latino New Urbanism: Building on Cultural Preferences," *Opolis* 1 (2005): 33–48; David R. Díaz and Rodolfo D. Torres, *Latino Urbanism: The Politics of Planning, Policy, and Redevelopment* (New York: New York University Press, 2012); Michael Rios, Leonardo Vazquez, and Lucrezia Miranda, eds., *Diálogos: Placemaking in Latino Communities* (New York: Routledge, 2012).

8. George J. Sánchez, *Becoming Mexican American: Ethnicity, Culture and Identity in Chicano Los Angeles, 1900–1945* (New York: Oxford University Press, 1993); William Deverell, *Whitewashed Adobe: The Rise of Los Angeles and the Remaking of Its Mexican Past* (Berkeley: University of California Press, 2004); Natalia Molina, *Fit to Be Citizens? Public Health and Race in Los Angeles, 1879–1939* (Berkeley: University of California Press, 2006).

9. Another part must be the study of Asian American urbanites. See, for example, Scott Kurashige, *The Shifting Grounds of Race: Black and Japanese Americans in the Making of Multiethnic Los Angeles* (Princeton, NJ: Princeton University Press, 2008); Charlotte Brooks, *Alien Neighbors, Foreign Friends: Asian Americans, Housing, and the Transformation of Urban California* (Chicago: University of Chicago Press, 2009); Wendy Cheng, *The Changs Next Door to the Diazes: Remapping Race in Suburban California* (Berkeley: University of California Press, 2013).

10. U.S. Census Bureau, "United States: 2020; Summary Population and Housing Characteristics," table 26; U.S. Census Bureau, 2020 Census Demographic Data Map Viewer, https://maps.geo.census.gov/ddmv/map.html;Werner Schink and David Hayes-Bautista, *Latino Gross Domestic Product Report: Quantifying the Impact of American Hispanic Economic Growth*, Latino Donor Collaborative (June 2017). Notably, between one-sixth and one-quarter of Latinos say that they are Afro-Latino or have substantial African ancestry; a significant (though declining) proportion of Latinos also categorize themselves as white.

11. A. K. Sandoval-Strausz, "Latino Landscapes: The Transnational Origins of a New Urban America," *Journal of American History* 101 (2014): 804–31; Vicki L. Ruiz, "Nuestra América: Latino History as U.S. History," *Journal of American History* 93 (2006): 655–72.

12. Mario T. García and Sal Castro, *Blowout! Sal Castro and the Chicano Struggle for Educational Justice* (Chapel Hill: University of North Carolina Press, 2011). The term *barrio* was used dozens of times in the 155 pages of *El plan de Santa Barbara* (1968); in the much briefer *El plan espiritual de Aztlán* (1969), it was used four times, each time the first in a series of words denoting, for example, "all levels of Chicano society—the barrio, the campo, the ranchero, the writer, the teacher, the worker, the professional."

13. María E. Pérez y González and Virginia E. Sánchez Korrol, *Puerto Rican Studies in the City University of New York: The First Fifty Years* (New York: Centro Press, 2021). See also Virginia Sánchez Korrol, "The Origins and Evolution of Latino History," *OAH Magazine of History* 10 (1996): 5–12; Frank Bonilla and Emilio González, "New Knowing, New Practice: Puerto Rican Studies," in *Structures of Dependency*, ed. Frank Bonilla and Robert Henriques Girling (Stanford, CA: Stanford University Press, 1973).

14. Juan Gómez-Quiñones and Luis Leobardo Arroyo, "On the State of Chicano History: Observations on Its Development, Interpretations, and Theory, 1970–1974," *Western Historical Quarterly* 7 (1976): 155–85; Lilia Fernández, "Urban History and the Construction of Social Difference," *Journal of Urban History* 41 (2015): 566–71.

15. Jesús Chavarría, "A Précis and Tentative Bibliography on Chicano History," *Aztlán* 1 (1970); Gómez-Quiñones and Arroyo, "On the State of Chicano History," 166–69; Alex M. Saragoza, "Recent Chicano Historiography: An Interpretive Essay," *Aztlán* 19 (1990): 1–77.

16. Albert Camarillo, *Chicanos in a Changing Society: From Mexican Pueblos to American Barrios in Santa Barbara and Southern California, 1848–1930* (Cambridge, MA: Harvard University Press, 1979); Richard Griswold del Castillo, *The Los Angeles Barrio, 1850–1890: A Social History* (Berkeley: University of California Press, 1979); Mario T. García, *Desert Immigrants: The Mexicans of El Paso, 1880–1920* (New Haven, CT: Yale University Press, 1981); Ricardo Romo, *East Los Angeles: History of a Barrio* (Austin: University of Texas Press, 1983); Rodolfo Acuña, *A Community under Siege: A Chronicle of Chicanos East of the Los Angeles River, 1945–1975* (Los Angeles: UCLA Chicano Studies Research Center, 1984); Korrol, *From Colonia to Community*. See also Camarillo's bibliographic work *Mexican Americans in Urban Society* (Berkeley, CA: Floricanto Press, 1986).

17. David Weber and Roger W. Lotchin, "The New Chicano History: Two Perspectives," *History Teacher* 16 (1983): 219–47, in which Weber's section was entitled "The New Chicano Urban History" and Lotchin's, "The New Chicano History: An Urban History Perspective."

18. Arthur Schlesinger Sr., *The Rise of the City, 1878–1898* (New York: Macmillan, 1933); Timothy Gilfoyle, "White Cities, Linguistic Turns, and Disneylands: The New Paradigms of Urban History," *Reviews in American History* 26 (1998): 175–204; Clay McShane, "The State of the Art in North American Urban History," *Journal of Urban History* 32 (2006): 582–97; Andrew Needham and Allen Dieterich-Ward, "Beyond the Metropolis: Metropolitan Growth and Regional Transformation in Postwar America," *Journal of Urban History* 35 (2009): 944–60.

19. Weber and Lotchin, "New Chicano History," 228.

20. See, for example, Bayrd Still, *Urban America: A History with Documents* (New York: Little, Brown, 1974); Charles N. Glaab and A. Theodore Brown, *A History of Urban America* (New York: Macmillan, 1976); Howard P. Chudacoff, *The Evolution of American Urban Society* (Saddle River, NJ: Prentice-Hall, 1981); Alexander B. Callow Jr., ed., *American Urban History:*

An Interpretive Reader with Commentaries (New York: Oxford University Press, 1982); Zane L. Miller and Patricia M. Melvin, *The Urbanization of Modern America: A Brief History* (New York: Harcourt Brace Jovanovich, 1987); Arthur P. Young, *Cities and Towns in American History: A Bibliography of Doctoral Dissertations* (New York: Greenwood Press, 1989); David R. Goldfield and Blaine A. Brownell, *Urban America: A History* (New York: Houghton Mifflin, 1990). One partial exception was Oscar Handlin's *The Newcomers* (1959), which grouped Puerto Ricans with Black people rather than addressing what made them distinct and, more notably, defined both as a problem. See Lorrin Thomas, "Oscar Handlin, *The Newcomers: Negroes and Puerto Ricans in a Changing Metropolis*," *Journal of American Ethnic History* 32 (2013): 46–52.

21. Albert Camarillo, interviewed by the author, March 31, 2023; email exchange with Richard Griswold del Castillo, April 27, 2023; email exchange with Mario García, March 28, 2023.

22. Camarillo interview; Ricardo Romo, interviewed by the author, March 14, 2023.

23. This and similar subsequent paragraphs are drawn from an issue-by-issue, article-by-article perusal of the entire run of the *Journal of Urban History*; a systematic reading of the Urban History Association's conference programs at its website (https://www.urbanhistory.org/Past-conferences); and a listing of prize winners (https://www.urbanhistory.org/Past-Awards). The 2006 proceeding are unavailable, so that number is unknown.

24. Sánchez, *Becoming Mexican American*; Deverell, *Whitewashed Adobe*; Molina, *Fit to Be Citizens?* See also Stephen J. Pitti, *The Devil in Silicon Valley: Race, Mexican Americans, and Northern California* (Princeton University Press, 2002).

25. Zaragoza Vargas, *Proletarians of the North: A History of Mexican Industrial Workers in Detroit and the Midwest, 1917–1933* (Berkeley: University of California Press, 1993); Zaragosa Vargas, *Major Problems in Mexican American History* (Stamford, CT: Cengage, 1999). See also Dionicio Valdés, *Al Norte: Agricultural Workers in the Great Lakes Region* (Austin: University of Texas Press, 1991).

26. Alejandro Portes and Alex Stepick, *City on the Edge: The Transformation of Miami* (Berkeley: University of California Press, 1993); María Cristina García, *Havana USA: Cuban Exiles and Cuban Americans in South Florida, 1959–1994* (Berkeley: University of California Press, 1996); Carmen Teresa Whalen, *From Puerto Rico to Philadelphia: Puerto Rican Workers and Postwar Economies* (Philadelphia: Temple University Press, 2001).

27. Sam Bass Warner, *Streetcar Suburbs: The Process of Growth in Boston, 1870–1900* (Cambridge, MA: Harvard University Press, 1978); Kenneth T. Jackson, *Crabgrass Frontier: The Suburbanization of the United States* (New York: Oxford University Press, 1985); Matt Garcia, *A World of Its Own: Race, Labor, and Citrus in the Making of Greater Los Angeles* (Chapel Hill: University of North Carolina Press, 2001). See also Gilbert G. Gonzales, *Labor and Community: Mexican Citrus Worker Villages in a Southern California County, 1900–1950* (Urbana: University of Illinois Press, 1994).

28. See, e.g., Monica Perales, *Smeltertown: Making and Remembering a Southwest Border Community* (Chapel Hill: University of North Carolina Press, 2010); Lilia Fernández, *Brown in the Windy City: Mexicans and Puerto Ricans in Postwar Chicago* (Chicago: University of Chicago Press, 2012); Angharad N. Valdivia and Matthew Garcia, eds., *Mapping Latina/o Studies: An Interdisciplinary Reader* (New York: Peter Lang, 2012); and Michael Innis-Jiménez, *Steel Barrio: The Great Mexican Migration to South Chicago, 1915–1940* (New York: New York University Press, 2013). Organization of American Historians awards for books on Latino urban history include Geraldo Cadava, *Standing on Common Ground: The Making of a Sunbelt Borderland* (Cambridge, MA: Harvard University Press, 2013); Eduardo Contreras, *Latinos and the Liberal City: Politics and Protest in San Francisco* (Philadelphia: University of Pennsylvania Press, 2019).

29. Jesse Hoffnung-Garskof, *A Tale of Two Cities: Santo Domingo and New York after 1950* (Princeton, NJ: Princeton University Press, 2008); Monica Perales, *Smeltertown: Making and Remembering a Southwest Border Community* (Chapel Hill: University of North Carolina Press, 2010); Cadava, *Standing on Common Ground*. See also A. K. Sandoval-Strausz, *Barrio America: How Latino Immigrants Saved the American City* (New York: Basic Books, 2019).

30. Gabriela F. Arredondo, *Mexican Chicago: Race, Identity, and Nation, 1916–1939* (Urbana: University of Illinois Press, 2008); Fernández, *Brown in the Windy City*; Innis-Jiménez, *Steel Barrio*; Omar Valerio-Jiménez, Santiago Vaquera-Vásquez, and Claire F. Fox, eds., *The Latina/o Midwest Reader* (Urbana: University of Illinois Press, 2017); Theresa Delgadillo, Ramón H. Rivera-Servera, Geraldo L. Cadava, and Claire F. Fox, *Building Sustainable Worlds: Latinx Placemaking in the Midwest* (Urbana: University of Illinois Press, 2022); Mike Amezcua, *Making Mexican Chicago: From Postwar Settlement to the Age of Gentrification* (Chicago: University of Chicago Press, 2022).

31. Hoffnung-Garskof, *Tale of Two Cities*; Llana Barber, *Latino City: Immigration and Urban Crisis in Lawrence, Massachusetts, 1945–2000* (Chapel Hill: University of North Carolina Press, 2017); Johana Londoño, *Abstract Barrios: The Crises of Latinx Visibility in Cities* (Durham, NC: Duke University Press, 2020); Johanna Fernández, *The Young Lords: A Radical History* (Chapel Hill: University of North Carolina Press, 2019).

32. Leon Fink, *The Maya of Morganton: Work and Community in the Nuevo New South* (Chapel Hill: University of North Carolina Press, 2003); Mary E. Odem and Elaine Lacy, eds., *Latino Immigrants and the Transformation of the U.S. South* (Athens: University of Georgia Press, 2009); Sarah McNamara, *Ybor City: Crucible of the Latina South* (Chapel Hill: University of North Carolina Press, 2023).

33. Andrew Wiese, *Places of Their Own: African American Suburbanization in the Twentieth Century* (Chicago: University of Chicago Press, 2004); Jerry González, *In Search of the Mexican Beverly Hills: Latino Suburbanization in Postwar Los Angeles* (New Brunswick, NJ: Rutgers University Press, 2017); Genevieve Carpio, *Collisions at the Crossroads: How Place and Mobility Make Race* (Berkeley: University of California Press, 2019); Bobby Cervantes, "Las Colonias: Latino Housing and American Poverty on the Modern Border," (PhD diss., University of Kansas, 2022).

34. Daniel D. Arreola, "Mexican American Housescapes," *Geographical Review* 78 (July 1988): 299–315; Daniel D. Arreola, *Tejano South Texas: A Mexican American Cultural Province* (Austin: University of Texas Press, 2002); Daniel D. Arreola, ed., *Hispanic Spaces, Latino Places: Community and Cultural Diversity in Contemporary America* (Austin: University of Texas Press, 2004); Lydia R. Otero, *La Calle: Spatial Conflicts and Urban Renewal in a Southwest City* (Tucson: University of Arizona Press, 2010); Eric Avila, *The Folklore of the Freeway: Race and Revolt in the Modernist City* (Minneapolis: University of Minnesota Press, 2014); Kelly Lytle Hernández, *City of Inmates: Conquest, Rebellion, and the Rise of Human Caging in Los Angeles, 1771–1965* (Chapel Hill: University of North Carolina Press, 2017). See also Carpio, *Collisions at the Crossroads*.

35. Arredondo, *Mexican Chicago*; Perales, *Smeltertown*; Fernández, *Brown in the Windy City*; Elizabeth R. Escobedo, *From Coveralls to Zoot Suits* (Chapel Hill: University of North Carolina Press, 2013); Delia Fernández-Jones, *Making the MexiRican City: Migration, Placemaking, and Activism in Grand Rapids, Michigan* (Urbana: University of Illinois Press, 2023); McNamara, *Ybor City*; Tiffany González, "Rabble-Rousers of the Community: Chicana Activism and the Mexican American Business and Professional Women of Austin," submitted to *Western Historical Quarterly* and cited with the author's permission.

36. Recent books by Chicana/o and Puerto Rican historians include Fernández, *The Young Lords*; George J. Sánchez, *Boyle Heights: How a Los Angeles Neighborhood Became the Future of*

American Democracy (Berkeley: University of California Press, 2021); Natalia Molina, *A Place at the Nayarit: How a Mexican Restaurant Nourished a Community* (Berkeley: University of California Press, 2022).

37. In the sense, of course, that in many cases the initial migrants were Anglos intruding into Mexico, the Caribbean, and Central America.

38. Lauria Santiago defined the problem as "when Latina/os are mentioned only as an afterthought or obligatory box-checking rather than taken up as an opportunity to rethink existing, mostly Black-white, paradigms of race" in an email exchange with the author, November 7, 2024.

Chapter One

1. National Advisory Commission on Civil Disorders (Kerner Commission), *Report of the National Advisory Commission on Civil Disorders* (Washington, DC: Government Printing Office, 1968), 1; Elizabeth Hinton, *America on Fire: The Untold History of Police Violence and Black Rebellion since the 1960s* (New York: Liveright, 2021), 2. On terminology, see Thomas Sugrue, *Sweet Land of Liberty: The Forgotten Struggle for Civil Rights in the North* (New York: Random House, 2008), 334; Malcolm McLaughlin, *The Long, Hot Summer of 1967: Urban Rebellion in America* (New York: Palgrave Macmillan, 2014), 12–16; Amanda I. Seligman, "'But Burn—No': The Rest of the Crowd in Three Civil Disorders in 1960s Chicago," *Journal of Urban History* 37, no. 2 (2011): 246–48. I agree with McLaughlin when he writes in *Long, Hot Summer*: "To refer to an outbreak of looting, fire setting, and street fighting as a riot is not necessarily to deny its broader significance. On occasions when 'rebellion' seems to imply a coherence lacking in a spontaneous uprising, the term 'riot' captures the chaos let loose by popular unrest. We should not abandon a perfectly useful word that can communicate the lack of conscious ambition that other terms for popular uprising imply" (15). In this chapter, as I have argued elsewhere, I position rioting as one aspect of broader communal uprisings, which often included marches, negotiations, vigils, and other related events. See Pedro A. Regalado, "The Washington Heights Uprising of 1992: Dominican Belonging and Urban Policing in New York City," *Journal of Urban History* 45, no. 5 (2019): 961–86.

2. National Advisory Commission on Civil Disorders, *Report*, 1, 16.

3. As A. K. Sandoval-Strausz has argued, this massive migration of Latinxs across the country represented "a transnational transformation of American cities" worthy enough to call for "a new phase in urban history." A. K. Sandoval-Strausz, "Latino Landscapes: Postwar Cities and the Transnational Origins of a New Urban America," *Journal of American History* 101, no. 3 (December 2014): 803.

4. U.S. Census Bureau, 1970 Census of Population Subject Reports, Persons of Spanish Origin, PC (2)-1C (June 1973), 1.

5. On the controversy that plagued the 1970 census, and the problem of counting more broadly, see Cristina Mora, *Making Hispanics: How Activists, Bureaucrats, and Media Constructed a New American* (Chicago: Chicago University Press, 2014), 83–118; Ray Hutchison, "Miscounting the Spanish Origin Population in the United States: Corrections to the 1970 Census and Their Implications," *International Migration* 22, no. 2 (1984): 73–89; Campbell Gibson and Kay Jung, "Historical Census Statistics on Population Totals by Race, 1790 to 1990, and by Hispanic Origin, 1970 to 1990, for the United States, Regions, Divisions, and States" (Working Paper No. 56, Population Division, U.S. Census Bureau, September 2002).

6. Gibson and Jung, "Historical Census Statistics," tables 5, 10, 33, 44. See "Table 1. Persons of Spanish Origin by Sex and Urban and Rural Residence: 1970," in U.S. Census Bureau, 1970 Census of Population Subject Reports, Persons of Spanish Origin, PC (2)-1C, 1.

7. Juan Flores and Pedro López Adorno, *Pedro Pietri: Selected Poetry* (San Francisco: City Lights Publishers, 2015); Lorna Dee Cervantes, "Beneath the Shadow of the Freeway," Latin American Literary Review 100, no. 10 (Spring 1977): 176–79.

8. National Advisory Commission on Civil Disorders, *Report*, 16. Until recently, the scale of this violence garnered little scholarly attention. See Llana Barber, "Latine Rebellions and Why They Matter," *American Historian* (December 2021): https://www.oah.org/tah/immigration-history/latine-rebellions-and-why-they-matter/#:~:text=The%20scores%20of%20Latine%20uprisings,affinity%20for%20violence%20or%20disorder; Aaron G. Fountain Jr., "Forgotten Latino Urban Riots and Why They Can Happen Again," *Latino Rebels*, May 6, 2016. For "Puerto Rican riots," see Aldo Lauria Santiago's blog posts on "Puerto Rican Labor" for the Center for Puerto Rican Studies (https://centropr-archive.hunter.cuny.edu/digital-humanities/puerto-rican-labor/puerto-ricans-riot-new-york-chicago-and-newark); Hinton, *America on Fire*; McLaughlin, *Long, Hot Summer of 1967*; Peter B. Levy, *The Great Uprising: Race Riots in Urban America during the 1960s* (Cambridge: Cambridge University Press, 2018).

9. For Lefebvre, the "right to the city" is the "right to freedom, to individualization in socialization, to habitat and to inhabit." Henri Lefebvre, *Writings on Cities*, ed. Eleonore Kofman and Elizabeth Lebas (Cambridge, MA: Blackwell, 1996), 173–74.

10. Lilia Fernandez, *Brown in the Windy City: Mexicans and Puerto Ricans in Postwar Chicago* (Chicago: University of Chicago Press, 2012), 163–67; Mervin Méndez, "Recollections: 1966 Division Street Riot," *Diálogo* 2, no. 1 (1997), including Méndez's interview of Donald Headly, 29–35. Puerto Rican editorialist quoted from Lorrin Thomas and Aldo A. Lauria Santiago, *Rethinking the Struggle for Puerto Rican Rights* (New York: Routledge, 2019), 77.

11. Homer Bigart, "Disorder Erupts in East Harlem; Mobs Dispersed," *New York Times*, July 24, 1967; Johanna Fernández, *The Young Lords: A Radical History* (Chapel Hill: University of North Carolina Press, 2020), 77; Cathy Lisa Schneider, *Police Power and Race Riots: Urban Unrest in Paris and New York* (Philadelphia: University of Pennsylvania Press, 2014), 57–58; Aldo Lauria-Santiago, "East Harlem in 1967," *Puerto Rican Riots* (blog), Center for Puerto Rican Studies at Hunter College, https://centropr-archive.hunter.cuny.edu/digital-humanities/puerto-rican-labor/puerto-ricans-riots-east-harlem-1967; Peter Khiss, "Puerto Ricans Lay Inaction to Mayor," *New York Times*, July 28, 1967.

12. Aldo Lauria-Santiago, "Lower East Side also in 1968," *Puerto Rican Riots* (blog), Center for Puerto Rican Studies at Hunter College; Victor Vanzi, "Police Fire Guns, Gas in New Paterson Riots," *Courier-Post* (Camden, NJ), July 6, 1968; Victor Vanzi, "Police Cut Forces in Paterson," *Courier-Post* (Camden, NJ), July 8, 1968.

13. "10 Arrested in Trenton Disturbances," *Central New Jersey Home News*, June 13, 1969; "Show of Force by Police Quiets Unrest in Trenton," *Asbury Park (NJ) Press*, June 14, 1969.

14. See Samuel Zipp, *Manhattan Projects: The Rise and Fall of Urban Renewal in Cold War New York* (New York: Oxford University Press, 2012); "Renewing Inequality," in *American Panorama: An Atlas of United States History*, ed. Robert K. Nelson and Edward L. Ayers (Richmond, VA: Digital Scholarship Lab, University of Richmond), https://dsl.richmond.edu/panorama/renewal/#view=0/0/1&viz=cartogram.

15. "Characteristics Directory of Projects as of June 30, 1965," *Urban Renewal Project Characteristics* (Washington, DC: Office of Program Planning; Program Data and Evaluation Branch), 41; Les Plosia, "Vandals Firebomb City Hall in Passaic," *Herald-News* (NJ), August 6, 1969; "Puerto Rican Area Again Hit by Strife in Passaic," *Janesville (NJ) Daily Gazette*, August 5, 1969; Sylvan Fox, "Passaic Has Third Night of Violence," *New York Times*, August 6, 1969.

16. Plosia, "Vandals Firebomb City Hall in Passaic"; "Puerto Rican Area Again Hit by Strife

in Passaic"; Ronald Sullivan, "Jersey Assembly Votes Police Aid," *New York Times*, August 6, 1969.

17. Fountain, "Forgotten Latino Urban Riots."

18. Lorena Oropeza, *Raza sí, guerra no: Chicano Protest and Patriotism During the Viet Nam War Era* (Berkeley: University of California Press, 2005), 145–60, esp. 172. This moratorium demonstration had its counterparts in cities across the West and Southwest: Edward J. Escobar, "The Dialectics of Repression: The Los Angeles Police Department and the Chicano Movement, 1968–1971," *Journal of American History* 79, no. 4 (March 1993): 1483–1514; Armando Morales, *Ando sangrando (I Am Bleeding): A Study of Mexican American-Police Conflict* (Fair Lawn, NJ: R. E. Burdick, 1972), 101. The activist Ernesto Vigil recalled that "hundreds" fought back with "sticks, rocks, fists, and bottles." He declared that the rally "ended in the largest urban uprising in California by people of color since the Watts uprising of 1965." Ernesto B. Vigil, *The Crusade for Justice: Chicano Militancy and the Government's War on Dissent* (Madison: University of Wisconsin Press, 1999), 139–40.

19. The Moratorium rebellion, what Rosalio Muñoz called a "police riot," became a pivotal moment in the Chicano movement's evolution and militancy. See Escobar, "Dialectics of Repression"; Oropeza, *Raza sí, guerra no*, esp. 174. Writing in 1972, the author of *Ando sangrando* observed that the origins of the riots in East Los Angeles began "when the Southwest Mexicans told the Anglos 'Mi casa es su casa' . . . . . . and the hospitable invitation was taken literally." Morales, *Ando sangrando*, 91. See also "El plan espiritual de Aztlán," *El grito del Norte* 2, no. 9 (July 6, 1969), 5.

20. "Deputy, Civilian Shot in Melee at East L.A.," *Los Angeles Times*, September 17, 1970; "Three Shot, Many Hurt as L.A. Chicanos Riot Again," *Desert Sun* (CA), September 1970; David Shaw and Johnny Mosqueda, "36 Chicanos Held in Window-Breaking Melee Downtown," *Los Angeles Times*, January 10, 1971. Before January was over, following another moratorium rally, police shot and killed one young man during a ferocious clash with police that left many injured and seventy stores "pillaged and nine businesses destroyed by fire." Paul Houston and Ted Thackrey Jr., "1 Slain, 25 Hurt in Violence after Chicanos' Rally," *Los Angeles Times*, February 1, 1971; Escobar, "Dialectics of Repression," 1505–6.

21. David Robles, "'It Was Us against Us': The Pharr Police Riot of 1971 and the People's Uprising against El Jefe Político," in *Civil Rights in Black and Brown: Histories of Resistance and Struggle in Texas*, ed. Max Krochmal and J. Todd Moye (Austin: University of Texas Press, 2021), 131, 138–39. On bystanders, see Seligman, "'But Burn—No': The Rest of the Crowd in Three Civil Disorders in 1960s Chicago," *Journal of Urban History* 37, no. 2 (2011): 230–55.

22. Howard Graves and Tom Fenton, "National Guard Mobilized to Curb Albuquerque riots," *Prescott (AZ) Courier*, June 14, 1971; Aaron Fountain, "U.S. Latino Urban Riots," libcom.org, June 13, 2016, https://libcom.org/article/us-latino-urban-riots-aaron-fountain.

23. Lauren Silverman, "How the Death of a 12-Year-Old Changed the City of Dallas," *All Things Considered* (NPR), July 24, 2013, https://www.npr.org/sections/codeswitch/2013/07/24/205121429/How-The-Death-Of-A-12-Year-Old-Changed-The-City-Of-Dallas. Katherine Bynum, "Civil Rights in the 'City of Hate': Black and Brown Organizing against Police Brutality in Dallas," in *Civil Rights in Black and Brown: Histories of Resistance and Struggle in Texas*, ed. Max Krochmal and J. Todd Moye (Austin: University of Texas Press, 2021), 222. See also Joel Zapata, "The South-by-Southwest Borderlands' Chicana/o Uprising: The Brown Berets, Black and Brown Alliances, and the Fight against Police Brutality in West Texas" in *Civil Rights in Black and Brown: Histories of Resistance and Struggle in Texas, ed.* Max Krochmal and J. Todd Moye (Austin: University of Texas Press, 2021), 93–114.

24. John Boyd, "Riots in Baltimore, Ferguson Recall Houston's Infamous Moody Park Riot," *Houston (TX) Chronicle*, April 28, 2015.

25. Fountain, "Forgotten Latino Urban Riots"; Gregg Lee Carter, "Hispanic Rioting during the Civil Rights Era," *Sociological Forum* 7, no. 2 (1992): 315.

26. Edwin Maldonado, "Contract Labor and the Origins of Puerto Rican Communities in the United States," *International Migration Review* 13, no. 1 (Spring 1979): 103–21; Daniel Sidorick, *Condensed Capitalism: Campbell Soup and the Pursuit of Cheap Production in the Twentieth Century* (Ithaca, NY: Cornell University Press, 2009), 92; Robert A. Poteete, "Puerto Ricans Harvest Jersey Tomato Crop," *New York Herald Tribune*, August 17, 1950. Puerto Ricans also settled in nearby Philadelphia. See Carmen Teresa Whalen, *From Puerto Rico to Philadelphia: Puerto Rican Workers and Postwar Economies* (Philadelphia: Temple University Press, 2001), 53–55; Rev. Roque Longo et al., *Puerto Ricans in Camden: A Report* (Camden, NJ: Our Lady of Fatima, Holy Name, June 1970).

27. In 1961, Campbell's employed only sixty-five Puerto Ricans of the several hundred it had employed just a decade earlier. See Joan Koss, "Puerto Ricans in Philadelphia: Migration and Accommodation" (PhD diss., University of Pennsylvania, 1965), 64; "Table 2. General Statistics for Standard Metropolitan Areas, Counties, and Urban Places: 1947 and 1939," *Census of Manufactures, 1947*, vol. 3, *Statistics by States* (Washington, DC: Government Printing Office, 1949–1950), 387; "Table 8. Statistics by Selected Industry Group and Industry for Selected Places: 1977 and 1972," *1977 Census of Manufactures*, vol. 3, *Geographic Area Statistics, Part 2. General Summary, Nebraska-Wyoming* (Washington, DC: Government Printing Office, 1977), 31–58; Howard Gillette, *Camden after the Fall: Decline and Renewal in a Post-Industrial City* (Philadelphia: University of Pennsylvania Press, 2005), 42.

28. Joseph R. McCarthy, "Two Patrolmen Charged in Beating of Motorist," *Courier-Post* (Camden, NJ), August 13, 1971; Bob Reichenbach, "3 Say They Saw Police Beating Man Who Died," *Courier-Post* (Camden, NJ), January 31, 1973.

29. They were part of a department that Black police officers said included "bullies who use their nightsticks as Nazi-like weapons for self-imposed law." "We are doubly appalled," they continued, "when incidents fomented by police carry racial overtones." "Black Police Lash Out at 'Nightstick Bullies' on Force," *Courier-Post* (Camden, NJ), August 14, 1971; Lauren Lahey, "'Justice Now!, ¡Justicia Ahora!': Interracial Coalitions and Camden, New Jersey's 1971 Riot," in *Civil Rights and Beyond: African American and Latino/a Activism in the Twentieth-Century United States* (Athens: University of Georgia Press, 2016), 158; McCarthy, "Two Patrolmen Charged in Beating of Motorist"; Renee Winkler, "Rioting Deepened Camden's Divisions," *Courier-Post* (Camden, NJ), February 1, 2007.

30. Kitty Capparella, "Yeager to Mario: '5 Minutes,'" *Courier-Post* (Camden, NJ), August 20, 1971.

31. Capparella, "Yeager to Mario"; Mike Wolk and Joseph Busler, "Both Sides Disclaim Riot Responsibility," *Courier-Post* (Camden, NJ), August 20, 1971.

32. Peter F. Finley, "More Fire Units Put on Alert to Assist Local Companies," *Courier-Post* (Camden, NJ), August 21, 1971; "Chronology of City Unrest," *Courier-Post* (Camden, NJ), August 22, 1971; "Burning Camden: A Hell for Cops," *Courier-Post* (Camden, NJ), August 21, 1971; Joseph H. Rodriguez, interviewed by the author, Camden, NJ, July 16, 2013.

33. Rodriguez interview; Mike Wolk and Joseph Busler, "Leaders of Riot Claim Nardi Waited Too Long" *Courier-Post* (Camden, NJ), August 20, 1971; Capparella, "Yeager to Mario"; "Here 'Own People'; Former Nun to Direct El Centro," *Courier-Post* (Camden, NJ), September 28, 1972; Gillette, *Camden after the Fall*, 56.

34. Gualberto "Gil" Medina, interviewed by the author, Saddle Brook, NJ, July 8, 2013.

35. Lahey, "'Justice Now!, ¡Justicia Ahora!,'" 160; "2 Killed in Camden Rioting; Sniper Fire Blamed," *The New York Times*, September 3, 1969; Gillette, *Camden after the Fall*, 83; James Jefferson and Joseph McCarthy, "Yeager Hints Riot a Possible Plot," *Courier-Post* (Camden, NJ), August 20, 1971.

36. Although journalists typically categorized uprisings like the one in Camden as either Puerto Rican or Black American, both groups united in forceful protest on many occasions, including in Camden and Patterson, New Jersey, and New Haven and Hartford, Connecticut, and beyond. Moreover, the complexity of Latinx racial classification is difficult to disentangle into neat threads: many Puerto Ricans were themselves Black, which likely shaped their experiences of police brutality but rarely appeared in local news reporting. As Laurie Lahey has written, "While the media and the few scholars who have considered this event characterized it as Latino, it was the product of interracial, African American-Latino cooperation." Lahey, "'Justice Now!, ¡Justicia Ahora!,'" 153–54; "Violence Erupts in Hill District," *New Haven (CT) Register*, August 30, 1967; Jose E, Cruz, *Identity and Power Puerto Rican Politics and the Challenge of Ethnicity* (Philadelphia: Temple University Press, 1998); "Firebombing Blamed on Earlier Shooting," *Progress Bulletin* (Pomona, CA), August 10, 1972; James M. Markham, "Curfew Is Continued in Quiet but Riot-Torn Camden," *New York Times*, August 23, 1971; Wolk and Busler, "Both Sides Disclaim Riot Responsibility."

37. "Partial List of Arrests in Camden," *Courier-Post* (Camden, NJ), August 20, 1971; Beth Durchschlag, "Looters Enjoy Field Days during Riots in Camden," *Courier-Post* (Camden, NJ), August 23, 1971; Jefferson, and McCarthy, "Yeager Hints Riot a Possible Plot."

38. Gillette, *Camden after the Fall*, 60, 95.

39. A sense of Latin American and Caribbean pan-ethnic identification had long been present among these groups in the United States. Here, I am referring to efforts at the federal level to create a voting bloc.

40. The books dealt with Mexico City, San Juan, and New York. See Emilio de Antuñano, "Mexico City as an Urban Laboratory: Oscar Lewis, the 'Culture of Poverty' and the Transnational History of the Slum," *Journal of Urban History* 45, no. 4 (April 2018): 813–30. Scholars would continue to research how Latinxs constituted a growing element of what would eventually be termed the nation's urban *underclass* and likewise part of the *inner city*, a signifier premised on popular perceptions of spatialized poverty and urban disorder. See Brian Eugenio Herrera, "Compiling *West Side Story*'s Parahistories, 1959–2009," *Theatre Journal* 64 (2012): 236–37; Michael B. Katz, ed., *The Underclass Debate: Views from History* (Princeton, NJ: Princeton University Press, 1993); Joan Moore and Raquel Pinderhughes, *In the Barrios: Latinos and the Underclass Debate* (New York: Russell Sage Foundation, 1993); Bench Ansfield, "Unsettling 'Inner City': Liberal Protestantism and the Postwar Origins of a Keyword in Urban Studies," *Antipode* 50, no. 5 (April 2018): 1166–85.

41. The CCOSSP was preceded by the Inter-Agency Committee on Mexican-American Affairs, which President Lyndon Johnson created in 1967 to assess the problems facing Mexican Americans. See Mora, *Making Hispanics*; Benjamin Francis-Fallon, *The Rise of the Latino Vote: A History* (Cambridge, MA: Harvard University Press, 2019); 115 Cong. Rec. H39394–95 (daily ed. December 16, 1969). Echoing his colleagues, William C. Cramer of Florida stated: "Americans of Spanish heritage have proved a law-abiding minority—and perhaps for this reason, we have been slow in recognizing their needs. Since they have not burned and rioted to draw attention to their problems, some have interpreted this as contentment with their lot." 115 Cong. Rec. H39395, 39399 (daily ed. December 16, 1969).

42. Similarly, amid a leadership change in the CCOSSP in 1970, "one California organization even suggested that replacing Castillo with a non-Mexican could lead to riots in Los Angeles," Cristina Mora writes in *Making Hispanics* (38). Francis-Fallon, *Rise of the Latino Vote*, 154; "Exhibit 4: Statement by Hon. Joseph M. Montoya, in Support of S.740, a Bill to Establish the Interagency Committee on Mexican-American Affairs," *Hearings before the Subcommittee on Executive Reorganization of the Committee on Government Operations*, U.S. Senate, 91st Cong., 1st sess., June 11 and 12, 1969 (Washington, DC: U.S. Government Printing Office), 17–18.

43. Francis-Fallon, *Rise of the Latino Vote*, 133.

44. Felix M. Padilla, *Puerto Rican Chicago* (South Bend, IN: University of Notre Dame Press, 1987), 160, 162; Mehrsa Baradaran, *The Color of Money: Black Banks and the Racial Wealth Gap* (Cambridge, MA: Harvard University Press, 2017), 191; Pedro A. Regalado, "They Speak Our Language . . . Business: Latinx Businesspeople and the Pursuit of Wealth in New York City," in *Histories of Racial Capitalism*, eds. Destin Jenkins and Justin LeRoy (New York: Columbia University Press, 2021). On the War on Poverty, see Annelise Orleck and Lisa Gayle Hazirjian, *The War on Poverty: A New Grassroots History, 1964–1980* (Athens, GA: 2011).

45. *Child Care and Child Development Programs, 1977–78: Hearings Before the Senate Subcommittee on Child and Human Development of the Committee on Human Resources*, U.S. Senate, 95th Cong., 2nd sess., February 20, 1978 (Washington, DC: U.S. Government Printing Office, 1978), 995–98.

46. In Chicago, home to Mexican Americans and Puerto Ricans, city leaders leveraged Puerto Rican rage in the Division Street uprising to "draw sharp distinctions between the city's two major Latino groups," notes Mike Amezcua. In Camden, the lingering perception among whites in nearby suburbs that the riot-torn city was a lost cause undermined demonstrators' transformative goals. Mike Amezcua, "A Machine in the Barrio: Chicago's Conservative Colonia and the Remaking of Latino Politics in the 1960 and 1970s," *The Sixties: A Journal of History, Politics, and Culture* 12, no. 1 (2019): 102–3.

47. Francis-Fallon, *Rise of the Latino Vote*; Barber, "Latine Rebellions and Why They Matter."

Chapter Two

1. William Booth, "Atlanta's Race against Time," *Washington Post*, April 20, 1996. Originally coined in a 1959 address by Mayor William B. Hartsfield, the "city too busy to hate" slogan painted an image of racial harmony in the desegregation era. The phrase also highlighted budding partnerships between local politicians, community leaders, and business interests that animated the development-centric "spirit of Atlanta." See Ed Hughes, "Must Tax People Who Use City, Hartsfield Declares," *Atlanta Journal*, September 2, 1959; "Mayor Vows Order in Desegregation," *Atlanta Journal*, April 6, 1961.

2. On Atlanta boosterism, Charles Ruthheiser writes, "Much like Los Angeles and other cities lacking any 'natural' advantages, such as a harbor or navigable ricer, Atlanta has from its inception been the object of a particularly intense form of boosterism, a creation of its own imagination." Charles Ruthheiser, *Imagineering Atlanta: The Politics of Place in the City of Dreams* (New York: Verso, 1996), 3, 18.

3. Steven R. Weisman, "Atlanta Selected over Athens for 1996 Olympics," *New York Times*, September 19, 1990. The image of Atlanta as a site of peaceful integration in the 1960s informed a continued booster representation of a city that was good for business and, by extension, good for Atlantans. Such top-down logic about urban development often came at the expense of Black, working-class, and low-income residents. See Maurice J. Hobson, *The Legend of Black Mecca:*

Politics and Class in the Making of Modern Atlanta (Chapel Hill: University of North Carolina Press, 2019).

4. After its establishment as a career center in 1977, the Mexican consulate became an official consulate general in 1992, contributing to the internationalizing efforts that characterized Atlanta in the years between winning the Olympic bid in 1990 and hosting the games in 1996. See "Mexican Consul Cites Region's Advances Due to Immigration from Her Country," *Global Atlanta*, July 16, 2007. A key legislative change was the passage of the Immigration Reform and Control Act of 1986, Pub. L. No. 99-603, 100 Stat. 3445.

5. Maus was a regular contributor to the *Mundo Hispánico* "Tribuna Pública" column in the 1990s, writing in with opinion pieces that included advocating for undocumented students' education rights and the right to driver's licenses for noncitizens. See especially columns from November 15, 1990, and February 15, 1991. See Dana Bultman, "The New Georgians 2001," uploaded May 20, 2014, YouTube video, 33:15, https://www.youtube.com/watch?app=desktop&v=jbSCk1qE5VA.

6. Johanes Roselló, "Transformaron Atlanta," *Mundo Hispánico*, July 7, 2016.

7. On the historical conflation of Mexicans with cheap labor, transience, hard work, and illegality, see Melita M. Garza, *They Came to Toil: Newspaper Representations of Mexicans and Immigrants in the Great Depression* (Austin: University of Texas Press, 2018); Natalia Molina, *How Race Is Made in America: Immigration, Citizenship, and the Historical Power of Racial Scripts* (Berkeley: University of California Press, 2014); Roselló, "Transformaron Atlanta"; David Wicker, "Atlanta Olympics—How the Olympics Drew Latinos to Atlanta," *Atlanta Journal-Constitution*, July 19, 2016.

8. Natalia Molina, "The Importance of Place and Place-Makers in the Life of a Los Angeles Community: What Gentrification Erases from Echo Park," *Southern California Quarterly* 97, no. 1 (2015): 69–111. See also Mary Odem, "Latin American Immigrants, Religion, and the Politics of Urban Space in Atlanta," in *Mexican Immigration to the U.S. Southeast: The Impact and Challenges* (Atlanta: Instituto de México, 2005), 141–56; Natalia Molina, *A Place at the Nayarit: How a Mexican Restaurant Nourished a Community* (Berkeley: University of California Press, 2022), 9.

9. Dolores Hayden, *The Power of Place: Urban Landscapes as Public History* (Cambridge, MA: MIT Press, 1997), 9, 16.

10. The majority of this development occurred north of the city center in white-flight counties such as Cobb and Gwinnett. "Sunbelt" is a flexible regional category that points to shared developmental processes, often dependent on Latinx migrant labor by the late twentieth century. See the introduction to *Sunbelt Rising: The Politics of Space, Place, and Region*, ed. Michelle Nickerson and Darren Dochuk (Philadelphia: University of Pennsylvania Press, 2011), 1–28.

11. Tera Hunter, *To 'Joy My Freedom: Southern Black Women's Lives and Labors after the Civil War* (Cambridge, MA: Harvard University Press, 1997); Allison Dorsey, *To Build Our Lives Together: Community Formation in Black Atlanta, 1875–1906* (Athens: University of Georgia Press, 2004); Kevin Kruse, *White Flight: Atlanta and the Making of Modern Conservatism* (Princeton, NJ: Princeton University Press, 2005).

12. U.S. Census Bureau, "Country of Origin and Nativity," 1970 Census, accessed via Social Explorer; U.S. Census Bureau, "Spanish by Specific Origin," 1980 Census, accessed via Social Explorer.

13. Scholars have often described the development of "new destinations" for Mexican migrants as beginning in the 1990s, as a result of the increased geographic mobility that citizenship afforded to previously undocumented workers. See Jorge Durand, Douglas S. Massey, and

Fernando Charvet, "The Changing Geography of Mexican Immigration to the United States: 1910–1996," *Social Science Quarterly* 18, no. 1 (March 2000): 1–15; Heather A. Smith and Owen J. Furuseth, eds., *Latinos in the New South: Transformation of Place* (London: Ashgate, 2006): 5; Navid Sabet and Christoph Winter, "The Political Economy of Immigrant Legislation: Evidence from the 1986 IRCA" (Working Paper No. 7611, CESifo, 2019).

14. For an early study on "Hispanic" residential patterns in Metro Atlanta, see John D. Hutcheson Jr. and Lino H. Dominguez, "Ethnic Self-Help Organizations in Non-Barrio Settings: Community Identity and Voluntary Action," *Journal of Voluntary Action Research* 15, no. 4 (1986): 13–22.

15. Census data recorded 7,164 Mexicans living in the ten-county Metro Atlanta region in 1980, making up about 30 percent of the overall "Spanish origin" population. U.S. Census Bureau, "Spanish by Specific Origin," 1980 Census, accessed via Social Explorer; Jorge Durand, Douglas S. Massey, and Emilio A. Parrado, "The New Era of Mexican Migration to the United States," *Journal of American History* 86, no. 2 (September 1999): 520; Pepe X., oral history interview by the author, August 1, 2016.

16. Cameron Lippard, "Building Inequality: A Case Study of White, Black, and Latino Contractors in the Atlanta Construction Industry" (PhD diss., Georgia State University, 2006), 19.

17. Julie Weise, *Corazón de Dixie: Mexicanos in the U.S. South since 1910* (Chapel Hill: University of North Carolina Press, 2015), chap. 4; Natalia Molina, *How Race Is Made*; Arthur Brice, "Atlanta's Other Underground," *Atlanta Journal-Constitution*, April 12, 1992.

18. Susan Harte, "Hispanics Have Filled a Void, but Contractors Say Better Training, Conditions Are Needed," *Atlanta Journal-Constitution*, June 20, 1999; Brice, "Atlanta's Other Underground."

19. Mina X., oral history interview by the author, July 16, 2018.

20. Mina X. interview.

21. This would change by the mid- to late 1990s as Latinx bricks-and-mortar places became a more common sight in Metro Atlanta.

22. Brenda Lopez Romero, oral history interview by the author, October 6, 2020, https://kaltura.uga.edu/media/t/1_dlahfwfi.

23. Here, "stepped migrations" points to the migratory practice of arriving and settling in one locale to work before moving on to a next location (rather than circular migration). See Anju Mary Paul, *Multinational Maids: Stepwise Migration in a Global Labor Market* (Cambridge: Cambridge University Press, 2017); Rubén Hernández-León, *Metropolitan Migrants: The Migration of Urban Mexicans in the United States* (Berkeley: University of California Press, 2008).

24. Ricardo X., oral history interview by the author, August 8, 2016.

25. Ricardo X. interview.

26. The author's research and own lived experiences suggest that migrants from Veracruz were among the earliest arrivals to Metro Atlanta and may have been recruited in even more direct ways by contractors.

27. Kevin Sack, "Atlanta: Day 1; Promised Renewal Has Been Less Than Olympian," *New York Times*, July 20, 1996; Michael Dobbins, Leon S. Eplan, and Randal Roark, *Atlanta's Olympic Resurgence: How the 1996 Games Revived a Struggling City* (Charleston, SC: History Press, 2021), 13; Rebecca J. Dameron and Arthur D. Murphy, "An International City Too Busy to Hate? Social and Cultural Change in Atlanta: 1970–1995," *Urban Anthropology and Studies of Cultural Systems and World Economic Development* 26, no. 1 (Spring 1997): 43–69; Ruthheiser, *Imagineering Atlanta*.

28. Alfredo Duarte, "Olimpiada cultural saluda a México," *Mundo Hispánico*, September 15, 1993; "Mexican Consul General: Multi-Cultural Activist," *Global Atlanta*, May 18, 1993; Arthur

Brice, "The Other Underground: From a Hard Life to New Challenges," *Atlanta Journal-Constitution*, April 12, 1992; Scott Bronstein, "Smyrna Police Violate Rights, Says Mexican Consul," *Atlanta Journal-Constitution*, July 20, 1991; Ralph Ellis, "Illegal Workers Feeling the Sting of SouthPAW," *Atlanta Journal-Constitution*, July 6, 1995.

29. Kathy Scruggs and Michelle Hiskey, "INS Sweeps Olympic Sites," *Atlanta Journal-Constitution*, January 13, 1995; Kathy Scruggs and Michelle Hiskey, "Local Olympics," *Atlanta Journal-Constitution*, January 12, 1995. Beginning in 1991, the Atlanta Labor Council planned for programs to train and hire unemployed community members. The lack of commitment to low-income local residents was also evident in the removal of public housing projects. See Harvey K. Newman, "Neighborhood Impacts of Atlanta's Olympic Games," *Community Development Journal* 34, no. 2 (April 1999): 151–59; Bert Roughton Jr., "Labor Unions Seek Role in Games Projects," *Atlanta Journal-Constitution*, January 30, 1991.

30. Ralph Ellis, "Illegal Workers Feeling the Sting of SouthPAW," *Atlanta Journal-Constitution*, July 6, 1995.

31. Wicker, "Atlanta Olympics."

32. Mexicans were by no means the only Latinx group migrating to Metro Atlanta at the close of the century, although they accounted for the majority of the Latinx population. This was an incremental increase, with Latinx people making up over 30 percent of the construction workforce by 2008. See Center for Construction Research and Training, CRTW Data Center, "Hispanic Employment in Construction," *CPWR Data Brief* 1, no. 1 (November 2009): 1–17; Lippard, "Building Inequality," 24; Center for Construction Research and Training, *The Construction Chart Book: The U.S. Construction Industry and Its Workers* (Silver Spring, MD: CPWR Center for Construction Research and Training, 2013), 53.

33. R. Robin McDonald and Ben Smith III, "Illegal Immigrants Are 'Rescued'—Packed: 34 Undocumented Workers Were Held in a Space Designed for Four Horses," *Atlanta Journal-Constitution*, May 23, 1996.

34. Pepe X. interview.

35. Natalia Molina, *How Race Is Made.*

36. Cobb County was the first in Georgia to sign on: Memorandum of Agreement No. 7151, signed on February 12, 2007, by Sheriff Neil Warren; Cecilia Menjívar and Daniel Kanstroom, *Constructing Immigrant "Illegality": Critiques, Experiences, and Responses* (New York: Cambridge University Press, 2013), 18.

37. "HB 87: Illegal Immigration Reform and Enforcement Act of 2011," Georgia General Assembly 2011–2012 Regular Session, at https://www.legis.ga.gov/api/legislation/document/2011 2012/116631.

38. Jesse Moss, "The Abandoned Vans of Atlanta," *New York Times*, May 7, 2019. https://www.nytimes.com/2019/05/07/opinion/ice-immigration-atlanta.html.

39. Michelle Nickerson and Darren Dochuk, eds., *Sunbelt Rising: The Politics of Space, Place, and Region* (Philadelphia: University of Pennsylvania Press, 2011), 14.

40. Description from Yehimi Cambrón's artist Instagram page (@ycambron); Yehimi Cambrón, "Monuments: Atlanta's Immigrants," https://www.yehimicambron.com.

Chapter Three

1. "53rd Puerto Rican/Hispanic Parade Celebrates Unity, Resiliency," *Newsday*, June 2, 2019; "Thousands Attend Puerto Rican Hispanic Day Parade in Brentwood," *News12*, June 3, 2019, https://www.news12.com/story/40578421/thousands-expected-at-puerto-rican-hispanic-day

-parade-in-brentwood. Vertical Files (hereafter VF), Hispanic Parade, Brentwood Public Library (hereafter BPL), Brentwood, NY; and VF, Hispanic Parade, Hispanic-Latino Collection, Special Collections, Long Island Studies Institute (hereafter LISI), Hofstra University, Hempstead, NY.

2. U.S. Census Bureau, American Community Survey, 5-Year Estimates, 2014–2018, table B03001. Figures are rounded to the nearest 100.

3. On Latinx suburbanization and racialization in Los Angeles and nationwide, see Genevieve Carpio and Andy Rutkowski, "Mapping LA-tinx Suburbia," *Boom California*, June 26, 2017, https://boomcalifornia.org/2017/06/26/mapping-la-tinx-suburbia/; Genevieve Carpio, *Collisions at the Crossroads: How Place and Mobility Make Race* (Berkeley: University of California Press, 2018). See also Matt Garcia, *A World of Its Own: Race, Labor, and Citrus in the Making of Greater Los Angeles* (Chapel Hill: University of North Carolina Press, 2001); Laura R. Barraclough, "South Central Farmers and Shadow Hills Homeowners: Land Use Policy and Relational Racialization in Los Angeles," *Professional Geographer* 61, no. 2 (2009): 164–86; Leland T. Saito, *Race and Politics: Asian Americans, Latinos, and Whites in a Los Angeles Suburb* (Champaign: University of Illinois Press, 1998); Wendy Cheng, *The Changs Next Door to the Diazes: Remapping Race in Suburban California* (Minneapolis: University of Minnesota Press, 2013); Jerry González, *In Search of the Mexican Beverly Hills: Latino Suburbanization in Postwar Los Angeles* (New Brunswick, NJ: Rutgers University Press, 2018); G. Aron Ramírez, "Business as Usual: Ethnic Commerce and the Making of a Mexican American Middle Class in Southeast Los Angeles, 1981–1995," *Journal of Urban History*, online publication, December 2022, https://doi.org/10.1177/00961442221139473; Becky M. Nicolaides, *The New Suburbia: How Diversity Remade Suburban Life in Los Angeles after 1945* (New York: Oxford University Press, 2023). On the Northeast, see Marilynn Johnson, "Revitalizing the Suburbs: Immigrants in Greater Boston since the 1980s," in *Immigration and Metropolitan Revitalization in the United States*, ed. Domenic Vitiello and Thomas J. Sugrue (Philadelphia: University of Pennsylvania Press, 2017), 67–79; Llana Barber, *Latino City: Immigration and Urban Crisis in Lawrence, Massachusetts, 1945–2000* (Chapel Hill: University of North Carolina Press, 2017).

4. Kenneth T. Jackson, *Crabgrass Frontier: The Suburbanization of the United States* (New York: Oxford University Press, 1985); Robert Fishman, *Bourgeois Utopias: The Rise and Fall of Suburbia* (New York: Basic Books, 1987); Delores Hayden, *Building Suburbia: Green Fields and Urban Growth, 1820–2000* (New York: Random House, 2003); Lizabeth Cohen, *A Consumers' Republic: The Politics of Mass Consumption in Postwar America* (New York: Knopf, 2003). Latinos are mostly missing from the formative histories of suburbanization, and they appear in only one chapter, by Michael Jones-Correa, in Kevin M. Kruse and Thomas J. Sugrue, eds., *The New Suburban History* (Chicago: University of Chicago Press, 2006). A noteworthy exception is Rosalyn Baxandall and Elizabeth Ewen, *Picture Windows: How the Suburbs Happened* (New York: Basic Books, 2000).

5. Audrey Singer, "Contemporary Immigrant Gateways in Historical Perspective," *Daedalus: The Journal of the American Academy of Arts and Sciences* 142, no. 3 (Summer 2013): 76–91; Michael B. Katz, Mathew J. Creighton, Daniel Amsterdam, and Merlin Chowkwanyun, "Immigration and the New Metropolitan Geography," *Journal of Urban Affairs* 32 (2010): 523–47.

6. William H. Frey, *The Rise of Melting Pot Suburbs*, Brookings Institution, May 26, 2015; William H. Frey, *Diversity Explosion: How New Racial Demographics Are Remaking America* (Washington, DC: Brookings Institution, 2018); Audrey Singer, *Twenty-First Century Gateways: Immigrant Incorporation in Suburban America* (Washington, DC: Brookings Institution, 2008). For influential alternatives, see Wei Li, *Ethnoburb: The New Ethnic Community in Urban America* (Honolulu: University of Hawai'i Press, 2012); R. L'Heureux McCoy, Natasha Warikoo,

Stephen A. Matthews, and Nadirah Farah Foley, "Resisting Amnesia: Renewing and Expanding the Study of Suburban Inequality," *RSF: The Russell Sage Foundation Journal of the Social Sciences* 9, no. 1 (2023): 1–30.

7. Cohen, *Consumers' Republic*; author's observations in October 2019 and January 2020; Kay Blough, "'Feels Like Home': They Come from All Over Latin America, but in Brentwood It's One Community," *Newsday*, July 29, 2012. The history of Latinx suburban businesses is ripe for further examination. For an essential starting point, see Ramirez, "Business as Usual"; and Nicolaides's chapter in this volume.

8. Author's observations, October 2019 and January 2020. On accessory housing, see Edna Negrón, "Concern over Housing Hispanics," *Newsday*, January 27, 1988, copy in VF, Brentwood: Housing, BPL. On Latinx workers, see James Duncan and Nancy Duncan, "Can't Live with Them; Can't Landscape without Them: Racism and the Pastoral Aesthetic in Suburban New York," *Landscape Journal* 22, no. 2 (2003): 88–98. There is a rich body of scholarship on Latinized urban landscapes essential for suburban historians. See A. K. Sandoval-Strausz, *Barrio America: How Latino Immigrants Saved the American City* (New York: Basic Books, 2019); Daniel D. Arreola, "Mexican American Housescapes," *Geographical Review* 78 (July 1988): 299–315; Victor M. Valle and Rodolfo D. Torres, *Latino Metropolis* (Minneapolis: University of Minnesota Press, 2000); Mike Davis, *Magical Urbanism: Latinos Reinvent the U.S. City* (New York: Verso Books, 2000); Daniel D. Arreola, ed., *Hispanic Spaces, Latino Places: Community and Cultural Diversity in Contemporary America* (Austin: University of Texas Press, 2004); David R. Diaz, *Barrio Urbanism: Chicanos, Planning, and American Cities* (New York: Routledge, 2005).

9. Author's observations, January 2020. On Long Island's parking-lot-based informal labor markets, see Sarah Garland, *Gangs in Garden City: How Immigration, Segregation, and Youth Violence Are Changing America's Suburbs* (New York: Nation Books, 2009), 141–43. On transportation to work, see U.S. Census Bureau, American Community Survey 5-Year Estimates, 2014–2018, table B01001I. About 1,100 Latinx residents of Islip walk to work.

10. Pepe Pertuz, "Tres ligas hispanas de Long Island se afilian en la Eastern New York," *El Diario La Prensa* (NY), January 4, 1996.

11. Michael H. Cottman, "Residents Fighting to Reopen Park," *Newsday*, July 17, 1986; Martin Weston and Scott Minerbrook, "600 March to Reopen Park in Brentwood," *Newsday*, July 22, 1986; "Study on Park," *Newsday*, April 28, 1987; Sharon Monahan, "Islip Ponders Future of Park," *New York Times*, September 13, 1987; Paula Park, "The Name of the Game Is Limbo: Deadlock Clouds Future of Closed Brentwood Park," *Newsday*, August 20, 1989; Katti Grey, "Dispute over Reopening Park," *Newsday*, September 2, 1990; Long Island Housing Partnership, *1992 Annual Report*, 3, https://www.lihp.org/Content/1992%20annual%20report.pdf.

12. "'Unscrupulous' Dumping at an Islip Town Park, Park Commissioner Resigns as DA Investigation Heats Up," *Newsday*, May 8, 2014; Sarah Armaghan and Sarah Crichton, "Exclusive: Town Was Warned: Dumping at Brentwood Park Was Reported to Islip by Ranger, Legislator and Residents," *Newsday*, May 12, 2014; Rick Chalifoux, "Informational Meeting Rife with Anger," *Suffolk County News*, May 22, 2014; "DA: Illegal Dumping Investigation Reveals Banned Pesticides, Dangerous Metals at 2 Suffolk County Locations," *CBS New York*, May 29, 2014; Victor Manuel Ramos, "Brentwood Residents Near Roberto Clemente Park Fear for Their Futures," *Newsday*, June 14, 2014; "Datre Jr. Pleads Guilty to Felony Charges," press release, County of Suffolk District Attorney's Office, March 30, 2016; Complaint, *Seggos v. Datre et al.*, No. 17-CCV-2684 (E.D.N.Y., filed May 4, 2017); Sophia Chang, "Residents Return to Newly Reopened Roberto Clemente Park," *Newsday*, July 31, 2017.

13. John R. Logan and Brian Stults, "The Persistence of Segregation in the Metropolis: New Findings from the 2010 Census," Census Brief Prepared for Project US2010 (2011), table 4, https://s4.ad.brown.edu/Projects/Diversity/Data/Report/report2.pdf.

14. On indexes of dissimilarity, see Karl Taeuber and Alma Taeuber, *Negroes in Cities: Residential Segregation and Neighborhood Change* (Chicago: Aldine Publishing Co., 1965); Douglas S. Massey and Nancy A. Denton, *American Apartheid: Segregation and the Making of the Underclass* (Cambridge, MA: Harvard University Press, 1992), 20. On Latino segregation, see Mary J. Fischer and Marta Tienda, "Redrawing Spatial Color Lines: Hispanic Metropolitan Dispersal, Segregation, and Economic Opportunity," in *Hispanics and the Future of America*, ed. Marta Tienda and Faith Mitchell (Washington, DC: National Academies Press, 2006); Daniel T. Lichter, Domenico Parisi, Michael C. Taquino, and Steven Michael Grice, "Residential Segregation in New Hispanic Destinations: Cities, Suburbs, and Rural Communities Compared," *Social Science Research* 39 (2010): 215–30; Douglas S. Massey and Jacob S. Rugh, "Segregation in Post-Civil Rights America: Stalled Integration or End of the Segregated Century?," *Du Bois Review* 11, no. 2 (2014): 205–32.

15. Indexes of dissimilarity were calculated under my direction by Andrew Beveridge, professor of sociology, Queens College, City University of New York, using block group data from the U.S. Census. Data available from the author upon request.

16. Town of Islip Community Development Agency, Town of Islip, Suffolk County, New York, *Analysis of Impediments to Fair Housing Choice* (hereafter Islip, *Analysis of Impediments*), 2010, ES-3-6, IV-4. See also the updated report published five years later: Islip, *Analysis of Impediments*, 2015, IV-3.

17. For example, Hauppauge, Holbrook, Islip Terrace, Ronkonkoma, and Bohemia all have small Latino populations but substantial tracts of houses, including rental properties, that are similar in size, amenities, and cost to those in parts of Brentwood, Central Islip, and North Bay Shore. Various studies have shown that socioeconomic differences between Latinos and whites cannot explain their segregation. See Islip, *Analysis of Impediments*, 2015, IV-3; U.S. Census Bureau, American Community Survey 5-Year Estimates, 2014–2018, table DP04. More generally, see Camille L. Zubrinsky and Lawrence Bobo, "Prismatic Metropolis: Race and Residential Segregation in the City of Angels," *Social Science Research* 25 (1996): 335–74.

18. A common hypothesis suggests that Latinos share a preference for living among other Latinos. This "birds of a feather flock together" view of housing segregation has solidified into a folk common sense about race and residence in the United States. It overlooks the fact that most Latinos—and other minority groups—do not prefer to live in ethnically homogeneous blocks and, indeed, exercise that preference by moving into majority-white neighborhoods when they have the opportunity. See Lawrence Bobo, "Attitudes on Residential Integration: Perceived Status Differences, Mere In-Group Preference, or Racial Prejudice?," *Social Forces* 74, no. 3 (1996): 883–909; Esther Havekes, Michael Bader, and Maria Krysan, "Realizing Racial and Ethnic Neighborhood Preferences? Exploring the Mismatches between What People Want, Where They Search, and Where They Live," *Population Research and Policy Review* 35 (2016): 101–26.

19. Virginia Sánchez Korrol, *Teaching U.S. Puerto Rican History* (Washington, DC: American Historical Association, 1999), 32; "Brentwood Puerto Ricans Proudly Maintain Heritage," *New York Times*, February 19, 1974.

20. Sarah J. Mahler, *American Dreaming: Immigrant Life on the Margins* (Princeton, NJ: Princeton University Press, 1995), 123.

21. Joshua Ruff, "Diasporas in Suburbia: Long Island's Recent Immigrant Past," *Long Island*

History Journal 21, no. 1 (2009): para. 13, https://lihj.cc.stonybrook.edu/2009/articles/diasporas-in-suburbia-long-islands-recent-immigrant-past/; Mark A. Torres, *Long Island Labor Camps: Dust for Blood* (Charleston, SC: History Press, 2021).

22. Lorrin Thomas, *Puerto Rican Citizen: History and Political Identity in Twentieth-Century New York City* (Chicago: University of Chicago Press, 2010), 69–72, 264.

23. Linda Gordon, *The Second Coming of the KKK: The Ku Klux Klan of the 1920s and the American Political Tradition* (New York: W. W. Norton, 2017); David M. Chalmers, *Hooded Americanism: The History of the Ku Klux Klan*, 3rd ed. (Durham, NC: Duke University Press, 1987); Kenneth T. Jackson, *The Ku Klux Klan and the City, 1915–1930* (New York: Oxford University Press, 1967).

24. Jane S. Gombieski, "Klokards, Kleagles, Kludds, and Kluxers: The Ku Klux Klan in Suffolk County, 1915–1928, Part I," *Long Island Historical Journal* 6, no. 1 (1993): 41–62; David Chalmers, *Hooded Americanism*, 256; "Long Island Sees Biggest Klan Crowd," *New York Times*, June 22, 1923; Jackson, *Ku Klux Klan and the City*, 178; "Klan Republicans Capture Suffolk," *New York Times*, April 13, 1924; Lenora Henson, "Ku Klux Klan," *Encyclopedia of New York State*, 847; Robert A. Caro, *The Power Broker: Robert Moses and the Fall of New York* (New York: Knopf, 1974), 148; Diana R. Gordon, *Village of Immigrants: Latinos in an Emerging America* (New Brunswick, NJ: Rutgers University Press, 2015), 48–49.

25. Garcia, *A World of Its Own*, 75–77, 91–92; Juan O. Sanchéz, *The Ku Klux Klan's Campaign against Hispanics: Rhetoric, Violence, and Response in the American Southwest, 1921–1925* (Jefferson, NC: MacFarland, 2018). A few hundred articles on the KKK appeared in *La Prensa*, New York's major Spanish-language newspaper, during the 1920s.

26. Thomas, *Puerto Rican Citizen*, 264. Schools in heavily Latino Brentwood and Central Islip were subject to lawsuits about the inadequacy of Spanish-language education. Earl Lane, "LI's Puerto Ricans: Closing the Language Gap," *Newsday*, November 10, 1971; *Cintron v. Brentwood U. Free Sch. Dist.*, 455 F. Supp. 57 (E.D.N.Y. 1978); "Civil Rights and Education: The Action on LI: Federal Agency Steps Up Bias Probes, from Bilingual Classes to Minority Hiring," *Newsday*, March 24, 1977. On perceptions of language-based discrimination, see Lourdes Torres, *Puerto Rican Discourse: A Sociolinguistic Study of a New York Suburb* (New York: Routledge, 2010), 30. On English-language-only campaigns, see Edna Negrón, "Hispanics to Fight English Bill," *Newsday*, December 18, 1988; Kathleen Kerr, "Verbal War on English Only," *Newsday*, February 15, 1989; Richard Pérez-Peña, "L.I. Veto Kills Bill to Require Use of English," *New York Times*, September 14, 1996.

27. Ruff, "Diasporas in Suburbia," 13, quoting "54 Puerto Rican Laborers Arrive for Suffolk Harvest," *Long Islander*, July 22, 1948. See also *Puerto Rican Farm Workers in the Middle Atlantic States: Highlights of a Study* (Washington, DC: U.S. Bureau Employment Security, 1954), The notion of heat tolerance dates back at least to Thomas Jefferson, *Notes on the State of Virginia* (1785).

28. Bob Greene, "Traffic in 'Slave' Domestics in LI Is Bared by State," *Newsday*, May 27, 1955; Emma Amador, "Organizing Puerto Rican Domestics: Resistance and Household Labor Reform in the Puerto Rican Diaspora after 1930," *ILWCH: International Labor and Working-Class History* 8 (Fall 2015): 67–86; Merida Rúa, *A Grounded Identidad: Making New Lives in Chicago's Puerto Rican Neighborhoods* (New York: Oxford University Press, 2012), chap. 1.

29. Mahler, *American Dreaming*, 109–10; Ann Markusen, Peter Hall, Scott Campbell, and Sabina Deitrick, *The Rise of the Gunbelt: The Military Remapping of Industrial America* (New York: Oxford University Press, 1991), 121–27.

30. Dave Hamilton, "LI's Puerto Ricans: Between Two Cultures," *Newsday*, November 10, 1971; Tim Keogh, *In Levittown's Shadow: Poverty in America's Wealthiest Postwar Suburb* (Chicago: University of Chicago Press, 2023), 61–62; Roger Waldinger and Thomas Bailey, "The Continuing Significance of Race: Racial Conflict and Racial Discrimination in Construction," *Politics and Society* 19 (1991): 291–324; Thomas J. Sugrue, "Breaking Through: The Troubled Origins of Affirmative Action in the Workplace," in *Color Lines: Affirmative Action, Immigration, and Civil Rights Options for America*, ed. John David Skrentny (Chicago: University of Chicago Press, 2001), 41–43.

31. Thomas J. Sugrue, *Sweet Land of Liberty: The Forgotten Struggle for Civil Rights in the North* (New York: Random House, 2008), 287; Alan Singer, *The Civil Rights Movement on Long Island: A Local History Curriculum Guide for Middle and High School Teachers*, in VF, Civil Rights, BPL; Charles F. Howlett, "The Long Island Civil Rights Movement in the 1960s, Part One: The Struggle to Integrate Public Schools," *Long Island Historical Review* 8, no. 2 (1996): 145–65; Joye Browne, "'The Movement' for Equality," *Newsday*, November 15, 1998; Christopher Verga, *Civil Rights on Long Island* (Charleston, SC: Arcadia, 2016). On the Black–Puerto Rican civil rights alliance in New York, see Sonia Song-Ha Lee, *Building a Latino Civil Rights Movement: Puerto Ricans, African-Americans, and the Pursuit of Racial Justice in New York City* (Chapel Hill: University of North Carolina Press, 2014).

32. Other Long Island businesses targeted by protesters included Abraham and Straus, Meadowbrook National Bank, Sealtest, and Howard Johnson's. Singer, *Civil Rights Movement*; Thomas A. Johnson, "Long Island Branch of CORE to Boycott Meadow Brook Bank," *Pittsburgh Courier*, February 17, 1963; Thomas Collins, "CORE Calls Boycott of Dairy in Job Bid," *Newsday*, June 14, 1963. To end protests, the merchants' association at Bay Shore's Gardiner Manor Shopping Center agreed to hire thirty-five African American and Puerto Rican workers. See "Shop Center, CORE Reach Job Accord," *Newsday*, August 31, 1964.

33. "CORE in Battle with L.I. Park Officials for Jobs," *Pittsburgh Courier*, July 13, 1963; "Islip Road Department Charged with Prejudice," *Newsday*, October 7, 1967; Town of Islip, EEO-4 Forms, 2017, Function 6, in author's possession; U.S. Census Bureau, American Community Survey 5-Year Estimates, 2014–2018, tables DP05 (overall population) and C24010I. See generally John R. Logan, Richard D. Alba, and Brian J. Stults, "Enclaves and Entrepreneurs: Assessing the Payoff for Immigrants and Minorities," *International Migration Review* 37 (2003): 344–88, 377; Steven P. Erie, *Rainbow's End: Irish Americans and the Dilemmas of Urban Machine Politics* (Berkeley: University of California Press, 1988); Peter K. Eisinger, "The Economic Conditions of Black Employment in Municipal Bureaucracies," *American Journal of Political Science* 26, no. 4 (1982): 754–71; Michael B. Katz and Mark J. Stern, *One Nation Divisible: What America Was and What It Is Becoming* (New York: Russell Sage Foundation, 2005), 93.

34. Sarah Mahler, *Salvadorans in Suburbia: Symbiosis and Conflict* (Boston: Allyn & Bacon, 1995), 56–70; Mahler, *American Dreaming*, 22–23, 108–15. See also Ruff, "Diasporas in Suburbia," 30; Baxandall and Ewen, *Picture Windows*, 241–42; and generally Roger Waldinger and Michael Lichter, *How the Other Half Works: Immigration and the Social Organization of Labor* (Berkeley: University of California Press, 2003); Cordelia Reimers, "Economic Well-Being," in *Hispanics and the Future of America*, ed. Marta Tienda and Faith Mitchell (Washington, DC: National Academies Press, 2006), 291–361.

35. On Latinx workers and working conditions in Islip and Long Island, see generally Jennifer Gordon, "We Make the Road by Walking: Immigrant Workers, the Workplace Project, and the Struggle for Social Change," *Harvard Civil Rights–Civil Liberties Law Review* 30 (1995):

407–50, 412–13; Gordon, *Suburban Sweatshops: The Fight for Immigrant Rights* (Cambridge, MA: Harvard University Press, 2005); Baxandall and Ewen, *Picture Windows*, 241–44; Gordon, *Village of Immigrants*, 57–59. On wage theft against Latinos, see *Campos v. Spot-Less Landscaping*, Case No. 10179395, July 27, 2017, New York State Division of Human Rights, https://dhr.ny.gov/sites/default/files/pdf/Commissioners-Orders/campos_v_spot_less_landscaping_etal.pdf.

36. Elaine Anne Pasquali, "From One Island to Another: The Story of Long Island Cubans," *Long Island History Journal* 2, no. 2 (1990): 267–70; Sarah Mahler, "First Stop: Suburbia," *NACLA Report on the Americas* 26, no. 1 (1992): 20–24.

37. Mahler, *Salvadorans in Suburbia*; Mahler, *American Dreaming*, chap. 2.

38. Javier Castaño, "Ecuadoreans and Colombians in New York," in *Latinos in New York: Communities in Transition*, ed. Sherrie Baver, Angelo Falcón, and Gabriel Haslip-Viera (South Bend, IN: University of Notre Dame Press, 2017).

39. Mahler, *Salvadorans in Suburbia*, 118; Mahler, "First Stop," 22; Torres, *Puerto Rican Discourse*, 2–4; Ruff, "Diasporas in Suburbia"; Barber, *Latino City*, 70–75.

40. Leo R. Chávez, *The Latino Threat: Constructing Immigrants, Citizens, and the Nation* (Palo Alto, CA: Stanford University Press, 2008); Douglas S. Massey and Karen A. Pren, "Origins of the New Latino Underclass," *Race and Social Problems* 4, no. 1 (April 2012): 5–7.

41. William Nack and Jim Scovel, "80 Students Boycott Classes at Central Islip," *Newsday*, September 30, 1969; "Protestors Picket Police in Bay Shore," *Newsday*, August 6, 1972; "Police Brutality Probe in Suffolk," *Newsday*, August 2, 1972; Howard Crook, "Klein versus Brutality Complaints," *Newsday*, August 23, 1972.

42. John McDonald, "Police Brutality Suit is Settled for $15,000," *Newsday*, March 16, 1978; "6 Brutality Cases Settled since '76 by Suffolk Co.," *National Law Journal*, June 11, 1979; Suffolk County Bar Association (SCBA), *Report of the Civil Rights Committee on Allegations of Police Brutality in Suffolk County*, January 1980.

43. SCBA, *Allegations of Police Brutality*; State of New York Commission of Investigation, *An Investigation of the Suffolk County District Attorney's Office and Police Department*, August 1989, https://nysl.ptfs.com/awweb/pdfopener?sid=CED9B60BF2C2D3D9E7F60D12B1A362CD&did=112422&fl=%2Flibrary1%2Fpdf%2F20027003.pdf; Rick Brand, "Police Rude to Caller Who Spoke Spanish," *Newsday*, April 12, 1989; "Black and Hispanic Officers File Discrimination Charges," *New York Times*, February 9, 1995; "U.S. Accuses Suffolk Police of Violating Bias Laws," *New York Times*, December 15, 1996.

44. *United States v. Suffolk County, Suffolk County Police Department et al.*, No. 83-CV-2737 (E.D.N.Y. 1983), https://www.clearinghouse.net/chDocs/public/EE-NY-0282-0001.pdf; *Lochren v. Suffolk County, Suffolk County Police Department*, No. 01-CV-03925 (E.D.N.Y., filed June 7, 2001), https://www.nyclu.org/en/nyclu-files-sex-discrimination-lawsuit-against-suffolk-county-police-department; U.S. Department of Justice, Agreement between the United States Department of Justice and Suffolk County Police Department, January 13, 2014, https://www.justice.gov/sites/default/files/crt/legacy/2014/01/23/suffolk_agreement_1-13-14.pdf. For public pressure on the Suffolk County Police Department, see "El DOJ tiene que intervenir en Suffolk," *El Diario La Prensa* (NY), September 3, 2009; Nicole Fuller and Michael O'Keefe, "Justice Department Releases Suffolk from Parts of Settlement on Treatment of Latinos," *Newsday*, May 24, 2024.

45. "New Responses to Soaring Bias Crimes," *New York Times*, October 19, 1997; Erik Holm, "Hate-Group Fliers in Islip Terrace," *Newsday*, February 15, 2001; Denise M. Bonilla, "2 More Students Suspended in Alleged Racial Attack," *Newsday*, September 25, 2003; "Tensions, Suspensions, 14 East Islip H.S. Pupils Disciplined after Hallway Brawl," *Newsday*, March 18, 2006; "Swastikas Painted on Islip High," *Newsday*, March 18, 2006. Cara Buckley, "Teenagers Violent

'Sport' Led to Killing of Ecuadorian Immigrant Marcelo Lucero," *New York Times*, November 20, 2008, A few days after Lucero's death, the United Northern and Southern Knights of the Ku Klux Klan distributed its newsletter, *The Klansmen's Voice*, to homes in Islip Terrace. Jennifer Maloney, "Islip Terrace: Klan's Unwelcome Delivery," *Newsday*, November 13, 2008; "White Teens Kill Hispanic Man in N.Y.," *Charleston Daily Mail*, November 10, 2008; "Latinos Increasingly Targeted for Hate Crimes," *Tell Me More* (National Public Radio), November 12, 2008; Raul Reyes, "Hot Rhetoric Fuels Latino Hate Crimes," *USA Today*, December 5, 2008; Annie Correal, "Víctimas de permanente acoso en L.I.," *El Diario La Prensa* (NY), September 3, 2009. See also BiasHelp's *Community Voices* newsletter (http://lincs.org/media-newsletters.php) and its annual reports (https://www.yumpu.com/en/biashelp). See also Southern Poverty Law Center, *Climate of Fear: Latino Immigrants in Suffolk County, New York*, September 1, 2009, https://www.splcenter.org/20090831/climate-fear-latino-immigrants-suffolk-county-ny.

46. *People ex rel. Wells v. Demarco*, N.Y.S. 3d (N.Y. App. Div. 2d Dep. Nov. 14, 2018).

47. Hannah Dreier, "Trapped in Gangland: How the MS-13 Crackdown Shattered Immigrant Lives," *ProPublica*, 2018, https://www.propublica.org/series/ms-13-on-long-island; Garland, *Gangs and Garden City*; Liz Robbins and Nadia T. Rodriguez, "The Gang Murders in the Long Island Suburbs," *New York Times*, July 12, 2017; Oliver Laughland, "Going Full Circle: Trump's MS-13 Crackdown Risks Unleashing New Cycle of Violence," *The Guardian*, July 28, 2017; Maggie Haberman and Liz Robbins, "Trump, on Long Island, Vows an End to Gang Violence," *New York Times*, July 28, 2017. "Editorial: La ley y el orden según Trump," *El Diario La Prensa* (NY), July 31, 2017; Sandra Peddie, "Despite Progress after Hate Crime, SPCD and Hispanics Still Struggle with Trust," *Newsday*, November 2, 2018. The civil rights group Latino Justice filed a harassment suit: *Plaintiffs #1-21 v. County of Suffolk; Suffolk County Police Department, et al.*, No. 15-CV-2431 (E.D.N.Y. Apr 29, 2015).

48. In 1948, the Department of Justice filed a brief in the landmark case *Shelley v. Kraemer*, highlighting restrictive covenants that categorized Puerto Ricans as "second-class citizens," suggesting that restrictions contribute to "resentment and bitterness against the United States." U.S. Department of Justice, brief as *amicus curiae*, *Shelley v. Kraemer*, 334 U.S. 1 (1948) at 3, 18–19. Puerto Ricans and other Latinos are seldom discussed in standard histories of restrictive covenants. See Robert Fogelson, *Bourgeois Nightmares: Suburbia, 1880–1930* (New Haven, CT: Yale University Press, 2005); John P. Dean, "Only Caucasian: A Study of Race Covenants," *Journal of Land and Public Utility Economics* 23 (1947): 429–30.

49. *Shelley v. Kraemer*, 334 U.S. 1 (1948); Richard R. W. Brooks, "Covenants without Courts: Enforcing Residential Segregation with Legally Unenforceable Agreements," *American Economic Review: Papers & Proceedings*, 101, no. 3 (2011): 360–65; Kenneth T. Jackson, "Race, Ethnicity, and Real Estate Appraisal: The Home Owners' Loan Corporation and the Federal Housing Administration," *Journal of Urban History* 6 (1980): 419–52; Louis Lee Woods II, "The Federal Home Loan Bank Board, Redlining, and the National Proliferation of Racial Lending Discrimination, 1921–1950," *Journal of Urban History* 38 (2012): 1036–59; Andrew Wiese, "Racial Cleansing in Suburbia: Suburban Government, Urban Renewal, and Segregation in Long Island, New York, 1945–1960," in *Contested Terrain: Power, Politics and Participation in Suburbia*, ed. Marc L. Silver and Martin Melkonian (Westport, CT: Greenwood Press, 1996), 61–69.

50. Carpio, *Collisions at the Crossroads*, 200–8, at 202.

51. Sam Washington, "Like a Dead End': Poverty Beset Carleton Park Has a Grim Past and Cloudy Future," *Newsday*, January 25, 1977.

52. Ken Moritsugu, "The Talk of Brentwood: Illegal Apartments are Focus of Race," *Newsday*, June 3, 1994.

53. Elizabeth Guanill, oral history interview conducted by Monte Rivera, June 18, 1974, Puerto Rican Oral History Project, 1976.001.025, Brooklyn Historical Society, Brooklyn, NY.

54. See, for example, "Venta de Lotes," *Ecos de Nueva York*, October 25, 1953, advertising ten lots in Bay Shore for $695 per half acre. On *colonias*, see Garcia, *World of Its Own*, chap. 2; Carpio, *Collisions at the Crossroads*, chap. 5, Bobby Cervantes, "Las Colonias: Latino Housing and American Poverty on the Modern Border" (PhD diss., University of Kansas, 2022).

55. George Vecsey, "Brentwood Puerto Ricans Proudly Keep Heritage," *New York Times*, February 19, 1974; Jack Altshul, "Yearning to Be Free: Hispanics," *Newsday*, July 4, 1976.

56. Alfonso A. Narvaez, "L.I. Puerto Rican Community Thriving," *New York Times*, November 12, 1972. On self-built communities, see Andrew Wiese, *Houses of Our Own: African American Suburbanization in the Twentieth Century* (Chicago: University of Chicago Press, 2004); Becky Nicolaides, *My Blue Heaven: Life and Politics in the Working-Class Suburbs of Los Angeles, 1920–1965* (Chicago: University of Chicago Press, 2002).

57. Josephine Festa and Gloria Tejada, oral history interview conducted by Monte Rivera, June 23, 1974, Puerto Rican Oral History Project, 1976.001.018, Brooklyn Historical Society, Brooklyn, NY.

58. "Islip Board Acts on Code Complaints," *Newsday*, July 9, 1947; "Civics Ask Further Probe on N. Bay Shore Housing," *Newsday*, December 30, 1947; Leon Guess, "To Caesar What Is Caesars," *Newsday*, August 5, 1947; Don Smith, "Old Slum Persists in Bay Shore," *Newsday*, February 12, 1963. Today the area is a mobile home park. Author's observations, January 2020.

59. Wiese, "Racial Cleansing in Suburbia," 62.

60. "Bare Prejudice in Suffolk Realty," *Newsday*, February 24, 1959.

61. "Charge Use of Realty Bias," *Newsday*, July 18, 1960.

62. Kenneth T. Jackson, "Suburbanization," in *Encyclopedia of New York State*, ed. Peter Eisenstadt (Syracuse, NY: Syracuse University Press, 2005), 1495–97; Roger Wunderlich, "Suffolk County," in *Encyclopedia of New York State*, 1497–1501.

63. U.S. Housing and Home Finance Agency, Intergroup Relations Service, *Fair Housing Laws: Summaries and Text of State and Municipal Laws* (Washington, DC: U.S. Government Printing Office, 1964), 138–55; Title VIII of the Civil Rights Act of 1968, 7 C.F.R. § 1901.203; Carole Ashkinaze, "Islip Passes Law against Housing Bias," *Newsday*, May 15, 1968; Islip Town Code, Chapter 26: Housing: Discriminatory Practices.

64. Massey and Denton, *American Apartheid*, 195–200; Robert G. Schwemm, "Private Enforcement and the Fair Housing Act," *Yale Law and Policy Review* 6 (1988): 375–92. On limits of fair housing enforcement, see Kathleen Kerr, "Decline of a Rights Panel: Suffolk Anti-Discrimination Agency's Power, Funds Have Ebbed," *Newsday*, April 18, 1988; Islip, *Analysis of Impediments*, 2015, III-11; ERASE Racism, *Racial Equity Report Card: Fair Housing on Long Island* (Syosset, NY: ERASE Racism, 2008), 5.

65. Diana Pearce, "Gatekeepers and Homeseekers: Institutionalized Patterns in Racial Steering," *Social Problems* 26 (1979): 325–34. "Claim Home Sale Bias," *Newsday*, August 3, 1963; "Mass Test of Brokers Brings LI Bias Charge," *Newsday*, November 11, 1963; quote from "Most LI Apartments for Whites Only," *Newsday*, May 20, 1968.

66. Susan Page, "Islip Town Charges Blockbusting," *Newsday*, May 18, 1977; Islip, *Analysis of Impediments*, 2010, II-26; John Yinger, *Housing Discrimination Study: Incidence of Discrimination and Variation in Discriminatory Behavior* (Washington, DC: U.S. Department of Housing and Urban Development, Office of Policy Development and Research, 1991); Michael Fix and Raymond J. Struyk, eds., *Clear and Convincing Evidence: Measurement of Discrimination*

in America (Washington, DC: Urban Institute Press, 1993); Margery Turner, Stephen L. Ross, George C. Galster, and John Yinger, *Discrimination in Metropolitan Housing Markets: National Results from Phase I HDS 2000* (Washington, D.C.: Urban Institute, 2002), https://www.huduser.gov/portal/Publications/pdf/Phase1_Report.pdf, IV-1; see also Margery Austin Turner and Stephen L. Ross, *Discrimination in Metropolitan Housing Markets: Phase I—Supplement* (Washington, D.C.: Urban Institute, 2003), https://www.huduser.gov/portal/Publications/pdf/phase1_supplement_final.pdf; ERASE Racism, *Long Island Fair Housing: A State of Inequity: Institutional and Structural Racism and Housing* (Syosset, NY: ERASE Racism, March 2005), 19–20, 42–43; ERASE Racism, *Racial Equity Report Card*, 4, 17; Islip, *Analysis of Impediments*, 2010, III-9, III-10; Islip, *Analysis of Impediments*, 2015, ES-5, III-9, III-10, III-11; *2015 Suffolk County Analysis of Impediments to Fair Housing*, July 2015, 9, 93, 110, https://suffolkcountyny.gov/Portals/0/formsdocs/ecodev/Community%20Development/AI%20final%20draft%202015.pdf?ver=2015-10-22-115354-200; "Long Island Divided," *Newsday*, November 17, 2019.

67. Islip, *Analysis of Impediments*, 2010, III-16, III-17; Christopher Niedt and Marc Silver, *Uneven Road to Recovery: Place, Race, and Mortgage Lending on Long Island* (Long Island Housing Services and National Center for Suburban Studies, Hofstra University, December 2014), 3, 10, 33; Brief of Defendants-Respondents Luis A. Turcios & Aurora Velasquez, Nationscredit Financial Services Corp. as Successor in Interest to *Equicredit Corp. of NY v. Turcios*, No. 2007-1187, 2008 WL 5509622 (N.Y. App. Div. March 27, 2008) (quoting lower court's opinion).

68. Mahler, *American Dreaming*, chap. 8; Edna Negrón, "Concern over Housing Hispanics," *Newsday*, January 27, 1988, copy in VF, Brentwood: Housing, BPL; "Islip Should Outlaw Bias in All Rental Housing," *Newsday*, May 13, 1992. By 1994, the Brentwood School District estimated that 40 percent of its students came from families living in accessory apartments. Mahler, "First Stop Suburbia," 24. See also Keogh, *In Levittown's Shadow*, chap. 3.

69. *Town of Islip, Five Year Consolidated Strategy and Plan Submission for Housing and Community Development Programs, 2015–2019*, http://www.islipcda.org/Plans/Final%202015-2019%20Con%20Plan.pdf, 34–36, 39, 83.

70. "Long Island Divided," *Newsday*, November 17, 2019.

71. Allison Roda, Amy Stuart Wells, Miya Warner, Bianca Baldridge, Jacquelyn Duran, Richard Lofton, Terrenda White, and Courtney Grzesilowski, "Why Boundaries Matter: A Study of Five Separate and Unequal Long Island Districts" (New York: Center for Understanding Race and Education, Teacher's College, Columbia University, July 2009); Amy Stuart Wells et al., *Divided We Fall: The Story of Separate and Unequal Suburban Schools 60 Years after* Brown v. Board of Education (New York: Center for Understanding Race and Education, Teachers College, Columbia University, 2014); Michael R. Glass, "Schooling Suburbia: The Politics of School Finance in Postwar Long Island" (PhD diss., Princeton University, 2020); ERASE Racism, *Heading in the Wrong Direction: Growing School Segregation on Long Island* (Syosset, NY: ERASE Racism, January 2015). See generally Justin Steil, Jorge de La Roca, and Ingrid Gould Ellen, "*Desvinculado y desigual*: Is Segregation Harmful to Latinos?," *Annals of the American Academy of Political and Social Science* 660, no. 1 (2015): 67–69; Erica Frankenberg, "The Role of Residential Segregation in Contemporary School Segregation," *Education and Urban Society* 45 (2013): 548–70; Anne Owens, "Unequal Opportunity: School and Neighborhood Segregation in the USA," *Race and Social Problems* (2020): 1–13.

72. I left Fire Island out of this analysis because it is such an outlier. It serves only twenty students and, as a result, has an unusually high per-pupil spending rate.

73. Enrollment calculated from New York State Education Department (NYSED), Data for

School Districts, https://data.nysed.gov/lists.php?type=district (reported as of June 30, 2017). Funding data from New York State Education Department, Fiscal Analysis and Research Unit, Fiscal Profiles, Master Files, 93–94 to 17–18, http://www.oms.nysed.gov/faru/Profiles/profiles_cover.html.

74. VF, Brentwood: Adelante; VF, Brentwood: Irizarry, Paul, BPL; Adelante of Suffolk County, Inc. Papers, Hispanic-Latino Collection, Special Collections, LISI. See "Mission Statement: CARECEN—NY," CARECEN NY, https://carecenny.wordpress.com/mission-statement/.

75. During one research trip to Islip, I went to simple *pupusería* in Brentwood where I purchased the namesake food—a traditional Salvadoran tortilla stuffed with cheese and beans—and washed it down with a Mexican cola. I also stopped at La Espiguita, a busy Colombian bakery where I bought a *pan queso*, a type of cheese bread, and a few Mexican tamales for my family before heading to the Long Island Railroad for my return train.

76. Marcherie Vázquez, "Lejos de la ciudad, pero cerca de Puerto Rico," *El Diario La Prensa* (NY), June 13, 1999. The parade's history is well documented in VF, Hispanic Parade, BPL; VF, Hispanic Parade, Hispanic-Latino Collection, Special Collections, LISI.

77. There is an intense debate about Latinidad. See especially Llana Barber's chapter in this volume.

Chapter Four

1. William H. Frey, "Melting Pot Cities and Suburbs: Racial and Ethnic Change in Metro America in the 2000s," *The State of Metropolitan America*, Brookings Institution Series 30, May 4, 2011, 7–10; William H. Frey, "Today's Suburbs Are Symbolic of America's Rising Diversity: A 2020 Census Portrait," Brookings Institution, June 15, 2022, https://www.brookings.edu/research/todays-suburbs-are-symbolic-of-americas-rising-diversity-a-2020-census-portrait/.

2. Audrey Singer, "Twenty-First-Century Gateways: An Introduction," in *Twenty-First Century Gateways: Immigrant Incorporation in Suburban America*, ed. Audrey Singer, Susan W. Hardwick, and Caroline B. Brettell (Washington, DC: Brookings Institution Press, 2008); Michael B. Katz, Matthew J. Creighton, Daniel Amsterdam, and Merlin Chowkwanyun, "Immigration and the New Metropolitan Geography," *Journal of Urban Affairs* 32, no. 5 (2010): 525; Kevin M. Kruse and Thomas J. Sugrue, eds., *The New Suburban History* (Chicago: University of Chicago Press, 2006); Matthew D. Lassiter and Christopher Niedt, "Suburban Diversity in Postwar America," *Journal of Urban History* 39, no. 1 (January 2013): 3–14; Becky M. Nicolaides and Andrew Wiese, eds., *The Suburb Reader* (New York: Routledge, 2006), esp. chaps. 7 and 14.

3. Becky M. Nicolaides, *The New Suburbia: How Diversity Remade Suburban Life in Los Angeles after 1945* (New York: Oxford University Press, 2024).

4. Wei Li, *Ethnoburb: The New Ethnic Community in Urban America* (Honolulu: University of Hawaiʻi Press, 2009).

5. Sarah Lynn Lopez, *The Remittance Landscape: Spaces of Migration in Rural Mexico and Urban USA* (Chicago: University of Chicago Press, 2015), 12.

6. Li, *Ethnoburb*; Leland T. Saito, *Race and Politics: Asian Americans, Latinos, and Whites in a Los Angeles Suburb* (Urbana: University of Illinois Press, 1998), 58–59; Yen Fen Tseng, "Chinese Ethnic Economy: San Gabriel Valley, Los Angeles County," *Journal of Urban Affairs* 16, no. 2 (1994): 169–89; Lucie Cheng and Philip Q. Yang, "Asians: The 'Model Minority' Deconstructed," in *Ethnic Los Angeles*, ed. Roger Waldinger and Mehdi Bozorgmehr (New York: Russell Sage Foundation, 1996), 324–33; Ed Soja, *Postmodern Geographies: The Reassertion of Space in Critical Social Theory* (New York: Verso, 1989).

7. Frey, "Melting Pot Cities and Suburbs," 7, 9; Nicolaides, *New Suburbia*, chap. 2.

8. Key works include Kenneth Jackson, *Crabgrass Frontier: The Suburbanization of the United States* (New York: Oxford University Press, 1985); Robert Self, *American Babylon: Race and the Struggle for Postwar Oakland* (Princeton, NJ: Princeton University Press, 2003); Matthew Lassiter, *The Silent Majority: Suburban Politics in the Sunbelt South* (Princeton, NJ: Princeton University Press, 2006); Kevin Kruse, *White Flight: Atlanta and Making of Modern Conservatism* (Princeton, NJ: Princeton University Press, 2007); David M. P. Freund, *Colored Property: State Policy and White Racial Politics in Suburban America* (Chicago: University of Chicago Press, 2007); Lisa McGirr, *Suburban Warriors: The Origins of the New American Right* (Princeton, NJ: Princeton University Press, 2001); Becky M. Nicolaides, *My Blue Heaven: Life and Politics in the Working-Class Suburbs of Los Angeles, 1920–1965* (Chicago: University of Chicago Press, 2002); Lily Geismer, *Don't Blame Us: Suburban Liberals and the Transformation of the Democratic Party* (Princeton, NJ: Princeton University Press, 2014).

9. Susan Hardwick, "Toward a Suburban Immigrant Nation," in *Twenty-First Century Gateways: Immigrant Incorporation in Suburban America*, ed. Audrey Singer, Susan W. Hardwick, and Caroline B. Brettell (Washington DC: Brookings Institution Press, 2008), 45. On Asian American suburbanization, see Charlotte Brooks, *Alien Neighbors, Foreign Friends* (Chicago: University of Chicago Press, 2009); Becky M. Nicolaides, "Introduction: Asian American Suburban History," *Journal of American Ethnic History* 34, no. 2 (Winter 2015): 5–17.

10. Deborah Dash Moore, *To the Golden Cities: Pursuing the American Jewish Dream in Miami and L.A.* (Cambridge, MA: Harvard University Press, 1994); Karen Brodkin, *How Jews Became White Folks and What That Says about Race in America* (New Brunswick, NJ: Rutgers University Press, 1998); David Roediger, *Working Toward Whiteness: How America's Immigrants Became White: The Strange Journey from Ellis Island to the Suburbs* (New York: Basic Books, 2006).

11. Min Zhou, Yen-Fen Tseng, and Rebecca Y. Kim, "Rethinking Residential Assimilation: The Case of a Chinese Ethnoburb in the San Gabriel Valley, California," *Amerasia Journal* 34, no. 3 (2008): 57–58; Emily Skop and Wei Li, "Asians in America's Suburbs: Patterns and Consequences of Settlement," *Geographical Review* 95, no. 2 (April 2005): 167–88. On the complexity of the assimilation process, also see George Sánchez, *Becoming Mexican American: Ethnicity, Culture, and Identity in Chicano Los Angeles, 1900–1945* (New York: Oxford University Press, 1995); Pierrette Hondagneu-Sotelo and Manuel Pastor, *South Central Dreams: Finding Home and Building Community in South L.A.* (New York: New York University Press, 2021), 13–19.

12. Eileen O'Brien, *The Racial Middle: Latinos and Asian Americans Living Beyond the Racial Divide* (New York: New York University Press, 2008); Lisa Lowe, *Immigrant Acts: On Asian American Cultural Politics* (Durham, NC: Duke University Press, 1996); Jerry González, *In Search of the Mexican Beverly Hills* (New Brunswick, NJ: Rutgers University Press, 2017), 9, 46–49.

13. Li, *Ethnoburb*.

14. Li, *Ethnoburb*, 100; Jan Lin and Melody Chiong, "How Chinese Entrepreneurs Transformed the San Gabriel Valley," PBS SoCal, May 20, 2016, https://www.kcet.org/shows/departures/how-chinese-entrepreneurs-transformed-the-san-gabriel-valley; Li, *Ethnoburb*; Chowkwanyun and Segall, "Rise of Majority Asian Suburbs"; Zhou, Tseng, and Kim, "Rethinking Residential Assimilation"; Skop and Li, "Asians in America's Suburbs," 173–74; Merlin Chowkwanyun and Jordan Segall, "The Rise of Majority Asian Suburbs," *Bloomberg CityLab*, August 24, 2012, https://www.bloomberg.com/news/articles/2012-08-24/the-rise-of-the-majority-asian-suburb; Willow Lung-Amam, *Trespassers? Asian Americans and the Battle for Suburbia* (Oakland: University of California Press, 2017). Unsurprisingly, ethnoburbs formed in metropolitan areas with

high proportions of immigrants, such as Los Angeles, the San Francisco or Silicon Valley, New York City, Houston, northern Virginia, Toronto, and Vancouver.

15. Discrimination was a critical catalyst in the formation of the Chinese ethnic economy. As many highly trained Chinese immigrants hit the glass ceiling, they left those American companies to start their own businesses. Saito, *Race and Politics*, 62.

16. Li, *Ethnoburb*, 106–10, 173; Willow Lung-Amam, "Malls of Meaning: Building Asian America in Silicon Valley Suburbia," *Journal of American Ethnic History* 34, no. 2 (Winter 2015): 18–53; Liz Cohen, *A Consumers' Republic: The Politics of Mass Consumption in Postwar America* (New York: Vintage Books, 2003); Susan Carpenter, "From Healing Hands Too Haute Handbags; Yes, Valley Boulevard in San Gabriel Is a Great Place for Dim Sum, but That's Only the Beginning," *Los Angeles Times* (hereafter *LAT*), March 31, 2005. See generally the website Dead Malls (www.deadmalls.com).

17. Although Proposition 13 set the property tax rate at 1 percent for everyone, in the context of rising home prices in California, it benefited those who stayed in their homes the longest. Homeowners of color, who gained access to the suburbs in significant numbers only after 1980, missed that initial fiscal advantage because they were largely excluded from white suburban neighborhoods for decades prior.

18. Myron Orfield and Thomas Luce, *California Metropatterns: A Regional Agenda for Community Stability in California* (Minneapolis: Metropolitan Area Research Corporation, April 2002), 10; Paul Feldman et al., "Thai Worker Sweatshop Probe Grows," *LAT*, August 9, 1995; Li, *Ethnoburb*, 133–43.

19. Saito, *Race and Politics*; Timothy Fong, *The First Suburban Chinatown: The Remaking of Monterey Park, California* (Philadelphia: Temple University Press, 1994); John Horton, *The Politics of Diversity: Immigration, Resistance, and Change in Monterey Park, California* (Philadelphia: Temple University Press, 1995).

20. Li, *Ethnoburb*; Zhou, Tseng, and Kim, "Rethinking Residential Assimilation"; Skop and Li, "Asians in America's Suburbs," 173–74. Lila Corwin Berman questions the linearity of suburban assimilation for white ethnic groups in *Metropolitan Jews: Politics, Race, and Religion in Postwar Detroit* (Chicago: University of Chicago Press, 2015).

21. Wilbur Zelinsky and Barrett A. Lee, "Heterolocalism: An Alternative Model of the Sociospatial Behaviour of Immigrant Ethnic Communities," *International Journal of Population Geography* 4 (1998): 281–98.

22. Emily Skop and Wei Li, "From the Ghetto to the Invisiburb: Shifting Patterns of Immigrant Settlement in Contemporary America," in *Multicultural Geographies: Persistence and Change in U.S. Racial/Ethnic Patterns*, ed. John W. Frazier and Florence Margai (Binghamton: State University of New York Press, 2003); Emily Skop, "Saffron Suburbs: Indian Immigrant Community Formation in Metropolitan Phoenix" (PhD diss., Arizona State University, 2002).

23. Becky M. Nicolaides and James Zarsadiaz, "Design Assimilation in Suburbia: Asian Americans, Built Landscapes, and Suburban Advantage in Los Angeles' San Gabriel Valley since 1970," *Journal of Urban History* 43, no. 2 (2017): 332–71.

24. Nicolaides and Zarsadiaz, "Design Assimilation"; Skop and Li, "From the Ghetto to the Invisiburb"; Denise Lawrence-Zúñiga, "Residential Design Guidelines, Aesthetic Governmentality, and Contested Notions of Southern California Suburban Places," *Economic Anthropology* 2, no. 1 (2015): 120–44; Willow Lung-Amam, "That 'Monster House' Is My Home: The Social and Cultural Politics of Design Reviews and Regulations," *Journal of Urban Design* 18, no. 2 (2013): 220–41; Gail Dubrow, "Deru Kugi Wa Utareru or the Nail That Sticks Up Gets Hit: The Archi-

tecture of Japanese American Identity, 1885–1942," *Journal of Architectural and Planning Research* 19, no. 4 (Winter 2002): 319–33.

25. On how the "suburbanization" of Latino people took two paths, see Jerry González, *Mexican Beverly Hills*, 70.

26. Wendy Cheng, *The Changs Next Door to the Díazes: Remapping Race in Suburban California* (Minneapolis: University of Minnesota Press, 2013), 59.

27. Genevieve Carpio, Clara Irazábal, and Laura Pulido, "Right to the Suburb? Rethinking Lefebvre and Immigrant Activism," *Journal of Urban Affairs* 32, no. 2 (2011): 197–98; Laura Barraclough, "Contested Cowboys: Ethnic Mexican Charros and the Struggle for Suburban Space in 1970s Los Angeles," *Aztlán* 37, no. 2 (Fall 2012): 95–124; González, *Mexican Beverly Hills*.

28. González, *Mexican Beverly Hills*; Gilda L. Ochoa, *Becoming Neighbors in a Mexican American Community: Power, Conflict, and Solidarity* (Austin: University of Texas Press, 2004).

29. G. Aron Ramirez, "Business as Usual: Ethnic Commerce and the Making of a Mexican American Middle Class in Southeast Los Angeles, 1981–1995," *Journal of Urban History* 50 (2022): 1113–34.

30. James Rojas, "The Enacted Environment of East Los Angeles," *Places* 8, no. 3 (Spring 1993): 42–53, https://escholarship.org/uc/item/84x3x9t2; James Rojas, "The Enacted Environment: The Creation of 'Place' by Mexicans and Mexican Americans in Los Angeles" (master's thesis, Massachusetts Institute of Technology, 1991); also see Daniel D. Arreola, "Mexican American Housescapes," *Geographical Review* 78 (July 1988): 299–315; Gustavo Leclerc, Raúl Villa, and Michael J. Dear, eds., *Latino Urban Cultures: La vida latina en LA* (Thousand Oaks, CA: SAGE Publications, 1999); Victor M. Valle and Rodolfo D. Torres, *Latino Metropolis* (Minneapolis: University of Minnesota Press, 2000); Daniel D. Arreola, ed., *Hispanic Spaces, Latino Places: Community and Cultural Diversity in Contemporary America* (Austin: University of Texas Press, 2004); David R. Díaz, *Barrio Urbanism: Chicanos, Planning, and American Cities* (New York: Routledge, 2005); Michael Rios, Leonardo Vázquez, and Lucrezia Miranda, eds., *Diálogos: Placemaking in Latino Communities* (New York: Routledge, 2012). A. K. Sandoval-Strausz describes similar patterns in *Barrio America: How Latino Immigrants Saved the American City* (New York: Basic Books, 2019), as do Lopez, *Remittance Landscape*, and Johana Londoño, *Abstract Barrios: The Crises of Latinx Visibility in Cities* (Durham, NC: Duke University Press, 2020).

31. Mary Helen Ponce described this vividly: "My father had a thing about fences . . . One year, I counted eight different fences on our property." Ponce, *Hoyt Street: An Autobiography* (Albuquerque: University of New Mexico Press, 1993), 13. On fences creating contained front yards, which fostered "strong social ties in shared public spaces," see Sandoval-Strausz, *Barrio America*, 276–77.

32. Rojas, "Enacted Environment of East Los Angeles"; George Sánchez, *Boyle Heights: How a Los Angeles Neighborhood Became the Future of American Democracy* (Oakland: University of California Press, 2021).

33. Nicolaides, *New Suburbia*, chap. 3.

34. Jon Teaford, *The American Suburb: The Basics* (New York: Routledge 2008), 123–24; Lassiter, *Silent Majority*; Nicolaides and Wiese, *Suburb Reader*; Monica Varsanyi, "City Ordinances as 'Immigration Policing by Proxy': Local Governments and the Regulation of Undocumented Day Laborers," in *Taking Local Control: Immigration Policy Activism in U.S. Cities and States*, ed. Monica W. Varsanyi (Stanford, CA: Stanford University Press, 2010), 135–36.

35. Max Felker-Kantor, *Policing Los Angeles: Race, Resistance, and the Rise of the LAPD* (Chapel Hill: University of North Carolina Press, 2018), 183; Zaragosa Vargas, *Crucible of Struggle*

(New York: Oxford University Press, 2011), chap. 11; Daniel HoSang, *Racial Propositions: Ballot Initiatives and the Making of Postwar California* (Berkeley: University of California Press, 2010).

36. Mark Villianatos, "A More Delicious City: How to Legalize Street Food," in *The Informal American City*, ed. Vinit Mukhija and Anastasia Loukaitou-Sideris (Cambridge, MA: MIT Press, 2014), 214.

37. "Street Vendors Finding It Harder to Ply Their Wares," *LAT*, September 23, 1990; "Local Laws '94," *LAT*, December 30, 1994. See also Nicolaides, *New Suburbia*, chap. 6.

38. Margaret Crawford, "The Garage Sales as Informal Economy and Transformative Urbanism," in *The Informal American City*, ed. Vinit Mukhija and Anastasia Loukaitou-Sideris (Cambridge, MA: MIT Press, 2014), 33.

39. "San Gabriel Valley Notebook: Azusa," *LAT*, December 10, 1981; "San Gabriel Valley Digest: Azusa," *LAT*, April 21, 1983; "Garage Sale Cop Cuts City in on Profits," *LAT*, May 10, 1990; "Garage Sale Savvy," *LAT*, May 23, 1990; "Not All Favor Restrictions on Garage Sales," *LAT*, December 3, 1993; "Proposed Rules Would Slam Door on Garage Sales as a Way of Life," *LAT*, December 26, 1993; "Council Moves to Put Curbs on Yard Sales," *LAT*, September 25, 1996; "Local Laws '98," *LAT*, December 29, 1998; "New Rules for Illegal Daily Yard Sales Approved by L.A. County Supervisors," *Los Angeles Daily News*, May 28, 2015; L.A. County Ordinance No. 94-0082, 1994 (on file with author); L.A. County Ord. 2019-0004 § 22.140.620—Yard Sales, https://library.municode.com/ca/los_angeles_county/codes/code_of_ordinances?nodeId=TIT22PLZO_DIV7STSPUS_CH22.140STSPUS_22.140.620YASA.

40. "Sign Law Would Require English in South Gate," *LAT*, October 20, 1985; "Letter to Editor: English Sign Law Example of Bias," *LAT*, November 3, 1985; "More Study Urged on Proposed Sign Ordinance," *LAT*, November 10, 1985; "English-Only Sign Bill Sidetracked," *LAT*, November 17, 1985; South Gate City Council minutes, December 18, 1985, 5; South Gate City Council minutes, January 13, 1986, 4; South Gate Ordinance No. 1718 (1986) (all municipal sources are from the City Clerk's Office, South Gate). Nearby Bellflower proposed a similar effort in 1987, which also met with Latino resistance ("Bellflower to Study Bid for English Signs," *LAT*, February 15, 1987). These English-only efforts mostly failed, but they primed the pump for "immigrant policy with far more violent and dehumanizing undertones," including Proposition 187, writes Daniel HoSang in *Racial Propositions*, 159.

41. "Hue and Cry over Color of Homes," *LAT*, September 22, 1998; "South Gate Council Postpones Vote," *LAT*, September 24, 1998; Nita Lelyveld, "Infusion of Fuchsia Rattles a California City's Staid Beige," *Philadelphia Inquirer*, October 5, 1998; Carol Morello, "California Town May Tone Down Loud House Hues," *USA Today*, November 6, 1998; South Gate Community Development "Agenda Bill" for city council, Item No. 7, August 31, 1998, South Gate City Clerk's Office. On San Marino, see Nicolaides and Zarsadiaz, "Design Assimilation."

42. These insights come from Sarah Lopez, "Cantera Stone and Mexican Masons: The Making of Migratory Landscapes in a Transnational Arena," in *Landscapes in the Making*, ed. Stephen Daniels and Dell Upton (Washington, DC: Dumbarton Oaks Research Library and Collection, 2025); Nicolaides and Zarsadiaz, "Design Assimilation"; Lopez, *Remittance Landscape*.

43. "Suburbia's Simmering Class Struggle," *LAT*, September 28, 1998.

44. Saito, *Race and Politics*, offers a comprehensive discussion of these battles.

45. Lopez, *Remittance Landscape*, 12; Saito, *Race and Politics*, 17–22; Li, *Ethnoburb*. These suburbs experienced a similar transformation nationally where Latinos migrated right into "urban crisis" cities that suffered from disinvestment, deindustrialization, and white flight, seizing opportunity where others abandoned it. See Sandoval-Strausz, *Barrio America*; Llana Barber,

Latino City: Immigration and Urban Crisis in Lawrence, Massachusetts (Chapel Hill: University of North Carolina Press, 2017).

46. On Downey around similar themes, see Ramirez, "Business as Usual."

47. William Fulton, *The Reluctant Metropolis: The Politics of Urban Growth in Los Angeles* (Point Arena, CA: Solano Press Books, 1997), 77; Mike Davis, "The New Industrial Peonage: Gambling Comes to the Southeast," *Heritage*, Fall 1991, 15–16.

48. Graham McNeill, "Deindustrialization and the Evolution of the Working-Class Suburban Dream in Southeast Los Angeles (1965–1990)" (unpublished seminar paper, Claremont Graduate University, 2014), 12–20.

49. Andy Pasmant, "South Gate's Bouncing Back," *Western City* (September 1986), 19–22, South Gate History Archive, Weaver Library, South Gate, CA (hereafter SGHWL), Box 6, File 39; South Gate, "Financial Assistance for Industries in South Gate," ca. 1989, Box 3, SGHWL; "South Gate Wins All-America City Honors," *LAT*, June 14, 1990; "The HON Company Contributes . . . ," *South Gate Progress* (Spring 1999), Box 6, File 37, SGHWL; Jacob Wegmann, "'We Just Built It': Code Enforcement, Local Politics, and the Informal Housing Market in Southeast Los Angeles County" (PhD diss., University of California, Berkeley, 2014), 83.

50. South Gate Chamber of Commerce, "Standard Industrial Survey Report," October 1970, SGHWL; "S. Gate's 606 Industries Provide Jobs for 25,000," *Huntington Park (CA) Daily Signal*, January 19, 1973, C9. On general economic trends in the southeast suburbs, see James R. Curtis, "Barrio Space and Place in Southeast Los Angeles, California," in *Hispanic Spaces, Latino Places: Community and Cultural Diversity in Contemporary America*, ed. Daniel D. Arreola (Austin: University of Texas Press, 2004), 136–40.

51. Fulton, *Reluctant Metropolis*, 261.

52. Anastasia Loukaitou-Sideris, "Regeneration of Urban Commercial Strips: Ethnicity and Space in Three Los Angeles Neighborhoods," *Journal of Architectural and Planning Research* 19, no. 4 (Winter 2002): 338–40; Terezia Nemeth, "Downtown on Parade: The Reshaping of a Traditional Retail Model," *Places* 8, no. 3 (1993): 39; "For Some, L.A. Fails to be a Refuge," *LAT*, May 9, 1992.

53. Jorge Leal, "Las Plazas of South Los Angeles," in *Post-Ghetto: Reimagining South Los Angeles*, ed. Josh Sides (Berkeley: University of California Press, 2012), 11–32; Clara Irazábal and Macarena Gómez-Barris, "Bounded Tourism: Immigrant Politics, Consumption and Traditions at Plaza Mexico," *Journal of Tourism and Cultural Change* 5, no. 3 (2007): 191; on La Curacao, see "Latino, yes, but with new tastes," *LAT*, May 28, 2008.

54. Bob Rodino, "Capturing the Latino Market: Repositioning for Fun and Profit," *California Centers* (Spring 1994): 44–46; Bob Rodino telephone interview with author, January 29, 2018.

55. "South Gate Wins All-America City Honors," *LAT*, June 14, 1990; Alvaro Huerta, "South Gate, California: The Latinization of a Formerly White, Blue Collar Suburb and a Case Study of Environmental Racism" (UCLA paper, June 9, 2004), 13; Coro Fellows Program in Public Affairs, *The Logic of South Gate: A Study of Its People, Institutions and Situations and the Outcomes of Their Interactions* (report for the South Gate Regional Advisory Group, 2005); South Gate Chamber of Commerce, Annual Progress Report, June 9, 1984, SGHWL.

56. "South Gate City Is Tops in Area for Entrepreneurs," *LAT*, October 23, 1994; Brent R. Keltner, Ellen M. Pint, Eugene Bryton, Cathy Krop, Robert Reichardt, William L. Spencer, and Suzanne Perry, *Sustaining Innovation in South Gate: A Framework for Restructuring City Government* (Santa Monica, CA: RAND Corporation, 1996); "Successful Latinos Team Up to Help Others Make It," *LAT*, July 24, 1983.

57. Thanks to Jorge Leal for pointing this out.

58. One could argue that Primestor had an ulterior motive in reaching this finding; I could not find additional sources to corroborate the results of its survey.

59. "A New Latino Clout, South Gate Shopping Center Goes Mainstream," *LAT*, September 24, 2015.

60. According to U.S. Census data, in Baldwin Park from 1980 to 2000, the Latino population increased from 58 percent to 79 percent, while the white population decreased from 35 percent to 7 percent, and the Asian population increased from 4 percent to 12 percent.

61. "Payday Advance Lenders Targeted," *LAT*, March 8, 2008; "Latino Yes, but with New Tastes," *LAT*, May 28, 2008; "New Latino Clout"; *South Gate Progress*, Spring 1999, Box 6, File 37, SGHWL; Tom Thienes, "Contributions toward the History of the City of South Gate, California" (unpublished manuscript for the Works Progress Administration, 1942), 123, SGHWL.

62. Li, *Ethnoburb*, 180; Lung-Amam, "Malls of Meaning," 18–53.

63. Coro Fellows Program in Public Affairs, *Logic of South Gate*, 7–8; U.S. Census Bureau, *1990 Census of Population: Social and Economic Characteristics, California*, 1065; U.S. Census Bureau, "Place of Work for Workers 16 Years and Over—Place Level [5]," Decennial Census, DEC Summary File 3, table P027, 2000.

64. Soja, *Postmodern Geographies*, 202.

65. For data, see "Los Angeles County Demographic Data Project 1950–2010," edited by Becky M. Nicolaides, USC Digital Library et al., 2024, https://doi.org/10.25549/lademo-oucl sto1757543.

66. Adam Goodman, *The Deportation Machine: America's Long History of Expelling Immigrants* (Princeton: Princeton University Press, 2020), 34 (by 1910, the typical deportee had transitioned from Asian to Mexican). For data from 2012, see Transactional Records Access Clearinghouse, Syracuse University, https://trac.syr.edu/immigration/reports/350/; Erika Lee, *The Making of Asian America: A History* (New York: Simon & Schuster, 2016).

67. Lopez, *Remittance Landscape*, 12.

68. Saito, *Race and Politics*; Cheng, *The Changs Next Door to the Díazes*.

69. Zoom conversation with Oscar Gutierrez, March 15, 2022.

Chapter Five

1. Established as El Paso's Second Ward in 1896, the neighborhood is bounded by Paisano Drive to the north, the Rio Grande to the south, Cotton Street to the east, and Santa Fe Street to the west. I use its historical names Segundo Barrio, Southside, and South El Paso interchangeably. Because most residents were born in El Paso or had lived there for decades, I use *Mexican American* to reflect their longtime residence and *Chicanx* for only those who claim the identity.

2. Southside Low-Income Housing Corporation (SLIHDC), Community Development Block Grant (CDBG) Proposal, February 6, 1979, 3, MS257, Box 3, Folder 3, Renate Caldwell Papers (hereafter Caldwell Papers), C. L. Sonnichsen Special Collections Department, University of Texas at El Paso Library (UTEP SCD); "Activist Group Offers South Side 'Self-Help' Plan," *El Paso Times*, December 8, 1978.

3. "City Council Approves Adobe Housing Project," *El Paso Herald-Post*, December 12, 1979; "La Campana Wins Debate; Project OK'd," *El Paso Times*, December 12, 1979.

4. I examine their holistic plan in my book *¡El Barrio No Se Vende! Grassroots Activism and Revitalization in El Paso* (Austin: University of Texas Press, forthcoming).

5. Albert Camarillo, *Chicanos in a Changing Society: From Mexican Pueblos to American Barrios in Santa Barbara and California* (Cambridge, MA: Harvard University Press, 1979);

Richard Griswold del Castillo, *The Los Angeles Barrio, 1850–1890: A Social History* (Berkeley: University of California Press, 1979); Mario T. García, *Desert Immigrants: The Mexicans of El Paso, 1880–1920* (New Haven, CT: Yale University Press, 1981); Ricardo Romo, *East Los Angeles: History of a Barrio* (Austin: University of Texas Press, 1983); and Arnoldo De León, *Ethnicity in the Sunbelt: Mexican Americans in Houston* (College Station: Texas A&M Press, 1989).

6. On Latinx displacement, see Lydia R. Otero, *La Calle: Spatial Conflicts and Urban Renewal in a Southwestern City* (Tucson: University of Arizona Press, 2010); Monica Perales, *Smeltertown: Making and Remembering a Southwestern Border Community* (Chapel Hill: University of North Carolina Press, 2010); Lilia Fernández, *Brown in the Windy City: Mexicans and Puerto Ricans in Postwar Chicago* (Chicago: University of Chicago Press, 2014); John Laslett, *Shameful Victory: The Los Angeles Dodgers, the Red Scare, and the Hidden History of Chavez Ravine* (Tucson: University of Arizona Press, 2015).

7. On barrio activism, see Mary Pardo, *Mexican American Women Activists: Identity and Resistance in Two Los Angeles Communities* (Philadelphia: Temple University Press, 1998); Mario Luis Small, *Villa Victoria: The Transformation of Social Capital in a Boston Barrio* (Chicago: University of Chicago Press, 2004); David Montejano, *Quixote's Soldiers: A Local History of the Chicano Movement, 1966–1981* (Austin: University of Texas Press, 2010); Fernández, *Brown in the Windy City*; Eric Avila, *Folklore of the Freeway: Race and Revolt in the Modernist City* (Minneapolis: University of Minnesota Press, 2014); Alyssa Ribeiro, "Forgotten Residents Fight Back: The Ludlow Community Association and Neighborhood Improvement in Philadelphia," in *Civil Rights and Beyond: African American and Latino/a Activism in the Twentieth-Century United States*, ed. Brian D. Behnken (Athens: University of Georgia Press, 2016); Abigail Rosas, *South Central Is Home: Race and the Power of Community Investment in Los Angeles* (Stanford, CA: Stanford University Press, 2019); Eduardo Contreras, *Latinos and the Liberal City: Politics and Protest in San Francisco* (Philadelphia: University of Pennsylvania Press, 2019); Johanna Fernández, *The Young Lords: A Radical History* (Chapel Hill: University of North Carolina Press, 2020); Felipe Hinojosa, *Apostles of Change: Latino Radical Politics, Church Occupations, and the Fight to Save the Barrio* (Austin: University of Austin Press, 2021); George J. Sánchez, *Boyle Heights: How a Los Angeles Neighborhood Became the Future of America Democracy* (Berkeley: University of California Press, 2021).

8. On Latinx urban revitalization, see Mike Davis, *Magical Urbanism: Latinos Reinvent the U.S. City* (New York: Verso, 2001); Fernández, *Brown in the Windy City*; Llana Barber, *The Latino City: Immigration and Urban Crisis in Lawrence, Massachusetts, 1945–2000* (Chapel Hill: University of North Carolina Press, 2017); A. K. Sandoval-Strausz, *Barrio America: How Latino Immigrants Saved the American City* (New York: Basic Books, 2019); Mike Amezcua, *Making Mexican Chicago: From Postwar Settlement to the Age of Gentrification* (Chicago: University of Chicago Press, 2022).

9. On civil rights and the War on Poverty, see Annelise Orleck, *Storming Caesar's Palace: How Black Mothers Fought Their Own War on Poverty* (Boston: Beacon Press, 2005); Susan Youngblood Ashmore, *Carry It On: The War on Poverty and the Civil Rights Movement in Alabama, 1964–1972* (Athens: University of Georgia Press, 2008); Robert Bauman, *Race and the War on Poverty: From Watts to East L.A.* (Norman: University of Oklahoma Press, 2008); William S. Clayson, *Freedom Is Not Enough: The War on Poverty and the Civil Rights Movement in Texas* (Austin: University of Texas Press, 2010); Annelise Orleck and Lisa Gayle Hazirjian, *The War on Poverty: A New Grassroots History, 1964–1980* (Athens: University of Georgia Press, 2011); and Michael Woodsworth, *Battle for Bed-Stuy: The Long War on Poverty in New York City* (Cambridge, MA: Harvard University Press, 2016).

10. Arlene Dávila, *Barrio Dreams: Puerto Ricans, Latinos, and the Neoliberal City* (Berkeley: University of California Press, 2004); Julia Rabig, *The Fixers: Devolution, Development & Civil Society in Newark, 1960–1990* (Chicago: University of Chicago Press, 2016); Brian D. Goldstein, *The Roots of Renaissance: Gentrification and the Struggle over Harlem* (Cambridge, MA: Harvard University Press, 2017); Johanna Lodoño, *Abstract Barrios: The Crises of Latinx Visibility in Cities* (Durham, NC: Duke University Press, 2020); Rebecca K. Marchiel, *After Redlining: The Urban Reinvestment Movement in the Era of Financial Deregulation* (Chicago: University of Chicago Press, 2020); Timo Schrader, *Loisada as Urban Laboratory: Puerto Rican Community Activism in New York* (Athens: University of Georgia Press, 2020); Thomas Sugrue and Andrew Diamond, *Neoliberal Cities: The Remaking of Postwar America* (New York: NYU Press, 2020); Benjamin Holtzman, *The Long Crisis: New York City and the Path to Neoliberalism* (New York: Oxford University Press, 2021); Claire Dunning, *Nonprofit Neighborhoods: An Urban History of Inequality and the American State* (Chicago: University of Chicago Press, 2022).

11. Oscar J. Martínez, *The Chicanos of El Paso: An Assessment of Progress* (El Paso: Texas Western Press, 1980), 5.

12. On borderland identities, see Gloria Anzaldúa, *Borderlands/La Frontera: The New Mestiza* (San Francisco, CA: Aunt Lute Books, 1987); David G. Gutiérrez, *Walls and Mirrors: Mexican Americans, Mexican Immigrants, and the Politics of Ethnicity* (Berkeley: University of California Press, 1995); Chad Richardson and Michael J. Pisani, *Batos, Bolillos, Pochos, and Pelados: Class and Culture on the South Texas Border* (Austin: University of Texas Press, 1999); Rodolfo Rosales, *The Illusion of Inclusion: The Untold Political History of San Antonio* (Austin: University of Texas Press, 2000); Pablo Vila, *Crossing Borders, Reinforcing Borders: Social Categories, Metaphors and Narrative Identities on the U.S. Mexico Frontier* (Austin: University of Texas Press, 2000); Geraldo L. Cadava, *Standing on Common Ground: The Making of a Sunbelt Borderland* (Cambridge, MA: Harvard University Press, 2013).

13. W. H. Timmons, *El Paso: A Borderlands History* (El Paso: Texas Western Press, 1990), 167; C. L. Sonnichsen, *Pass of the North: Four Centuries on the Rio Grande* (El Paso: Texas Western Press, 1968).

14. El Paso Bureau of Information, *The city and county of El Paso, Texas, containing useful and reliable information concerning the future of great metropolis of the Southwest; its resources and advantages for the agriculturist, artisan and capitalist* (El Paso: Times Publishing Co., 1886), 6–7, http://hdl.handle.net/2027/uc2.ark:/13960/t7kp8682z; and "Only a Few Years Ago El Paso Was a Frontier Town; Today a City of Progress and Modernity," *El Paso Herald*, January 27, 1912. On Anglo dominance through the built environment, see Chris Wilson, *The Myth of Santa Fe: Creating A Modern Regional Tradition* (Albuquerque: University of New Mexico Press, 1997); Daniel D. Arreola, *Tejano South Texas: A Mexican American Cultural Province* (Austin: University of Texas Press, 2002); William Deverell, *Whitewashed Adobe: The Rise of Los Angeles and the Remaking of its Mexican Past* (Berkeley: University of California Press, 2004); Phoebe S. Kropp, *California Vieja: Culture and Memory in a Modern American Place* (Berkeley: University of California Press, 2006); Otero, *La Calle*; Shine Trabucco, "Returning to Roots: The History of Adobe and Earthen Architecture in San Antonio" (PhD diss., University of Houston, expected 2025); Ralph Newlan, *Adobe in Texas: An Historic Context, Annotated Bibliography and Survey Methodology*, Historical Studies Report prepared for the Texas Department of Transportation Environmental Affairs Division (November 2008), 13–15, https://ftp.dot.state.tx.us/pub/txdot-info/env/toolkit/420-01-gui.pdf.

15. Edwin C. Eckel, *Portland Cement Materials and Industry in the United States*, Bulletin 522 for the U.S. Geological Survey in the Department of the Interior (Washington, DC: Government

Printing Office, 1913), 344–47, https://www.google.com/books/edition/Portland_Cement_Materials_and_Industry_i/UO2A3JK_vagC?hl=en&gbpv=1; L. A. Wilson, *The Immigrants Guide to Texas Giving Descriptions of Counties, Towns and Villages with Valuable Historical and Statistical Information* (Dallas: Wilmans Bros. Printers, 1889), 88, https://babel.hathitrust.org/cgi/pt?id=loc.ark:/13960/t1qf90g17&seq=1; "We Will Be Happy," *El Paso Times*, November 25, 1883; "Vale the Adobes; Rise the Skyscraper," *El Paso Herald*, February 10, 1910; El Paso Chamber of Commerce, *El Paso, What Is It and Why?* (El Paso: El Paso Printing Co., 1914), 8, https://babel.hathitrust.org/cgi/pt?id=hvd.hwhj54&seq=5.

16. On Mexican migrants and community formation in El Paso, see Oscar J. Martínez, *Border Boom Town: Ciudad Juárez since 1848* (Austin: University of Texas Press, 1978); Mario T. García, *Desert Immigrants*; Vicki Ruiz, *From Out of the Shadows: Mexican Women in Twentieth Century America* (New York: Oxford University Press, 2008), chap. 2; Monica Perales, *Smeltertown: Making and Remembering a Southwest Border Community* (Chapel Hill: University of North Carolina Press, 2010); Julian Lim, *Porous Borders: Multiracial Migrations and the Law in the U.S.-Mexico Borderlands* (Chapel Hill: University of North Carolina Press, 2017), chap. 2.

17. "Council Decided on Early Cleanup of Chihuahuita," *El Paso Herald*, August 20, 1914; "Council Condemns Unsanitary Huts," *El Paso Times*, September 11, 1914; "Destruction That Means Progress," *El Paso Herald*, August 14, 1914; "Chihuahuita Clean-Up Campaign Inaugurated," *El Paso Times*, October 10, 1917; "Enforced Baths for Chihuahuita Inhabitants Fail to Make a Strong Appeals to the Victims," *El Paso Herald*, October 16, 1917. On race and public health on the border, see David Dorado Romo, *Ringside Seat to a Revolution: An Underground Cultural History of El Paso and Juárez: 1893–1923* (El Paso: Cinco Puntos Press, 2005), 193–244; Alexandra Minna Stern, *Eugenic Nation: Faults & Frontiers of Better Breeding in Modern America* (Berkeley: University of California Press, 2005), chap. 2; Ann R. Gabbert, "Defining the Boundaries of Care: Local Responses to Global Concerns in El Paso Public Health Policy, 1881–1941" (PhD diss., University of Texas at El Paso, 2006); John Mckiernan-González, *Fevered Measures: Public Health and Race at the Texas-Mexico Border, 1848–1942* (Durham, NC: Duke University Press, 2012), chaps. 5 and 7; Lina-Maria Murillo, "Birth Control on the Border: Race, Gender, Religion and Class in the Making of the Birth Control Movement, El Paso, Texas, 1937–1973" (PhD diss., University of Texas at El Paso, 2016).

18. "Model Tenements Provide Homes for Many Families," *El Paso Herald*, August 29, 1914; "Leads West in Number of Big Structures," *El Paso Herald*, January 27, 1917; "Apartments and Tenements Erected in El Paso during Year at Cost of $50,000," *El Paso Herald*, August 25, 1917.

19. Martínez, *Chicanos of El Paso*, 8–11.

20. "The Barrio: Another World," *El Paso Herald-Post*, June 7, 1985. Chapter 2 of *¡El Barrio No Se Vende!* discusses placemaking in the barrio.

21. Robert E. Alexander, *Urban Development Manual for the City of El Paso: A Handbook for Community Planning*, May 1968, 40–57. American Planning Association, Texas Chapter: The History of Planning in Texas Project (hereafter APA-TX History of Planning Project), Box 7, Folder 1, Alexander Architectural Library, University of Texas at Austin.

22. Better Communities Corporation, *Revitalization Plan for the South El Paso Project Area*, August 1976, 2. APA-TX History of Planning Project, Box 7, Folder 1; La Campaña Pro La Preservación del Barrio (La Campaña), Manifesto from the Community of South El Paso, 1975, 1, MEChA Movimiento Estudiantil Chicano de Aztlán (El Paso) Records, MS254, Box 7, Folder 34, UTEP SCD.

23. Oscar Lozano, oral history interview with the author, December 27, 2018, El Paso, TX; City of El Paso, Urban Development Action Grant (UDAG) proposal submitted to the U.S.

Department of Housing and Urban Development, January 1978. El Paso Department of City Planning Records (hereafter City Planning Records), MS204, Box 6, Folder 27, UTEP SCD; Nestor Valencia, oral history interview with the author, August 1, 2018, Anthony, NM; "UDAG Slashed 62 Percent," *El Paso Times*, June 24, 1978; "$2.3 Million Approved for UDAG in El Paso," *El Paso Herald-Post*, July 10, 1978; "HUD Officials Tell Why Request Was Pared Down," *El Paso Herald-Post*, July 12, 1978.

24. Valencia interview, 2018; "HUD takes money back," *El Paso Herald-Post*, September 9, 1981. This episode is detailed in chapter 4 of *¡El Barrio No Se Vende!*

25. SLIHDC, CDBG Proposal, Exhibit: SLIHDC History, February 6, 1979, 19, and SLIHDC By-Laws, ca. 1979, both in Caldwell Papers, Box 3, Folder 3; La Campaña, "The Barrio:" A Positive View, June 1978, 6, and La Campaña, A Community Protest and A Community Alternative to Regenerate the Barrio, June 1978, 17, both in Caldwell Papers, Box 2, Folder 4.

26. La Campaña, A Community Protest, June 1978, 18; "Activist Group Offers South Side 'Self-Help' Plan," *El Paso Times*, December 8, 1978; Mack Caldwell, Interview Questions for the SLIHDC, ca. 1978. Caldwell Papers, Box 3, Folder 3.

27. Lozano interview, 2018; "La Campana tries to pull poor together," *El Paso Times*, April 1, 1981; Classified Ad, "Industrial Property 714 S. Mesa," *El Paso Times*, November 8, 1981; "SLIHDC Legal Notice," *El Paso Times*, April 26, 1980.

28. City of El Paso, UDAG Revised Application, Attachment #1: Dwelling Units, May 1978, Caldwell Papers, Box 3, Folder 11; "$1.5 Million Facelift Approved for El Paso Tenements," *El Paso Herald-Post*, September 15, 1981; City of El Paso, *El Segundo Barrio—Neighborhood Revitalization Strategy*, February 9, 2010, 12, Vertical Files, El Paso Public Library; City of El Paso Office of Grants and Urban Affairs, South El Paso Survey: Techniques and Findings, May 1978, 3, Caldwell Papers, Box 13, Folder 32; SLIHDC, Regeneración del Barrio CDBG Proposal, December 9, 1980, 10, Caldwell Papers, Box 2, Folder 13.

29. SLIHDC, Community Development Program Proposal, ca. 1978, 12, and SLIHDC, Neighborhood Revitalization and Economic Development Project CDBG Proposal, February 6, 1979, 16, both in Caldwell Papers, Box 3, Folder 3, UTEP SCD; "La Campana Tries to Pull Poor Together," *El Paso Times*, April 2, 1981.

30. Lozano interview, 2018; "Activist Group Offers South Side 'Self-Help' Plan," *El Paso Times*, December 8, 1978; SLIHDC, Regeneración del Barrio CDBG Proposal, December 9, 1980, 5. Caldwell Papers, Box 2, Folder 3, UTEP SCD.

31. La Campaña, Jardines del Barrio Proposal, ca. 1977, 1. Chicano Vertical Files, UTEP SCD; "Alternativas," *El Mestizo*, July 1980; Lozano interview, 2018.

32. SLIHDC, Neighborhood Self-Help Development Grant Proposal, May 1980, 51. Caldwell Papers, Box 2, Folder 3; Mack Caldwell, "Regeneración del Barrio: Alternative Urban Public Housing in El Segundo Barrio," in *Future Visions of Urban Public Housing: An International Forum*, ed. Wolfgang F. E. Preiser, David P. Varady, and Francis P. Russell (New York: Routledge Revivals, 2016), 167.

33. "Adobe Makes a Comeback," *El Paso Times*, August 12, 1979; "Get Back to the Land," *Texas Monthly*, March 1981, 133; On adobe's "comeback," see Wilson, *Myth of Santa Fe*; Lawrence A. Herzog, *From Aztec to High Tech: Architecture and Landscape across the Mexico-United States Border* (Baltimore: Johns Hopkins University Press, 1999); Lyle Massey and James Nisbet, *The Invention of the American Desert: Art Land, and the Politics of the Environment* (Berkeley: University of California Press, 2021).

34. "A Home for All Seasons," Southwestern Homes open house ad, *El Paso Times*, December 20, 1981; "El Paso's First Passive Solar Adobe Home," open house ad, *El Paso Times*, May 4,

1980; "Southwestern Homes Open House," ad, *El Paso Times*, August 21, 1982; "Is Adobe Suited for El Paso?," *El Paso Times*, May 19, 1979; "Adobe Makes Comeback," *El Paso Times*, August 12, 1979; "City Hopes for Adobe Brick Industry Funding," *El Paso Herald-Post*, November 16, 1979.

35. "Use of Adobe In Army Structures To Be Protested," *El Paso Times*, April 11, 1919; "City Delays Adobe Project," *El Paso Herald-Post*, December 4, 1979; "City Council Approves Adobe Housing Project," *El Paso Herald-Post*, December 12, 1979; "That Snug and Warm Adobe Isn't, Bureaucrats Say," *El Paso Herald-Post*, November 15, 1979; "Builder Protests Adobe Ban with 'Common Sense,'" *El Paso Times*, November 23, 1979; "Feds May Have Bricked Up Adobe Project," *El Paso Times*, December 4, 1979; "Adobe Builder Refutes Claims of Inefficiency," *El Paso Herald-Post*, November 21, 1979.

36. See Martínez, *Chicanos of El Paso*, table 7, "Residential Patterns in the Best Neighborhoods by Surname, 1965–1975"; "EP Men Cash In on Solar Competition," *El Paso Times*, January 4, 1979; "Adobe Abode Solves Problem of High Utility Bills," *El Paso Times*, January 26, 1979; "Adobe + Sun = Bargain Home," *El Paso Times*, December 8, 1980; Lozano interview, 2018; "Code Proposal Eases Restrictions on Use of Adobe," *El Paso Times*, January 20, 1980; "HUD Begins Study into Future Uses for 'Lowly' Adobe," *El Paso Times*, December 26, 1980; "Housing Projects Pass Inspection," *El Paso Herald-Post*, January 28, 1982.

37. "Adobe May Be Housing Answer," *El Paso Herald-Post*, December 12, 1980; Caldwell, "Regeneración del Barrio," 165–66; SLIHDC, Community Development Program Proposal, ca. 1978, 3, Caldwell Papers, Box 3, Folder 3; La Campaña, A Community Protest, June 1978, 17, Caldwell Papers, Box 2, Folder 4.

38. SLIHDC, Neighborhood Self-Help Development Grant Proposal, May 1980, 54, Caldwell Papers; Caldwell, "Regeneración del Barrio," 168–70.

39. James Thomas Rojas, "The Enacted Environment: The Creation of 'Place' by Mexicans in East Los Angeles" (master's thesis, Massachusetts Institute of Technology, 1991); Mike Davis, *Magical Urbanism*; David R. Diaz, *Barrio Urbanism: Chicanos, Planning, and American Cities* (New York: Routledge, 2005); David R. Diaz and Rodolfo Torres, *Latino Urbanism: The Politics of Planning, Policy, and Redevelopment* (New York: New York University Press, 2012); Michael Rios and Leonardo Vazquez, *Diálogos: Placemaking in Latino Communities* (New York: Routledge, 2012); A. K. Sandoval-Strausz, "Viewpoint: Latino Vernaculars and the Emerging National Landscape," *Buildings and Landscapes: Journal of the Vernacular Architecture Forum* 20, no. 1 (Spring 2013): 1–18; Jesus J. Lara, *Latino Placemaking and Planning: Cultural Resilience and Strategies for Reurbanization* (Tucson: University of Arizona Press, 2018); Sandoval-Strausz, *Barrio America*; Lodoño, *Abstract Barrios*.

40. Caldwell, "Regeneración del Barrio," 168; SLIHDC, Regeneración: Neighborhood Self-Help Development Grant Application, May 20, 1980, 44–46, Caldwell Papers, Box 3, Folder 3.

41. SLIHDC, Regeneración: Neighborhood Self-Help Development Grant Application—Organizational History, May 20, 1980, 35–37, and Regeneración Neighborhood Self-Help Development Grant Application, May 20, 1980, 55, both in Caldwell Papers, Box 3, Folder 3; City of El Paso Office of Federal Grants and Urban Affairs, South El Paso Survey Techniques and Findings—South El Paso (SEP) Population and Household Chronology, May 16, 1978, City Planning Records, Box 13, Folder 23.

42. SLIHDC, Regeneración del Barrio CDBG Proposal, December 9, 1980, 5, Caldwell Papers; SLIHDC, Aviso de La Corporación de Vivienda del Segundo Barrio, 1981, Chicano Vertical Files, UTEP SCD.

43. "Barrio Residents Get Dream of Better Home," *El Paso Times*, October 16, 1988; "Cash Runs Short, but Tenants Pitch In on Task," *El Paso Times*, October 16, 1988.

44. SLIHDC, Regeneración del Barrio CDBG Proposal, December 9, 1980, 3–4; "South Side Group Gains Credibility," *El Paso Times*, September 20, 1992.

45. "Barrio Residents Get Dream of Better Home"; "Cash Runs Short, but Tenants Pitch In on Task."

46. Oscar Lozano, oral history interview with the author, February 24, 2014, El Paso, TX; "Segundo Barrio Residents Dream of New Homes," *El Paso Times*, December 22, 1995; "Segundo Barrio, primera casa . . ." *El Paso Herald-Post*, October 9, 1997; Nestor Valencia, oral history interview with the author, July 27, 2017, Anthony, NM.

47. "Businesses Closing In on Poverty-Stricken Residential District," *El Paso Times*, December 3, 1990; City of El Paso Department of Planning, Research & Development Urban Design Division, *The South El Paso Zoning Rollback—1986*, November 1986, 53, City Planning Records, Box 24, Folder 15; Carmen Felix, untitled speech regarding the Special Residential Revitalization District overturn, ca. 1991, Chicano Vertical Files, UTEP SCD; Alicia Chacón to Mayor Suzanne Azar, May 1, 1991, Chicano Vertical Files, UTEP SCD; "City May Bend on Downtown Residential Zoning," *El Paso Herald-Post*, December 21, 1990.

48. On neoliberal cities, see Dávila, *Barrio Dreams*; Jonathan Soffer, *Ed Koch and the Rebuilding of New York City* (New York: Columbia University Press, 2010); Kim Phillips-Fein, *Fear City: New York's Fiscal Crisis and the Rise of Austerity Politics* (New York: Metropolitan Books, 2017); Sugrue and Diamond, *Neoliberal Cities*.

49. SLIHDC, Regeneración: Neighborhood Self-Help Development Grant Application, May 20, 1980, 38, Caldwell Papers.

50. SLIHDC, Regeneración del Barrio CDBG, December 9, 1980, 3, Caldwell Papers. Local bankers and investors make it clear that their commitment to financing low-income housing depended on "qualified borrowers." See City of El Paso, UDAG, Part II: The South El Paso Revitalization Program, January 1978, City Planning Records, Box 6, Folder 27. On late twentieth-century policies, see Jon C. Teaford, *The Rough Road to Renaissance: Urban Revitalization in America, 1940–1985* (Baltimore: Johns Hopkins University Press, 1990); John F. Bauman, Roger Biles, and Kristin M. Szylvian, *From Tenements to the Taylor Homes: In Search of an Urban American Housing Policy in Twentieth-Century America* (University Park: Pennsylvania State University Press, 2010); Roger Biles, *The Fate of Cities: Urban America and the Federal Government, 1945–2000* (Lawrence: University Press of Kansas, 2011); Tracy Neumann, *Remaking the Rust Belt: The Postindustrial Transformation of North America* (Philadelphia: University of Pennsylvania Press, 2016); Keeanga-Yamahtta Taylor, *Race for Profit: How Banks and the Real Estate Industry Undermined Black Homeownership* (Chapel Hill: University of North Carolina Press 2019).

51. Juan Montes, a Chicanx activist and La Campaña member, testified on HUD's lack of oversight. Juan Montes, Testimony before Senate Subcommittee on Housing and Urban Affairs, March 1983, U.S. Senate, Committee on Banking, Housing, and Urban Affairs, *Hearings on Funding Authorizations for Housing and Community Development Programs for Fiscal Year 1984*, 99th Cong., 1st sess., March 1983, 253–88; "City's Spending Gets Stiff HUD Criticism," *El Paso Herald-Post*, November 28, 1978; "Community Development—A Rebuilding," *El Paso Times*, April 19, 1979.

52. "City Council Kills Housing Funds; Irate Southsiders Scream Protest," *El Paso Times*, April 9, 1980; "Housing Cut Angers Southsiders," *El Paso Times*, April 3, 1980; "Council Puts Off Housing Project 1 More Time," *El Paso Times*, April 8, 1987; "3 Years Later, City OKs South Side Housing Project," *El Paso Times*, May 20, 1987; "Groundbreaking Today Ends Fight for South Side Housing Project," *El Paso Times*, September 5, 1987; "Grants," *El Paso Times*, August 13, 1989.

53. Victor Vega to the City of El Paso's Chief Administrator Officer and Aldermen, April 8, 1980, Chicano Vertical Files, UTEP SCD.

54. On neighborhood groups transitioning to CDCs, see Alexander von Hoffman, *House by House, Block by Block: The Rebirth of America's Urban Neighborhoods* (New York: Oxford University Press, 2003); Rabig, *Fixers*; Goldstein, *Roots of Renaissance*; Holtzman, *Long Crisis*; and Dunning, *Nonprofit Neighborhoods.*

55. On NCLR funding Chicanx/Latinx CDCs, see Benjamin Marquez, "Mexican-American Community Development Corporations and the Limits of Directed Capitalism," *Economic Development Quarterly* 7, no. 3 (1993): 287–95; John Chávez, *Eastside Landmark: A History of the East Los Angeles Community Union* (Stanford, CA: Stanford University Press, 1998); Montejano, *Quixote's Soldiers*; Cristina Mora, *Making Hispanics: How Activists Bureaucrats, and the Media Constructed a New American* (Chicago: University of Chicago Press, 2014); Small, *Villa Victoria*; Contreras, *Latinos and the Liberal City*; and "Latino Community Development: Histories of Economic and Social Justice," http://stmupublichistory.org/lcd/. For El Paso's Chicanx CDCs, see Joel Zapata, "Women's Grassroots Revitalization of South El Paso: La Mujer Obrera's Challenge to Gentrification and Neglect," *Río Bravo: A Journal of the Borderlands*, no. 1 (2014): 42–68; Sandra I. Enríquez, "'A Totality of Our Well-Being': The Creation and Evolution of the Centro de Salud Familiar La Fe in South El Paso," in *Civil Rights in Black and Brown: Histories of Resistance and Struggle in Texas*, ed. Max Krochmal and J. Todd Moye (Austin: University of Texas Press, 2021), 177–96.

56. "Grant Awarded for Low-Income Housing," *El Paso Times*, September 12, 1992; "South Side Group Gains Credibility," *El Paso Times*, September 20, 1992; "Low-Cost Housing Project Builds Hopes," *El Paso Times*, 1995.

57. Letter to the Editor, "Southside Corporation Delays Development," *El Paso Times*, July 10, 1988; "Segundo Barrio, primera casa . . . ," *El Paso Herald-Post*, October 9, 1997.

58. On NAFTA in the Ciudad Juárez–El Paso region, see Victor M. Ortiz-Gonzalez, *El Paso: Local Frontiers at a Global Crossroads* (Minneapolis: University of Minnesota Press, 2004); Zapata, "Women's Grassroots Revitalization of South El Paso"; and Oscar J. Martínez, *Ciudad Juarez: The Saga of a Legendary Border City* (Tucson: University of Arizona Press, 2018); City of El Paso, *El Segundo Barrio—Neighborhood Revitalization Strategy*, February 9, 2010, 20; "At Least 25,000 Homes Needed," *El Paso Herald-Post*, June 21, 1997; Elizabeth J. Mueller, *Building Community Development Capacity in El Paso: A Report to the Ford Foundation*, December 1998, 12, Center for Urban Policy Research, Rutgers University, https://cupr.rutgers.edu/products/building-community-development-capacity-in-el-paso/; Texas Low Income Housing Information Service, *Housing in Texas: A Living Crisis, Texas Solutions*, 2000, 44–51, https://texashousers.org/wp-content/uploads/2011/06/living-in-crisis-report.pdf.

59. "El Paso Community Dialogue," in *Housing in Texas: A Living Crisis, Texas Solutions*, 2000, 48–51, https://texashousers.org/wp-content/uploads/2011/06/living-in-crisis-report.pdf; U.S. Department of Housing and Urban Development, Case Study—Organización Progresiva de San Elizario, n.d., https://www.hud.gov/sites/documents/19565_OPSE.PDF; "Home, Sweet Home," *El Paso Times*, 1997; "Brighter Future," *El Paso Times*, November 5, 2002; "Building a Dream," *El Paso Times*, February 11, 2003; "Families Help to Build Adobe Homes in San Eli," *El Paso Times*, January 3, 2006.

60. "El Paso: It's a Strange and Distant Place," *El Paso-Herald Post*, September 8, 1983; "Debunking Right-Wing Myths about the Southern Border," *Immigration Hub*, October 14, 2021, https://theimmigrationhub.org/debunking-rightwing-myths-about-the-southern-border.

61. City of El Paso, Texas, "Economic Snapshot Overview," https://www.elpasotexas.gov

/economic-development/economic-snapshot/snapshot-overview/; U.S. Census Bureau, QuickFacts for El Paso City and El Paso County, Texas, https://www.census.gov/quickfacts/fact/table/elpasocitytexas,elpasocountytexas/PST045222. HACEP recently rebranded to Housing Opportunity Management Enterprises, or HOME, to remove the stigma associated with public housing. Why the Largest Housing Authority in Texas Has a New Name," *El Paso Inc.*, July 25, 2021; "About HOME," HOME, https://www.ephome.org/housing/about_hacep/index.php.

62. "El Paso Migrant Street Releases Imminent as Numbers Rise, Shelter Operators Fear," *El Paso Matters*, September 14, 2023, https://elpasomatters.org/2023/09/14/el-paso-migrant-en counters-rise-border-patrol-sacred-heart/; "El Paso's Segundo Barrio named in National Register of Historic Places," *El Paso Times*, November 6, 2021.

Chapter Six

1. Eleanor Swertlow, "Cleric Calls Cops Lax, Hints Vigilante Group," n.d. (no newspaper title included), clip in New York City Mission Society, 1976–77, RBF Box 732, Folder 4388, Rockefeller Archives, Sleepy Hollow, NY (hereafter Rockefeller Archives).

2. Acción Cívica Evangélica, New York City Mission Society, 1976–77, RBF RG 3.1-GRANTS, Box 732, Folder 4388, Rockefeller Archives.

3. David Vidal, "Hispanic Protestant Church Group Forges New Role for the Spanish-Speaking in New York City's Affairs," *New York Times*, August 2, 1976; George Dugan, "Lower East Side Churches Mobilize against Vandalism and Fires," *New York Times*, October 31, 1976. See also Leo Grebler, Joan W. Moore, and Ralph Guzman, *The Mexican American People: The Nation's Second Largest Minority* (New York: Free Press, 1970), 447–53, which hypothesized that those on the margins of the church hierarchy tended to be at the center of broader social welfare programs.

4. Kim Phillips-Fein, *Fear City: New York's Fiscal Crisis and the Rise of Austerity Politics* (New York: Picador, 2017), 4.

5. Phillips-Fein, 93, 68.

6. Sherrie Baver, Angelo Falcón, Gabriel Haslip-Viera, eds., *Latinos in New York: Communities in Transition*, 2nd ed. (South Bend, IN: University of Notre Dame Press, 2017), 27.

7. Felipe Luciano, interview with author, New York City, July 11, 2018.

8. Piri Thomas, *Savior, Savior, Hold My Hand* (Garden City, NY: Doubleday, 1972), 325–27. Carter's Little Liver Pills were well-known patent medicine.

9. Jon Butler, *God in Gotham: The Miracle of Religion in Modern Manhattan* (Cambridge, MA: Harvard University Press, 2020), 112.

10. Benjamin Holtzman, *The Long Crisis: New York City and the Path to Neoliberalism* (New York: Oxford University Press, 2021), 4.

11. Thomas, *Savior, Savior*, 19–21.

12. Interesting also to note that the NCC failed miserably with Latino churches and in connecting to the issues that matter most to Latinos. For more on this, see Mark Wild, *Renewal: Liberal Protestants and the American City after World War II* (Chicago: University of Chicago Press, 2019).

13. Brian J. Miller, "'Jungles of Terror' to 'God Will Begin a Healing in This City': Billy Graham and Evangelicals on Cities and Suburbs," *Journal of Urban History* 48, no. 2 (2022): 302–18.

14. The story of Nicky Cruz looms large in Latino churches because it came out of a Latino context and because of Cruz's gang involvement and drug culture. See Nicky Cruz, *Run, Baby, Run* (Plainfield, NJ: Bridge Logos Publishers, 1968).

15. Kenneth A. Briggs, "Pentecostalism Rises Like a Phoenix from the Slums" *New York Times*, February 20, 1975.

16. For more on Mama Leo and the history of Pentecostalism in New York City, see Elizabeth D. Ríos, "'The Ladies Are Warriors': Latina Pentecostalism and Faith-Based Activism in New York City," in *Latino Religions and Civic Activism in the United States*, ed. Gastón Espinosa et al. (Oxford: Oxford University Press, 2005); Gastón Espinosa, *Latino Pentecostals in America: Faith and Politics in Action* (Boston: Harvard University Press, 2014).

17. Ríos, "The Ladies Are Warriors," 203–04.

18. Ríos, 204.

19. For more on the history of Pentecostalism, see Arlene M. Sánchez Walsh, *Latino Pentecostal Identity*; Daniel Ramírez, *Migrating Faith*; Gastón Espinosa, *Latino Pentecostals in America*; and Lloyd Barba, *Sowing the Sacred.*

20. Robert Orsi, *Gods of the City: Religion and the Urban Landscape* (Bloomington: Indiana University Press, 1999), 43.

21. Gastón Espinosa, "El Azteca: Francisco Olazábal and Latino Pentecostal Charisma, Power, and Faith Healing in the Borderlands," *Journal of the American Academy of Religion* 67, no. 3 (1999): 614.

22. Sonia Song-Ha Lee, *Building a Latino Civil Rights Movement: Puerto Ricans, African Americans, and the Pursuit of Racial Justice in New York City* (Chapel Hill: University of North Carolina Press, 2016), 3.

23. Johanna Fernández, "Radicals in the Late 1960s: A History of the Young Lords Party, 1969–1974" (PhD diss., Columbia University, 2005), 27, 33–34.

24. Lee, *Building a Latino Civil Rights Movement*, 46.

25. Johanna Fernández, *The Young Lords: A Radical History* (Chapel Hill: University of North Carolina Press, 2020), 1. See also Felipe Hinojosa, *Apostles of Change: Latino Radical Politics, Church Occupations, and the Fight to Save the Barrio* (Austin: University of Texas Press, 2021).

26. Luis Aponte-Parés, "Lessons from El Barrio—The East Harlem Real Great Society/Urban Planning Studio: A Puerto Rican Chapter in the Fight for Urban Self-Determination," *New Political Science* 20, no. 4 (1998): 401.

27. Raymond Rivera, *Liberty to the Captives: Our Call to Minister in a Captive World* (Grand Rapids, MI: Eerdmans Publishing, 2012), 88–89.

28. Rivera, 89.

29. Rivera, 90.

30. Rivera, 47; "Community Development Program and Application," C49.65 CDPA April 1975, New York Municipal Archives, New York City.

31. Rivera, *Liberty to the Captives*, 47.

32. John T. McGreevey, *Parish Boundaries: The Catholic Encounter with Race in the Twentieth Century* (Chicago: University of Chicago Press, 1996), 162.

33. Gustavo Gutiérrez, *A Theology of Liberation*, rev. ed. (New York: Orbis Books, 1988); Phillip Berryman, *Liberation Theology* (New York: Pantheon, 1996).

34. See, for example, the work of Matthew J. Cressler, "'Real Good and Sincere Catholics': White Catholicism and Massive Resistance to Desegregation in Chicago, 1965–1968," *Religion and American Culture* 30, no. 2 (2020): 273–306.

35. Justin D. Poché, "Race and Catholicism in American History," *Oxford Research Encyclopedia of Religion*, February 26, 2018, 277 and 294.

36. Ronald J. Sider, "Evangelism, Salvation, and Social Justice: Definitions and Interrelationships," *International Review of Mission* 64 (1975): 254–55. See also David Kirkpatrick, *A Gospel*

for the Poor: Global Social Christianity and the Latin American Evangelical Left (Philadelphia: University of Pennsylvania Press, 2019).

37. Orlando E. Costas, *The Church and Its Mission: A Shattering Critique from the Third World* (Wheaton, IL: Tyndale House Publishers), 308–9. In the past twenty years, scholars such as Arlene Sánchez-Walsh, Gastón Espinosa, and Daniel Ramírez have published important works on the role of Pentecostals in social movements. These scholars point out that even as Pentecostals have maintained a complex relationship with society and culture, their social service engagements, always couched within an evangelical message of salvation, are an important form of Latina/o religious politics.

38. New York City Poverty Areas (Maps and Boundary Descriptions), New York City Council against Poverty, C831.58 pam copy 1, NY Municipal Archives, New York City; Edward C. Burks, "Puerto Ricans Say Poverty Program Neglects Them," *New York Times*, February 25, 1970.

39. Charles Molina Jr., *Youth Labor Markets for Puerto Rican-Latin American Youth Labor Market in New York City*, n.d., Arawak Consulting Corp, New York, Report prepared for the Office of the Assistant Secretary for Policy, Education, and Research, U.S. Department of Labor, New York Municipal Archives, New York City.

40. Frances X. Clines, "Puerto Rican Poverty Charge Denied," *New York Times*, November 15, 1969.

41. "Blacks Continue Antipoverty Rift: Puerto Ricans Assailed—Lindsay Plot Is Seen," *New York Times*, December 18, 1969.

42. Edward C. Burks, "Puerto Ricans Say Poverty Program Neglects Them," *New York Times*, February 25, 1970.

43. Burks, "Puerto Ricans Say."

44. Burks.

45. David Vidal, "Hispanic Protestant Church Group Forges New Role for Spanish-Speaking in New York City's Affairs," *New York Times*, August 2, 1976.

46. Glenn Fowler, "Beame Names Erazo to Fill Terry post," *New York Times*, December 30, 1973.

47. Fowler.

48. Fowler.

49. RBF RG 3.1—Grants, Box 732, Folder 4388, New York City Mission Society Acción Cívica Evangélica 1976–1977, Rockefeller Archives.

50. "Memorandum," May 15, 1976, from W. Gerald Davenport, subject: New York City Mission Society–Acción Cívica Evangélica. Rockefeller Archives.

51. Kenneth A. Briggs, "Pentecostalism Rises Like a Phoenix from the Slums," *New York Times*, February 20, 1975.

52. Kenneth A. Briggs, "Seminary Finds Success Isn't Just an Academic Issue," *New York Times*, December 18, 1976.

53. Rev. Raymond Rivera, interview with author, Latino Pastoral Action Center, New York City, May 19, 2022.

54. For more on the failures of liberal Protestantism and the religious left with relation to Latinos, see Mark Wild, *Renewal: Liberal Protestants and the American City after World War II Theology* (Chicago: University of Chicago Press, 2019), 216.

55. Holtzman, *Long Crisis*, 10.

56. Holtzman, 11.

57. "Youth-Job Program Assailed in Report," *New York Times*, March 28, 1977.

58. "Response to U.S. Rep. Elizabeth Holtzman's Report on New York City's 1976 Summer Youth Employment Program, March 27, 1977," New York City Mission Society, Acción Cívica Evangélica 1976–77, RBF RG 3.1-GRANTS, Box 732, Folder 4388, Rockefeller Archives.

59. Rios, "Ladies Are Warriors," 209.

60. Mark Warren, *Dry Bones Rattling: Community Building to Revitalize American Democracy* (Princeton, NJ: Princeton University Press, 2001); Mario T. Garcia, *Father Luis Olivares, a Biography* (Chapel Hill: University of North Carolina Press, 2018).

61. Kenneth A. Briggs, "Pentecostalism Rises Like a Phoenix from the Slums," *New York Times*, February 20, 1975.

Chapter Seven

1. See the piece described and more of Martinez Dominguez's work at his blog (http://feegz.wordpress.com). On his problems with the term *Latino*, see "Without Any Words in It," Harlem One Stop, video, NYXT, https://www.nyxt.nyc/blog/haiti-dominican-republic-graffiti/; Carlos Jesus Martinez Dominguez, *Talk Your Sh*t!* podcast, July 22, 2021, https://youtu.be/O7yvUR2WkU0.

2. Tatiana Flores, "'Latinidad Is Cancelled': Confronting an Anti-Black Construct," *Latin American and Latinx Visual Culture* 3, no. 3 (2021): 59; Alan Pelaez Lopez, @MigrantScribble, tweet no longer available on X but included in Julissa Arce, *You Sound Like a White Girl: The Case for Rejecting Assimilation* (New York: Flatiron Books, 2022), 146. See also "Afro-indigenous Poet Alan Pelaez Lopez Breaks Down Why Blackness Is Radical in Latinidad," *The Root*, https://youtu.be/bb4XGUA7kcU.

3. Llana Barber, *Latino City: Immigration and Urban Crisis in Lawrence, Massachusetts, 1945–2000* (Chapel Hill: University of North Carolina Press, 2017).

4. Rodolfo F. Acuña, review of *Latino City* in *Journal of American History* 105, no. 2 (September 2018): 458–59.

5. For key texts in this debate, see Cristina Beltrán, *The Trouble with Unity: Latino Politics and the Creation of Identity* (Oxford: Oxford University Press, 2010); G. Cristina Mora, *Making Hispanics: How Activists, Bureaucrats, and Media Constructed a New American* (Chicago: University of Chicago Press, 2014); Juana María Rodríguez, *Queer Latinidad: Identity Practices and Discursive Spaces* (New York: New York University Press, 2003); Arlene Dávila, *Latinos, Inc.: The Marketing and Making of a People* (Berkeley: University of California Press, 2012); Arlene Dávila, *Latino Spin: Public Image and the Whitewashing of Race* (New York: New York University Press, 2008). Chicago has been a key site to explore pan-ethnicity owing to its distinctive postwar population of both Mexicans and Puerto Ricans. See Felix M. Padilla, *Latino Ethnic Consciousness: The Case of Mexican Americans and Puerto Ricans in Chicago* (Notre Dame, IN: University of Notre Dame Press, 1985); Lilia Fernández, *Brown in the Windy City: Mexicans and Puerto Ricans in Postwar Chicago* (Chicago: University of Chicago Press, 2012); Nicholas De Genova and Ana Y. Ramos-Zayas, *Latino Crossings: Mexicans, Puerto Ricans, and the Politics of Race and Citizenship* (New York: Routledge, 2003). On related debates in Asian American Studies, see, e.g., Jay Caspian Kang, *The Loneliest Americans* (New York: Crown, 2021).

6. For key texts on the urban history of stateside Puerto Ricans in this era, see Lorrin Thomas, *Puerto Rican Citizen: History and Political Identity in Twentieth-Century New York City* (Chicago: University of Chicago Press, 2010); Lorrin Thomas and Aldo Lauria Santiago, *Rethinking the Struggle for Puerto Rican Rights* (New York: Routledge, 2019); Fernández, *Brown in*

the Windy City; Carmen Teresa Whalen, *From Puerto Rico to Philadelphia: Puerto Rican Workers and Postwar Economies* (Philadelphia: Temple University Press, 2001); Johanna Fernández, *The Young Lords: A Radical History* (Chapel Hill: University of North Carolina Press, 2020); Felipe Hinojosa, *Apostles of Change: Latino Radical Politics, Church Occupations, and the Fight to Save the Barrio* (Chicago: University of Chicago Press, 2021); Rose Muzio, *Radical Imagination, Radical Humanity: Puerto Rican Political Activism in New York* (Albany: State University of New York Press, 2017); Sonia Song-Ha Lee, *Building a Latino Civil Rights Movement: Puerto Ricans, African Americans, and the Pursuit of Racial Justice in New York City* (Chapel Hill: University of North Carolina Press, 2016); Vanessa Rosa, "Colonial *Projects*: Public Housing and the Management of Puerto Ricans in New York City, 1945–1970," in *Critical Dialogues in Latinx Studies: A Reader*, ed. Ana Y. Ramos-Zayas and Mérida M. Rúa (New York: New York University Press, 2021), 186–96.

7. Barber, *Latino City*.

8. Barber.

9. Eduardo A. Contreras, *Latinos and the Liberal City: Politics and Protest in San Francisco* (Philadelphia: University of Pennsylvania Press, 2019); Fernández, *Young Lords*, 132; Padilla, *Latino Ethnic Consciousness*.

10. Beltrán, *Trouble with Unity*, 19, 127; Milagros Ricourt and Ruby Danta, *Hispanas de Queens: Latino Panethnicity in a New York City Neighborhood* (Ithaca, NY: Cornell University Press, 2002). Or "Latinismo" as Felix Padilla defined it: Padilla, *Latino Ethnic Consciousness*; Beltrán, *Trouble with Unity*, 157.

11. Cathy Booth, "Miami: The Capital of Latin America," *Time*, June 24, 2001. The literature on U.S. intervention in Latin America is vast. A good starting point on U.S. Latines is Juan González, *Harvest of Empire: A History of Latinos in America* (New York: Penguin Books, 2022). See also Yveline Alexis, *Haiti Fights Back: The Life and Legacy of Charlemagne Péralte* (New Brunswick, NJ: Rutgers University Press, 2021); Alan McPherson, *The Invaded: How Latin Americans and Their Allies Fought and Ended U.S. Occupations* (Oxford: Oxford University Press, 2014).

12. On the "decade of the Hispanic" and the term's popularization, see Frank del Olmo, "Latino 'Decade' Moves into '90s" *Los Angeles Times*, December 14, 1989, and Mora, *Making Hispanics*; Juan Flores, *From Bomba to Hip Hop: Puerto Rican Culture and Latino Identity* (New York: Columbia University Press, 2000), 149; "The Puerto Rican Exception" is a chapter in neoconservative Linda Chavez's book *Out of the Barrio: Toward a New Politics of Hispanic Assimilation* (New York: Basic Books, 1991), 139–59. Flores discusses it in *From Bomba to Hip Hop*, 155. The classic "culture of poverty" text was Oscar Lewis, *La Vida: A Puerto Rican Family in the Culture of Poverty—San Juan and New York* (New York: Random House, 1965). See also Whalen, *From Puerto Rico to Philadelphia*, 198–206, 238–41. Flores cites the work of Nathan Glaser, Daniel Patrick Moynihan, and Oscar Lewis. Flores, *From Bomba to Hip Hop*, 154–55.

13. Flores, *From Bomba to Hip Hop*, 156, 164.

14. De Genova and Ramos-Zayas, *Latino Crossings*.

15. There were also substantial Puerto Rican communities in the Midwest. Gilberto Marzán, Andrés Torres, and Andrew Luecke, "Puerto Rican Outmigration from New York City: 1995–2000," Centro de Estudios Puertorriqueños, Hunter College, Policy Report 2, no. 2 (Fall 2008), 3; Carmen Teresa Whalen, "Colonialism, Citizenship, and the Making of the Puerto Rican Diaspora," in *The Puerto Rican Diaspora: Historical Perspectives*, ed. Carmen Teresa Whalen and Victor Vázquez Hernández (Philadelphia: Temple University Press, 2005), 1–42, quote at 2; Marzán, Torres, and Luecke, "Puerto Rican Outmigration from New York City," 2.

16. U.S. Census, "Table 33. New York—Race and Hispanic Origin for Selected Large Cities and Other Places: Earliest Census to 1990," 2005, https://www2.census.gov/library/working

-papers/2005/demo/pop-twps0076/nytab.pdf. On New York suburbanization, see Rosalyn Fraad Baxandall and Elizabeth Ewen, *Picture Windows: How the Suburbs Happened* (New York: Basic Books, 2000).

17. On Puerto Ricans in the urban crisis, see Thomas, *Puerto Rican Citizen*; Thomas and Lauria Santiago, *Rethinking the Struggle for Puerto Rican Rights*; Fernández, *Brown in the Windy City*; Whalen, *From Puerto Rico to Philadelphia*; Fernández, *Young Lords*; Hinojosa, *Apostles of Change*; Muzio, *Radical Imagination, Radical Humanity*; Lee, *Building a Latino Civil Rights Movement*; Rosa, "Colonial *Projects*." On the vast literature on African American migration to cities, see Isabel Wilkerson, *The Warmth of Other Suns: The Epic Story of America's Great Migration* (New York: Vintage Books, 2011); Donna Jean Murch, *Living for the City: Migration, Education, and the Rise of the Black Panther Party in Oakland, California* (Chapel Hill: University of North Carolina, 2010); Thomas J. Sugrue, *The Origins of the Urban Crisis: Race and Inequality in Postwar Detroit* (Princeton, NJ: Princeton University Press, 2005).

18. My arguments here—that structural anti-Black racism shaped the experiences of Puerto Ricans and that Puerto Ricans shared many experiences with African Americans in northeastern cities during the crisis era—are not incompatible with scholars' findings that Latines, including Puerto Ricans, have also perpetuated various forms of anti-Blackness, directed at Afro-Latines and African Americans. See Tanya Katerí Hernández, *Racial Innocence: Unmasking Latino Anti-Black Bias and the Struggle for Equality* (New York: Beacon Press, 2022).

19. A. K. Sandoval-Strausz, *Barrio America: How Latino Immigrants Saved the American City* (New York: Basic Books, 2019). It bears repeating that poverty, racialized disinvestment, and segregation in U.S. cities have continued into our contemporary era of gentrification. The end of the urban crisis era in the mid-1990s did not bring an end to all of the defining elements of that crisis.

20. U.S. Census, "Persons of Spanish Origin in the United States: 1979," 13; Douglas S. Massey and Nancy A. Denton, "Residential Segregation of Mexicans, Puerto Ricans, and Cubans in Selected U.S. Metropolitan Areas," *Social Science Research* 73, no. 2 (January 1989): 73, 77.

21. Anna M. Santiago and George Galster, "Puerto Rican Segregation in the United States: Cause or Consequence of Economic Status?," *Social Problems* 42, no. 3 (August 1995): 361–89, at 376. Puerto Rican and Black segregation from each other was unusually high in Chicago: Massey and Denton, "Residential Segregation," 75–76. See also De Genova and Ramos-Zayas, *Latino Crossings*, 51.

22. Frank D. Bean and Marta Tienda, *The Hispanic Population of the United States* (New York: Russell Sage Foundation, 1987), 176–77. Interestingly, the "Puerto Rican exception" of higher segregation from white people than Black people disappeared in places like Miami, Chicago, and Los Angeles, where Puerto Ricans were not the main Latine group. "This pattern is consistent with the idea that Anglos see all Hispanics as members of the locally dominant group no matter what their ethnic background, and react to them on that basis." Massey and Denton, "Residential Segregation," 76.

23. U.S. Commission on Civil Rights, "Puerto Ricans in the Continental United States: An Uncertain Future," October 1976, 52, 57, 59, 64, 61, https://files.eric.ed.gov/fulltext/ED132227.pdf.

24. Andres Torres and Frank Bonilla, "Decline within Decline: The New York Perspective," in *Latinos in a Changing U.S. Economy: Comparative Perspectives on Growing Inequality*, ed. Rebecca Morales and Frank Bonilla (Newbury Park, CA: Sage Publications, 1993), 85–108, at 96.

25. Whalen, *From Puerto Rico to Philadelphia*, 206.

26. Puerto Rican Forum, "A Study of Poverty Conditions in the New York Puerto Rican Community," 1970, ii, 1, 41; Lee, *Building a Latino Civil Rights Movement*, 46–52.

27. Clara Rodríguez, "Economic Factors Affecting Puerto Ricans in New York," in History Task Force, Centro de Estudios Puertorriqueños, *Labor Migration under Capitalism: The Puerto Rican Experience* (New York: Monthly Review Press, 1979), 197–221, at 205; Lee, *Building a Latino Civil Rights Movement*, 215; U.S. Commission on Civil Rights, "Puerto Ricans in the Continental United States," 8, 9, 44, qtd. in Julio Morales, *Puerto Rican Poverty and Migration: We Just Had to Try Elsewhere* (New York: Praeger, 1986), 22, 39.

28. Puerto Rican Forum, "Study of Poverty Conditions," 1; Nicholas Lemann, "The Other Underclass," *Atlantic*, December 1991.

29. Quoted in Morales, *Puerto Rican Poverty and Migration*, 39 (emphasis added to highlight the level of surprise implicit in the assertion); Andrés Torres, *Between Melting Pot and Mosaic: African Americans and Puerto Ricans in the New York Political Economy* (Philadelphia: Temple University Press, 1995), 5.

30. Nelson Denis, *War against All Puerto Ricans: Revolution and Terror in America's Colony* (New York: Nation Books, 2015); Jesús Colón, *A Puerto Rican in New York, and Other Sketches* (New York: International Publishers, 1991), 499–501; Pedro Pietri, "Puerto Rican Obituary," Poetry Foundation, https://www.poetryfoundation.org/poems/58396/puerto-rican-obituary.

31. Sidney W. Mintz, *Worker in the Cane: A Puerto Rican Life History* (New York: W. W. Norton, 1974). On migrants' efforts to "flee the cane," see Gina M. Pérez, *The Near Northwest Side Story: Migration, Displacement, and Puerto Rican Families* (Berkeley: University of California Press, 2004); César J. Ayala and Rafael Bernabe, *Puerto Rico in the American Century: A History since 1898* (Chapel Hill: University of North Carolina Press, 2007), chaps. 5 and 7; James L. Dietz, *Economic History of Puerto Rico: Institutional Change and Capitalist Development* (Princeton, NJ: Princeton University Press, 1986), 99–142; César Ayala, "The Decline of the Plantation Economy and the Puerto Rican Migration of the 1950s," *Latino Studies Journal* 7, no. 1 (Winter 1996): 62–90; Laura Briggs, *Reproducing Empire Race, Sex, Science and U. S. Imperialism in Puerto Rico* (Berkeley: University of California Press, 2003); Ana María García, *La Operación* (1982).

32. Ayala and Bernabe, *Puerto Rico in the American Century*, chap. 9. Note the term *Operation Bootstrap* was not used until 1949. Ramón Grosfoguel, "Migration and Geopolitics in the Caribbean: The Cases of Puerto Rico, Cuba, the Dominican Republic, Haiti, and Jamaica," in *Free Markets, Open Societies, Closed Borders? Trends in International Migration and Immigration Policy in the Americas*, ed. Max J. Castro (Miami: North-South Center Press, 1999), 228; César Ayala, "The Decline of the Plantation Economy and the Puerto Rican Migration of the 1950s," *Latino Studies Journal* 7, no. 1 (Winter 1996): 62–90, at 75; Grosfoguel, "Migration and Geopolitics in the Caribbean"; Ayala, "Decline of the Plantation Economy"; Edgardo Meléndez, *Sponsored Migration: The State and Puerto Rican Postwar Migration to the United States* (Columbus: Ohio State University Press, 2017).

33. Meléndez, *Sponsored Migration*. Meléndez is adamant, however, that individual Puerto Rican emigration began before the state organized to assist it. Grosfoguel, "Migration and Geopolitics in the Caribbean," 228; Meléndez, *Sponsored Migration*, 29, 108–11; Ayala and Bernabe, *Puerto Rico in the American Century*, 194.

34. Whalen, "Colonialism, Citizenship, and the Making of the Puerto Rican Diaspora"; Denis, *War against All Puerto Ricans*, chap. 2; Marilisa Jiménez García, *Side by Side: U.S. Empire, Puerto Rico, and the Roots of American Youth Literature and Culture* (Jackson: University Press of Mississippi, 2021); Meléndez, *Sponsored Migration*, 56–58; Edgardo Meléndez, *The "Puerto Rican Problem" in Postwar New York City: Migrant Incorporation from the U.S. Colonial Periphery* (New Brunswick, NJ: Rutgers University Press, 2023).

35. Cecilia Márquez has demonstrated how the racialization of Latines varied by region and changed over time, and specifically how non-Black Latines in the postwar U.S. South managed to access various forms of privilege through their racialization as distinctly not Black. Cecilia Márquez, *Making the Latino South: A History of Racial Formation* (Chapel Hill: University of North Carolina Press, 2023).

36. Rodríguez, "Economic Factors Affecting Puerto Ricans in New York," 210; C. Wright Mills, Clarence Senior, and Rose Kohn Goldsen, *The Puerto Rican Journey: New York's Newest Migrants* (1950; New York: Russel & Russell, 1967), 87. This idea of Latines being somehow "between" Black and white mistakes socioeconomic indicators for racial formation. Latines are no more "between" Blacks and whites than Asian Americans are somehow "above" white people in the racial hierarchy as a result of their higher median incomes. Each racial category has its own history and construction—there is not simply one type of racism of which different groups experience more or less. Anti–Puerto Rican racism profoundly shaped Dominican experiences in New York City, Ramón Grosfoguel argues in *Colonial Subjects: Puerto Ricans in a Global Perspective* (Berkeley: University of California Press, 2003), chap. 5, written with Chloe S. Georas.

37. Torres, *Between Melting Pot and Mosaic*; Fernández, *Young Lords*, esp. chap. 8; Frederick Douglass Opie, *Upsetting the Apple Cart: Black-Latino Coalitions in New York City from Protest to Public Office* (New York: Columbia University Press, 2015); Lee, *Building a Latino Civil Rights Movement*; Milagros Denis-Rosario, "Asserting Their Rights: Puerto Ricans in Their Quest for Social Justice," *Centro Journal* 24, no. 1 (Spring 2012): 44–67. Pablo "Yoruba" Guzmán, "Before People Called Me a Spic, They Called Me a N———," *Afro-Latin@ Reader: History and Culture in the United States*, ed. Miriam Jiménez Román and Juan Flores (Durham, NC: Duke University Press, 2010), 235–43.

38. Fernández, *Young Lords*, 243; Torres, *Between Melting Pot and Mosaic*, 3; Lee, *Building a Latino Civil Rights Movement.*

39. See Torres, *Between Melting Pot and Mosaic*; Fernández, *Young Lords*, esp. chap. 8; Opie, *Upsetting the Apple Cart*; Denis-Rosario, "Asserting Their Rights"; Thomas and Lauria-Santiago, *Rethinking the Struggle for Puerto Rican Rights*; Muzio, *Radical Imagination, Radical Humanity.* On grassroots connections between Black and Puerto Rican communities in New York City, see Juan Flores, *From Bomba to Hip Hop* and *The Diaspora Strikes Back: Caribeño Tales of Learning and Turning* (New York: Routledge, 2009); *From Mambo to Hip Hop: A South Bronx Tale* (2006).

40. Elizabeth Hinton, *America on Fire: The Untold History of Police Violence and Black Rebellion since the 1960s* (New York: Liveright, 2021); Aaron G. Fountain Jr., "Forgotten Latino Urban Riots and Why They Can Happen Again," *Latino Rebels*, May 6, 2016, https://www.latinorebels.com/2016/05/02/forgotten-latino-urban-riots-and-why-they-can-happen-again/. As I have noted elsewhere, "The diversity of these rebellions is noteworthy. Big cities and small; rust belt and sunbelt; Caribbean Latines, Central Americans, and Chicanos; immigrants, colonial subjects, and U.S. Americans; across the country, and throughout the urban crisis era . . . they were both *widespread* and *persistent*." Llana Barber, "Latine Rebellions and Why They Matter," *American Historian* (December 2021): 30–36. See also Thomas and Lauria-Santiago, *Rethinking the Struggle for Puerto Rican Rights*; Fernández, *Young Lords*; Muzio, *Radical Imagination, Radical Humanity*; Hinojosa, *Apostles of Change.*

41. Muzio, *Radical Imagination, Radical Humanity*; Miguel "Mickey" Melendez, *We Took the Streets: Fighting for Latino Rights with the Young Lords* (New Brunswick, NJ: Rutgers University Press, 2005); Thomas and Lauria-Santiago, *Rethinking the Struggle for Puerto Rican Rights.*

42. Nicholas Lemann, "The Other Underclass," *Atlantic*, December 1991; Francisco L. Rivera-Batiz and Carlos Santiago, *Puerto Ricans in the United States: A Changing Reality* (Washington, DC: National Puerto Rican Coalition, 1994), 28–30. This is true of both mean and median household income per capita.

43. Income here is mean household income per capita. Rivera-Batiz and Santiago, *Puerto Ricans in the United States*, lii, 33–35.

44. Thomas and Lauria-Santiago, *Rethinking the Struggle for Puerto Rican Rights*.

45. Barber, *Latino City*, chap. 6; Max Felker-Kantor, "Latinx Criminality," *Oxford Research Encyclopedia of American History*, June 20, 2022, https://doi.org/10.1093/acrefore/9780199329175.013.651. See also Kelly Lytle Hernández, *City of Inmates: Conquest, Rebellion, and the Rise of Human Caging in Los Angeles, 1771–1965* (Chapel Hill: University of North Carolina Press, 2017); Elana Zilberg, *Space of Detention: The Making of a Transnational Gang Crisis between Los Angeles and San Salvador* (Durham, NC: Duke University Press, 2011).

46. Flores, *From Bomba to Hip Hop*, 156.

47. On the Puerto Rican debt crisis, see the Puerto Rico Syllabus, https://puertoricosyllabus.com; Naomi Klein, *The Battle for Paradise: Puerto Rico Takes on the Disaster Capitalists* (Chicago: Haymarket Books, 2018).

48. Marisol Lebrón and Yarimar Bonilla, eds., *Aftershocks of Disaster: Puerto Rico before and after the Storm* (Chicago: Haymarket Books, 2019); Klein, *The Battle for Paradise*. Frequent English-language coverage of this activism can be found at *Latino Rebels*, https://www.latinorebels.com. Bad Bunny and Bianca Graulau have also drawn attention to this activism with the short documentary *Aquí vive gente*, released as part of the music video for the song "El apagón." For Puerto Rican activism in historical context, see Marisol Lebrón, *Policing Life and Death: Race, Violence, and Resistance in Puerto Rico* (Oakland: University of California Press, 2019); Denis, *War against All Puerto Ricans*.

Chapter Eight

1. The chant translates to "The people, united, will never be defeated!" Ryan Osborne, "'It's Scary': Hundreds Protest Fort Worth's Failure to Join SB4 Lawsuit," *Fort Worth Star-Telegram*, August 1, 2017; Sandra Baker, "Protesters Allege Racism after Fort Worth Council Refuses to Join SB4 Lawsuit," *Fort Worth Star-Telegram*, August 15, 2017; Max Krochmal, "Protesters, the Council and the Many Meanings of Racism," *Fort Worth Star-Telegram*, August 18, 2017.

2. Census 2020 Preliminary Data, accessed via Social Explorer. We use *Latinx* as a substitute for *Hispanic*. All other groups (white, Black, and Asian) are those listed as "Non Hispanic [insert race] Alone." The leading histories of Fort Worth acknowledge but deemphasize the city's nonwhite populations and its regional connections to the histories of Jim Crow and Juan Crow: Ty Cashion, *The New Frontier: A Contemporary History of Fort Worth & Tarrant County* (San Antonio, TX: Tarrant County Historical Society, 2006); Richard F. Selcer, *Fort Worth: A Texas Original!* (Austin: Texas State Historical Association, 2004); Victoria L. Buenger and Walter L. Buenger, *Texas Merchant: Marvin Leonard & Fort Worth*, Kenneth E. Montague Series in Oil and Business History 11 (College Station: Texas A&M University Press, 1998); Julia Kathryn Garrett, *Fort Worth: A Frontier Triumph* (Fort Worth: Texas Christian University Press, 1996); Tarrant County Historical Society, *Fort Worth and Tarrant County: An Historical Guide*, ed. Carol E. Roark (Fort Worth: Texas Christian University Press, 2003). Studies in African American and Mexican American history include Bob Ray Sanders, *Calvin Littlejohn:*

Portrait of a Community in Black and White (Fort Worth: Texas Christian University Press, 2009); Carlos Eliseo Cuéllar, *Stories From the Barrio: A History of Mexican Fort Worth* (Fort Worth: Texas Christian University Press, 2003); Richard F. Selcer, *A History of Fort Worth in Black & White: 165 Years of African-American Life* (Denton: University of North Texas Press, 2015); Cecilia N. Sanchez Hill, "¿Mi tierra, también? Mexican American Civil Rights in Fort Worth, 1940–1990s" (master's thesis, University of Texas at Arlington, 2016); Peter Charles Martinez, "Ready to Run: Fort Worth's Mexicans in Search of Representation, 1960–2000" (PhD diss., University of North Texas, 2017). The classic history of the city is entirely Anglo-centric: Oliver Knight, *Fort Worth, Outpost on the Trinity* (Norman: University of Oklahoma Press, 1953).

3. On the insular, interlocking nature of local political and business leaders and the "Fort Worth Way," see Katie Sherrod, "Who Runs Fort Worth," *D Magazine*, November 1995, https://www.dmagazine.com/publications/d-magazine/1995/november/power-who-runs-fort-worth/.

4. Luke Ranker, "Can United Fort Worth Be a Major Player? This Election May Test Its Strength," *Fort Worth Star-Telegram*, January 14, 2019.

5. Jacob W. Olmstead, *The Frontier Centennial: Fort Worth and the New West* (Lubbock: Texas Tech University Press, 2021). The "waiting room" metaphor is from Dipesh Chakrabarty, *Provincializing Europe: Postcolonial Thought and Historical Difference*, rev. ed. (Princeton, NJ: Princeton University Press, 2007).

6. Cuéllar, *Stories from the Barrio*, 3.

7. "Mexicans Celebrate Their Independence and Aid Red Cross," *Fort Worth Star-Telegram*, September 16, 1917, 8; "100 Strike On New Refinery For More Pay," *Fort Worth Star-Telegram*, August 2, 1919, 1; "6,000 Fort Worth Mexicans Observe Independence Day," *Fort Worth Star-Telegram*, September 17, 1924, 6.

8. "Mexican Idle Less; Protest over Arrests," *Fort Worth Star-Telegram*, May 27, 1924, 8.

9. "Mexicans to Start on Work in Park," *Fort Worth Star-Telegram*, May 9, 1921, 1.

10. Peter Martinez, "Colonia Mexicana: Mexicans Subject to Modern Empire in Fort Worth, Texas," *Journal of South Texas* 33, no. 1 (Spring 2019): 56–72.

11. "A School Building Program, Fort Worth, Texas," February 1930, Billy Sills Archives, Fort Worth Independent School District Administration Building, Fort Worth, TX (private collection).

12. "Mexican Home Solution Near," *Fort Worth Star-Telegram*, May 28, 1939.

13. Marshall Lynam, "GI Forum—It's Hitting Heavy Blows at the Enemy—Prejudice," *Fort Worth Press*, August 19, 1957.

14. Doug Clarke, "California Business Assailed by Chavez," *Fort Worth Star-Telegram*, November 27, 1969.

15. Jim Vachule, "S-T Supplement Assailed At Meeting of CAA," *Fort Worth Star-Telegram*, July 28, 1970.

16. "S-T Supplement Receives Praise," *Fort Worth Star-Telegram*, July 30, 1970.

17. Reinaldo "Renny" Rosas, interview by Caleigh Prewitt and P. J. Theberge, Civil Rights in Black and Brown (CRBB) Oral History Project, https://crbb.tcu.edu/interviews/9/interview-with-renny-rosas; Eva Bonilla, interview by Caleigh Prewitt and P. J. Theberge, CRBB, https://crbb.tcu.edu/interviews/2/interview-with-eva-bonilla; Jose Gonzales, interview by Caleigh Prewitt and P. J. Theberge, CRBB, https://crbb.tcu.edu/interviews/6/interview-with-jose-gonzales; Folder "Business. Organizations—Hispanic Chamber of Commerce," 008-016-405, Tarrant County Archives; Gilbert Garcia and Sam Garcia, *Hispanic Directory: Fort Worth—Tarrant County*, Folder "Cultures—Mexican Americans—Directories, 1983–1984," Tarrant County Archives. Also see Caleigh Prewitt and P. J. Theberge, *¡Viva la raza! Documenting Tarrant County's Mexicano Activism*,

ed. Max Krochmal (Fort Worth: Texas Communities Oral History Project, Texas Christian University, 2013), https://fortworthmexicanoactivism.wordpress.com. See also Arnoldo de León, *Ethnicity in the Sunbelt: Mexican Americans in Houston*, rev. ed. (College Station: Texas A&M University Press, 2001), chaps. 11–12.

18. Decennial Census of the United States, 1970, 1980, 1990, 2000, 2010, and 2020 (preliminary data), Social Explorer and Census.gov.

19. Polytechnic Heights statistics refer to a constant geographic area based on the sum of 2010 census tracts 1035, 1037.01, and 1037.02. Fort Worth's city limits grew over time and are defined according to the contemporary boundaries in each year. For 1970, see Census tracts 35, 37.1, and 37.2.

20. Miss Nell Bratton, ed., "A History of Polytechnic," 1933 (quotations); William Ludwig, "Polytechnic Was a Barren Prairie in 1852," *Handley Herald*, January 21, 2009—both in Folder "Communities—Polytechnic," Subject Files, Tarrant County Archives. See also Donah Tucker, interview by Briana Salas, Fort Worth, November 4, 2021; Buster Alison, interview by Evaliza Fuentes, Fort Worth, November 12, 2021; Estrus Tucker, interview by Lucius Seger, November 16, 2021; Reba Henry, interview by Lucius Seger, Fort Worth, October 18, 2021; Ramon Romero Jr., interview by Evaliza Fuentes, Fort Worth, November 15, 2021, especially 20:30–20:40—all in Memories of Poly Oral History Project, Special Collections, Texas Christian University, and accompanying website (https://memoriesofpoly.wordpress.com) (this beta website was accessed August 13, 2022). See Sara Horsfall, *A Neighborhood Portrait: Polytechnic Heights of Inner City Fort Worth* (Austin, TX: Sunbelt Eakin, 2002); Scott Cummings, *Left Behind in Rosedale: Race Relations and the Collapse of Community Institutions* (Boulder, CO: Westview Press, 1998). See also Becky Nicolaides's discussion in this volume of ethnic Asian and Mexican majority areas.

21. In that same decade (the 1970s), Fort Worth as a whole also experienced a slight *decline* of roughly 8,300 people, even as the Black population increased by 8,900 and the Latinx population grew by roughly 15,000. Put another way, had it not been for the growth of the city's Black and Brown communities, Fort Worth might have lost nearly 10 percent of its population—in the midst of a booming Sunbelt county that grew by 20 percent over the same span.

22. Eric Harrison, "Poly Is . . . but What without Wesleyan?," *Fort Worth Star-Telegram*, May 9, 1982, 1A, 6A, at 6A.

23. Robert V. Camuto, "A Bitter Struggle to Abolish Blight," *Fort Worth Star-Telegram*, August 7, 1989, 1, 6, at 6; Estrus Tucker interview by Seger; Elizabeth Campbell, "Church Plans to Aid Hispanics," *Fort Worth Star-Telegram*, December 1, 1984, 9E; and "Noticia por todos," *Poly Herald* 10 (March 1980 [actually 1981]), Neighborhood Housing Services newsletter, folder "Communities—Polytechnic," Subject Files, Tarrant County Archives. The Spanish is simply horrendous.

24. Henry, interview by Seger. On policing, see Briana Salas, "The Development and Decline of Murder Worth," *Memories of Poly*, https://memoriesofpoly.wordpress.com/murder-worth.

25. Camuto, "Bitter Struggle," 1.

26. Poly's decline and rebound ran countercyclically to Tarrant County as a whole.

27. U.S. Census Bureau, Decennial Census 2000, "Nativity by Citizenship Status," "Place of Birth for the Foreign-Born Population," "Year of Entry for the Foreign-Born Population," and "Hispanic or Latino by Specific Origin."

28. U.S. Census Bureau, Census 2000, "Language Spoken at Home, Population 5 Years and Over," *Profile of Selected Social Characteristics: 2000*, Summary File 3, Matrices P18, P19, P21, P22, P24, P36, P37, P39, P42, PCT8, PCT16, PCT17, and PCT19.

29. Ramon Romero Jr., interview by Evaliza Fuentes, Fort Worth, November 15, 2021, Memories of Poly Oral History Project, 1:30–2:00.

30. Romero interview by Fuentes, 12:00–12:30.

31. Romero interview by Fuentes; "Texas House Member: Biography," Texas House of Representatives, https://house.texas.gov/members/member-page/?district=90.

32. Representative Ramon Romero Jr., "I know my work has only been made possible thanks to the community that raised me . . . ," Facebook, September 15, 2022, 2:08 p.m., https://www.facebook.com/RepRamonRomero.

33. Romero interview by Fuentes, 51:00–51:20.

34. Toni Ruiz, interview by Evaliza Fuentes, Fort Worth, November 24, 2021, Memories of Poly Oral History Project, 20:30–22:00.

35. Giovanni Rojero, interview by Evaliza Fuentes and Max Krochmal, Fort Worth, November 16, 2021, Memories of Poly Oral History Project, 44:20 (first quote), 1:13:08–1:16:23 (second quote), 46:04–48:28 (third and fourth quotes). We use *second-generation* to refer to the U.S.-born children of adult immigrants.

36. Troy Phillips, "Extended Family," *Fort Worth Star-Telegram*, March 17, 2000, 18D; Eric Zarate, "Breakthrough Season—Polytechnic Ready for First Playoff Game in Girls Soccer," *Fort Worth Star-Telegram*, March 15, 2001, 14; Michelle Melendez, "Pick of Ivy League Crop Is Poly Student's Reward," *Fort Worth Star-Telegram*, May 15, 2000, 1.

37. Anna M. Tinsley, "Polytechnic High Students March Forward with Academic Gains," *Fort Worth Star-Telegram*, November 1, 2009, B1.

38. Diane Smith, "Student Activists Join in Protests," *Fort Worth Star-Telegram*, March 28, 2006, B1.

39. Alex Branch and Diane Smith, "Tarrant Students Take to the Streets," *Fort Worth Star-Telegram*, March 29, 2006, A1 (all quotations); "Schools Make Walkout into Chance for Learning," *Fort Worth Star-Telegram*, March 29, 2006, A10.

40. Diane Smith, "Speaking Up—Children of Immigrants Add Their Voices to a Chorus of Change," *Fort Worth Star-Telegram*, April 30, 2006: B1. We borrow "right to be" from Kelly Lytle Hernandez, *City of Inmates: Conquest, Rebellion, and the Rise of Human Caging in Los Angeles, 1771–1965* (Chapel Hill: University of North Carolina Press, 2017).

41. Johnson quoted in Branch and Diane Smith, "Tarrant Students Take to the Streets."

42. Bud Kennedy, "Marching to City Hall Does Little," *Fort Worth Star-Telegram*, March 30, 2006. For one partial exception to the general rule of adult condescension, see city council member Sal Espino, "Making Vital Points," *Fort Worth Star-Telegram*, March 31, 2006, B11.

43. Mercedes Olivera, "2006 Mega-March in Dallas Energized a New Generation of Latinos," *Dallas Morning News*, April 15, 2016, https://www.dallasnews.com/news/2016/04/15/2006-mega-march-in-dallas-energized-a-new-generation-of-latinos/.

44. Diane Smith, "5th-graders' Punishment Investigated," *Fort Worth Star-Telegram*, May 9, 2006, B1.

45. Diane Smith, "Teacher Quits after Probe of Punishment," *Fort Worth Star-Telegram*, August 8, 2006, B1.

46. Diane Smith, "Nearly 15,200 Fort Worth Students Missed Class on 'A Day without Immigrants,'" *Fort Worth Star-Telegram*, February 23, 2017, https://www.star-telegram.com/news/local/fort-worth/article134586229.html; Domingo Ramirez Jr., Diane Smith, and Ryan Osborne, "Students March in Fort Worth in Support of 'Dreamers': 'The School's Got My Back,'" *Fort Worth Star-Telegram*, September 7, 2017, https://www.star-telegram.com/news/local/fort-worth

/article171516952.html; "Cutting Class for a Protest: A Real-World Lesson," editorial, *Fort Worth Star-Telegram*, September 7, 2017, https://www.star-telegram.com/opinion/editorials/article171874987.html.

47. Hanaa' Tameez, "Race and Culture Task Force presents final recommendations for equity to City Council," *Fort Worth Star-Telegram*, December 4, 2018; Luke Ranker, "Fort Worth to Adopt Race and Culture Report, but What's Next?," *Fort Worth Star-Telegram*, December 12, 2018.

48. "Commissioner Devan Allen Statement on 287(g) Vote," Tarrant County, Texas, June 18, 2019, https://www.tarrantcounty.com/en/commissioner-2/news/2019/commissioner-devan-allen-statement-on-287-g--vote.html; Max Krochmal, "Tarrant Sheriff Needs to Give Straight Story on Immigration Program's Costs, Drawbacks," *Fort Worth Star-Telegram*, June 17, https://www.star-telegram.com/opinion/opn-columns-blogs/article231638593.html.

49. See this volume's introduction for an extended discussion of this emerging literature and its historiographical origins.

50. We borrow phrases from Eric R. Wolf, *Europe and the People Without History* (Berkeley: University of California Press, 1982), and David Gutiérrez, *Walls and Mirrors: Mexican Americans, Mexican Immigrants, and the Politics of Ethnicity* (Berkeley: University of California Press, 1995).

51. The classic, if often mischaracterized, formulation of the generational model is Mario T. Garcia, *Mexican Americans: Leadership, Ideology, & Identity, 1930–1960* (New Haven, CT: Yale University Press, 1989). Reviews of the historiography include Pedro A. Cabán, "Moving from the Margins to Where: Three Decades of Latino Studies," *Latino Studies* 1 (2003): 5–35; Alex M. Saragoza, "Recent Chicano Historiography: An Interpretive Essay," *Aztlán* 19 (1990): 1–77. One recent synthesis acknowledges the many continuities tying the Chicano generation to the Mexican American generation: Marc Simon Rodriguez, *Rethinking the Chicano Movement* (New York: Routledge, 2015), 10, 16–17, 23–92. See also Ana Raquel Minian, *Undocumented Lives: The Untold Story of Mexican Migration* (Cambridge, MA: Harvard University Press, 2018), chaps. 5–6, 8. Perhaps no city has experienced as dramatic a demographic and cultural revolution as Houston, where the historical *colonia* comprised just 7 percent of the city's population as late as 1960. By 2020, the Census counted 44.5 percent of its residents as Hispanic or Latino (of all races). Arnoldo de León, *Ethnicity in the Sunbelt*, 147, 235.

52. See, e.g., Abigail Rosas, *South Central Is Home: Race and the Power of Community Investment in Los Angeles* (Stanford, CA: Stanford University Press, 2019); Albert M. Camarillo, "Navigating Segregated Life in America's Racial Borderhoods, 1910s–1950s," *Journal of American History* 100, no. 3 (December 2013): 645–62. For an early articulation of anti-Blackness as foundational, see Frank Wilderson III, "Gramsci's Black Marx: Whither the Slave in Civil Society?," *Social Identities* 9, no. 2 (2003): 225–40. Most works in Latinx urban history center on neighborhoods that were formerly dominated by "white ethnics," with would-be Black residents appearing as distant threats.

53. For the new map, see "Redistricting," City of Fort Worth, https://www.fortworthtexas.gov/government/redistricting. The analysis of the map is our own. Also see Rachel Behrndt, " 'Begrudging Acceptance': Compromise Map Prompts Community Response, Rumors of Possible Candidates," *Fort Worth Report*, March 31, 2022, http://fortworthreport.org/2022/03/31/begrudging-acceptance-compromise-map-prompts-community-response-rumors-of-possible-candidates/. The city mapmakers' cracking of the barrios mirrors a similar practice in Islip, New York, yet Latinx residents of Fort Worth have achieved a greater degree of influence, due to both the community's longevity and the recent grassroots organizing led by UFW. On Islip, see Sugrue's chapter in this volume.

54. The newly elected councilwoman Jeanette Martinez is the body's first Latina member. A "proud daughter of Mexican immigrants," Martinez serves as executive administrator to Roy C. Brooks, a long-serving county commissioner who supported the non-renewal of the Tarrant County's 287(g) immigration enforcement agreement. An African American and the son of a renowned civil rights leader, Brooks serves as an important ally to the city's poor and nonwhite communities, in sharp contrast to his colleague, police union chief Manny Ramirez. Still, Brooks is no outsider to the city's political elite. See "Jeanette Martinez: District 11 City Council Member," City of Fort Worth, https://www.fortworthtexas.gov/government/elected-officials/jeanette-martinez.

Chapter Nine

1. "Mexico en Chicago," editorial, *Correo Mexicano* (Chicago), October 23, 1926.

2. Chicago Field Notes dated June 24, 1926, Manuel Gamio Papers, Bancroft Library, University of California, Berkeley; U.S. Census Bureau, Fifteenth Census of the United States, 1930, table 626, Washington, DC: National Archives and Records Administration, 1930, accessed via Ancestry.com, 1930 United States Federal Census.

3. "Mexico en Chicago."

4. The following are examples of scholarship examining the significance of ethnic restaurants in general and Mexican in particular and the communities they served: José M. Alamillo, *Making Lemonade out of Lemons: Mexican American Labor and Leisure in a California Town, 1880–1960* (Urbana: University of Illinois Press, 2006); M. Bianet Castellanos, "Idealizing Maya Culture: The Politics of Race, Indigeneity, and Immigration Among Maya Restaurant Owners in Southern California," *Diálogo* 18, no. 2 (2015): 67–78; Krishnendu Ray, *The Ethnic Restaurateur* (London: Bloomsbury Publishing, 2016); Jose A. Vasquez-Medina, "'Cooking Mexican': Negotiating Nostalgia in Family-Owned and Small-Scale Mexican Restaurants in the United States," in *Food Across Borders*, ed. E. Melanie DuPuis, Matt Garcia, and Don Mitchell (New Brunswick, NJ: Rutgers University Press, 2017), 64–78.

5. Meredith E. Abarca, "*Charlas Culinarias*: Mexican Women Speak from Their Public Kitchens," *Food and Foodways* 15, nos. 3–4 (2007): 183–212.

6. Jeffrey M. Pilcher, *Planet Taco: A Global History of Mexican Food* (New York: Oxford University Press, 2017); Jeffrey M. Pilcher, "Who Chased Out the 'Chili Queens'? Gender, Race, and Urban Reform in San Antonio, Texas, 1880–1943," *Food and Foodways* 16, no. 3 (2008): 173–200. See also the introduction to the then new journal *Global Food History*, in which the founding coeditors Katarzyna Cwiertka, Megan Elias, and Jeffrey Pilcher argue for the importance of looking at food history writ large and ensuring scholarly cross-pollination. By ignoring the work of scholars outside of history who are working on "similar problems in other times and places," scholars practice a "provincialism that duplicates efforts and stifles progress." Katarzyna J. Cwiertka, Megan J. Elias, and Jeffrey M. Pilcher, "Editorial Introduction: Writing Global Food History," *Global Food History* 1, no. 1 (2015): 5–12.

7. Lori A. Flores, "The Career of Chef Zarela Martinez and a Changing Mexican Foodscape in New York City, 1981–2011," *Food, Culture & Society* 26, no. 2 (2021): 241–64.

8. Natalia Molina, *A Place at the Nayarit: How a Mexican Restaurant Nourished a Community* (Oakland: University of California Press, 2022), 25.

9. Molina, 96.

10. Molina, 10.

11. Molina, 8.

12. Molina, 8.

13. Molina, 134.

14. Molina, 10.

15. Molina, 12.

16. Molina, 10.

17. Molina, 162.

18. Molina, 124.

19. Molina, 85.

20. Molina, 38.

21. Record Group 85, Records of the Immigration and Naturalization Service, microfilm roll 76, Bureau of the Census, Fifteenth Census of the United States, 1930 (Washington, DC: National Archives and Records Administration, 1930), table 626, accessed via Ancestry.com, 1930 U.S. Federal Census; "El Puerto de Veracruz advertisement," *Noticia Mundial* (Chicago), September 16, 1927. Drury worked as a reporter at the *Los Angeles Record* before returning to Chicago to work at the *Daily News*. For more on the relationship between the Mexican community in Chicago and Hull House, see Cheryl Ganz and Margaret Strobel, *Pots of Promise: Mexicans and Pottery at Hull-House, 1920–40* (Urbana: University of Illinois Press, Chicago, 2004). The City of Chicago technically recognizes community areas and not neighborhoods, but many Chicagoans ignore city boundaries and refer to neighborhood instead. For example, the New City community area is known as the neighborhood of Back of the Yards. I use the terms *neighborhood* and *community area* interchangeably in this chapter.

22. Miranda Zarzuela Program, 1930, Box 18, Drury-Neville Collection, 552:9, Newberry Library; advertisement for El Foco Rojo, *Mexico* (Chicago), January 7, 1927; advertisement for El Porvenir Restaurant, *La Noticia Mundial*, October 16, 1927, 5; "Un auto atropelló a un agente de La Prensa" *La Prensa*, June 8, 1932. The *La Prensa* article mentions an accident in front of Venus Restaurant and that the establishment is owned by Miranda.

23. For more on the various Mexican neighborhoods in Chicago, see Michael Innis-Jiménez, *Steel Barrio: The Great Mexican Migration to South Chicago, 1915–1940* (New York: New York University Press, 2013).

24. Robert C. Jones and Louis R. Wilson, *The Mexican in Chicago* (Chicago: Comity Committee of the Chicago Church Federation, 1931), 10; Robert Shackleton and Herbert Pullinger, *The Book of Chicago* (Philadelphia: Penn Publishing Co., 1920), 320. For more on the relationship between the Mexican community in Chicago and Hull House, see Ganz and Strobel, *Pots of Promise*.

25. Advertisement for El Puerto de Veracruz, *La Noticia Mundial* (Chicago), September 16, 1927, 5; El Puerto de Veracruz, business card, 1930, Drury-Neville Collection, Newberry Library.

26. *La Prensa* (San Antonio, TX), August 9, 1931; Xavier Mondragon, "Macaroni versus Chile Con Carne!," *La Prensa de San Antonio* (TX), February 7, 1932. For more on the influence of *La Prensa* as a national newspaper, see Melita M. Garza, *They Came to Toil: Newspaper Representations of Mexicans and Immigrants in the Great Depression* (Austin: University of Texas Press, 2018), 39.

27. Bruce Grant, "Little Mexico in Chicago! Gayety, Color and Strumming Guitars," *Chicago Sunday Times*, May 26, 1935, in *Chicago Foreign Language Press Survey*, 1935, ed. Works Progress Administration, Newberry Library Archives, Chicago.

28. John Drury, *Dining in Chicago* (New York: John Day Co., 1931); Unpublished notes, 1930, Box 16, Folder 522, Drury-Neville Collection, Newberry Library.

29. Tour flyer, 1938, Drury-Neville Collection, Newberry Library.

30. Drury, *Dining in Chicago*, 71.

31. Vicki L. Ruiz, "Citizen Restaurant: American Imaginaries, American Communities," *American Quarterly* 60, no. 1 (March 2008): 1–21.

32. Molina, *Place at the Nayarit*, 68.

33. Carlos Cortéz, "Requiem for a Street," in *Crystal-Gazing the Amber Fluid and Other Wobbly Poems* (Chicago: Charles H. Kerr, 1990), 27–29.

34. Deborah Kanter, *Chicago Católico: Making Catholic Parishes Mexican* (Urbana: University of Illinois Press, 2020). For example, Kanter establishes that Chicago-area Catholic churches often served as mediating institutions among different ethnicities.

Chapter Ten

1. Emmett Auglin, Mr. X field report (L402), 1; Author unknown, Jose Mendes field report (D186), both in box 1, folder 13, Paul Radin Papers, 1934–1936, San Francisco History Center, San Francisco Public Library. Staff with the San Francisco Relief Administration often attempted to maintain anonymity. Auglin did not disclose the individual's name and just identified him as Mr. X.

2. This discussion uses *LatinX* conceptually and interpretatively. Capitalizing the *X* moves us beyond simply replacing the *o/a* in *Latino/a* with an *x* in the name of gender neutrality and inclusivity. The *X* points us to locations and temporalities unbounded by identities or present-day social categories.

3. *Latine* is a gender-neutral term for people of Latin American descent; *Latino/a/X studies* refers to the academic field. *Latine* and *Latinx* share a similar commitment to gender inclusivity but differ in their provenance, linguistic sensibilities, and currency in the U.S. academy. See "Keywords: A Critical Reflection," Latinx/e/a/o Studies Library Guide, Latin American Library, Tulane University, last updated July 21, 2023, https://libguides.tulane.edu/latinos/keywords; Paloma Celis Carbajal, "From Hispanic to Latine: Hispanic Heritage Month and the Ties That Bind Us," New York Public Library (blog), 2020, https://www.nypl.org/blog/2020/09/29/hispanic-heritage-month-terms-bind-us.

4. See, e.g., Nicole Guidotti-Hernández, "Affective Communities and Millennial Desires: Latinx, or Why My Computer Won't Recognize Latina/o," *Cultural Dynamics* 29, no. 3 (2017): 141–59; Salvador Vidal-Ortiz and Juliana Martínez, "Latinx Thoughts: Latinidad with an X," *Latino Studies* 16, no. 3 (2018): 384–95.

5. Ed Morales, "Why I Embrace the Term Latinx," June 30, 2018, https://edmorales.net/2018/06/30/why-i-embrace-the-term-latinx/; Nicholas De Genova, "Latino Studies, Latino/a/X Futures: Provocations toward a Prospectus," *Cultural Dynamics* 31, nos. 1–2 (2019): 16, 24.

6. Claudia Milian, *LatinX* (Minneapolis: University of Minnesota Press, 2019), 4.

7. Multiple disciplinary analyses inform this assessment, including Gary R. Mormino and George E. Pozzetta, *The Immigrant World of Ybor City: Italians and Their Latin Neighbors in Tampa, 1885–1985* (Urbana: University of Illinois Press, 1987); James R. Barrett and David Roediger, "Inbetween Peoples: Race, Nationality, and the 'New Immigrant' Working Class," *Journal of American Ethnic History* 16, no. 3 (Spring 1997): 3–44; Walter Mignolo, *The Idea of Latin America* (Malden: Blackwell Publishers, 2005); Cybelle Fox and Thomas A. Guglielmo, "Defining America's Racial Boundaries: Blacks, Mexicans, and European Immigrants, 1890–1945," *American Journal of Sociology* 118, no. 2 (September 2012): 327–79; Claudia Milian, "Latin," in *Keywords*

for Southern Studies, ed. Scott Romine and Jennifer Rae Greeson (Athens: University of Georgia Press, 2016), 179–88.

8. Kirsten Silva Gruesz, "The Gulf of Mexico System and the 'Latinness' of New Orleans," *American Literary History* 18, no. 3 (Autumn 2006): 490.

9. For a short introduction to postwar metropolitan history, see Amanda Seligman, "Producing the North American Metropolitan Landscape," *Journal of Urban History* 34, no. 4 (May 2008): 695–703; Andrew Needham and Allen Dieterich-Ward, "Beyond the Metropolis: Metropolitan Growth and Regional Transformation in Postwar America," *Journal of Urban History* 35, no. 7 (October 2009): 944–45, 960.

10. Dependency, world-systems, and postcolonial theories have variously guided Latin American historians' assessments. For introductions to these frameworks, see Louis A. Pérez Jr., "Dependency," *Journal of American History* 77, no. 1 (June 1990): 133–42; Gilbert M. Joseph, "Close Encounters: Toward a New Cultural History of U.S.–Latin American Relations," in *Close Encounters of Empire: Writing the Cultural History of U.S.–Latin American Relations*, ed. Gilbert. M. Joseph, Catherine C. LeGrand, and Ricardo D. Salvatore (Durham, NC: Duke University Press, 1998), 3–46; Fernando Coronil, "After Empire: Reflections on Imperialism from the Américas," in *Imperial Formations*, ed. Ann Laura Stoler, Carole McGranahan, and Peter C. Perdue (Santa Fe, NM: SAR Press, 2007), 241–71.

11. Coronil, "After Empire," 242; Thomas Bender, "Globalization: City vs. Nation-State?: Responses to Question of U.S. Empire and Urban History," *NeoAmericanist* 5, no. 1 (Winter 2010): 13.

12. Milian, *LatinX*, 6.

13. De Genova, "Latino Studies," 17.

14. Paul F. Lachance, "The 1809 Immigration of Saint-Domingue Refugees to New Orleans: Reception, Integration, and Impact," *Louisiana History* 29, no. 2 (Spring 1988): 109–12; Jennifer Spear, *Race, Sex, and Social Order in Early New Orleans* (Baltimore: Johns Hopkins University Press, 2009), 184; Raushana Johnson, "From Saint-Domingue to Dumaine Street: One Family's Journeys from the Haitian Revolution to the Great Migration," *Journal of African American History* 102, no. 4 (Fall 2017): 429–30.

15. The inclination to include Haitians in explorations of Latina/e/o/x America presents a new and important direction in Latino/a/X studies. See, e.g., Sophie Maríñez, "The Quisqueya Diaspora: The Emergence of Latina/o Literature from Hispaniola," in *The Cambridge History of Latina/o American Literature*, ed. John Morán González and Laura Lomas (Cambridge: Cambridge University Press, 2018), 561–81; Fredo Rivera, "Precarity + Excess in the *Latinopolis*: Miami as Erzulie," *Cultural Dynamics* 31, nos. 1–2 (2019): 62–80.

16. The 1810 census counted 17,742 residents; the 1820 census enumerated 27,176. Historians have used municipal and parish records to estimate the number of migrants. See Campbell Gibson, U.S. Census Bureau, "Population of the 100 Largest Cities and Other Urban Places in the United States, 1790–1990" (Working Paper No. POP-WP027, June 1998), tables 4 and 5, https://www.census.gov/library/working-papers/1998/demo/POP-twps0027.html; Lachance, "1809 Immigration," 112, 125–27; and Spear, *Race, Sex, and Social Order*, 184.

17. Spear, *Race, Sex, and Social Order*, 180; Benjamin Henry Latrobe, *Impressions Respecting New Orleans* (1818–1820), cited in Spear, *Race, Sex, and Social Order*, 180, 294.

18. Nathalie Dessens, "The Saint-Domingue Refugees and the Preservation of Gallic Culture in Early American New Orleans," *French Colonial History* 8 (2007): 57–59.

19. William Claiborne to Robert Smith, August 5, 1809, in Lachance, "1809 Immigration," 115.

20. Silva Gruesz, "Gulf of Mexico System," 469.

21. Michel Gobat, *Empire by Invitation: William Walker and Manifest Destiny in Central America* (Cambridge, MA: Harvard University Press, 2018), 3–8, 164, 190–91.

22. Gobat, 152–53, 165–70.

23. "No Such Word as Fail," *El Nicaragüense*, September 6, 1856, cited in Gobat, *Empire by Invitation*, 152.

24. Oscar Lewis, *San Francisco: Mission to Metropolis* (Berkeley, CA: Howell-North Books, 1966).

25. Edward Dallam Melillo, *Strangers on Familiar Soil: Rediscovering the Chile-California Connection* (New Haven, CT: Yale University Press, 2015), 2–3.

26. Susan Lee Johnson, *Roaring Camp: The Social World of the California Gold Rush* (New York: W. W. Norton & Co., 2000); Marilyn S. Johnson, *The Second Gold Rush: Oakland and the East Bay in World War II* (Berkeley: University of California Press, 1993); Robert O. Self, *American Babylon, Race and the Struggle for Postwar Oakland* (Princeton, NJ: Princeton University Press, 2003).

27. Melillo, *Chile-California Connection*, 69–70.

28. Bender, "Globalization," 13.

29. Jason M. Colby, *The Business of Empire: United Fruit, Race, and U.S. Expansion in Central America* (Ithaca, NY: Cornell University Press, 2011), 53.

30. See, e.g., Gerald Poyo, "The Cuban Experience in the United States, 1865–1940: Migration, Community, and Identity," *Cuban Studies* 21 (1991): 24–25.

31. John McQuaid, "Link between Honduras, N.O. Has Rich History," *New Orleans Times-Picayune*, February 24, 1991, A-31.

32. Glenn A. Chambers, *From the Banana Zones to the Big Easy: West Indian and Central American Immigration to New Orleans, 1910–1940* (Baton Rouge: Louisiana State University Press, 2019), 11.

33. McQuaid, "Link between Honduras, N.O.," A-32.

34. "Nueva Orleans donde comienza la America hispana" and "New Orleans Gateway to Latin America," taglines, *La Voz Latina* and *The Latin Voice*, September 13, 1935, 1.

35. Colby, *Business of Empire*; Luis E. Henao, *The Hispanics of Louisiana* (New Orleans: Latin American Apostolate, 1982), 17.

36. Daniel E. Bender and Jana K. Lipman, eds., *Making the Empire Work: Labor and United States Imperialism* (New York: New York University Press, 2015).

37. Chambers, *From the Banana Zones*, 129, 132.

38. Julie Weise, "Mexican Nationalisms, Southern Racisms: Mexicans and Mexican Americans in the U.S. South, 1908–1939," *American Quarterly* 60, no. 3 (September 2008): 749, 751.

39. Chambers, *From the Banana Zones*, 13, 134.

40. Mormino and Pozzetta, *Immigrant World of Ybor City*, 51, 55; Sarah McNamara, "Borderland Unionism: Latina Activism in Ybor City and Tampa, Florida, 1935–1937," *Journal of American Ethnic History* 38, no. 4 (Summer 2019): 11.

41. Milian, *LatinX*, 2.

42. Lorrin Thomas, *Puerto Rican Citizen: History and Political Identity in Twentieth-Century New York City* (Chicago: University of Chicago Press, 2010), 27–28.

43. Mormino and Pozzetta, *Immigrant World of Ybor City*, 10.

44. Nancy Raquel Mirabal, "Telling Silences and Making Community: Afro-Cubans and African-Americans in Ybor City and Tampa, 1899–1915," in *Between Race and Empire: African-Americans and Cubans before the Cuban Revolution*, ed. Lisa Brock and Digna Castañeda Fuertes (Philadelphia: Temple University Press, 1998), 51.

45. Mormino and Pozzetta, *Immigrant World of Ybor City*, 241; Barrett and Roediger, "Inbetween Peoples," 8–9, 29.

46. Mormino and Pozzetta, *Immigrant World of Ybor City*, 11, 91.

47. For my earlier treatment of latinidad, see my *Latinos and the Liberal City: Politics and Protest in San Francisco* (Philadelphia: University of Pennsylvania Press, 2019), 11–12, 41–43, 113–17.

48. Gary R. Mormino, "The Reader and the Worker: *Los Lectores* and the Culture of Cigarmaking in Cuba and Florida," *International Labor & Working-Class History* 54 (Fall 1998): 11; McNamara, "Borderland Unionism," 11.

49. A. K. Sandoval-Strausz, "Latino Landscapes: Postwar Cities and the Transnational Origins of a New Urban America," *Journal of American History* 101, no. 3 (December 2014): 808.

50. Mormino and Pozzetta, *Immigrant World of Ybor City*, 10; National Park Service, U.S. Department of Interior, "El Centro Español de Tampa," in *The American Latino Heritage Discover Our Shared Heritage Travel Itinerary*, https://www.nps.gov/nr/travel/american_latino_heritage/El_Centro_Espanol_de_Tampa.html.

51. Mormino, "Reader and the Worker," 3.

52. Milian, *LatinX*, 21.

53. Joseph P. Sánchez, "The National Park Service and American Latino Heritage," n.d., https://www.nps.gov/nr/ travel/american_latino_heritage/National_Park_Service_and_American_Latino_Heritage_Over_Time.html.

54. National Park Service, "Vieux Carré Historic District New Orleans, Louisiana," https://www.nps.gov/nr/travel/american_latino_heritage/Vieux_Carre_Historic_District.html.

Chapter Eleven

1. *Zig-Zag Libre*, March 23, 1963, Exile Periodicals Collection, Cuban Heritage Collection (hereafter CHC), University of Miami, Coral Gables, FL.

2. Seymour Topping, "Soviet Warns Washington on Attacks in Caribbean," *New York Times*, March 30, 1963; U.S. Department of State, *Foreign Relations of the United States, 1961–1963*, vol. 11, *Cuban Missile Crisis and Aftermath* (Washington, DC: Government Printing Office, 1996), 732, https://history.state.gov/historicaldocuments/frus1961-63v11/d300; Tad Szulc, "British Capture 17 Cuban Exiles and Raiding Boat," *New York Times*, April 2, 1963.

3. "Collins Suggests New Cuba," *Miami Herald*, March 10, 1963.

4. "Cosas de nuestro exilio," *Zig-Zag Libre*, March 23, 1963, Exile Periodicals Collection, CHC.

5. Lilia Fernández, *Brown in the Windy City: Mexicans and Puerto Ricans in Postwar Chicago* (Chicago: University of Chicago Press, 2012), 26.

6. Fernández, *Brown in the Windy City*, 24. Fernández's insights complement those of Carmen Teresa Whalen, who notes that Puerto Rico's shift from agriculture to industry urbanized many Puerto Ricans both at home and as they moved to cities in the continental United States. American imperialism thus drove these processes and, as Fernández notes, reracialization and exploitation in American cities. See Carmen Teresa Whalen, *From Puerto Rico to Philadelphia: Puerto Rican Workers and Postwar Economies* (Philadelphia: Temple University Press, 2001), 2.

7. Llana Barber, *Latino City: Immigration and Urban Crisis in Lawrence, Massachusetts, 1945–2000* (Chapel Hill: University of North Carolina Press, 2017), 54.

8. Barber, *Latino City*, 57.

9. A. K. Sandoval-Strausz, *Barrio America: How Latino Immigrants Saved the American City* (New York: Basic Books 2019), 132, 144–47, 258–59.

10. Sandoval-Strausz, *Barrio America*, 235–42.

11. Paul A. Kramer, "The Geopolitics of Mobility: Immigration Policy and American Global Power in the Long Twentieth Century," *American Historical Review* 123, no. 2 (April 2018): 396–99.

12. Jesse Hoffnung-Garskof, "The Immigration Reform Act of 1965," in *The Familiar Made Strange: American Icons and Artifacts after the Transnational Turn*, ed. Brooke L. Blower and Mark Philip Bradley (Ithaca, NY: Cornell University Press, 2015), 128–29.

13. Some examples include Meredith Oyen, *The Diplomacy of Migration: Transnational Lives and the Making of U.S.-Chinese Relations in the Cold War* (Ithaca, NY: Cornell University Press, 2015); Carl J. Bon Tempo, *Americans at the Gate: The United States and Refugees during the Cold War* (Princeton, NJ: Princeton University Press, 2008); Maddalena Marinari, Madeline Y. Hsu, and María Cristina García, eds., *A Nation of Immigrants Reconsidered: U.S. Society in an Age of Restriction, 1924–1965* (Urbana: University of Illinois Press, 2019).

14. Influential histories of the U.S.-Mexico borderlands and the Chicano movement have detailed the influence of the Cold War on Latinos. Geraldo L. Cadava shows how the Cold War became entwined with longer-standing patterns in the Arizona-Mexico borderlands area and older U.S.-Mexico relations. Cold War anxieties could help address the growing nativism in Arizona and maintain both U.S. and Mexican governments' interests regarding the Bracero Program. The Cuban Revolution could foster fears of potential migrants from Mexico, whereas Sonoran students could draw inspiration from it even while critiquing Castro's repression of democracy. Likewise, David Montejano's study of the Chicano Movement in San Antonio, Texas, showed how many of the movement's members status as Vietnam veterans helped mold their activism, as did the inspiration they drew from Cuba's revolution—an association that drew pointed rebukes and accusations of communism from local critics. See Geraldo L. Cadava, *Standing on Common Ground: The Making of a Sunbelt Borderland* (Cambridge, MA: Harvard University Press, 2013); David Montejano, *Quixote's Soldiers: A Local History of the Chicano Movement, 1966–1981* (Austin: University of Texas Press, 2010).

15. This is not to suggest that the field of Latino urban history does not already have some engagement with the effects of the Cold War. Barber notes that the patterns she describes in relation to Puerto Ricans and Dominicans in Lawrence were experienced by other Latin American nations, particularly during the Cold War and its aftermath, thus making the "harvest of empire" framework applicable in other situations. See Barber, *Latino City*, 69. Sandoval-Strausz draws on Mary Dudziak's *Cold War Civil Rights: Race and the Image of American Democracy* (Princeton, NJ: Princeton University Press, 2000) to recount how concerns about Soviet propaganda helped move policymakers toward the construction of a new immigration regime that went beyond the restrictions of the National Origins Act quota system. See Sandoval-Strausz, *Barrio America*, 134.

16. Raymond A. Mohl, "Miami: The Ethnic Cauldron," in *Sunbelt Cities: Politics and Growth since World War II*, ed. Richard M. Bernard and Bradley R. Rice (Austin: University of Texas Press, 1983), 62–63. In 1960 the *Herald* reported that the growth Dade's suburban areas had "rocketed to the nation's top at 158 per cent." "Metro Government: What It Costs . . . And Will Cost . . . And Why," *Miami Herald*, October 18, 1960.

17. N. D. B. Connolly, *A World More Concrete: Real Estate and the Remaking of Jim Crow South Florida* (Chicago: University of Chicago Press, 2014), 249.

18. Bon Tempo, *Americans at the Gate*, 122.

19. Alejandro Portes and Ariel C. Armony, *The Global Edge: Miami in the Twenty-First Century* (Oakland: University of California Press, 2018), 66.

20. Lars Schoultz, *That Infernal Little Cuban Republic: The United States and the Cuban Revolution* (Chapel Hill: University of North Carolina Press, 2009), 91.

21. Schoultz, *That Infernal Little Cuban Republic*, 118.

22. Schoultz, 145–48.

23. Bon Tempo, *Americans at the Gate*, 109.

24. Bon Tempo, *Americans at the Gate*, 115–16.

25. María de los Angeles Torres, *In the Land of Mirrors: Cuban Exile Politics in the United States* (Ann Arbor: University of Michigan Press, 1999), 72.

26. García, *Havana USA*, 13.

27. Tracy S. Voorhees, "Report to the President of the United States on the Cuban Refugee Problem," 1961, Folder T. S. Voorhees President's Representative for Cuban Refugees—Documents—Reports—TSV Final of Jan 18, 1961, Box P, Tracy S. Voorhees Papers (hereafter Voorhees Papers), Special Collections and University Archives, Rutgers University, New Brunswick, NJ.

28. David Kraslow, "Commission to Assist in Handling Refugees," *Miami Herald*, October 25, 1960.

29. Juanita Greene, "New Group to Aid Cuban Refugees," *Miami Herald*, October 12, 1960.

30. Greene and Jones, "Cubans in Exile, Who Can Help?," *Miami Herald*, October 2, 1960.

31. The specific connections and the logic by which Kennedy administration officials justified this involvement, as well as the long-term consequences of these policy choices, are at the core of my recent monograph. See Mauricio Castro, *Only a Few Blocks to Cuba: Cold War Refugee Policy, the Cuban Diaspora, and the Transformations of Miami* (Philadelphia: University of Pennsylvania Press, 2024).

32. Mauricio Castro, "Object Lesson: 'All the Help I Needed, I Got Here': Miami's Freedom Tower and the Freedom Tower's Miami," *Buildings & Landscapes: Journal of the Vernacular Architecture Forum* 23, no. 1 (Spring 2016): 19.

33. Bon Tempo, *Americans at the Gate*, 68.

34. I write about the specifics of these ambitions and how they make Miami fit into other patterns in American urban development, a topic outside the scope of this chapter, in *Only a Few Blocks to Cuba*.

35. Don Shoemaker to John S. Knight, James L. Knight, Alvah Chapman Jr., George Beebe, and Lee Hills, January 10, 1966, Folder 73, Dade County, Subseries 3.1, Series 3, Don Shoemaker Papers 1937–1998 (hereafter Shoemaker Papers), Southern Historical Collection, Louis Round Wilson Library Special Collections, University of North Carolina, Chapel Hill, NC; George Volsky, "Cuban Refugees Mark '61 Invasion," *New York Times*, April 18, 1971.

36. One such vow appeared in April of 1963 in Miami's largest Spanish-language newspaper, *Diario Las Américas*, as a political advertisement that acknowledged the ultimate authority of the U.S. government in matters of raids launched from its territory but also asked for understanding in the exile goal of fighting "the regime that enslaves our homeland." See "De 'Cuba libre' al exilio," *Diario Las Américas*, April 19, 1963.

37. Luis V. Manrara, "The Truth about Cuba Committee, INC.: It's Motives, Organization and Goals," September 22, 1988, Folder 2—TACC History by L.V. Manrara, Box 118, The Truth about Cuba Committee 1961–1975, CHC.

38. Max Freedman, "Cuba's Future Will Be Decided—but In Cuba," *Miami Herald*, April 16, 1963.

39. Jonathan C. Brown, *Cuba's Revolutionary World* (Cambridge, MA: Harvard University Press, 2017), 64–68.

40. Jesse Hoffnung-Garskof, *A Tale of Two Cities: Santo Domingo and New York after 1950* (Princeton, NJ: Princeton University Press, 2008), 34–35.

41. Ramona Hernández and Sophia Monegro, "Dominican Americans," *Oxford Bibliographies*, https://www.oxfordbibliographies.com/view/document/obo-9780199913701/obo-9780199913701-0015.xml.

42. Hoffnung-Garskof, *Tale of Two Cities*, 72–73.

43. Hoffnung-Garskof, 75.

44. Paul Hofmann, "Rising Hispanic Migration Heightens City Tensions," *New York Times*, April 4, 1966.

45. "Illegal Status of Dominicans Shaping Their Lives in the City," *New York Times*, November 9, 1971.

46. "Illegal Status."

47. Hoffnung-Garskof, *Tale of Two Cities*, 80.

48. Hoffnung-Garskof, 120.

49. "Dominicans Picketed over Jailings," *New York Times*, July 20, 1975.

50. Andrea Elliott, "For Dominicans, a New York Vote Cast Homeward," *New York Times*, May 17, 2004.

51. David Cruz, "Dominican New Yorkers Broaden Political Base as More Gain the Right to Vote," *Gothamist*, May 4, 2021, https://gothamist.com/news/dominican-new-yorkers-broaden-political-base-more-gain-right-vote.

52. Kyle Longley, *In the Eagle's Shadow: The United States and Latin America*, 2nd ed. (Wheeling, IL: Harlan Davidson, 2009), 286–93.

53. Longley, 303–4.

54. Ana Patricia Rodríguez, "Becoming 'Wachintonians,'" *Washington History* 28, no. 2 (Fall 2016): 4.

55. Ivonne Gonzalez, interview by Blanca Henriquez, March 11, 2019, transcript, Center for Global Migration Studies, University of Maryland, College Park, https://archiveofimmigrantvoices.omeka.net/items/show/80.

56. Karlyn Barker, "New Wave of Salvadoran Immigrants Revives Call for Refugee Status," *Washington Post*, February 18, 1989.

57. Andrew Friedman, *Covert Capital: Landscapes of Denial and the Making of U.S. Empire in the Suburbs of Northern Virginia* (Berkeley: University of California Press, 2013), 261–63.

58. Friedman, *Covert Capital*, 263–67.

59. David Pedersen, *American Value: Migrants, Money, and Meaning in El Salvador and the United States* (Chicago: University of Chicago Press, 2013), 38–39.

60. Jennifer S. Light, *From Warfare to Welfare: Defense Intellectuals and Urban Problems in Cold War America* (Baltimore: Johns Hopkins University Press, 2003), 5.

61. Margaret Pugh O'Mara, *Cities of Knowledge: Cold War Science and the Search for the Next Silicon Valley* (Princeton, NJ: Princeton University Press, 2005), 6.

62. Patrick Vitale, *Nuclear Suburbs: Cold War Technoscience and the Pittsburg Renaissance* (Minneapolis: University of Minnesota Press, 2021), 6.

Chapter Twelve

1. Although Cuban émigrés are classified as refugees, I use the term *immigrants* interchangeably to highlight the commonality of their experiences with other groups who come to the United States and seek incorporation into society. Monika Gosin, *The Racial Politics of Division: Interethnic Struggles for Legitimacy in Multicultural Miami* (Ithaca, NY: Cornell University Press, 2019).

2. Alex Stepick, Guillermo Grenier, Max Castro, and Marvin Dunn, *This Land Is Our Land: Immigrants and Power in Miami* (Berkeley: University of California Press, 2003); Alejandro Portes and Rubén G. Rumbaut, *Immigrant America: A Portrait* (Berkeley: University of California Press, 2006); Mary C. Waters, *Black Identities: West Indian Immigrant Dreams and American Realities* (Cambridge, MA: Harvard University Press, 1999); Alex Stepick and Carol Dutton Stepick, "Diverse Contexts of Reception and Feelings of Belonging," *Forum Qualitative Sozialforschung/Forum: Qualitative Social Research* 10, no. 3 (2009); Philip Kasinitz, John Mollenkopf, and Mary Waters, "Becoming American/Becoming New Yorkers: Immigrant Incorporation in a Majority Minority City," *International Migration Review* 36, no. 4 (2002): 1021.

3. Evelio Grillo, *Black Cuban, Black American: A Memoir* (Houston, TX: Arte Público Press, 2000); Susan D. Greenbaum, *More Than Black: Afro-Cubans in Tampa* (Gainesville: University Press of Florida, 2002); Christina D. Abreu, *Rhythms of Race: Cuban Musicians and the Making of Latino New York City and Miami, 1940–1960* (Chapel Hill: University of North Carolina Press, 2015); José I. Fusté, "Translating Negroes into Negros: Rafael Serra's Trans-American Entanglements between Black Cuban Racial and Imperial Subalternity, 1895–1909," in *Afro-Latinos in Movement: Critical Approaches to Blackness and Transnationalism in the Americas*, ed. Petra R. Rivera-Rideau, Jennifer A. Jones, and Tianna S. Paschel (New York: Palgrave Macmillan, 2016); Jesse Hoffnung-Garskof, *Racial Migrations: New York City and the Revolutionary Politics of the Spanish Caribbean* (Princeton, NJ: Princeton University Press, 2019).

4. Clara E. Rodríguez, *Changing Race: Latinos, the Census, and the History of Ethnicity in the United States* (New York: NYU Press, 2000); C. Alison Newby and Julie Dowling, "Black and Hispanic: The Racial Identification of Afro-Cuban Immigrants in the Southwest," *Sociological Perspectives* 50, no. 3 (2007): 343–66; José Itzigsohn, *Encountering American Faultlines: Race, Class, and the Dominican Experience in Providence* (New York: Russell Sage Foundation, 2009).

5. Thomas D. Boswell and James R. Curtis, *The Cuban-American Experience: Culture, Images, and Perspectives* (Totowa, NJ: Rowman and Allanheld, 1984), 71; Nathan Connolly, *A World More Concrete: Real Estate and the Remaking of Jim Crow South Florida* (Chicago: University of Chicago Press, 2016); Melanie Shell-Weiss, *Coming to Miami: A Social History* (Gainesville: University Press of Florida, 2009); Gosin, *Racial Politics of Division*.

6. Between 2010 and 2020, the percentage of Latinxs in the area remained stable at 48 percent, according to U.S. Census Bureau, State and County QuickFacts, http://quickfacts.census.gov/qfd/states/06/06037.html.

7. Newby and Dowling, "Black and Hispanic"; Alan A. Aja, *Miami's Forgotten Cubans: Race, Racialization, and the Miami Afro-Cuban Experience* (New York: Palgrave Macmillan, 2016); Devyn Spence Benson, *Antiracism in Cuba: The Unfinished Revolution* (Chapel Hill: University of North Carolina Press, 2016); Monika Gosin, "'A Bitter Diversion': Afro-Cuban Immigrants, Race, and Everyday-Life Resistance," *Latino Studies* 15, no. 1 (2017): 4–28; Gosin, *Racial Politics of Division*; María Cristina García, *Havana U.S.A.: Cuban Exiles and Cuban Americans in South Florida, 1959–1994* (Berkeley: University of California Press, 1996); Kelly Woltman and K. Bruce Newbold, "Of Flights and Flotillas: Assimilation and Race in the Cuban Diaspora," *Professional Geographer* 61, no. 1 (2009); Emily H. Skop, "Race and Place in the Adaptation of Mariel Exiles," *International Migration Review* 35, no. 2 (2001): 449–71.

8. García, *Havana U.S.A.*; Isabel Molina-Guzman, "Rescuing Elián: Gender and Race in Stories of Children's Migration," in *Immigrant Rights in the Shadows of Citizenship*, ed. Rachel Ida Buff (New York: New York University Press, 2008), 179–89; Antonio López, "Cosa de blancos: Cuban-American Whiteness and the Afro-Cuban Occupied House," *Latino Studies* 8, no. 2 (2010), 220–243; Aja, *Miami's Forgotten Cubans*; Antonio López, *Unbecoming Blackness: The Di-*

aspora Cultures of Afro-Cuban America (New York: NYU Press, 2012); Gosin, *Racial Politics of Division*.

9. Luis Noe-Bustamante, Antonio Flores, and Sono Shah, "Facts on Hispanics of Cuban Origin in the United States, 2017," Pew Research Center, https://www.pewresearch.org/hispanic/fact-sheet/u-s-hispanics-facts-on-cuban-origin-latinos/; Jynnah Radford and Luis Noe-Bustamante, "Facts on U.S. Immigrants, 2017," Pew Research Center, June 3, 2019, https://www.pewresearch.org/hispanic/2019/06/03/facts-on-u-s-immigrants-2017-data/. California has recently been edged out by Texas, and as of this writing is now tied with New Jersey for having the third-largest Cuban population in the United States. Mohamad Moslimani, Luis Noe-Bustamante, and Sono Shah, "Facts on Hispanics of Cuban Origin in the United States, 2021," Pew Research Center, https://www.pewresearch.org/race-and-ethnicity/fact-sheet/u-s-hispanics-facts-on-cuban-origin-latinos/.

10. David Córdova Jr. and Richard C. Cervantes, "Intergroup and Within-Group Perceived Discrimination among U.S.-Born and Foreign-Born Latino Youth," *Hispanic Journal of Behavioral Sciences* 32, no. 2 (2010): 259–75; Jessica Lavariega Monforti and Gabriel R. Sanchez, "The Politics of Perception: An Investigation of the Presence and Sources of Perceptions of Internal Discrimination Among Latinos," *Social Science Quarterly* 91, no. 1 (2010): 245–65.

11. Miriam Jiménez Román and Juan Flores, introduction to *The Afro-Latin@ Reader: History and Culture in the United States*, ed. Miriam Jiménez Román and Juan Flores (Durham, NC: Duke University Press, 2010), 1–18; Petra R. Rivera-Rideau, Jennifer A. Jones, and Tianna S. Paschel, *Afro-Latin@s in Movement: Critical Approaches to Blackness and Transnationalism in the Americas* (New York: Palgrave Macmillan, 2016); Silvio Torres-Saillant, "Problematic Paradigms: Racial Diversity and Corporate Identity in the Latino Community," in *Latinos: Remaking America*, ed. Marcelo Suárez-Orozco (University of California Press, 2002), 435–55; Torres-Saillant, "Inventing the Race: Latinos and the Ethnoracial Pentagon," *Latino Studies* 1, no. 1 (2003): 123–51; Torres-Saillant, "Divisible Blackness: Reflections on Heterogeneity and Racial Identity," in *The Afro-Latin@ Reader: History and Culture in the United States*, ed. Miriam Jiménez Román and Juan Flores (Durham, NC: Duke University Press, 2010), 453–65; G. Cristina Mora, *Making Hispanics: How Activists, Bureaucrats, and Media Created a New American* (Chicago: University of Chicago Press, 2014); Cristina Beltrán, *The Trouble with Unity: Latino Politics and the Creation of Identity* (New York: Oxford University Press, 2010); Arlene Dávila, *Latinos Inc.* (Berkeley: University of California Press, 2001); Nilda Flores-Gonzalez, "The Racialization of Latinos: The Meaning of Latino Identity for the Second Generation," *Latino Studies Journal* 10, no. 3 (1999): 3–31; Suzanne Oboler, *Ethnic Labels, Latino Lives: Identity and the Politics of (Re)Presentation* (Minneapolis: University of Minnesota Press, 1995); Shalini Puri, *The Caribbean Postcolonial: Social Equality, Post/nationalism, and Cultural Hybridity* (New York: Springer, 2004); Ruth Rama, "Latin America and the Geographical Priorities of Multinational Agro-Industries," *Geoforum* 27, no. 1 (1996): 39–52; Edward Telles, "Mexican Americans and the American Nation: A Response to Professor Huntington," *Aztlán: A Journal of Chicano Studies* 31, no. 2 (2006): 7–23.

12. Eugenio M. Rothe and Andrés J. Pumariega, "The New Face of Cubans in the United States: Cultural Process and Generational Change in an Exile Community," *Journal of Immigrant & Refugee Studies* 6, no. 2 (2008): 255; Jorge Duany, "Reconstructing Racial Identity: Ethnicity, Color, and Class among Dominicans in the United States and Puerto Rico," *Latin American Perspectives* 25, no. 3 (1998): 147–72; Nancy A. Denton and Douglas S. Massey, "Racial Identity among Caribbean Hispanics: The Effect of Double Minority Status on Residential Segregation," *American Sociological Review* 54, no. 5 (1989): 790–808; William A. J. Darity and Patrick L. Mason, "Evidence on Discrimination in Employment: Codes of Color, Codes of Gender," *Journal of Economic Perspectives* 12, no. 2 (1998): 63–90; Clara E. Rodríguez, *Changing Race: Latinos, the*

Census, and the History of Ethnicity in the United States (New York: New York University Press, 2000).

13. Alejandro Portes and Robert L. Bach, *Latin Journey: Cuban and Mexican Immigrants in the United States* (Berkeley: University of California Press, 1985); Alejandro Portes and Min Zhou, "The New Second Generation: Segmented Assimilation and Its Variants," *Annals of the American Academy of Political and Social Science* 530, no. 1 (1993): 74–96; Frank D. Bean and Gillian Stevens, *America's Newcomers and the Dynamics of Diversity* (New York: Russell Sage Foundation, 2003); Aja, *Miami's Forgotten Cubans*; Skop, "Race and Place"; Rothe and Pumariega, "New Face of Cubans"; Nancy Raquel Mirabal, "'Ser de aquí': Beyond the Cuban Exile Model," *Latino Studies* 1 (2003): 366–82; Devyn Spence Benson, "Cuba Calls! African American Tourism, Race, and the Cuban Revolution, 1959–1961," *Hispanic American Historical Review* 93, no. 2 (May 2013): 239–71.

14. For a discussion regarding processes of data collection in Cuba that may result in a "whitening" of the population, and a discussion of scholarly perspectives that place in doubt the 2002 Cuban census data point that put the white population of Cuba at 65 percent, see Danielle P. Clealand, *The Power of Race in Cuba: Racial Ideology and Black Consciousness during the Revolution* (New York: Oxford University Press, 2017), 15.

15. López, *Unbecoming Blackness*; Gosin, *Racial Politics of Division*.

16. López, *Unbecoming Blackness*; Benson, *Antiracism in Cuba*, 153–97; Gosin, *Racial Politics of Division*; Mark Q. Sawyer, *Racial Politics in Post-revolutionary Cuba* (Cambridge: Cambridge University Press, 2006); Aline Helg, *Our Rightful Share: The Afro-Cuban Struggle for Equality, 1886–1912* (Chapel Hill: University of North Carolina Press, 1995); Frank Andre Guridy, *Forging Diaspora: Afro-Cubans and African Americans in a World of Empire and Jim Crow* (Chapel Hill: University of North Carolina Press, 2010); Danielle P. Clealand, "When Ideology Clashes with Reality: Racial Discrimination and Black Identity in Contemporary Cuba," *Ethnic and Racial Studies* 36, no. 10 (2013): 1619–36; Clealand, *Power of Race in Cuba*; Devyn Spence Benson, "Owning the Revolution: Race, Revolution, and Politics in Havana and Miami, 1959–1963," *Journal of Transnational American Studies* 4, no. 2 (2012): 1–30; Benson, "Cuba Calls!"; Ada Ferrer, *Insurgent Cuba: Race, Nation, and Revolution, 1868–1898* (Chapel Hill: University of North Carolina Press, 1999); Alejandro de la Fuente, *A Nation for All: Race, Inequality, and Politics in Twentieth-Century Cuba* (Chapel Hill: University of North Carolina Press, 2001).

17. Benson, *Antiracism in Cuba*, 152.

18. Gosin, *Racial Politics of Division*; Stepick et al., *This Land Is Our Land*; Alejandro Portes and Alex Stepick, *City on the Edge: The Transformation of Miami* (Berkeley: University of California Press, 1993); Skop, "Race and Place"; García, *Havana U.S.A.*; Benson, *Antiracism in Cuba*.

19. Aja, *Miami's Forgotten Cubans*; Elizabeth M. Aranda, Sallie Hughes, and Elena Sabogal, *Making a Life in Multiethnic Miami: Immigration and the Rise of a Global City* (Boulder, CO: Lynne Rienner, 2014).

20. Monika Gosin, "No Choice but Unity: Afro-Cuban Immigrants Building Community in Los Angeles," in *Latinx Belonging: Community Building and Resilience in the United States*, ed. Jennifer Bickham Mendez and Natalia Deeb-Sosa (Tucson: University of Arizona Press, 2022), 73–92.

21. She is referring to La Presencia Cubana en Los Angeles, a festival focused on celebrating Cuban culture. The festival was started in 1993 by Adolfo V. Nodal and Aurelio de la Vega. It was held near the Jose Martí Plaza and monument in Echo Park, Los Angeles (Adolfo Nodal, personal interview).

22. I recount more of these positive experiences in Gosin, "No Choice but Unity."

23. Newby and Dowling, "Black and Hispanic"; Julie A. Dowling and C. Alison Newby, "So Far from Miami: Afro-Cuban Encounters with Mexicans in the U.S. Southwest," *Latino Studies* 8, no. 2 (2010): 76–94.

24. Gosin, *Racial Politics of Division.*

25. Dávila, *Latinos, Inc.*

26. Wendy D. Roth and Nadia Y. Kim, "Relocating Prejudice: A Transnational Approach to Understanding Immigrants' Racial Attitudes," *International Migration Review* 47, no. 2 (2013): 330–73; Newby and Dowling, "Black and Hispanic"; Christina Sue, *Land of the Cosmic Race: Race Mixture, Racism, and Blackness in Mexico* (New York: Oxford University Press, 2013).

27. Toni Morrison, *Playing in the Dark: Whiteness and the Literary Imagination* (Cambridge, MA: Harvard University Press, 1992); Toni Morrison, "On the Backs of Blacks," in *Arguing Immigration: The Debate Over the Changing Face of America*, ed. Nicolaus Milla (New York: Simon and Schuster, 1994), 97–100; Helen B. Marrow, *New Destination Dreaming: Immigration, Race, and Legal Status in the Rural American South* (Stanford, CA: Stanford University Press, 2011); López, *Unbecoming Blackness*; Gosin, *Racial Politics of Division*; Lavariega Monforti and Sanchez, "Politics of Perception."

28. Dowling and Newby, "So Far from Miami"; Newby and Dowling, "Black and Hispanic"; Lavariega Monforti and Sanchez, "Politics of Perception."

29. Gordon W. Allport, *The Nature of Prejudice*, 25th anniversary ed. (Boston: Addison-Wesley, 1979); Thomas F. Pettigrew, "Prejudice," in *The Harvard Encyclopedia of American Ethnic Groups*, ed. Stephan Themstrom, Ann Orlov, and Oscar Handlin (Cambridge, MA: Belknap Press of Harvard University Press, 1980), 820–29; Gosin, "Bitter Diversion," 6.

30. Gosin, *Racial Politics of Division*; Aihwa Ong, *Buddha Is Hiding: Refugees, Citizenship, the New America* (Berkeley: University of California Press, 2003); Herbert J. Gans, "The Possibility of a New Racial Hierarchy in the Twenty-First-Century United States," in *The Cultural Territories of Race: Black and White Boundaries*, ed. Michele Lamont (Chicago: University of Chicago Press, 1999), 371–90; Herman Gray, *Watching Race: Television and the Struggle for "Blackness"* (Minneapolis: University of Minnesota Press, 1995); Bonnie Urciuoli, *Exposing Prejudice: Puerto Rican Experiences of Language, Race, and Class* (Boulder, CO: Westview, 1996).

31. Gosin, *Racial Politics of Division.*

32. Gosin, "Bitter Diversion" and *Racial Politics of Division*; Córdova and Cervantes, "Intergroup and Within-Group Perceived Discrimination," 259–75.

Contributors

LLANA BARBER is the Rudolph J. Vecoli Endowed Chair in Immigration History and the director of the Immigration History Research Center at the University of Minnesota. She is the author of *Latino City: Immigration and Urban Crisis in Lawrence, Massachusetts, 1945–2000* (University of North Carolina Press, 2017).

MAURICIO CASTRO is assistant professor of history and chair of Latin American studies at Centre College. He specializes in the intersection of political, urban, and immigration history. His book *Only A Few Blocks to Cuba: Cold War Refugee Policy, the Cuban Diaspora, and the Transformations of Miami* (University of Pennsylvania Press, 2024) recounts how the U.S. government embraced Cuban migration as a strategic Cold War asset, investing heavily in Miami and fundamentally transforming it.

EDUARDO CONTRERAS is associate professor of history at Hunter College and the CUNY Graduate Center. He is the author of *Latinos and the Liberal City: Politics and Protest in San Francisco* (University of Pennsylvania Press, 2019). He is now at work on "Central American Labor and U.S. Empire: From the Gold Rush to the Early 1930s," an investigation of working people's responses to U.S. corporate enterprises in Central America.

SANDRA I. ENRÍQUEZ is an associate professor of history and director of the Public History Emphasis at the University of Missouri–Kansas City. Enríquez is completing her first book, *¡El Barrio No Se Vende! Grassroots Activism and Revitalization in El Paso* (forthcoming from University of Texas Press), and has published pieces on Chicanx grassroots movements centered on housing and access to health care. Enríquez promotes Kansas City and Midwest history through public-facing research and collaborative projects.

MONIKA GOSIN is an associate professor of ethnic studies at the University of California, San Diego. Her research and teaching focuses on African American and Latinx relations, Afro-Latinx immigrant experiences in the United States, and race, gender, and representation in media. She is the author of *The Racial Politics of Division: Interethnic Struggles for Legitimacy in Multicultural Miami* (Cornell University Press, 2019).

FELIPE HINOJOSA is the John and Nancy Jackson Endowed Chair in Latin America & Professor of History at Baylor University. He is the author of two books—*Latino Mennonites* (Johns

Hopkins University Press, 2014) and *Apostles of Change* (University of Texas Press, 2021)—and an edited collection titled *Faith & Power* (NYU Press, 2022). He is working on a book on the Latinx civil rights movement and American democracy from the 1960s to the 1990s.

MICHAEL D. INNIS-JIMÉNEZ is professor in the Department of American Studies at the University of Alabama. He earned his PhD in history from the University of Iowa and writes about Latinx food and foodways, Mexican Chicago, Latinx communities in the American South, Mexican migration to the American Midwest and South, and the racialization of Latinx communities. He also writes about labor and the urban environment. He is at work on *Made in Chicago: Mexican Food, Tourism, and Cultural Identity* (University of Texas Press, in progress).

MAX KROCHMAL is professor of history and director of justice studies at the University of New Orleans. He is the author of *Blue Texas: The Making of a Multiracial Democratic Coalition in the Civil Rights Era* (University of North Carolina Press, 2016) and *Civil Rights in Black and Brown: Histories of Resistance and Struggle in Texas* (University of Texas Press, 2021). His work has been supported by the National Endowment for the Humanities, a Fulbright-García Robles Fellowship, and the Andrew W. Mellon Foundation.

BECKY M. NICOLAIDES is a historian of American suburbia. Her books include *The New Suburbia: How Diversity Remade Suburban Life in Los Angeles after 1945* (Oxford University Press, 2024), *My Blue Heaven: Life and Politics in the Working-Class Suburbs of Los Angeles* (University of Chicago Press, 2002), and *The Suburb Reader* (Routledge, 2006, 2016), coedited with Andrew Wiese. Becky has consulted extensively for the City of Los Angeles, and is a research affiliate at the Huntington-USC Institute on California and the West.

PEDRO A. REGALADO is assistant professor of history at Stanford University. He is a historian of twentieth-century America, interested in immigration, cities, and capitalism. His book manuscript, *Nueva York: Making the Modern City*, is a spatial and economic history of New York City's Latinx community during the twentieth century, from the "pioneers" who arrived after World War I to the panoply of Latinx people who rebuilt the city in the wake of the 1975 fiscal crisis.

ILIANA YAMILETH RODRIGUEZ (she/they) is an assistant professor of history at Emory University, where she researches and teaches Latinx history. Their interdisciplinary historical research considers matters of race, ethnicity, labor, and migration. Specifically, Rodriguez's work investigates the placemaking practices of Latinx people living and working in the U.S. South. Their current project, *Mexican Atlanta*, traces the history of Metro Atlanta's ethnic Mexican community formation alongside the region's broader Latinx histories beginning in the mid-twentieth century.

CECILIA N. SÁNCHEZ HILL earned her PhD in history at Texas Christian University. Her dissertation, "Brown Erasure: Mexican Americans and the Teaching of History in Cold War Texas," combines history, ethnic studies, and curriculum studies to demonstrate how politicians and educators have used schooling as a tool of white supremacy to maintain social hierarchies. She also partnered with an interdisciplinary team of TCU scholars to cocreate *Latinx Studies Curriculum in K-12 Schools: A Practical Guide*.

A. K. SANDOVAL-STRAUSZ is director of the Latina/o Studies Program and professor of history at Penn State University and the president of the Urban History Association. His published works include *Hotel: An American History* (Yale University Press, 2007), *Barrio America: How Latino Immigrants Saved the American City* (Basic Books, 2019), and, coedited with Nancy H. Kwak, *Making Cities Global: The Transnational Turn in Urban History* (University of Pennsylvania Press, 2018).

THOMAS J. SUGRUE is Silver Professor of Social and Cultural Analysis and History at New York University and the director of the NYU Cities Collaborative. His books include *The Origins of the Urban Crisis* (Princeton University Press, 2014); *Sweet Land of Liberty: The Forgotten Struggle for Civil Rights in the North* (Random House, 2008); *The New Suburban History* (University of Chicago Press, 2006); and *Immigration and Metropolitan Revitalization* (University of Pennsylvania Press, 2017). His current project is *Rent: An American History*.

Index

The letter *f* following a page number denotes a figure.